All line drawn illustrations by Jessa Dawson,
modeled from photographs taken by Doug Dawson
or courtesy of courses acknowledged in the illustration captions.
Maps and cover design by Rory Vance
from photographs by Doug Dawson.
Cover photo taken from Number 10 tee at
Quail Lodge Resort and Golf Club, Carmel, CA.

Published by Sureshot Productions, Los Altos, CA
Printed by Transcontinental Printing in Louiseville, Canada

Northern California's

Best 100 Public Golf Courses

. . . and golf planning guide

BY **Doug Dawson**

ILLUSTRATIONS BY
Jessa Dawson

Forward

Northern California's Best 100 Public Golf Courses by Doug Dawson is an important book for those seeking great new golf experiences in Northern California, and offers excellent insight on which courses are either the best in quality, or the best in value. In good times or hard times, quality golf courses endure to lift the sporting spirit, and what better way to find an outlet for the joy of the game than using his advice to find new places to play.

I am pleased to have our design work in Northern California included in the listings he provides. We craft each golf course to our client's needs . . . and tailor it to their particular topography. As you can tell from our many differing designs included herein, the possibilities are endless. The golfing gypsies amongst the readers should have a great time trying them all. Doug Dawson has spent over two years researching and assembling the data you will find in this unique reference tome and I will refer to this book myself, over the years, when I'm looking for another fun opportunity to experience our endlessly fascinating sport.

Robert Trent Jones, Jr.

Acknowledgements

Three disparate events, which happened over the past 52 years, combined to motivate my writing this epistle . . .

Back in 1956, at the ripe age of ten, my mother and father, Carl and Velma Dawson pushed me to learn the game of golf. They struggled, because I wasn't interested and rebelled against it. I hated not being able to hit the ball into the air, and besides, baseball and football with my buddies was a lot more fun. However, by the age of 12, after four years of skipping church to earn 10 cents a hole pulling my mother's cart around Stanford Golf Club, they took me to Lake Tahoe for a week at Glenbrook Resort. This was heaven because what was then called *American Plan* meals meant my new friend Tucker Trautman and I could eat all we wanted off the hotel's menu. That never happened at home! We also played all the unsupervised golf we wanted and then swam in the lake. Golf . . . with a buddy . . . no pressure from adults . . . no one else on the course . . . and I could even get the ball off the ground! I finally became hooked and must thank them all for starting and pushing this life-long habit.

Jump shift to the early '70's, at age 22, in the barracks of Coast Guard OCS, Yorktown, Virginia. On a cold weekend night in the early fall I had an epiphany that would further affect my future: Why am I delaying proposing to my college sweetheart, Jesssa Vogt? My long term plan to complete three years of military service, two of business school and a couple for work experience before marriage, seemed naive and very dumb. I think she wants to get married, I love her, so let's get on with it! Thank you Jess for saying "I do" and also allowing me Saturday mornings for the next several years to keep plugging away with my abbreviated golf swing.

Then in the mid-'90's another piece of life's puzzle fell into place. I met a businessman from Long Island, Sam Feinberg. He was a bootstrap entrepreneur who I worked with closely for twelve years. He showed me that being your own boss, while scary, can be awfully rewarding too. After 35 years in the corporate world, the last couple being very frustrating, his example gave me the courage to do something new and exciting. So, I retired in order to have time to write my first book. (For those who think writing and leisure are synonymous . . . NOT. Writing and research end up being 10-12 hours-a-day jobs. Only the time of day varies from normal paid work.)

Several good friends and family members also deserve multitudes of thanks for assisting and cheerleading this project:

First and foremost, Jess, now forty years a Dawson, continues to be a pillar of advice, understanding, talent and love. She drew all the illustrations, handled the related scanning and computer enhancements, volunteered to edit, kept me on-track and comforted me consistently over the two-year project period. Dear, thank you and I'll try to mend my many bad habits.

Next come my friends in the Sun Valley Gang and golfing buddies at Menlo CC. They spurred me on and even let me win a few bucks in the process. Since this book is a self-published effort I expect them to now generate lots of great marketing ideas and help spread the word about how useful the guide is for choosing new courses to try. Thanks also to the many club pros and club managers who gave freely of their time, sharing insight about the game and their courses.

I received editing help from many independent experts, most of all Will Ray from Camino Medical Foundation, but also from my sister Kay and step-mother Vicky Dawson. Any awkwardness or goofs found by readers are not the editor's fault but mine, since I tend to over-control the publishing and editing process.

Rory Vance, an ex-associate at Smurfit-Stone, gets great kudos for the map designs and the cover layouts.

Daughters Leslie and Ali actively assisted in setting up the business and marketing ends of our self-publishing project, and I expect they will be continuing helpers. My other daughter Erin kept us *real* by produced our first grandchild along the way. Thanks also to siblings Stan, Barbara and friends Sherm Waldman and Jim Kunkel for lodging me on several of my itinerant golf research escapades.

Mark Solteau and Robert Trent Jones Jr. were very helpful in suggesting ways to avoid pitfalls of the publishing process. Their encouragement came at the right time to get me back on track.

And last, but not least, I'd like to thank my ex-business associate John Lamb for being an inspiration. Not only has he shown me and others how golf can be used to bring all sorts of people close together in comradeship and business, but his personal fortitude and enthusiastic personality are models almost impossible to duplicate. Keep that handicap up buddy.

Table of Contents

Chapter 2 (Cont.).....The Best 100 Courses

Chapter 3.................The Rest of the Courses...............221

Chapter 3 (Cont.).......The Rest of the Courses

Chapter 3 (Cont.).......The Rest of the Courses

Chapter 4.................Not so Public Courses.................323

Chapter 5......Trip Planning and Value Courses..........335

Chapter 6........Glossary and Local Golf Trivia............367

Chapter 7........Index and Ordering Information..........389

For Tootsie, with love

Preface

Right here, in our own Northern California backyard, world-class golf is within a few hours' drive. Yet, large groups of players know little about these public courses. Members of private clubs, visiting tourists and everyday golfers, who normally play day-in and day-out with the same group of friends, need a guide to expand their horizons. Nicknamed the **Best 100**, my book suggests that venturesome players don't have to travel as far as Scotland, South Carolina, Arizona or Hawaii to have a great golf experience. Northern California is a special place already, offering oceans, bays, lakes, mountains, rivers and valleys in plenitude. Why not stay nearer home and exploit everything Northern California has to offer, great golf included?

The **Best 100** is a one-of-a-kind travel guide. It is the only book current and available to review all 219 Northern California eighteen-hole public access golf courses, other than the Northern California Golf Association (NCGA) Blue Book. Unlike others, it *ranks and reviews* the top 100 openly public courses, plus five more with less access for non-members, *reviews* the remaining 115, and provides both positive and negative commentary about them all.

Most golf guides published today include very little subjective commentary about the style and quality of the courses they list. Rarely are concerns or weaknesses discussed. Why? Perhaps authors or publishers are afraid that a bad review will hurt ad sales and business associations will prevent them from being completely honest. Maybe they fear the ridicule of friends or legal problems. Or perhaps they're too modest, too unsure of their opinions to be presumptuous enough to publish them, even to help others find the best quality courses.

Just as critics make judgments about movies and books, I feel golf courses deserve discriminating review. After all, don't golfers deserve the same quality of critique before they pay +/- $50 for a 4-5 hour golf game, as moviegoers who pay $10 for a 2-hour feature film? I think they do. So I attempt to give basic background information about the courses, followed by pro-and-con discussion in short essays. I give basic data on course statistics, course style, pricing, contact information, and location. I've also organized courses by region to make travel planning easy and calculated which are the best values. In the final chapter, I include a small glossary of terms, with lists of best holes and other "bests" on our courses. This last chapter also has enough golf trivia to fuel clubhouse or party conversation—and enough resources for further study to fill rainy afternoons when golfers can only dream, not play.

Don't expect these write-ups to be filled with nasty commentary. I am basically an optimist, at least about golf. Most of what you read emphasizes the positive. Negative comments are expressed in terms that are honestly descriptive rather than destructively critical. My goal is to provide information and opinions that help you make better choices of where to play. Trashing a venue is best left to trashy critics, and only a few courses get anything close to that treatment here. An Internet chain mail I received recently philosophized: "When you wake up in the morning you have two choices—you can either be in a good mood or a bad mood; it is your choice." I choose to be in a good mood when I write. The old adage, "A bad day on the course is better than the best day in the office," is a huge overstatement, but being happy when writing about golf isn't hard and it makes the task of writing a first book easier.

I have played a lot of golf, much of it in Northern California, for about 50 years, and have strong opinions about many of the best courses. These opinions needed tempering, since other players often have different thoughts. The truth is forged through discussion, listening, and looking at data to bring new facts to light. In order to make my rankings as objective as possible, I developed an original rating system.

This system is unrelated to the "Slope" or "Course Ratings" printed on scorecards. Slope and Course Rating systems are created for a different purpose. They allow accurate handicapping of players with differing skill levels. Their systems use mandatory rules and predetermined formulas that quantify values for yardage, terrain, water hazards, trees, fairway width, bunker position, rough height, recovery location, wind conditions, type of greens, etc. Teams of volunteers are trained how to complete the ratings and then play all the courses at least once every six years. When needed, some courses are re-rated more often than others. The end result is a set of numbers that consistently and accurately allow fair competition between players of different skill levels. They also give a good indication of how tough each course plays.

My book has a different purpose. It strives to rate *quality*. While *difficulty* is certainly a good indicator of the challenge presented by a course and helps me double-check some findings, other important factors come into play that help golfers decide where to shell out their hard earned cash. They include:

- The distinction of layout and design
- Course condition
- Beauty of location
- The clubhouse, pro shop, bar, restaurant, water fountains, and rest rooms
- History of amateur and professional tournament play
- Walk-ability
- Practice facilities, including driving range, chipping areas and putting greens

Cost was eliminated as a primary criterion in the quality rankings. For those interested in greens fees, a list is provided in the charts following each review. I also developed a value scale that combines quality and cost together into one rating. It is used to calculate lists of Best Value Courses in Chapter Five.

This guide was created without utilizing the huge rating crews engaged by state golf associations. Instead, **I played all the courses myself, at as close to 6500-yards total yards as possible, to give the study some consistency**. I've played golf all over the world on all kinds of courses and have a better than average skill of the game. My judgment comes through the eyes of a player who hits drives about 200 yards in the air, flies a seven iron 150 yards, and maintains a handicap between six and eight. Other players of varying skills— some women, some men, some kids—often joined me to make sure that opposing comments and attitudes were heard and included. I usually teamed with local club members or frequent players to get the history and foibles of a particular course. I also interviewed local pros and owners to get their perspective.

My comments reflect, to a degree, the quality of maintenance conditions and weather the day I played each course. Unfortunately, to rate 220 courses within only fifteen months, meant having imperfect conditions at times, and the month of play is listed at the end of each article. When greens or fairways had just been aerated (*i.e.* punched and sanded), I gave more weight to comments of pros and fellow players than my own observations. When weather was variable I did further research on standard conditions before commenting about it. Fortunately, I have been on many of the courses multiple times, helping gain a broader and more balanced view.

I hope that the result of this work is a useful, up-to date guide for all eighteen-hole public-access courses in Northern California. It includes municipal, public, semi-private, resort and even a few struggling private courses. Admittedly, access may need to be bought by staying at resorts, playing in charity tournaments, or settling for non-prime starting-times. But all the courses listed herein do have some sort of public access, at least part of the time.

Unfortunately for country club members, the **Best 100** does not review several fine private courses. Maybe that subject can be addressed in a sequel to this book. Members of clubs deserve to know that many quality public facilities have been built in the last decade. In truth, it is country club members who are missing out on the opportunity to play the wonderful, new—and often-refurbished—public facilities reviewed here. I hope this book will help change that.

Good luck on finding your own favorite courses. May *Northern California's Best 100 Public Golf Courses* start you on a new adventure.

Chapter 1:
How They Were Chosen

A great golf course has some combination of six characteristics. When added together, they determine overall quality and make it possible to create comparisons and rankings. These traits include: (1) design excellence, including the need for accurate shot-making; (2) the beauty of the surroundings; (3) course condition; (4) the quality of facilities and service; (5) the variety or uniqueness of the experience; and (6) history and tradition. For some players, familiarity, or knowing-the-course, is important as well: the better golfers know the course, the more fun, success and advantage they have. To others, the cost of play is an important consideration.

This book not only guides players to where they can play but also speaks to the culture and emotions of the game, because golf is unlike most other sports. People of unequal skills—young and old, the best of the pros and the most average of amateurs—can play together in the same group and have an enjoyable, fair competition. Golf isn't so much a game of strength or speed, but an activity where well-practiced coordination gives a better advantage than training-room bulk. The Tiger Wood Generation may change things, but most golfers still avoid the gym.

For some, playing golf is a way to unwind from work or get out of the house to enjoy the outdoors in the company of friends. For others, it's a way to make new business contacts, develop important business relationships, sometimes close profitable business deals. For a few, it can also be about betting and winning at a game where victory can mean money or notoriety. For everyone, however, golf is a contest in which honesty and honor are taken for granted, where players call penalties on themselves and scores must be posted accurately using the old-fashioned honor system.

And whatever their particular age or motivation, most golfers admit that a course's design and its immediate surroundings are a big part of their experience. Given a chance to play in a really beautiful setting, most golfers seize the opportunity and enjoy it to the hilt.

I wrote *Northern California's Best 100 Public Golf Courses*—the **Best 100** for short—to help golfers venture forth, try new experiences, and choose where to play, whether in their own community or while traveling Northern California. Before writing the book, I played every course, most of them during the past 24 months. After playing each round, I rated the course numerically, using 29 values in the categories described below.

My top 105 courses are listed and reviewed in detail in Chapters 2 and 4; the remaining 115 get briefer reviews in Chapter 3. Each individual course measurement was compared to other **Best 100** courses of the same type for fairness and consistency, and tentative final rankings were compared to those of national publications such as *Golf Digest*. A final test—what people understand intuitively when you say, "I-know-it-when-I-see-it"—was then applied to make subjective adjustments. I'm a trained engineer but also a golfer. My hunches and feelings come from 50 years playing the sport. The emotions of a golfer sometimes trump the analysis of my quantitative mind.

Design and Beauty

In many ways a golf course can be compared to a beautiful garden. Augusta National, perhaps the best example, evolved from an abandoned nursery. Bobby Jones (Robert Tyre Jones), the famed Grand Slam winner of 1929, and Alister MacKenzie, Augusta's visionary architect, sculpted fairways through much of the existing flora, and then wound them around Rea's Creek, a series of ponds, and the natural canyons that were part of the site's existing topography. The two creators made famous use of azaleas, rhododendrons, and dogwoods to fashion a floral tapestry that is at its peak in mid-April, when the Masters' tournament unfolds. The colors of blooming trees, along with lush fairways and soft southern pine, combine to make each arena of their course like a well-framed theatre design.

Northern California may not have the same profusion of fragrant flowering shrubbery, but we have our share of spectacular plant species. Giant cypresses at Harding Park, Ponderosa pines around burgeoning North Tahoe courses, redwoods towering above fairways at Boulder Creek and Beau Pre, and various oak species dotting foothill courses, all present California native plants in their own glorious style. The disappearing ice plant of Spyglass Hill, the grasses of Saddle Creek and Cinnabar, and the reeds or cattails of Stevinson Ranch and Teal Bend, each add their own unmistakable texture, and make our anthology of Northern California courses as majestic as the finest of master's paintings.

Beyond the near view of trees and flowers, the vistas of the far horizon enhance many a golf experience. Pebble Beach is Northern California's gem in this category, offering views of the Pacific Ocean, Carmel Beach, steep cliffs, and dolphins or otters playing in the surf. Indeed, hitting a shot across the rocks and waves that wash the inlets of Sand Dollar Cove is itself a time-stopping moment rarely forgotten by those who experience it. More than one golfer claims that a poor score at Pebble Beach was caused by the powerful distraction of sand, sea, and cliffs.

Other locations can be just as magnificent. The mountains of the Sierra Nevada provide a majestic backdrop for courses such as Coyote Moon and

Graeagle Meadows. In the grassy foothills, golden summer pastures and vineyards thick with grapes enhance venues such as The Ranch, Wente Vineyards, Saddle Creek, and Hunter Ranch. There, courses mingle serenely with oaks and grazing cattle, while adjacent narrow canyons frame views of the cityscape not far away. In California's Central Valley, from Redding in the north to Porterville in the south, many courses follow rivers, where views of distant mountains add sublime contrast to waterfowl and reed shorelines running right alongside fairways.

For the quintessential golfer, however, flora, fauna, and natural vistas are just adjuncts, compared to the essential heart and muscle of the golf holes themselves. True, fairway curves and aesthetics must mesh with the local environment, but they should also be shaped and sculpted to provide a golfing perspective, shot-making challenge, and in the best case, an experience not to be seen on other courses.

The view from a tee box enables golfers to plan their attack and appreciate the walk or ride they are about to take. They like to see where the risks are set, what the mental challenges will be, how much fun or dread awaits them. The length of the rough, the danger provided by lakes and creeks, the twists and undulations of the fairway, the placement of trees or rocks, the expanse of hazards—all combine to define the upcoming test.

Near the green, new challenges loom. Depth and placement of bunkers, elevation and mounding of putting surfaces, shape and mowing of the apron, location of the pin, and speed of putts: these features—called the green complex—will determine most of the strokes taken on each hole.

High-quality golf venues usually display a range of difficulty within their 18-holes. For instance, the first five at Pebble Beach present far fewer demands than the final 13. Their lengths are shorter, giving average golfers a greater chance at success before playing the ocean holes, notorious for testing concentration and skill. Spyglass Hill has similar variation: holes two through five play short but narrow. On these the primary challenge is to keep shots in play, avoiding the need to recover from sandy footprints or ice plant. The rest of the course is tree-lined, bunker-guarded, and undulating, with a heavy primary rough and some of the toughest greens in the state. Variations like these make the game more interesting . . . glory on one hole, disaster on the next. Added to creative design and unusual beauty, this special mix helps put Pebble and Spyglass at the top of the **Best 100** rankings.

Throughout the upcoming reviews, I use technical terms and golf jargon to describe course styles. Some of these get immediate explanation. Others are explained in the glossary found in Chapter 6.

Course condition

When golfers arrive in the parking lot and unload their clubs, they already have an idea of whether or not their course experience will be memorable. The trees, contours, and initial glimpses of fairways, bunkers, and roughs by the roadway give the golfer his or her first clues. Is the setting well groomed, raked, and cut, with leaves and cut grass swept from the ground? Do bare spots appear? Do roped off areas protect players from leaking pipes that soak the turf? Do fairways look smooth, consistent, and solid green, with evidence of regular mowing? Are greens dry of dew, with aprons and fringes neatly trimmed?

The funny thing about course condition is that, as with residential architecture, expectations will vary depending where in the world one plays the game. In Europe, travelers can often anticipate small rooms and minimal indoor living space. In New Mexico, one expects adobe walls and earthen structures; in New England traditional, center-hall interiors and Cape Cod house styles; in California, ranch homes today, bungalows in an earlier era. Golf architecture also varies from locale to locale and from one era to another. In Scotland, where irrigation rarely exists, courses often show dry spots, lots of roll, and the rough seems irregular, if cut at all. Yet these conditions, unkempt as they seem, become part of the course's charm. In India, my father told me of golf courses with no grass at all. Lines of small rocks bordered the dirt fairways, and when a ball came to rest within these boundaries, the caddy unrolled a carpet, dropped the ball on it, and that became a fairway lie. Shots landing outside the rocks were played down, wherever they lay.

By contrast, Americans seem pretty spoiled when it comes to course condition. We may not expect perfect grooming, but we sure appreciate it, and we want the condition to be consistent throughout the course. Tee boxes need to be level; they need to have good-looking, thick, short cut grass. They should be firm enough that tees can be placed in the ground easily but also stand steadily. Clear access is needed from tee to fairway: a path off the tee should be trimmed so that long grass or shrubbery doesn't scratch players' legs or ruin or pants and shoes.

Fairways and roughs have become particularly important. We like a nice soft walking surface, but one that allows shots to roll. We also prefer to keep our shoes clean, out of the mud and away from grass clippings. In other words, we want the ball to bounce, stay clean, and get a little extra distance, but not roll into a hazard. One problem that prevails on several warm climate courses is that, though these criteria are met, mowers shave the grass so short that the ball sits down, very close to the ground, as if on pavement. Pros actually like the resulting *tight lies*, because they allow good players to *pinch* the ball and apply backspin. But for the other 95 percent of us, tight lies just make for thinly hit shots.

An exception is Kikuyu grass, a wiry variety that stays green with little care or water. When Kikuyu is cut short, the ball appears to sit up, but its blades grow so tough that they decelerate club-head speed significantly. The result is that shots land short, or a four iron must be used to hit the same distance as a six to make up for the nasty drag of the grass. The sudden need for more strength can dishearten the average golfer, who begs for every extra inch of shot length.

The condition of roughs and traps, though not as critical as fairways, has a lot to do with good scores and bad luck. Most of us don't want to rely on good luck to get a normal lie. How often has the ball ended up in a footprint or an un-repaired divot or a patch of rough where the grass grain makes it nearly impossible to hit? These concerns don't mean that all rough should be cut short, or that all trap shots should be easy . . . If you hit deep into the woods or into a patch of rough where one expects to lose the ball, the natural result needs to be accepted. But it is being confronted by un-groomed parts of the cut rough, or bunkers without sand or raking, that can create understandable frustration.

Yet even a course with poor tees, ratty roughs, well-tromped traps, or patchy fairways can make amends with great greens. This is where real scoring takes place and where poor lies in the fairway can be almost forgiven. The first criterion for a great green is consistency. The speed and firmness need to be equal throughout each green or apron and from one green to the next. Players need to have confidence that the ball will behave as he or she expects when hitting approaches, chips, and putts. The practice green should be the same speed as greens on the course. Next in priority is speed, measured with a StimpMeter, a short platform from which a ball rolls down a slope onto the putting surface and the number of feet the ball rolls is measured. A six-foot roll means a slow green; a 12-foot roll means professional speed. Average is probably about an eight or nine, and club tournaments often see greens cut and rolled to 10.5 or so.

Every player has his or her personal preference on speed, but one physical fact prevails: the ball has a better chance of going in the hole on a fast green. This occurs because a slow green requires that putts be hit hard. When a fast-moving ball hits the edge of the cup, it will usually rim the cup and stay out due to higher momentum. The same ball, moving slower on a fast green, often falls into the cup. Greens should also be clean, devoid of bare spots, and swept of leaves, needles, sand, and bird droppings. Nothing is quite as distracting as taking the time to brush debris away, or worrying about whether a leaf will blow into the line of a putt. Finally, what treatise on green condition would be complete without the universal warning: "Repair ball marks!"? Imagine all the perfect conditioning executed by the greens crew, undone by an uncaring or unknowledgeable golfer. The conscientious golfer repairs his damage, then looks for other marks to fix as well.

Facilities and service

Like it or not, a big part of everyday golf experience relates to comfort and attitude. Driving from the street to the pro-shop on a nicely paved entrance road sets up a much better expectation of what is to come than broken cement, cracking asphalt, or potholes. A snack shop that sells a cup of coffee for $1.50 rather than three bucks puts me in a slightly better mood. A course ranger who barks at us to speed up after a particularly frustrating hole is asking for a red face, or worse. Settling bets in a nice lounge is more relaxing and congenial than doing it in the parking lot.

Most U.S. golfers prefer a comfortable clubhouse with a decent restaurant to a shack. We like to have clean bathrooms, maybe even lockers, and restrooms on the course too. Drinking water should be free and available on the course. Pro-shop and restaurant staff members should be friendly, merchandise plentiful, and prices reasonable. Fast speed-of-play is extremely important: starting-times should be nine or 10, not seven or eight minutes apart, and rangers should actively try to assist and accelerate slower groups. Courses should not overbook tournaments, and players should show up on time or face the consequences.

Every quality course needs an easily accessible practice range, preferably one with groomed turf and good mats, but no cage-nets. It should have a large putting green that duplicates the texture and speed of greens on the course. A real treat for the players who can afford it is to have caddies available. For the rest of us, walking should be relatively easy, with short distances from green to tee, and carts should be allowed to drive on most fairways and in the parking lots.

Not all of the above will be available at a low-priced golf facility. But the standard is actually attained at some of Northern California's best-valued courses. (See Chapter 5 for a list of *top value,* courses and Chapter 6 for how the *value* calculations were made.)

Variety and uniqueness

How many holes have you played that can be described as follows? . . . A 385-yard par-four, with a flat fairway, a trap at 200 yards on one side and bunkers at front corners of the green; or . . . a 400-yard par-four, sharp dog leg left, with a bunker at 190-yards down the left side and 210 down the right, and more bunkers surrounding the green?

Yes, these are the prosaic features of the courses we play every day. However, add sloping hills, fairway mounds, a creek, a forest, overhanging trees, an old stone fence, a vineyard, some tightly cut aprons, a multi-tiered green with four or five different pin locations, a rock outcropping bordering the green-side bunker or a lake, and an entirely different image comes to mind. Mere prose becomes poetry.

We live in a time of such poetry, when courses can be constructed to fulfill the vivid vision of architects and entrepreneurs, much as artists in paint and stone once fulfilled the demands of princes and popes for beauty, sublimity, and significance. This doesn't mean the older courses were poorly designed. In fact, some of the finest were built many years ago, or have been remodeled to recreate their original layouts. But as time progresses and population grows, good, new, natural golf-course terrain becomes too rare, too costly, or too remote to attract much play. Yet golfers still yearn to play on holes like the ones they see on TV. They want that shot down a 100-foot cliff, or across a river to a small green perched on a tiny peninsula. They want grass tufts, split rail fences, and waterfalls to surround the playing areas. They want distinctly shaped bunkers like the pots—the deep, small, round bunkers—of St. Andrews. Or they want to play a hole mimicking Pebble Beach's eighteenth . . . on their own river's bend. Many courses meet these expectations. Many are in Northern California.

History and tournament play

Golf tournaments usually select the best courses for their competitions. They provide the most challenge, have the best maintenance, attract the best players, and bring in the biggest galleries. For this reason, tournament-play makes sense as one of my ranking criteria. Tournaments that count can be amateur or professional, drawing from the nation, the state, the county, or local high schools, with smaller draws having less weight in my quality rating.

Golfers like to play courses where famous shots have been hit or where well-publicized dramas have unfolded. For example, take San Francisco's Harding Park. The rebuilt course had its tournament debut at the World Golf Championships of 2005; it was here that John Daly and Tiger Woods fought their fabulous head-to-head dual. Tied going into the 72nd hole, a difficult par-four, each successfully hit a high-risk 350-yard drives across a tree-covered corner, resulting in easy wedges to the green. Both got par, and then repeated identical performances on first play-off hole. Next they moved out to the course to number 15, where they tied again. Then at 16, a very short par-four, Daly went for the green, but faded his drive to the right, behind the trees. Tiger played safe with an iron. Daly paced and cogitated for several minutes—all caught dramatically on TV--then decided to go for it. He hit a miraculous wedge over a monster cypress tree, barely clearing both the tree and a bunker, and got closer to the pin than Wood's easy pitch shot. Woods missed his putt and Daly came close but skidded by four feet. Then, to everyone's surprise, Daly missed his comeback putt, providing an anticlimactic end to a Battle of the Titans that those watching wanted to see go on and on. This story holds the same drama as the legendary finishes of Jack Nicklaus and Tom Watson in consecutive U.S. Opens at Pebble Beach. Each makes us want to try the same shots ourselves, or at least see the spots where they happened and imagine what our own result would be.

Ours is a cerebral sport. That's not to say that baseball, football, tennis, track or gymnastics don't demand equal mental acuity. On the contrary, they all exert heavy pressure, demand good memory and quick recall, and require leadership skills as well as tough physical training. But unlike basketball, for example, good golf depends more on a player's state-of-mind in the moment than on conditioned prowess or inherited IQ. Players who hit fairways, hit greens, recover from disaster, and then sink putts under pressure are the ones who win. Physical strength and prowess get players on the stage, but *confidence*—having a clear idea of what shot is needed and knowing that one has the ability *at that moment* to pull it off—such *confidence in-the-moment* is what golf audiences really love. And they understand it best when it is delivered on familiar courses or by familiar faces. No wonder the sport pays such homage to individual performance, to self-satisfaction, and to tradition. Old courses that have seen successes are often more revered than new ones. The oldest tournaments, developed by the original icons of the game, become the Majors and the most sought after victories on the Tour. The British Open, the U.S. Open, and the Masters' return again and again to the tournament venues of the past.

****

The numerical system used to create *quality ratings* of the **Best 100** assigns 120 points to Design, 100 to Condition, 70 to Facilities/Service, 50 to Beauty, 25 to Tradition, and 25 to Uniqueness, for a total of 390 points. Each of the six primary categories is then subdivided into twenty-nine specific sub-topics for individual scoring. Examples include:

- Overall beauty of surroundings
- Fairway condition
- Green design (shape, slope, size)
- Practice facilities
- Walk-ability

Rankings will vary from year to year. The time that elapses between writing this book and distributing it to readers will be enough for a few things to change. Course maintenance and conditions will adjust, going from rock-hard to swamp-wet, or from hot and dry to cold and blustery. Trees will blow down, fairway mowing will change pattern, greens keepers will come and go, and management will move on. Few things stay the same for long at most golf courses. For these reason, the last date I played each course is noted as a reference point for the reader.

By way of warning, permit me a comment about prices shown in the summary charts following each review. Most courses change greens fees annually, some more frequently. Many have 10-15 categories of play. Prices shown on our **Best 100** charts were published in print or on line, or quoted in conversation, on the dates I have indicated. Changes and special deals make perfect accuracy impossible. Make sure to check pro shops or websites for up-to-date information. The price charts I used to calculate value ratings described in Chapters 5 and 6 reflect summer prices for 2008. Further information on pricing and discounts can be found in Chapter 6 under the headings "Websites," and "Value Ratings."

Finally, it took me 15 months to play 220 courses and 10 to write and edit this book. Can anyone think of a better way to spend two years?

Chapter 2:
The Best 100 Courses

<u>No. 1: Pebble Beach</u>

Pebble Beach, Augusta National, and St. Andrews may be the most famous golf courses anywhere in the world. *Golf Digest Magazine* ranked Pebble Number One early in the '00's, before the historic tree overlooking the eighteenth green died and had to be replaced. Today, it's still a great course by any standard, certainly the best public access course in Northern California. The expanse of natural coastline, sculptured green complexes,* mammoth bunkers, and mesmerizing vistas provide everything that players are conditioned to expect.

Less well known is that Pebble's length, short for a U.S. Open venue, allows average golfers to enjoy the same sense of accomplishment as the pros. Even novices can experience occasional success with some truly memorable swings—like hitting over the ocean inlet to the eighth green, approaching across the huge trap in front of the fourteenth green, clearing the bunkers on the picturesque seventeenth, or facing the threat of a hook into the Pacific Ocean on number eighteen. For those who can afford the almost $500 greens fee, almost any level golfer can have a great time.

Here, then, are suggestions, impressions, and bits of info from a guy who remembers playing 36 holes at Pebble Beach for $10 a day in the mid 1960s, and who still manages to wangle his way to a bi-annual round at this best-of-the-best:

1. The preferred weather on the Monterey Peninsula starts in September and lasts through early June. July and August can be chilly and foggy, with visibility infrequently reduced to no more than 75 yards. Don't expect weather at the start of a round to be like conditions at the finish during these months, although Pebble's summer weather is often clearer and warmer than its sister courses, Spanish Bay and Spyglass Hill.
2. Some people criticize the first five holes because they play more easily than the rest. Instead of complaining, concentrate on scoring well, because after these first few, other easy holes are few and far between.
3. If you want a foursome starting time, remember to reserve a room at the Resort at Pebble Beach or the Inn at Spanish Bay a year in advance.

(Single players, on the other hand, will find they can sometimes walk on without a starting time. Also, the '08/'09 recession has lowered fees and increased starting time flexibility.)

4. Pebble's greens are small, making long putts rare. Players who find the feel of speed and break will have a lot of success, and a lot of fun.

5. The grain on greens almost always breaks west, toward the setting summer sun. Why? During the summer, fog often obscures the sunlight till late in the day. Because grass blades tend to grow toward the light, the afternoon sun pulls them in that direction.

6. Holes eight, nine, and ten are considered by many the most beautiful and most difficult three-hole stretch in the world. (Amen Corner at Augusta could make the same claim.) Seven, seventeen, and eighteen are also top-notch holes.

7. Pebble Beach caddies are experienced, expensive, and cocky. But if you want to score well, their putting tips and advice can be worth it.

8. Highly recommended: Invite your non-playing spouse, friend, or significant other to accompany you on the course or to drive the cart. It's the most beautiful walk in the world, especially on sunny days, and will save you money. The alternative—shopping the day away in nearby Carmel—can be really expensive.

Number eight green and number ten fairway at Pebble Beach, looking west toward Carmel-by-the-Sea. Holes number four to number ten and seventeen and eighteen all border on the Pacific Ocean.

One feature of this book is to identify holes of distinctive character on every top course. At Pebble Beach, that's a monumental challenge. Other writers have already described the multitude of choices: For example, number eighteen, with its expansive scenic view of the ocean, the beauty of the homes lining its right side, and the risky nature of each and every shot, tops many lists. According to Jack Nicklaus, number eight was once the best hole he ever played. Its spectacular approach shot, directly over a 160-yard chasm of surf, cliff, bunkers, and apron, remains as dramatic as any golf scene in the world. Number seventeen, the difficult par-three where both Tom Watson and Jack Nicklaus secured their U.S. Open victories, gets its share of votes. Seven, the short par-three that extends all the way to the edge of the ocean on a small peninsula, also qualifies; Sam Snead once putted his 100-yard drive into the front bunker, just to keep it safely out of the wind. Number nine, the most difficult hole at Pebble Beach, skirts along 440 rolling yards of cliffs overlooking the Pacific. The approach—often over 200 yards—requires the player to cross a monstrously deep bunker and a tiny apron to reach a very small green. Numbers seven and eighteen are said to be the most often-photographed golf holes in America.

Judiciously, therefore, I will avoid picking the best hole on this best of courses, instead pointing out the one that is most underrated—par-four, number eleven—the challenge that starts the turn back toward the clubhouse. Demanding precision on the green-approach, it's nonetheless played easily by long and medium hitters alike. It begins with a blind, uphill drive, which is to say, you can't see the area where the ball lands. You'll feel tempted to aim down the shorter right side of the treeless dogleg, but that would be a mistake, because the right side creates a difficult approach over deep bunkers. Besides, the hole is short enough to use a medium iron on the second shot from the opposite side of the fairway. The smartest approach target is the front edge, avoiding trouble entirely, even playing short for an easy uphill chip. But what fun would that be, especially when a birdie is possible on the number-four handicap hole? There's nothing like a little success on a tricky hole before you head back into the prevailing wind of Pebble's final stretch.

If the course has a weakness, other than the cost of play, it's the erratic condition of the greens, so at odds with the exclusive setting. Lately some pros have been quite critical of this anomaly. Also, although it's one of the most beautiful places in the world, management demands that players take an expensive caddy if they choose to walk the course. The extra cost pushes most people into carts, and carts must stay on paths. Humph . . . another reason to bring along a buddy to do the driving! *Review based on frequent play, most recently in July '07.*

*See Chapter 6 for definitions of various golf terminologies, including a definition of *green complexes*.

Pebble Beach Golf Links:		
1700 17-Mile Drive	**Reservations:**	800 654-9300
P. O. Box 658	**Golf Shop:**	831 647-6500
Pebble Beach, CA 93953	**Fax**	831 662-8795
	www.pebblebeach.com	
Managed by: Pebble Beach Company	**Architect:**	Jack Neville

Location:	On the Monterey Peninsula: Take State Rt. 68 exit at the top of the hill, north off State Rt.1. Follow signs to Pebble Beach. After going through entrance gate, take lower fork and follow signs to Pebble Beach Golf Links.
Style:	Links w/ tenth hole away from clubhouse. Slightly hilly terrain, some shots over ocean, some forced carries. Panoramic views of ocean. Well bunkered small greens. Caddies or carts required.
Other info:	Resort golf course. Players usually need to book a room in Lodge at Pebble Beach or Inn at Spanish Bay to get a reserved foursome starting time. However, the proshop will allow walk-on singles and the public-at-large if course is not booked. Business events should reserve 12 months in advance. Cart fee included for resort guests.

Greens Fees as of 10/08:	Weekends	Weekdays	Twilight	Seniors	Carts/person
	$495	$495	No Savings	No savings	$35

Course ratings	Men	Par	Rating	Slope	Yardage	Women	Par	Rating	Slope	Yardage
	Blue	72	73.8	142	6742	White	72	76.6	135	6116
Pebble Beach	Gold	72	72.3	137	6350	Red	72	71.8	129	5198
	White	71	71.2	134	6116					

NO. 2: Spyglass Hill

Preferred by many golfers over Pebble Beach, Spyglass Hill is one of the world's premier courses. But it can also be a challenging test of patience and skill. As a course member, I enjoy inviting one and two-handicappers to play, then watch them shoot ten strokes above their normal score. It happens time and again, partly because they seem too proud to ask for advice.

At Spyglass, you have to make shots that are smart rather than risky, aim for safe parts of the green, and be adept with bunker shots and chipping finesse. Unlike many other California courses—where difficulties come from steep canyons, multiple creek crossings, and environmentally protected spaces—the obstacles at Spyglass are more conventional. They include deep bunkers, elevated greens, tightly cut aprons, rolling terrain, tree-lined fairways, strategically placed ponds, sand dunes, and a deep third cut of rough, all challenges that easily make up for the course's relatively short yardage. Greens will be missed and close misses roll down embankments into heavy grass. Chipping back close to the pin is very difficult, but it is also the key to good scores. And don't forget the ice plant, a quirky little succulent that adds an element of ambience or terror to the experience, depending on your point of view.

There are many good reasons to love this course: On most days, particularly days before and after tournaments, maintenance crews keep the course in outstanding condition. Its proximity to the ocean makes for spectacular views on holes one through five, and no two holes are remotely similar. Indeed, most players agree that there isn't a weak hole, and several rank among the toughest anywhere on the PGA tour. (In 1999, Spyglass hosted the final qualifying rounds of the U.S. Amateur. Because the greens were slightly firmed and rolled, the second cut of rough was allowed to grow an extra inch, and the aprons were trimmed quite short, the average score ballooned to 79!) And, Pebble Beach Company, owner of the course, continues to improve conditions. Even in wet winters, and despite problems with tree disease, it remains a year-round challenge.

The tee on par-three, number three at Spyglass Hill has a spectacular view of the Pacific Ocean, nearby Cypress Point and Monterey Peninsula Golf Courses, and Seal Rock.

Spyglass boasts many special holes, and most critics consider it architect Robert Trent Jones Sr.'s best design. The toughest are numbers six, eight, and sixteen, where the fairways thread through Monterey Pines to bunkered, elevated, and undulating greens. The best-looking holes are four and fourteen, where the greens offer borders of mounded dunes, a stone-lined pond, and tall pines. All par-threes measure short from the middle tees (120 to 165-yards), but appear picturesque and demand accuracy. My personal favorite hole is four, a short 350-yard par-four with an open-appearing driving area, a wonderful links-style view of sand and ocean (and gorgeous homes), and a scary need for accuracy on the approach. The green looks like a funnel or a diagonally shaped trough set between high dunes. It's less than 12 yards wide and at least 50 yards long. The pin frequently sits hidden, so only the top of the flag can be seen.

However, because of its special artistry, most connoisseurs choose hole number one as the premier design on this premier course. Its layout is a reverse image of the course itself. Pine trees closely guard the first two-thirds of a 550-yard (middle tee), downhill fairway that curves and slopes, mirroring the last 13 holes of the course. The final one-third plays out among dunes, bunkers, and clusters of ice plant, with an ocean view, exactly like the next four holes. Due to the downhill lies, a tree-lined driving chute, and bunkers surrounding the green, newcomers usually score poorly on number one. Combine these features with another fast, undulating, 50-yard putting surface, and you have a classic introduction to what's coming.

Don't be frustrated with a bad start; just accept it as part of the experience. Feel super with a par and make hay on the next four shorter holes, because you'll need a cushion for what comes after them. In the end, settle for shooting well above your normal score. *Review based on frequent play over the years, last in June '09.*

Spyglass Hill Golf Course:

Stevenson Drive and Spyglass Hill Road		Reservations:	800 654-9300
P. O. Box 658		Golf Shop:	831 625-8563
Pebble Beach, CA 93953		Fax:	831 622-1308
		www.pebblebeach.com	
Managed by:	Pebble Beach Company	Architect:	Robert Trent Jones, Sr.
Location:	On the Monterey Peninsula. Take State Rt. 68 exit north off State Rt.1. Follow signs to Pebble Beach. After going through entrance gate, take lower fork and follow signs to Spyglass Hill Golf Course.		
Style:	Dunes and ocean views on first five holes. Next thirteen are hilly and in the forest. Large greens. Walking OK but a fairly long trek. Good driving range where balls are included in greens fee.		
Other info:	Resort golf course. Players usually need to book a room in Lodge at Pebble Beach or Inn at Spanish Bay to get a reserved foursome starting time, but arranging a time is much easier than at Pebble. Call Del Monte Golf course to find out about the Dukes club, a way to save on greens fees at Del Monte, Spyglass Hill, and Spanish Bay. Cart fee included for hotel guests only.		

Greens Fees as of 11/08:	Weekends	Weekdays	Twilight	Senio	Carts/pe	Carts/person
	$330	$330	Call proshop	No savings	Included	

Course ratings	Men	Par	Rating	Slope	Yardage	Women	Par	Rating	Slope	Yardage
	Blue	72	75.5	147	6953	White	73	76.8	140	6114
Spyglass Hill	Gold	72	73.2	144	6354	Red	73	72.9	133	5329
	White	72	71.4	137	6123					

No. 3: Pasatiempo

Pasatiempo is a lesser-known top ranked course that every serious golfer needs to play. Found just off Highway 17 north of downtown Santa Cruz, it fully lives up to it's name ("passing time")—so fully, in fact, that some golfers say if they had only one course to play for the rest of their lives, this would be it. Although less demanding than more famous courses down the Monterey Peninsula, it was designed by famed architect Alister MacKenzie, near the home where he lived, giving aficionados an opportunity to play one of his classics in an easily accessible location.

The roughs are not too rough, the par-fives are not too long or too tight, and the surrounding homes are not too close. The tree-lined fairways are trimmed high enough to allow a player to swing under them, and total length is only 6,500 yards from the back tees. Newcomers will find some easy holes and some tough holes, and that they will need to use every club in their bag. To top it off, Pasatiempo's elevation above the Pacific Ocean summer fog belt offers great vistas of majestic Monterey Bay, stretching south to Carmel and Pebble Beach.

Pasatiempo's greens are one of its major distinctions. Because they're large and undulating, often fast and usually in great shape, approach shots challenge on almost every hole, from the downhill 450-yard par-four number one to the deep barranca and bunker-protected par-three eighteenth. Stately cypress trees lining the fairways sit far enough into the rough to allow decent recoveries from small driver errors, but the multiple greenside bunkers quickly bring golfers back to reality.

A major course renovation was completed late in 2007. Although overall length and fairway layouts remain relatively unchanged, trees were thinned or removed, fairway bunkers were added or amended, and the drainage was improved. Bunker designs and placement around the greens were revamped to restore the unique ambience of MacKenzie's original 1929 design. The re-creations are elegant and imaginative, with bright white-colored bunker sand contrasting brightly against dark green, enlarged greens. The visuals are stunning, but be careful: the sandy hazards and greens are more intimidating than ever.

The club is actually a corporation in which each member owns a true, fully tradable share of stock, currently valued between $200,000 and $300,000, plus annual dues. The course qualifies as semi-private, meaning that members and their guests have playing rights during prime time, but the public can play in periods of lesser demand. Big increases in public-access greens fees over the past few years have funded much of the ambitious renovation effort.

Pasatiempo has an august tournament history, especially for college-level competition. The revered Grand Slam winner Bobby Jones joined the first foursome on opening day in 1929. Tiger Woods and Julie Ingster, among other contemporary pros, played here in during their developing years.

As at Spyglass and Pebble Beach, choosing a best hole isn't easy. Par-fours in particular show superior design, with many highlights. Number eight plays short at only 340-yards but demands an extremely accurate drive and a well-controlled shot to a shallow and narrow reverse L-shaped green. Numbers ten and eleven are among the most challenging-yet-fair par-fours in Northern California, usually making or breaking a good score. And, with its newly designed green and bunkers, number ten is now the best hole on the course.

Yet others disagree. Ben Hogan claimed number sixteen was the best two-shot hole he ever played, and the updated green is now a rare four-tiered surface that drops nearly 10 feet from back-to-front. Its drive is especially challenging. Standing on the tee, golfers feel they should aim straight up a hill on a blind dogleg left. But if hit to what seems to be a safe spot, the ball may roll over into hidden trees or go out-of-bounds. Deceptively, the correct shot placement looks perilous, down the left side toward a creek, aimed at a distant tall tree. *Knowing* you need to hit it left has to overcome *wanting* to hit it down the center. I think this psychological disparity is what made Hogan like the hole so well.

Number sixteen green at Pasatiempo has a four-tier green four-putted by Stanford junior Tiger Woods during the Western Intercollegiate Tournament. It was once Ben Hogan's favorite two-shot hole.

Three of the four par-threes also make for terrific adventure. The first of these one shot opportunities, number three, requires most players to hit a hefty wood up a steep hill between bunkers to a long, two-tier green. Next, number five green slopes so steeply that three-putting often seems like the norm. Finally, locals consider the last hole, a rare par-three eighteenth, as the course's new signature design. It requires a carry of about 160 yards over a deep barranca, where a face bunker now extends down into the creek. Another sharply sloped green, steep hillside, along with even more bunkers, together create room for additional errors. The few approaches that land directly below the hole yield easy birdies. But not many! *Review based on frequent play, last with interview in January '08.*

Pasatiempo Golf Course:

20 Clubhouse Road
Santa Cruz, CA 95060

Golf Shop:	831 459-9155
Fax:	831 459-9157
www.pasatiempo.com	

| **Managed by:** | Private local ownership | **Architect:** | Alister MacKenzie |

Location: Fifteen miles south of San Jose off State Rt. 17. Follow frontage road past Pasatiempo Inn. Turn right on Pasatiempo Dr; clubhouse is on the right, a half mile up the hill.

Style: Mildly hilly course with tree-lined holes. Very difficult, fast greens, lots of bunkers and creeks.

Other info: Semi-private course with access to the public, usually in late morning/early pm. Excellent Hollands house restaurant on the hill above clubhouse.

Greens Fees	Weekends	Weekdays	Twilight	Seniors	Carts/person
as of 10/08:	$200	$200	None	None	$30

Course ratings	Men	Par	Rating	Slope	Yardage	Women	Par	Rating	Slope	Yardage
	Blue	70	72.2	139	6511	White	73	76.6	139	6173
Pasatiempo	White	70	70.4	135	6142	Green	72	74.0	134	5681
	Red	68	68.3	130	5680	Green Sh.	72	73.6	133	5623

No. 4: Poppy Hills

Poppy Hills, home course of the Northern California Golf Association (NCGA), provides a fine—if somewhat controversial—golf experience. For years it joined Spyglass Hill and Pebble Beach as one of three legs of the PGA's February ATT Pro-Am. But in each of the last few tournaments scores went up, averaging higher totals than at either of the other two famous venues. This created some frustration among the participants and started rumors about Poppy Hills' being taken out of the ATT rotation; and May '09 press reports confirm this will happen. Meanwhile, it remains a top course and a top value for quality golf in Northern California.

Robert Trent Jones Jr., son of the architect at nearby Spyglass Hill, designed Poppy Hills in 1986. Cut from a forest of native Monterey pines, it possesses its share of hilly lies, deep forest, heavy rough, and tight OB stakes. The forest obscures views of the ocean and surrounding hills, and thanks to sharp doglegs, severe fairway slopes, and a few well-placed bunker groups, it requires more target-placement shots than either Pebble or Spyglass. You come to Poppy Hills for golf, not sightseeing. The clubhouse accommodates NCGA headquarters; so, well-conditioned grounds, a first-rate pro-shop, a good lunch shop, and a nearby practice facility help make an excellent clubhouse complex.

While many holes such as the par-five number eighteen (illustrated on the next page) appear unique and picturesque, the real jewels at Poppy Hills are its greens. They can be made as fast as the tournament dictates. Typically huge and multi-terraced, they also feature undulations that can spell big trouble; because of their excessive firmness and speed, the NCGA came under criticism when the course opened in 1986. Fortunately, they are rarely kept in their original super-fast state anymore.

Poppy Hills is also home to many Norcal Championship tournaments. For most of us who are members, this means the NCGA Zone Sectionals. NCGA members, 175,000 strong, vie each year to qualify for playing both Poppy Hills and Spyglass Hill in one tournament. We earn this honor by winning a home-course competition, then travel to Monterey for two days of high-quality golf. (Starting in 2009, Spyglass Hill co-hosts only the Finals of the Zone competitions. The Bayonet Golf Course in Seaside replaces Spyglass as the new alternate Sectional course.)

A heads-up to those playing in Zone tournaments for the first time—the NCGA is a super-stickler for the rules. In particular, pay attention to two that you may not be aware of: Don't stand behind or in front of the line of your partner's shot or putt, or officials will zealously assess a two-stroke penalty. Also after trudging behind slower groups for seven holes, you'll have to sprint to keep up with the group in front of you to finish the nines. Teams that fall behind on the last hole (of each nine) face severe penalties.

NCGA Headquarters overlook the par-five eighteen at Poppy Hills. The green is reachable in two by a high-risk approach but is a devil to putt.

Like most well-designed modern courses in Northern California, Poppy Hills has a great layout, with few holes looking the same. The par-fives In particular are lots of fun and a challenge for all levels of play. They tease the long hitters to go for the green in two, yet play long and twisty enough that shorter second and third shots need to be well placed.

As at Papa Jones' Spyglass Hill nearby, the best hole here, a par-four playing around 380 yards, comes on number one. The drive is easy if you want a long 180-yard shot into a well-trapped, well-mounded, creek-protected green. If you try to cut the corner to save 50-60 yards, the drive becomes much riskier, providing a good test at the start of your round. It lets you know Poppy Hill will be no pushover. *Review based on play several times, most recently in June '08.*

Poppy Hills Golf Course:

3200 Lopez Road	**Reservations:**	831-625-2035
P. O. Box 1157	**Golf Shop:**	831-622-8239
Pebble Beach, CA 93953	**Fax:**	831-626-5421
	www.poppyhillsgolf.com	
Managed by: The NCGA	**Architect:**	Robert Trent Jones Jr.

Location: On the Monterey Peninsula. Take State Rt. 68 exit off State Rt. 1. Follow signs to to Pebble Beach. After going through entrance gate, take lower fork and follow signs to Poppy Hills Golf Course.

Style: Hilly, tree lined, with many target-style holes. Big Greens kept at moderate to fast speeds.

Other info: Public golf course. Home of the NCGA. NCGA members receive special rates on greens fees at about 50% of non-member prices. Members must show evidence of NCGA membership at check-in. Tee times are arranged through a very efficient voice mail system.

Greens Fees 10	Weekends	Weekdays	Twilight	Seniors	Carts
Non-NCGA	$200	$200	$65	No Savings	$17
NCGA membe	$70	$55	$30	No Savings	$17

Course ratings:	Men	Par	Rating	Slope	Yardage	Women	Par	Rating	Slope	Yardage
	Black	72	74.3	144	6857	White	73	76.0	141	6175
Poppy Hills	Blue	72	71.3	141	6561	Gold	72	71.9	131	5421
	White	72	71.0	134	6175					
	Gold	72	67.6	126	5421					

No. 5: Old Greenwood

North Lake Tahoe, particularly the area around the old stagecoach stop of Truckee, has seen huge growth in the last two decades. Located just south of Interstate-80 about two miles east of town, Old Greenwood is among the newest and most affluent of the area's golf club developments. Lightly forested Ponderosa pine and gentle rolling terrain provide a casual home to elegant mountain-style architecture. Homes have good views of fairways but sit far enough from play to be unobtrusive, and beautiful back nine-views balance the occasional annoyance of front-nine freeway noise along a couple of early fairways.

Jack Nicklaus designed the highly challenging course, which opened in 2004. Some holes are so intimidating that standing on their tee brought back memories of my earlier, anxious experiences navigating their terrain. Landing areas often sit past strategically located trees and bunkers designed to trap anything slightly off line. With the exception of par-five number-two and all the par-threes, each hole positions bunkers near the same shot-grabbing distance from the tee. With sand on one side and water hazards or trees on the other, straight tee shots become a must. Thank goodness a 5,400-foot elevation gives shots an extra 5% in distance, providing a helpful boost with the long layout.

As the course has matured, it's lost the unforgiving tight fairway lies of earlier years. Today they are merely firm, and beautifully manicured. The short roughs also show good grooming. The deep primary rough may look like a stand of harmless, well-spaced grass tufts, but don't be fooled. It holds two to three-foot high blue sagebrush, a dense woody foliage that grabs club-heads rigidly. Finding balls in this tough vegetation can be like needles in a haystack, so sure to bring an extra supply.

Green approaches present another challenge. Picturesque deep bunkers, many with steeply inclined aprons, protect diagonally angled greens. Surfaces still firm from their recent construction remain difficult to hold. Each offers an avenue to roll the ball on, but constricted openings in front usually head rolling shots away from the pin, not towards it.

The sixth hole at Old Greenwood is typical of a difficult Nicklaus layout. The second shot on this long par-five often needs to be aimed over the water and then faded back to the fairway.

A significant design strength comes from the variety and challenge presented by sophisticated par-fives. Each one plays tough-but-fair, rewarding good shots while penalizing bad ones. Especially entertaining is the sixth, which offers a challenge on each shot. If hit too far, drives may reach a lake, but most land in the bail-out position behind a small stand of trees. Once behind the trees, the next shot has to be sliced out over the lake and then return to the fairway. Even after two perfect shots, bunkers and a lake protect the green's left flank, a hill guards the right and back, and putts are forced to negotiate an undulating green. I suggest studying the course yardage book before playing each hole; you will need it.

Par-five, number ten represents the first of our toughest par-fives in the **Best 100**.* Nicklaus positioned several shallow marshy lakes and a stream along the entire left side of the left-hand dogleg. Complicating matters, pines stand interspersed among these lakes, so a ball going that direction will likely hit a limb and drop into one of the hazards. The player's only hope is that the good Lord will land the deflection in the rough, rather than the water. Deep bunkers and tall rough protect the right side, where the drive needs a draw and the second shot has to land with pinpoint accuracy. After navigating the first two or three shots, you'll discover that the green itself is small, undulating, and surrounded by all sorts of nasty new trouble. Bottom line: Old Greenwood may look like a resort, but it plays like a top-quality, tournament-caliber course.

My un-requested advise for its management and members is to convince the PGA or USGA to bring in a big open national tournament and show the quality of their course to the rest of the golfing world. *Review based on play twice, last with interview in July '08.*

*See Chapter 6 for a list of the toughest holes in Northern California. Pebble Beach and Spyglass Hill are not included in the choices in order to give recognition to other lesser-known challenges throughout the state.

Old Greenwood Golf Club:

12915 Fairway Drive	**Reservations:**	800-754-3070
Truckee, CA 96161	**Golf Shop:**	530-550-7010
	www.oldgreenwood.com	

Managed by:	Tahoe Mountain Club	**Architect:**	Jack Nicklaus
Style:	Gently rolling terrain; pine lined fairways; extensive bunkering; large firm terraced greens.		
Location:	Two miles east of Truckee on I-80. Take exit 190 and turn south on Prosser Village Road. Entrance to Fairway Drive is very near the exit.		
Other info:	Semi-private resort golf course. Local residents can purchase "Tahoe twosome" pass for savings of 25% to 40% on greens fees.		

Greens Fees as of 10/08:	Weekends	Weekdays	Twilight	Seniors	Carts/person
	$185	$185	$100	No savings	Included

Course ratings	Men	Par	Rating	Slope	Yardage	Women	Par	Rating	Slope	Yardage
Old Greenwood	4 Trees	72	75.2	140	7518	1 Tree	72	69.8	133	5419
	3 Trees	72	72.7	137	6944					
	2 Trees	72	70.4	128	6457					

No. 6: Stevinson Ranch

Northern California boasts all types of wonderful golf course terrain. Traditionally, the coastal areas around Monterey top everyone's list. But the mountain topography of Lake Tahoe has gained growing recognition over the last 10 years. Golden, grass-covered foothills stretching north from San Luis Obispo to Redding have also provided excellent sites for some classically Californian venues. However, the least-known region remains the vast agricultural Central Valley, where creating modern golf courses from flat topography still proves challenging. Lots of dirt needs to be moved, and manmade lakes and creeks have to be excavated. George Kelly, owner of Stevinson Ranch, with his architect, John Harbottle III, did just that in 1995, giving Northern California its best Central Valley tournament venue, well worth a special trip to play.

The Savannah Course, as it's known on the Stevinson webpage, is situated equidistant from Los Banos, Merced, and Modesto, about a half hour from each. The site lies close to marshlands and sloughs where duck hunting has long been a major sporting activity. Receiving Certified Signature Sanctuary status from the National Audubon Society was an important step in the development process for the venue.

Like the land of links along the coast, the land in this area is considered unfit for most forms of agriculture. Although the loamy, sandy soil can't hold enough water to grow crops, it's perfect for grass, and several sod-farms that grow the turf for NFL football lie within a good, long two-iron distance of the course perimeter.

The eighth at Stevinson Ranch is a short par-four with a very long green, tightly protected by bunkers and sloped aprons. It's an example of the varied designs found on this spacious layout.

Stevinson plays tough. Even at the shorter 6093-yard resort tees, bunkers and other hazards make for challenging play by men; women encounter similar trouble from their 5400-yard tee blocks. The intermediate men's set, at 6646-yards, is a big jump for middle-distance golfers. Further obstacles are created by ball-gobbling sloughs, where the reeds and grasses are so thick that ball-hunts usually prove pointless. The third cut of Bermuda rough often stands shin-deep, a challenge for both finding and swinging. Lakes with railroad-tie bulkheads and pin-positions within 15 feet of the water require critically accurate shots.

The ultimate difficulty, however, comes from the greens themselves--fast, usually at 12 on the StimpMeter,* with curious broad, tightly cut collars, sometimes spreading out five-ten yards adjacent to putting surfaces. They're trimmed so short that most players putt rather than chip because of their ultra-tight lies.

Ample spaces lie between the holes, allowing the course to be extended to over 7,200 yards. Size and length, good maintenance, a great practice area, and fast greens, together make Stevinson Ranch an excellent venue for competition.

Even service details entice repeat play. On hot days a cart shows up on the back nine with cold wet towels to wipe the sweat that develops on a warm day. You may find that you'll need the towel for more than the heat since the design of the last three holes is among the finest anywhere in the **Best 100.** Par-three sixteen requires a long iron or wood over water to a diagonally shaped green, well protected by bunkers. Seventeen, a medium length par-four, heads both the drive and the second shot over lakes to a small green. Each shot requires risk and accuracy, especially the approach to a pin position located close to the water. Finally, eighteen sets up a short par-five, flirting with water and heavy bushes down one side and out-of-bounds down the other, toward a deeply undulating fairway and multi-bunkered, creek-protected green. Mastering this complex is a real accomplishment, especially in competitive events.

U.S. Open and U.S. Senior Open Qualifying Tournaments regularly take over the course. (If you plan to participate or watch, plan for a 30-minute commute, because local lodging is sparse.) At these events, players who have won lesser tournaments come to Stevinson for a chance to win one or two spots in the finals. For example, the 2008 Senior Open Qualifier had a spot for one golfer to go to the big show. Rick Burgess of Colusa birdied five of the last six difficult holes to tie Don Thames of Rancho Murieta for the position. Thames had to sink a wedge on the final hole to reach the playoff, then sink a sweaty downhill slider to win. This constituted high golf drama for a course 20 miles from any big town, and proved the Championship caliber of Stevinson Ranch once again. *Review based on play twice, most recently in August '08.*

* See Chapter 6 for definitions of golf terminology, including the green speed-measuring devise called a "StimpMeter."

Stevinson Ranch Golf Club, Savannah Course:

2700 North Van Clief		**Reservations:**	877-752-9276
Stevinson, CA 95374		**Golf Shop:**	209-668-8200
		Fax:	209-668-6909
		www.stevinsonranchgolf.com	
Managed by:	Greenway Golf	**Architect:**	John Harbottle
Style:	Flat terrain with graded contours. Lakes and creeks are common. Few trees. Fast greens with unusual collars 5 to 10 yards wide.		

Location:	Midway between Merced and Gustine, and Los Banos and Turlock. Near junction of State Rts. 168 and 140. Take Rt. 140 east 2 miles to Van Clief and turn north about 2 miles.
Other info:	Cabins available for overnight rentals.

Greens Fees as of 7/08:	Weekends	Weekdays	Twilight	Seniors	Carts
	$90	$70	50%	-$30 Tuesdays	Included

Course ratings:		Men	Par	Rating	Slope	Yardage	Women	Par	Rating	Slope	Yardage
Stevinson Ranch	Black		72	75.2	143	7135	White	73	75.5	131	6093
	Gold		72	74.4	139	7060	Green	72	71.9	124	5461
	Blue		72	72.7	129	6646					
	White		71	70.2	122	6093					

No. 7: Coyote Moon

A granite outcropping protrudes from bunkers situated behind a gracefully elevated green. In a small den created by a rocky crevasse, coyotes spend the winter; come spring, young pups romp and play, stealing golfers' balls. These artful predators have lent their name to Coyote Moon, a wonderful north Tahoe course that opened in 1998. Its layout offers a prime example of how modern golf design can be adapted to a mountain venue. The setting is well-maintained, moderately sculpted, and it boasts holes with stunning ridgeline vistas. At the same time it retains the feel of traditional tree-lined design, without tricked-up hazards or too many bunkers adding unwarranted difficulty. Coyote Moon represents a throw back to days when courses were built without houses surrounding them. One hopes that the inevitable pressure to build, build, build can be resisted, or least delayed.

Number thirteen at Coyote Moon, par-three 195-yards, is one of the **Best 100's** *prettiest holes. The drop from tee to green is steep, so subtract 2 1/2 clubs for the shot.*

The back nine, where you'll find most of the special holes, is uniquely scenic and requires a lot of shot control. Every hole is distinct, many with sudden changes in elevation, steeply up or steeply down. Number thirteen, a par-three, stands out as Coyote Moon's signature hole, providing a dramatic vista of the distant mountain ranges north of Lake Tahoe. In the foreground, a 196-yard (blue tees) shot heads downhill across a riverbed lined with pine and aspen, and fills with glorious Sierra colors in the fall. The steep drop is a bit scary, so hit about 2½ clubs less than normal to compensate for the drastic change. The holes fore and aft also appear particularly picturesque. Number twelve flaunts those coyote-filled boulders, as the focal point at the end of a scenic uphill par-five. Number fourteen, an extremely tight, short par-four, forces a very short 185-yard drive to avoid the wide, woodsy riverbed waiting to eat up balls hit even slightly off line. A 125-yard approach follows the drive, heading over the river to a small green, archetypal of twisty mountain design.

The front nine has less drama but is still fun to play, offering multiple vistas and providing a good warm-up. Number four is the exception, in a class of its own as one of the toughest par-fours holes anywhere in the **Best 100**. A long dogleg from an elevated tee, it circles around a steep hill on the left. To avoid falling off a sharp slope to the right, your drive needs to stay on the left, but the tee box acts like a magnet connected to the trees on the hill, pulling all shots slightly off line into the forest. Even with a good drive, a long second needs to be hit perfectly to a highly elevated green. A miss of putt number one usually leaves at least 15 feet back up for a second try. Bogey on four is a very good score.

Although reasonably difficult, Coyote Moon remains an area favorite for Tahoe, like Pasatiempo in San Francisco's South Bay. Location and beauty balance long holes and a deep, undeveloped rough. If it had a driving range instead of nets, it would rank even higher in the **Best 100**. *Review based on play twice, most recently with interviews in July '08.*

Coyote Moon Golf Course:

10685 Northwoods Boulevard	**Golf Shop:**	530 587-0886
Truckee, CA 96161	**Fax:**	530 550-7059
	www.coyotemoongolf.com	

Managed by:	Tahoe Mountain Club. **Architect:** Brad Bell
Style:	Rolling topography w/ many tight, tree lined fairways. Gorgeous mountain scenery. Well guarded greens. Difficult walk due to hills from green to tee.
Location:	In Truckee. Take I-80 exit 184 and go north to Donner Pass Rd. Then turn left and go 1/2 mile and turn right on Northwood Blvd. Course is on the right about 1/2 mile up the hill.
Other info:	No driving range, nets only for warm-up.

Approx. Greens	Weekends	Weekdays	Twilight	Seniors	Carts
Fees as of 10/08	$160	$160	$100	No savings	Included

Course ratings:	Men	Par	Rating	Slope	Yardage	Women	Par	Rating	Slope	Yardage
Coyote Moon	Black	72	73.7	136	7061	White	74	74.4	142	6106
	Blue	72	70.9	134	6555	Gold	69	68.4	127	4965
	White	69	68.9	129	6106					

No. 8: The Ridge

The final hole at The Ridge requires an accurate drive to avoid both water and sand. This course is one of the best values in the foothills east of metropolitan Sacramento.

The historic town of Auburn and metropolitan Sacramento are home to several excellent public-access courses. For first-rate quality and overall value, The Ridge ranks number one. The relatively low greens fees may be partially attributable to an area price war, which began late in 2007, so golfers wanting a really good deal should plan to play soon.

The Ridge offers numerous outstanding features. Robert Trent Jones Jr., creator of its rugged design, built in enough variety to engage players on almost every shot. Although a couple of holes display similarities, such as sharing opposite sides of the same creek, strategies for play differ on each. Doglegs go left and right, on both short holes and long holes. Long par-fives head downhill; shorter ones head up. The par-threes measure differing lengths, and the par-fours vary widely in difficulty. Shorter holes have severe greens with multiple tiers, and longer ones are flatter, compensating for the challenge of reaching them.

The course condition rivals that of a good country club. Roughs and fairways look freshly mown, and the rye grass is well fertilized, thick, and green. Ten to 20-yard wide roughs mean that hardpan under the oaks sits well off the fairway and rarely comes into play. Greens stay at a Stimp speed of between 9 and 10, pretty fast on these undulating surfaces, but not overly punishing. Aprons and tees show good maintenance and are a pleasure for chips and drives.

Because The Ridge is hilly, walking can be work, but cart cost is included with greens fees and most players ride. Diehards who want the exercise and choose to walk will find that Jones has mitigated the distance between green and tee. It's certainly shorter than at nearby Whitney Oaks.

As with other Top Ten courses, choosing the best hole at The Ridge presents a challenge. Every candidate is interesting, picturesque, and fun. Number thirteen, a 400-yard par-four, heads straight uphill and requires a well-placed drive followed by a long fairway wood to reach an elevated green. A steep mound in front protects the putting surface, making it the toughest hole on the course. Later, a reed bordered lake, contoured fairway, and beautiful bunkers, give number eighteen (shown in the drawing on the previous page) the *most photogenic* prize.

One has to look hard for weaknesses. Straight drivers have a huge advantage, because landing areas appear narrow and greens are well protected by bunkers and hazards. The white tees and lady's tees get a big break in distance, taking away much of the worry felt at the rear teeing areas. Players who don't like hilly courses or hate non-level lies may think twice about playing, as might those who hit the ball way off-line. Some purists will gripe about noise from nearby Bell Road, but it's a small price to pay, on just a few holes, for the beauty, interest, and challenge of the well-trimmed landscape at this wonderful venue. *Review based on play in October '07.*

The Ridge Golf Club:

2020 Golf Course Road		**Golf Shop:**	530 888-7888
Auburn, CA 95602		**Fax:**	530 888-8870
		www.ridgegc.com	
Managed by:	Western Care Construction	**Architect:**	Robert T. Jones, Jr.
Style:	Fairways wind through oak covered hills. Walking OK but not easy. Moderate sized highly undulating greens. Landing areas well protected by bunkers. Excellent condition.		
Location:	In Auburn, 25 miles northeast of Sacramento. Take I-80 to Bell Road exit. Go about one mile west. Then turn north on New Airport Road.		
Other info:	Public course, very good value.		

Greens Fees	Weekends	Weekdays	Twilight	Seniors	Carts
as of 11/08:	$60	$50	$50/$40	$40	Included

Course ratings:	Men	Par	Rating	Slope	Yardage	Women	Par	Rating	Slope	Yardage
	Gold	71	73.1	137	6734	White	71	73.5	134	5855
The Ridge	Blue	71	71.2	133	6345	Red	71	70.7	128	5354
	White	71	68.7	127	5855	Green	71	68.5	123	4954

No. 9: Links at Spanish Bay

The Inn at Spanish Bay occupies a 500-acre resort tract built by Pebble Beach Company in the mid-1980s. The five-star resort is comprised of hotel rooms, condominiums, restaurants, pools, tennis courts, and the Links at Spanish Bay golf course. For many years the property operated as a sand quarry, but its easy access and the market demand for high-quality, links-style golf made it a natural for development.

Today, Spanish Bay ranks in *Golf Digest's* Top 100 U. S. Courses, but critical acclaim was slow in coming. The design team of Tom Watson, Sandy Tatum, and Robert Trent Jones Jr. received mixed reviews as a result of the extreme nature of the course. The greens had excessive breaks and undulations, and the grass covering them was an unusual coarse strain that was often bumpy and usually slow. The dunes surrounding the fairways were heavily trodden, and hitting from them proved difficult. An exposed course setting, open to the ocean winds, made playing colder and more uncomfortable than at other nearby resorts. At the time, the average American golfer hadn't yet grown accustomed to these hardy Scottish virtues, and the course's reputation suffered.

But times changed, and Spanish Bay now ranks at the forefront of the golfing community, in part because the Scottish style is now "in," in part because the course matured. Its fairways now feel lush and roll well, even in wet weather. Grasses on greens have been converted to the more traditional bent variety and stay in pristine condition. Sandy areas to the sides of the roughs feature coverings of mature native vegetation, plus several environmental-protection stakes, set to keep golfers out. Plantings have filled out and offer greater protection from the wind. As a result, Spanish Bay is now considered a fun golf experience—but usually to those who like challenging drive placements, creative green approach-shots, and crazy putting on greens that still feature many of their quirky, original mounds.

Spanish Bay is also a course with real risk/reward opportunities. The longest tees are only 6,800 yards and the whites are around 6000. This leaves more chances to drive the ball close on par-fours, or go for the par-fives in two, than can be found on many big-name courses. But taking chances is risky and misses can ruin a score. For example, the first hole is a short par-five, tempting players to take a second shot at the green over an area heavy with native grasses and low shrubs. Who wants to play it safe with a medium iron on the second shot of the day? Only the smart golfers! Holes two, three, five, six, and nine also look attractive for attempting risky drives, but playing it safe remains the smart, winning choice.

Despite the course's severe target-golf characteristics, several well-designed holes deserve mention. Number six, a medium length par-four dogleg, gives the player a complete view of the complex arrangement of bunkers, hollows, and ridges leading from the tee to the distant green. Because shots ending closer to the elevated, bunkered green make the approach much easier, this expansive view helps determine how much corner to cut. An even better (read "tougher") hole comes at thirteen, a 550-yard downhill par-five, usually directly into the wind. Breezy afternoons easily amplify hook or slice spins. Although the elevation drops continuously from tee to green, undulations seem to push straight shots off line, toward the edges of the fairway. The green sits at the focal point of a tightening, funnel-shaped approach, an area beset by numerous, nasty hazards. The surface may appear normal from a distance, but a reverse terrace, where the middle level lies lower than the front, can fool and frustrate an approach or chip.

The proximity of the course to the ocean, at the cove named "Spanish Bay," can make play a real treat. No shots have to be hit over saltwater, and it's unlikely that one would land in the bay, but the mist blown up by the breaking waves is beautiful, and close views of the surf beat those at Pebble Beach. Golfers lucky enough to play on days when the sky is clear blue, the water is emerald green, and the winds are calm will have an unforgettable experience—one that has helped the course achieve its national rating. For all those other times when the temperature drops and the fog rolls in, Spanish Bay provides a Spartan "Scottish encounter." *Review based on play several times, most recently in November '07.*

The Links at Spanish Bay:

2700 17-Mile Drive	Reservations: 800 654-9300
P. O. Box 658	Golf Shop: 831 647-7495
Pebble Beach, CA 93953	Fax: 831 644-7956
	www.pebblebeach.com

Managed by:	Pebble Beach Co. **Architect:** Jones Jr, Tatum, Watson
Style:	Oceanside views. Holes wind through sand dunes and some trees. Greens have unusual shapes and steep slopes. Hilly terrain but easy walking. Can be windy. Beautiful ocean views throughout course.
Location:	On the Monterey Peninsula. Take State Rt. 68 exit off State Rt. 1. Follow Rt. 68 through town for five miles. Turn left onto Seventeen Mile Drive and take first right into Spanish Bay.
Other info:	Resort golf course. Players usually need to book a room in Lodge at Pebble Beach or Inn at Spanish Bay to get a reserved foursome starting time, but arranging a time is much easier than at Pebble. Call Del Monte Golf course to find out about the Dukes club, a way to save on greens fees at Del Monte, Spyglass Hill, and Spanish Bay. Cart fee included for hotel guests. Driving range located at Spyglass Hill, via 10 minute shuttle.

Greens Fees	Weekends	Weekdays	Twilight	Seniors	Carts
as of 11/08:	$295	$295	$175	No savings	Included

Course ratings:	Men	Par	Rating	Slope	Yardage	Women	Par	Rating	Slope	Yardage
Spanish Bay	Blue	72	74.1	146	6779	White	72	75.6	137	5922
	Gold	72	72.0	137	6336	Red	72	72.1	129	5332
	White	72	70.3	129	5922					

No. 10: Sevillano Links

They call the town of Corning, located 90 minutes north of Sacramento on Interstate-5, Olive Town. The country's largest table olive processor, Bell Carter Foods, is headquartered there, and nearby Butte County produces 80 percent of the olives grown in California. No wonder owners of nearby Rolling Hills Casino named its new golf course for the queen of the olive family, the jumbo variety called Sevillano.

Michael Stark's design for Sevillano Links Golf Course is certainly regal. When I played in July 2008, it was the finest-conditioned golf course in the **Best 100**, possibly the finest anywhere in Northern California. Even premier private venues such as Cypress Point, San Francisco Golf Club, and The Preserve in Carmel Valley don't feature fairways, roughs, bunkers, aprons and greens more beautifully maintained than those I experienced that day at Sevillano Links. Whether or not management can keep them at the same high level remains to be seen, but they were a true joy.

John Daly joined the project along the way, and the course begun by Stark eventually became a John Daly Signature Course. Along with input for the final layout and style, Daly came with a novel idea. Why not set up a series of tees and additional target fairways so the course could be played at 10,000 yards, not just 7,800? Par from this super stretch would be 90, with all holes par-fives. The expansive property, measuring more than 400 acres, could easily accommodate the concept and became a reality. Pro Brian Dahmer then tested the idea during a late 2008 NCGA outing: To judge from the logistical difficulties created by crossing fairways plus the resulting seven-and-a-half-hour rounds, the next extra-length tournament may have to be reduced to the original 7,800-yard maximum length.

For non-tournament players, the course's flexibility is more forgiving. Ladies play at 5,500 yards and men can choose the length that suits their ability. The typical test for macho guys is 6,813 yards, which is plenty, placing most bunkers out of reach for 200 to 240-yard hitters. Since Sevillano is a links-style course, without trees or sharp elevations to improve depth perception, it's helpful to consult the yardage book before hitting drives. Most holes have doglegs, so incorrectly directed shots can easily find their way through fairways into high grass. At a few locations, cutting corners becomes obligatory.

One of the special pleasures at Sevillano comes from enjoying the course's gently rolling scenery, particularly the subtle differences among the colors of its prolific flora. The fairways use hybrid Bermuda grass of one color, the bluegrass roughs sport a contrasting hue, and the Bent grass greens have striations that feature a small 18-inch band of rye-grass outside the Bent collar to prevent the Bermuda from growing into putting surfaces. For continuity, dry 12-inch-high golden range grasses form the exterior border, complemented by wheat-colored bunker sand. The only flaw in this otherwise perfect picture comes in a yard-wide stretch of tall, unruly green rough sitting at the inside edge of the native range grass. Balls bouncing through the second-cut of rough are often lost in this three-foot wide border. (Cutting the grass back to a six-inch height would maintain plenty of challenge without making it so difficult to find balls.)

The diverse design of the last four holes presents a final pleasure. Unlike the first fourteen, which derive their definition from gently mounded grass dunes and raised or sunken greens, elevations change more steeply on the final four. A 60-acre lake adds a pastoral touch first seen on the fifteenth hole, built with a double fairway to lure players toward a slightly shorter line at the 540-yard up-hill dogleg. (Don't do it! The shorter distance is illusion.) The sixteenth hole, a photogenic medium length par-three, extends into the lake, making accuracy critical on the drive. Number seventeen, a long par-four, tempts players to hit the drive hard and cut its dogleg, but an errant drive can hook into the lake, go out-of-bounds through the fairway, or land in bunkers at the corner. Finally, number eighteen is a Daly-size signature hole, more than 600 yards in length, with the last 220 yards all-uphill to an elevated green. Grip-it-and-rip-it!

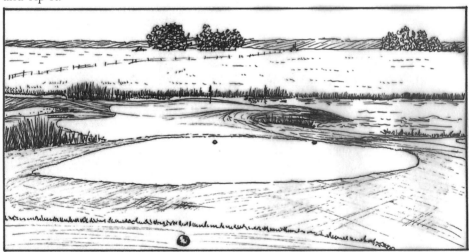

Par-three number sixteen at Sevillano Links provides one of the few water-threatened shots on this new John Daly Signature Course. Jumbo tees offer 7,800-yards for the intrepid amongst us.

Sevillano may be a long way from urban areas, but it truly represents a wonderful golf experience. Next time, rather than flying to Bandon Dunes, Bend, Portland or Seattle, drive up I-5. Take a few extra hours and play golf on the way. Sevillano, at Rolling Hills Casino is one choice, but an hour north sits Gold Hills in Redding, and then another hour north are Mt. Shasta Resort and Lake Shastina, also good courses. As a matter of fact, why not just forget

Oregon altogether and stay-and-play right in California? *Review based on play and interviews in June '08.*

Sevillano Links at Rolling Hills Casino

2657 Barham Avenue	**Golf Shop:**	530-528-4600
Corning, CA 96021	**Fax:**	530-528-4601
	www.sevillanolinks.com	
Managed by:	Rolling Hills Casino	**Architect:**	Michael Stark

Style:	Links type layout, no trees, slightly rolling hills. Lots of dogleg fairways require lay-up shots or knowledge of where to cut across. Plenty of bunkers and excellent large greens.
Location:	Near Corning, 60 miles south of Redding on I-5. Take Liberal Ave exit and head west to frontage road. Turn south and driveway is within 1/4 mile.
Other info:	Resort Golf Course. Special prices are available in winter and summer months. Stay-and-play deals are very reasonable; all proshop for details. Course can be extended to par 90 and 10,000-yard length for special events.

Greens Fees as of 10/08:	Weekends	Weekdays	Twilight	Seniors	Carts/person
	$69	$59	$59/$49	No Savings	Included

Course ratings:	Men	Par	Rating	Slope	Yardage	Women	Par	Rating	Slope	Yardage
	Daly	72	78.0	140	7815	Challenge	72	76.1	125	6259
Sevillano	Champ.	72	75.9	138	7359	Olive	72	71.7	118	5418
Links	Tournament	72	73.4	130	6799					
	Challenge	72	70.4	125	6259					

No. 11: Eagle Ridge

Playing Gilroy's Eagle Ridge for the first time, a golfer walking from the pro-shop to the first tee thinks, "Wow, this is going to be great!" The striped fairway sports diagonal reverse-mown bands of green; the rough's edges appear sharp and well-tended; an expanse of emerald hues, extending from the center of the fairway to the road landscaping well beyond, look inviting and ready. But next you see the bunkers—deep, defined, strategically placed, 92 in number on later count. Then, addressing the first tee shot at a distance of 375 yards, you notice a flag tucked away on a small terrace in the distance, just behind a series of insidious sand pits yawning ahead. "Wow," indeed. This one is going be a real challenge!

On balance, Eagle Ridge plays as a difficult but fair course. The lush vegetation is trim, the fairways and roughs kept prim-and-proper, reminding veterans of Palm Desert courses of their springtime prime. Despite a couple of canyons with big drop-offs to the side, gullies are generally few and far between. Drive landing areas are wide and roughs broad, so stray shots have a fair chance to stay in play. The course's chief distinction consists of bunkers and steep mounds or hills surrounding almost every green. Tee shots generally present minimal problems, but green approaches can be devilish.

Take number one again: Its fairway undulates evenly, but bunkers sit out of reach for most 200-220 yard hitters. The narrow rolling green is kidney-shaped, with sand on all but the right front edge, plus a steep hill in back. The approach shot, although not long, needs to land on the green because missing it easily adds two chips or an extra putt.

Number nine plays the opposite, with few bunkers and a flat fairway that looks no wider than a country road. Eventually, it widens behind a hill, but hitting safely there only complicates matters because oaks growing in crossing creek threaten the long approach shot from that side. Number fifteen also presents a narrow driving slot, requiring a drive that is both straight and long enough to reach the fairway, 220-yards from the blue tees. Hit it hard and hit it dead-straight, then clear the bunker in the front-center of the figure-eight shaped green with an 80 yard wedge.

The ninth at Eagle Ridge, one of the few holes without severe bunkers around the green, requires a straight drive. The course offers several views of Gilroy and Santa Clara Valley.

Both the golf and the setting provide spectacular experiences. A few front nine fairways have homes at their perimeters, evidence that the course was built to attract well-heeled buyers. But the houses don't intrude on the game, and drops and rises in elevation on most holes provide panoramic views of the town of Gilroy and surrounding Santa Clara Valley. Vineyards cover the lower slopes, oak forests, and upper ridges; and the middle of the course provides a natural animal habitat, away from houses. If you see fox and coyote crossing the fairway, enjoy the relief from the rigors of your last hole.

In summary, keeping the ball in play, hitting straight drives, and meeting the test of challenging shots on interesting greens should put Eagle Ridge on your *repeat-play* list, especially if you know how to wedge out of deep bunkers . *Review based on play several times, most recently in August '08.*

Eagle Ridge Golf Course:

2951 Club Drive	Golf Shop:	408 846-4531
Gilroy, CA 95020	Fax:	408 846-4532
	www.eagleridgegc.com	

Managed by:	Monterey Golf Mgmt Group	Architect: Miller/ Fream & Dale
Style:	Rolling terrain, with several elevated views of the Santa Clara Valley. Tremendous amount of bunkers, many surrounding undulating greens. Walking is allowed but not easy.	
Location:	In Gilroy, about 20 miles south of San Jose via US 101. Take State Rt. 152 West exit from 101 and follow through town to Santa Teresa Blvd. Turn left and go 1/2 mile; then turn right into course complex.	
Other info:	Excellent condition. Difficult course.	

Greens Fees	Weekends	Weekdays	Twilight	Seniors	Carts
as of 7/08:	$95	$70	$65/$55	None	$18

Course ratings:	Men	Par	Rating	Slope	Yardage	Women	Par	Rating	Slope	Yardage
	Black	72	74.3	140	6971	White	74	76.8	143	6290
Eagle Ridge	Blue	72	72.7	139	6665	Gold	73	75.2	138	5959
	White	72	71.0	133	6290	Green	72	73.0	135	5546
	Yellow	72	69.4	130	5959	Red	72	70.7	125	5102

NO. 12: Hunter Ranch

Located near the northern border of San Luis Obispo County, the town of Paso Robles has become quite the destination for vacationers, wine enthusiasts, and Californians looking for a more laid-back life style. High-class chefs have been attracted to new restaurants, prompted by the burgeoning wine trade and lower cost of entry. Retirees come for the good weather, coastal access, and relatively reasonable housing prices. Indeed, golfers are finally discovering some great courses and reasonable greens fees along the Central Coast.

San Luis Obispo County stretches for 60 miles along the ocean. Via U.S. 101 from Paso Robles to Santa Maria, it offers a variety of leisure-time activities and beautiful side trips. The Santa Lucia Mountains form a barrier from the Pacific, so the north end of the county is mild-to-hot in the summer. But the coastal towns of San Luis Obispo, Pismo Beach and Morro Bay, fed by ocean winds, enjoy temperate summers and relatively warm winters. California Polytechnic State University, San Luis Obispo (Cal Poly), creates many of the cultural activities and beaches dominate much of the real estate. Wineries abound the entire length of the highway and five of the **Best 100's** top courses flourish in the county.

Hunter Ranch Golf Course, located approximately three miles east of Paso Robles on the road to Fresno, tops the list. Its design, especially on the front nine, represents a return to traditional layout, where holes follow the natural terrain and fairways wander gracefully through stands of 100-year-old oaks. The position of bunkers encourages moderate driver accuracy, and greens set on hillsides rather than on hilltops provide artistically framed approach shots.

The back nine offers more extreme design. An elevated tee on number ten starts a series of target-style shots, structured by lakes and creeks, sharp doglegs, and tight driving zones. Holes eleven through thirteen—all difficult par-fours—will make or (more likely break) most golfers' rounds. Eleven requires a straight drive, followed by a daunting 180-yard approach down to

This first hole suggests a flowing route through the gentle slopes east of Paso Robles. Hunter Ranch is Northern California's best example of how good design combines with native oaks and grassland to make a first-rate golf course.

what looks at first like a small island green. The next hole offers a sharp uphill dogleg, with a narrow drive landing-area set far across a lake. The 200-yard green approach has to clear a creek, squeeze between trees, and land on a gently elevated green. Number thirteen completes the section with a tight drive and a long, tunnel-like approach to a green set atop a hill. Other holes on this side play well, but provide less opportunity for a ball to run off the hill into trouble.

Despite some real anxiety created by these back-nine holes, Hunter Ranch deserves its top billing in the **Best 100**. Its relaxed setting encourages casual and friendly golf. It offers excellent design and maintenance, quality food and service, convenient location—and a great starting point for your first trip to

California's growing Central Coast. *Review based on play several times, most recently with interviews in September '07.*

Hunter Ranch Golf Course:

4041 Highway 46 East	**Golf Shop:**	805 237-7444
Paso Robles, CA 93446	**Fax:**	805 237-7430
	www.hunterranchgolf.com	
Managed by: Vaquero Energy Co.	**Architect:**	Hunter Resources

Style:	Low rolling foothills covered with live oak. Few if any steep hills, so walking is pleasant. Landing areas range from broad to very tight. Very nicely shaped green complexesd with moderately sized contours on putting surfaces.
Location:	Due east of U.S. 101 in Paso Robles. Drive about 4 milesfrom the State Rt. 46 exit, and course is on the right.
Other info:	Managed in tandem with La Purisima Golf course, near Solvang. Annual membership cost of $250 gets big discounts. Part of the Central Coast Golf Trail.

Greens Fees as of 7/08:	Weekends	Weekdays	Twilight	Seniors	Carts
	$79	$60	$62/$43	no savings	$21

Course ratings:	Men	Par	Rating	Slope	Yardage	Women	Par	Rating	Slope	Yardage
	Blue	72	72.7	138	6716	White	72	75.6	136	6292
Hunter Ranch	White	72	70.9	130	6292	Red	72	72.0	128	5639

No. 13: Darkhorse

A rumor is floating around that this fabulous course is called "Darkhorse" because no one had ever used the name before. Well, six short years after the course was completed in 2002, that long-shot label may have proved more prophetic than any advertising executive would have dreamed. The real estate collapse that began in 2005 finally put the facility into the ownership of its mortgage holder, Owen Financial. Meanwhile, management tries hard to make ends meet in Auburn's over-supplied golf market. With a price war on greens fees underway in the area, golfers who want to take advantage of the chance to experience a top-notch course cheaply should play while the taking is good.

The Darkhorse property is located east of State Rt. 49, halfway between Auburn and Grass Valley. Directional signage along the way is poor. As you drive, keep reminding yourself that there is indeed a golf course at the end of the long, twisting Combie Road, but pay attention to speed limit signs along the way or pay the consequences. And once there, don't be too surprised that the clubhouse consists of a row of neatly organized trailers. Someday a fine structure will certainly be built in their place, but internationally renowned courses such as Ireland's Ballybunion and Carnoustie in Scotland operated successfully for many years from even humbler quarters.

In fact, comparing Darkhouse with these world-class venues isn't an exaggeration. It possesses the course design, conditioning, and layout to become a great golf destination—once enough players have found their way to experience its extraordinary qualities. At 1,500 feet, the air is cooler and clearer than in the Sacramento Valley below. Ponderosa pines and black oaks begin to mingle gently with valley oaks and sycamores. They provide a magic mountain ambience, augmented by sloping hills, shallow canyons, and steep climbs between holes.

Surprisingly, despite the financial difficulties, Empire Golf maintains the course with dedication. Beautiful greens feature bent grass and typically run very fast; and fairways are mowed two or three times a week. Even if the grass seems a little long, the ball sits up quite well. Except on some outside perimeters, roughs are also evenly cut, but the ground between tee and green on par-threes has some lumpy textures, so walkers need to be careful. Aprons are gorgeously consistent, making for easy chipping or bump-and-run shots. Indeed, the only real disappointment is the erratic condition of the bunkers, which are so numerous and steep that Empire's short-staffed greens crews can't keep them all in optimal shape.

Number seven is the second of four excellent par-fives at Darkhorse in Auburn. This one requires a well-placed second shot to set up a short iron to the lake-protected green.

Every hole at Darkhorse has its own special space and style. Few fairways run adjacent to one another; when they do, large distances separate them. Fairway bunkers add to the ambience but are frequently so deep that wedges must be used for recovery shots. To balance this penalty, they're wider set than normal, giving drivers some leeway. Greens measure longer than they look, often set in elevated positions with raised surrounds acting as a backstop. Darkhorse is one of the few high-quality **Best 100** courses where approaches should miss long, not short.

Par-fives provide many of the course's highlights. Number eleven is the *piece de resistance*. It heads uphill, well over 550 yards, with tall trees protecting the corners of a double dogleg. The huge green has numerous bumps and terraces. In fact, no one in the pro-shop ever heard of its having been reached in two shots from the tips. Number four, a past signature par-five, also plays long and slightly uphill. The fairway is well protected by the hillsides, a creek, deep rough, and plenty of bunkers, as well as by a 100-foot oak tree framing the elevated, bunker-guarded green. Others at seven and eighteen, are a bit shorter, and can be reached in two with high-risk shots over water. Care to try?

Like Stevinson Ranch, this course is worth a special trip. *Review based on play and interview in October '07.*

Darkhorse Golf Course:

24150 Darkhorse Dr.	**Golf Shop:**	530 269-7900
Auburn, CA 95602-8917	**Fax:**	530 269-7903
	www.darkhorsegolf.com	

Managed by:	Empire Golf	**Architect:**	Keith Foster
Style:	Hilly Terrain, where nearly every hole has its own private canyon. Deep bunkers protect elevated greens and fairways. Oak and pine forests line many fairways. Walking allowed but is somewhat challenging.		
Location:	Off State Rt. 49, between Auburn and Grass Valley. Go north from Auburn ten miles and turn right on Combie Rd. Follow carefully, about four miles to the golf entrance on the left.		
Other info:	Good condition. Clubhouse consists of upgraded pre-fab buildings.		

Greens Fees	Weekends	Weekdays	Twilight	Seniors	Carts/person
as of 10/08:	$69	$49	$55/$35	$42	Included

Course ratings:	Men	Par	Rating	Slope	Yardage	Women	Par	Rating	Slope	Yardage
	Black	72	75.0	139	7096	Blue	72	76.4	137	6364
	Copper	72	72.2	136	6653	White	72	73.6	133	5903
Darkhorse	Blue	72	70.9	130	6364	Jade	72	68.3	122	4978
	White	71	68.8	126	5903					

No. 14: Monarch Dunes

Strictly speaking, Monarch Dunes should not be included in a book about Northern California golf courses. The NCGA and SCGA, governing bodies for men's and some women's golf in Northern and Southern California, have agreed upon what seems an arbitrary and impractical border between the two organizations. Apparently they believe that southern San Luis Obispo County has more in common with the south than the north. As a veteran traveler I disagree, and annexed five additional courses, south of the San Luis River into the **Best 100,** creating a Central Coast region from Paso Robles down through Santa Maria.

This locale finds many quaint towns with unique names, interesting shopping, wineries, beaches, and golf courses. Multitudes flock here for vacations and retirement, and we northerners need to know that a whole new territory of wonderful golf waits to be conquered . . . only three hours drive from San Jose.

Hunter Ranch Golf Course in Paso Robles, leads the group with a No. 12 ranking. Next in line comes Monarch Dunes Old Course, off State Rt. 1, in Nipomo, about twenty miles south of San Luis Obispo, and three miles north of the small town of Guadalupe. Not more than twenty years ago, Nipomo was best known for its farms and excellent steak house, Jocko's. (Jocko's Steakhouse, the Hitching Post in Casmalia, the Far Western Tavern in Guadalupe, and McLintocks Saloon in Pismo Beach, are a group of wonderful steak houses serving special local beef in the Santa Maria Barbeque style.) Today, Nipomo has doubled in size to become a major retirement area with 57 golf holes at two separate facilities.

The approach to a eucalyptus-framed green on par-five number six at Monarch Dunes, is steep and dramatic. The course has many such picturesque settings.

Kemper Sports manages Monarch Dunes as part of a Trilogy Homes residential real estate development. The complex operates two courses—The Old Course, a traditional eighteen-hole facility completed in 2005, and The Challenge, a new 12-hole par-three course, which just opened in 2008.

The Challenge Course presents a unique experience, well worth trying. Its novel design could in fact create a whole new golf category for quick two-hour rounds. Full of difficult par threes varying from 82 to 202-yards, the setting looks like a jagged, grass-tuft covered moonscape. Highly undulating greens, plus hair-raising pin positions make good short-game skills mandatory, unless you are just looking for lots of fun. Time will tell how well it succeeds, but it was filled to capacity on a foggy Thursday afternoon in late 2008.

The other venue, Monarch Dune's full sized Old Course, supplies the primary treat. It also uses fields full of bunkers, mostly of normal style, but a few show the same jagged features found on The Challenge. Grass clumps— actually long rye varieties trodden into thick mats—surround small bunkers that look like mini bomb craters blasted out of dirt piles. Balls, landing on the heavy grass, rarely sink down underneath the long grass shafts, and usually stay on top. But don't be fooled, the irregular surface still makes hitting very tricky.

Bunker style is only one of several distinctions here. Eroded dunes have been shaped into large grass-covered hills or depressions at the edges of nearly every fairway. This contouring appears natural in most cases and adds a rolling texture to the flow of the course. Green aprons often sit on exaggerated mounding, reminiscent of links courses in the British Isles.

A large eucalyptus-covered hill juts above the center of the course. It forms the focal point for several holes, which either climb up its slope, or find greens set against its face. One of the most distinctive and photogenic par fives in the **Best 100** is found here, number six pictured on the prior page. The hole starts gently enough, heading up a narrowing fairway chute. After traversing a small portal, the view opens to a broad vista of golfing delight. A lake sits below, to the right of a crescent shaped fairway, which narrows beneath the tree-covered hill. Ahead is the green, on a highly elevated spot about a third the way up. Protecting the fringe are bunkers and steep slopes, which make chipping a challenge. The green surface is no slouch either, it's over twice as long as wide and is severely sloped, back to front like a raked stage. The entire setting offers a grand theatrical appearance.

Greens throughout represent a real challenge and joy. If they have been rolled and double cut none are smoother, faster or trickier in the **Best 100**. Even though most possess severe slopes with large mounds and terraces, each has many possible pin positions. Such conditions force approach shots to be aimed below the pin, or putting becomes a nightmare.

Kemper Sports keeps everything in great shape. With its unique style and fast rolling greens you will love it or hate it. Most experienced golfers come down on the "love" side. *Review based on play twice, last with interview in September '08.*

Monarch Dunes Old Course:

1606 Trilogy Parkway	**Golf Shop:**	805 343-9459
Nipomo, CA 93444	**Fax:**	805 343-0913
	www.monarchdunesgolf.com	
Managed by: Kemper Sports	**Architect:**	Damian Pascuzzo

Style:	Graded sand dunes surrounded by eucalyptus groves and some housing. Large elevated bunkers line many fairways. Greens can be very fast and have big undulations. Mildly rolling terrain accented with various hazards.
Location:	Course is about 3 miles west of U.S. 101, fifteen miles south of San Luis Obispo. Easiest access is off State Rt. 1, at Louise Lane, about three miles north of Guadalupe and five miles south of Arroyo Grande.
Other info:	Course is not an NCGA affiliate. The adjacent twelve-hole Challenge Course is a unique experience of interesting par-three holes.

Approx. Greens	Weekends	Weekdays	Twilight	Seniors	Carts
Fees as of 11/08	$78	$57	$51/$30	$40 weekdays	$17

Course ratings:	Men	Par	Rating	Slope	Yardage	Women	Par	Rating	Slope	Yardage
Monarch Dunes	Black	71	73	137	6810	White	71	75.6	146	5821
	Gold	71	70.7	135	6337	Bronze	71	73.2	136	5320
	White	71	68.5	128	5821	Green	71	69.2	132	4702

No. 15: Bayonet

For years Bayonet was an unpublicized Monterey Bay jewel because its location on a military base restricted public-at-large play. Only pros, tuning up their games for tournaments at nearby Pebble Beach, along with guests and active/retired military personnel, could get access. Then, about a decade ago, Ft. Ord Army Base closed, the land became public, and golfers worldwide could see what they had been missing.

Now the 400-acre property, which houses both the Bayonet and Black Horse courses, finds another change underway, this time to an upscale resort. The Fairmont Hotel organization is building a luxury hotel on the site of the old driving range; about 125 new home sites are zoned and ready; and an extensive re-vamping of the courses is nearly complete. As of this writing in March '09, both the front nine of the Bayonet and the back side of Black Horse were finished and open. Golfers played these two together as one course while the other two nines complete construction. An extensive new driving range was already open. The composite course gives an exciting look at how the changes will impact the final products, which open mid-2009.

Judging from the quality of rehab on Bayonet's front nine, the renovated course will not disappoint. The new front side gives a superb update of the old one. For instance, though the layout of par-five number one remains generally the same, nuances improve it. Fairway bunkers have been enlarged to add visual appeal and difficulty . . . they look taller, wider and much whiter than before. The green has been moved further to the right, and now sits partially hidden by a row of old cypress trees. It gives long hitters a riskier shot at reaching home in two. The new elevated putting surface has bunkers set below, and utilizes bent grass rather than the old *poa anna* variety. All green complexes and fairways have been redesigned and re-graded with new bunkers. Contractors eradicated the Kikuyu grass, which had infested much of the course, another vast improvement.

Hole sequencing was adjusted and augmented. Old number three, the ultra-long 590-yard par-five, now plays number eight. Numbers three and nine received entirely new designs. Three is an excellent, short 330-yard par-four, requiring that a very accurate drive avoid a wide fairway bunker on the left side and trees on the right. The approach, to its double-tiered hillside green, heads over deep bunkers.

The new number nine replaced a hole that pro Al Geiberger once said was the longest par-four he ever played. It remains a doozie, one of the **Best 100's** toughest. The drive, though fairly open, faces out-of-bounds and new homes on the right, but the real difficulty comes on the long approach. This second shot, usually at least 200-yards, must clear or land between a series of artfully banked cross-bunkers in front of a green elevated a good 40 feet above the drive landing area. The kidney shaped surface finds a backbone hump in is middle, just to keep putting interesting. To the designer's credit, normal men's tees have been shortened to a mere 388-yards, with the ladies at 350, giving mere mortals a bit of a chance. Those who play at the tips find them at 476-yards, even longer than Geiberger's old nemesis.

Number nine on the reconstructed Bayonet course remains a doozie. Its approach is steeply uphill, over multiple bunkers to a spine humped green.

While the front nine gets the recent buzz, the old back nine forms the backbone of this course. Holes eleven, twelve and thirteen, nicknamed Combat Corner, are as thorny as any group of par-fours anywhere. General Robert McClure, who supervised the original construction in 1954, played left-handed, with a big, long slice. He designed the doglegs on holes eleven, twelve and fifteen to fit his trajectory, and judging from their length, he hit the ball a long way before it started to slice. Current re-designers must be careful to retain the famous character on these holes by not shortening their tees. Well-trimmed cypresses line their narrow fairways, and old-style, subtly breaking greens dominate the rest of the nine. As is usual with many of our better courses, good scores comes from good chipping, straight shots and a lot of one-putts. Accuracy trumps length on most holes at Bayonet.

If the kinds of changes already seen on the front nine continue on the back, *i.e.* eliminating the Kikuyu, and modernizing the bunkers and green complexes, Bayonet will continue as one of California's premier courses. If only we can afford to play it after the hotel opens! *Review based on play several times, last with interviews in Sept '08.*

Bayonet Golf Course:

1 McClure Way		**Golf Shop:**	831 899-7271
Seaside, CA 93955		**Fax**	831 899-7169
		www.bayonetblackhorse.com	
Managed by:	Seaside Resort Development	**Architect:**	Gen Robt McClure
Location:	North of Monterey in Seaside, off State Rt. 1. Take Main Entrance Gate to Fort Ord. Turn right on N S Road and follow signs to Golf Courses.		
Style:	Rolling landscape with cypress trees lining most fairways. Well placed bunkers in fairways and around greens. Greens are moderate in size but have many undulations.		
Other info:	Resort golf course currently being rebuilt. In late 2008 the front side of a renovated Bayonet course combined with the back side of a brand new Black Horse Course. Ratings below are for the old Bayonet course.		

Greens Fees as of 11/08:	Weekends	Weekdays	Twilight	Seniors	Carts/person
	$138	$100	$120/$82	-$27	included

Course ratings:	Men	Par	Rating	Slope	Yardage	Women	Par	Rating	Slope	Yardage
	Gold	72	75.3	138	7130	White	75	77.0	135	6318
Bayonet	Blue	72	73.4	135	6771	Red	72	70.4	123	5591
	White	72	71.3	133	6318					

No. 16: Diablo Grande: Ranch

Back in the 1990's, Donald Panoz, founder of Elan Pharmaceuticals and first owner of Diablo Grande, bought the 33,000 acre Oak Flat Ranch. The huge property sits eight miles west of Patterson, off Interstate-5, about 20 miles south of Tracy. His vision was to build an entire community, starting with construction of the Ranch course in 1996, designed by Dennis Griffiths. In 1998 he added the Legends course. These two projects formed the initial phase of a development planned to consume about half of the original land purchase.

Unfortunately, financial and membership problems occurred over the years, ending in his sale of the property to World International, LCC, in October 2008. With the assistance of Laurus Corporation, World bought the property for $20 million, down from an asking price of $150 million.* Whether the name stays the same, or the new owners continue with plans for a resort and more home development is still unsettled, but the golf courses remain in operation.

The Ranch course is the tougher, narrower, and longer of the two courses, at least from the middle men's tees. It is also less popular, probably because of its difficulty. However, unlike some cruel courses such as The Bridges in San Ramon, or The Ranch in San Jose, Diablo Grande's Ranch course, offer a fair test, in a relatively conventional but very picturesque setting.

The difficulty comes because of long holes and hazards in awkward positions. Par-five number twelve illustrates well: Besides the impressive 600-plus-yard length, Griffiths located a wide creek crossing 240-yards from the blue tee box. This position forces long hitters to lay-up, leaving a second shot to traverse a 150-yard wide gully. Even a successful second may leave a 200-yard-plus approach to the green; and this shot needs to hook around or fly over a tall tree on the way. Reaching the green in three is difficult so par becomes a gift and bogey is a respectable score.

While more long, thorny holes arrive at fourteen and fifteen, the rest of the layout is playable. Numbers one thru five wander through hillside oak forests where cattle once grazed under the trees. Numbers six thru eleven display characteristic California rolling topography, with lakes, gullies, bunkers and grassland replacing the trees, forming picturesque backdrops. Tee shots seem to stay suspended in front of the golden tapestry behind. All holes prove interesting, with no two remotely alike. Most use small, devilish, but negotiable, obstacles to add interest.

Fairways, roughs, bunkers and greens were in excellent shape when I played. Walking proved fairly level, though a few hills and distance from green to tee combine to give a very good workout. Fairway turfs combine rye and blue grass, and greens use the traditional bent variety.

Due to its rural location, several native animals add an unusual element, usually in the fall. At dusk and at night, raccoons and wild boar sometimes root-out grubs and worms from the lush fairways. Generally limited to just a few holes, parts of fairways then look like freshly tilled farmland and become ground-under-repair.

Bring your "A-game" to the Ranch course, and you should be most impressed. *Review based on play and interview in September '07.*

---

* See *The Patterson Irrigator* article by James Leonard dated October 10, 2008

for more information about recent history and the sale.

Diablo Grande Winery and Resort, Ranch Course:

9521 Morton Davis Drive	**Golf Shop:**	209 892-4653
Patterson, CA 95363	**Fax**	209 892-4136
	www.diablogrande.com	
Managed by: Sierra Golf Management	**Architect:**	Dennis Griffiths
Location:	Drive south from Tracy on Interstate-5 about 25 miles to Diablo Grande Exit. Head west seven miles, thru gate, and turn right onto Morton Davis Drive. Then turn left again on Morton Davis Circle.	
Style:	Rolling, oak covered foothills. Some trees come into play, but most shots are open. Greens are moderate size, some with terracing, and are well protected by bunkers and slopes.	
Other info:	Course has just come out of bankruptcy and changed ownership. Special price available to play both courses in one day.	

Greens Fees	Weekends	Weekdays	Twilight	Seniors	Carts/person
as of 11/08:	$65	$49	none	none	included

Course ratings:	Men	Par	Rating	Slope	Yardage	Women	Par	Rating	Slope	Yardage
Diablo Grande Ranch	Black	72	75.4	138	7246	White	73	77.7	137	6381
	Blue	72	74.1	135	6932	Gold	72	72.7	128	5496
	White	72	71.6	129	6381	Red	71	70.0	124	5112

No. 17: Cypress Ridge

Like its neighbor Monarch Dunes, Cypress Ridge does not belong in the Northern California Golf Association. Its site is too far south. But the course plays so well, and sits so close to the NCGA's San Luis Obispo southern border, that it deserves a ranking in our **Best 100**. Northern Californians need a persistent reminder that many high quality, moderately priced courses can be found along the Central Coast.

Cypress Ridge forms an integral part of a high quality housing development built in 1999. It's situated on an old 390-acre dairy farm, about fifteen miles south of San Luis Obispo, two miles from the ocean. Tour pro Peter Jacobsen, joined partner Jim Hardy, to build his first California course here. The result is a beauty, routed nicely through homes, dunes, a couple of strategically placed lakes, and groves of cypress, and eucalyptus. Six holes find homes inconspicuously placed on both sides of fairways, another six have them on one side only, and the remainder sees no homes at all. The overall layout yields a broad sense of privacy and spaciousness, as if you were on the course alone. Wildlife appreciates it too, with its Certified Signature Sanctuary status from Audubon International.

Jacobsen courses present a unique quality. His theory, "since a golf ball is round, you should be able to roll it around the course." means no forced carries and lots of bump-and-run opportunities. He creates difficulty other ways by using slopes, mounds, trees and elevation changes. Everyone has a chance to succeed and have fun on his courses.

He also camouflages the direction balls break on the greens. For instance, balls seem to roll uphill on downhill par-threes two and seventeen. When standing on either tee or putting surface the altitude drop on each fairway makes the green appear higher in back than in front. This illusion fools golfers because putts break towards the rear. Even course pros have a hard time reading the smooth well-maintained greens.

Cypress Ridge tries hard to maintain a competitive pedigree by hosting several open amateur tournaments. It's a home practice course for Cal Poly* and many college matches. Pro mini-tours have stopped to try it, and the facility hosts local U.S. Open qualifying events. Many high quality players and publications give it rave reviews.

This short 288-yard hole, number seven at Cypress Ridge, can be driven if one has the guts and accuracy. Otherwise hit a lay-up down and a short iron up to the tiny green.

To me, the main attributes include (1) the excellent, relatively soft, very green appearance of the entire layout, (2) hole's design variation—all different and all playable, and 3) the sophisticated small, un-terraced, hard-to-read greens. These combine to make a fun course, perhaps a little quirky in spots, which should keep repeat golfers entertained for years. *Review based on play in September '07.*

*California Polytechnic State University, San Luis Obispo

Cypress Ridge Golf Course:

780 Cypress ridge Parkway	**Golf Shop:**	805 474-7979
Arroyo Grande, CA 93420	**Fax:**	805 474-7975
	www.cypressridge.com	
Managed by: Lucadia	**Architect:**	Jacobsen/Hardy

Style:	Hilly terrain about two miles from the ocean. Many holes surrounded by expensive homes. Greens often elevated. Extensive bunkering throughout course.
Location:	About 18 miles south of San Luis Obispo. Take U.S. 101 to E. El Campo Exit. Turn right (south) and go 1 1/2 miles to Los Berros Rd. Turn left and go about 200 feet and make immediate right on W. El Campo Rd. Go 1 1/2 miles to S Halcyon Rd. Turn left and then turn right on Cypress Ridge Pkwy.
Other info:	Not a member of the NCGA. Audubon Certified Signature Sanctuary

Approx. Greens	Weekends	Weekdays	Twilight	Seniors	Carts
Fees as of 10/08	$68	$55	$43/$30	None	$17

Course ratings:	Men	Par	Rating	Slope	Yardage	Women	Par	Rating	Slope	Yardage
	Black	72	72.9	134	6803	White	72	75.0	131	5838
Cypress Ridge	Blue	72	71.2	129	6443	Red	72	70.7	122	5087
	Combo	72	70.0	126	6140					
	White	72	68.5	124	5838					

No. 18: Wente Vineyards

The word "gourmet" perfectly describes Wente Vineyards. The clubhouse provides gourmet sandwiches, the winery next door serves some of the best gourmet meals in the South Bay, the adjoining concert venue hosts gourmet entertainment, and the Greg Norman 1998 designed course offers gourmet views of local vineyards, Livermore Valley and the nearby hillsides.

Surroundings for all these activities are first class, a Livermore Valley version of the restaurant and golf competition up in the Napa Valley. Wineries abound, and the oak covered knolls appear lush . . . green in the spring and gold in the summer and fall. Winding through the hills, over the top of them, and covering small flat openings between them are the well-kept fertile fairways of one of the California's premier public courses.

The front nine of The Course at Wente Vineyards starts mildly enough, with a highly elevated tee looking southeast to a small valley, holding five relatively easy holes. After this short stint the fun begins. Number six presents a short par-four—uphill, with an extremely narrow funnel shaped fairway—followed by a downhill par-three that gives a breath-taking view of the Livermore Valley, Mt. Diablo, and a couple of long holes, which head into the wind.

Next comes Lombard Street. Its true! A cart path between nines climbs a hill just as long and steep as its San Francisco namesake, making about as many turns. The views up on top become even more spectacular than the one at number seven. Each of the next five hillside holes shows unique character; some golfers will enjoy them, others will think them over-tricked. For instance, number ten measures only 300-yards long, but its small highly sloped green is too risky to attack directly from the tee. This means a 180-yard lay-up and then a wedge. What fun is that? I guess it's all in the putting.

Whatever the opinions, the 2007 Nationwide tour stop at Wente saw no players break par. Hole number fourteen, a 180-yard downhill par-three, caused several double-digit scores on a simple looking hole. If you miss the green, apron or bunkers here, just re-load. The high tournament scores put it on our list of the **Best 100** toughest par-threes. For that matter, don't hit the ball in the rough anywhere on the course. Rumors abound that greens-keepers add extra fertilizer to roughs to make their long grasses super-thick for t5he young pros that frequent the facility.

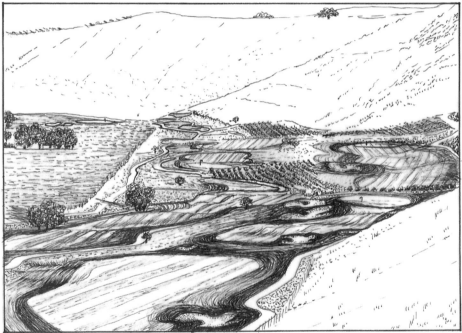

View of Wente Vineyards from the seventh tee, including numbers nine, ten, sixteen and seventeen. The clubhouse and The Restaurant nearby both serve wonderful gourmet food. Illustration modeled from photo supplied by Wente.

The final four holes head down on the flats again, through the vineyards, with a tailwind or perhaps a crosswind finally helping. Thank goodness for small favors, but watch out for the multiple ponds on number eighteen. Then, have a glass of some fine Wente Reserve before a designated-driver partner takes you back home. It's a great layout, in excellent condition, except . . . the distance up Lombard Street kind of prevents walking the course. And who likes super heavy rough? *Review based on play several times, last in May '07.*

The Course at Wente Vineyards

5050 Arroyo Road
Livermore, CA 94550

Golf Shop: 925 456-2475
Fax 925 456-2490

www.wentegolf.com

Managed by:	Wente Vineyards	**Architect:**	Greg Norman
Location:	In the hills south of Livermore. Take Interstate-580 to N. Livermore exit, turn south go to the fifth light. Turn right on Portola. At first light turn left on North L St./Arroyo Rd. Course gate is five miles ahead, on the left.		
Style:	Hilly oak and grass covered terrain. Vineyards abut several fairways. Beware of thick, heavy rough. Many elevated views of Livermore Valley. Some very steep climbs between holes so carts are advised.		
Other info:	Adjacent to Wente restaurant and concert venue. Food is great at golf shop & restaurant.		

Greens Fees as of 10/08:	Weekends	Weekdays	Twilight	Seniors	Carts/person
	$105	$85	$75/$55	None	Included

Course ratings:	Men	Par	Rating	Slope	Yardage	Women	Par	Rating	Slope	Yardage
Wente Vineyards	Black	72	75.8	145	7167	Blue	76	76.4	136	6233
	Gold	72	73.9	141	6837	White	72	73.6	130	5686
	Blue	72	71.6	131	6259	Red	72	69.4	122	4975
	White	72	68.7	124	5625					

No. 19: Half Moon Bay, Ocean Course

Half Moon Bay houses the San Francisco Peninsula's premier public golf courses. The Old Course built in 1974, and the Ocean Course reviewed here, both offer excellent and elegant venues. Many Silicon Valley executives and even regular tourists consider them the best facilities within a forty-five minute drive of San Francisco and SF airport.

Built in 1994, The Ocean Course is the newer and the better choice for pure golf. Some might disagree with this conclusion because the layout shows more exposure to weather and wind than the Old Course. However, the Ocean eighteen shows more distinction, variation, and seaside scenery because fairways gracefully wind through a dune-like countryside. Hole designs follow a gentle rhythm, consistent with tranquil views of the Pacific Ocean. The nearby Ritz Carlton Hotel adds a noble quality to the natural landscape, in contrast to the housing and condo development enveloping several holes on the Old Course.

In my opinion, the Ocean Course has the feel of what an American golfer would expect to find on a good Scottish links . . . sand dunes, rolling terrain, undulating greens, deep picturesque bunkers and long roughs. Many Americans are actually disappointed by play in Scotland. The cold, windy weather combines with dry and sometimes scruffy conditions to dash the comforts we come to expect. Prickly gorse fills roughs and no power carts means walking the fairways. Heaven forbid!

View from the Ritz Carlton Hotel of the Pacific Ocean and numbers 16 and 17 at Half Moon Bay Ocean Course. The LPGA Samsung World Championships were held here in October 2008.

Half Moon Bay resolves the expectation vs. truth by simulating the appearance, but grooming to U. S. aesthetic expectations. Shots hold well on the greens. The wind blows, but rarely as strongly as in the British Isles. Players have the option of riding or walking; and walking The Ocean's mildly rolling terrain comes close to what you might really experience overseas.

It has other differences too. The fairways show little mounding, much greener turf, and a softer feel underfoot. Chip-and-run shots rarely need to be used at Half Moon Bay. Prickly gorse is non-existent, but take care to avoid our own native poison oak. Bunkers seem deep, but not like the ones on St. Andrews where a stance is often one foot in the sand and a knee on the lip. Hazards can usually be seen, rather than the sneaky hidden obstacles in the British Isles. However, Half Moon Bay has no caddy program, so players must rely on guidebooks purchased in the pro-shop. Reading putts is an unsolvable mystery.

After completing your links-like experience, the clubhouse bar sits within a short walking of the Ritz Carlton, one of the SF Peninsula's finest hotels. Scotland in our own backyard, with carts and an evening afterglow; what could be more satisfying? And no eight-hour plane ride to Glasgow required! *Review based on play several times, last in August '08.*

Half Moon Bay Golf Links, Ocean Course

2 Miramontes Point Road	**Golf Shop:**	650 712-2200
Half Moon Bay, CA 94019	**Fax**	650 726-9039
	www.hmbgolflinks.com	

Managed by:	Kenmark Real Eastate Group	**Architect:** Arthur Hills
Location:	Just south of Half Moon Bay. Take State Rt. 92 west to Half Moon Bay. Turn south on State Rt. 1 and drive 2 miles to Miramontes Pt. Road. Turn right and then right again near Ritz Carlton roundabout, to the proshop. Valet parking may be needed if top lot is full.	
Style:	Links style with gently rolling hills and dunes. The ocean can be seen from most holes. Can be windy and cold. Fairways and greens are well manicured. Relatively flat lies. Greens usually hold approaches. Bunkers abound and can be deep. Few, if any trees.	
Other info:	Resort golf course adjacent to Ritz Carlton. 36 holes. Ocean Course is is the tournament venue, Old Course is more resort in style. Cheaper greens fees if you book less than 14 days in advance.	

Greens Fees	Weekends	Weekdays	Twilight	Seniors	Carts/person
as of 10/08:	$205	$180	$102/$90	No savings	Included

Course ratings:	Men	Par	Rating	Slope	Yardage	Women	Par	Rating	Slope	Yardage
Half Moon Bay Ocean	Black	72	72.2	131	6649	White	73	75.8	136	6041
	Blue	70	70.7	128	6303	Gold	72	72.5	129	5464
	White	70	69.4	126	6041	Red	71	69.0	119	4872

No. 20: Chardonnay

Silverado Resort may have provided the Napa Valley's first big time golf-resort destination, but Chardonnay Golf Club became the area's first course built to feature modern, undulating fairways and sophisticated green complexes. Silverado North is a classically designed course, with broad, relatively flat fairways lined by gorgeously mature trees, in dramatic contrast with Chardonnay's hilly, contoured fairways, and open, links-like feel. The lakes at Chardonnay look more dangerous, the roughs seem thicker, and vineyards physically touch the course at every chance. Playing Chardonnay, you know you're in wine country.

Designer Algie Pullet created Chardonnay's original 18-hole course in 1987. With the help of Sandy Tatum, they expanded it to 36 holes in 1992. The new 18-hole course started as a private property called the Shakespeare Course, but operated out of the same clubhouse as the original Chardonnay. Unlike the poet, this Shakespeare didn't last long, and one of the two nines was sold to Eagle Vines, a development next door (see Course No. 78.) Thus Chardonnay became a 27-hole public facility, comprised of three nines named Meadows, Lakes, and Vineyard.

Twenty-seven holes may seem like an odd combination, but the course's management likes it, citing several advantages:

• More players can start at peak times.

- Tournaments can host larger groups.
- Marshals have the flexibility to move players to another nine when play runs slow.
- Course condition improves, since play spreads over more holes.
- Members have more options for holes to play.
- When a tournament covers one set of 18 holes, non-tournament players can still play the other nine.

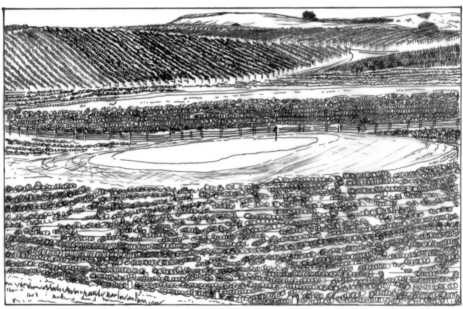

Chardonnay's number five on the Meadows Nine presents a classic wine country par-three, where vineyards replace water at an island-style green.

Chardonnay's new ownership inherited a deteriorated infrastructure where general course maintenance had been neglected and some of the most distinctive holes had been sold. Quick changes were required, starting with course conditions and maintenance style. Brown spots and wet spots were eliminated. Roughs around greens and next to fairways were cut evenly. Cart paths and parking lots were repaired and re-paved. At the same time, the new owners changed the hardscape by turning the creek into a lake in front of the final green on the Meadows nine.

Additional changes planned for the greens may be even more significant. Currently, putting surfaces look long, narrow, and undulating, surrounded by mounded aprons covered in moderate rough. Some seem like gently twisted slalom slopes meandering between greenside bunkers. Approach shots and longer putts must use the banked mounds as backboards to bounce balls close to the hole. Management thinks that these unusual shapes give too much advantage to low-handicap players who can chip well. In order to equalize play and win back average players, they plan to broaden parts of some greens by cutting down the apron roughs and expand the collars, creating tightly shaved fringes that force all players to putt, not chip.

Golfers who liked Chardonnay before and return to play today will be very happy with the current state of the course. Management has succeeded in restoring the facility to its former status as the premier challenge-course in Napa Valley. Like a fine wine, Chardonnay offers physical beauty, top condition, and continued improvement from year to year. *Review based on play several times, most recently with interviews in August '08.*

Chardonnay Golf Club:

2255 Jameson Canyon Road	**Reservations:**	800 788-0136	
P. O. Box 3779	**Golf Shop:**	707 257-1900 or 707 257-8950	
Napa, CA 94558	**Fax**	707 257-0613	
	www.chardonnaygolfclub.com		

Managed by:	Local, private **Architect:** Algie Pullet
Location:	Between Napa and Vallejo on State Rt. 12. Take State Rt. 29 north from Vallejo and turn right onto Rt. 12. Go 1 1/2 miles to second light. Turn right into club complex. See website for other options.
Style:	Mix of hills and gently roling terrain, surrounded by vineyards. Broad, well bunkered fairways. Greens are quite distinctive and can be very long with lots of slopes. Moderate walking difficulty.
Other info:	Semi-private golf course with 27 holes. Lots of private tournament play. Excellent condition, but can be very windy, especially when San Francisco is foggy in the summer. See web site for monthly changes in greens fees.

Greens Fees	Weekends	Weekdays	Twilight	Seniors	Carts/person
as of 10/08:	$84	$64	$70/$50	No savings	Included

Course ratings:	Men	Par	Rating	Slope	Yardage	Women	Par	Rating	Slope	Yardage
Chardonnay	Black	72	73.8	141	6751	White	72	75.2	132	6015
Lakes/Meadow	Blue	72	72.7	136	6492	Red	72	71.8	126	5361
s	White	72	70.3	127	6015					

No. 21: Saddle Creek

The southern Gold Country foothills, stretching from Sonora to Jackson, have matured nicely as a locale for golf tourism and retirement living. Long established courses such as Castle Oaks (Ione), Greenhorn Creek (Angels Camp), Mountain Springs (Sonora), Pine Mountain Lake (Groveland), La Contenta (Valley Springs) and Micke Grove (Lodi) join the list as ranked **Best 100** golf venues.

At the top of the list sits Saddle Creek Resort, a Castle and Cooke project near lake Tulloch, located in Copperopolis, between State Rts. 120 and 4. The resort forms part of a nicely developed semi-gated community just south of the old copper-mining town. Big, beautiful homes perch above some of the holes, but many fairways wander through totally rural settings. The whole property seems a good blend of development, resort facilities, and pastoral oak covered foothill landscape.

Copperopolis, about 50 miles east of Stockton, has witnessed a full-blown re-birth. Developers decided the town needed a newly constructed, old-fashioned motif, so they built a new town square about two miles from old downtown. It's site lies adjacent to Rt. 4, so motorists can easily see what's going on. The drive from there to golf takes about five minutes.

Saddle Creek's top area ranking fits right in with the new up-scale—but still small-town—image. The course may not be everyone's favorite, but golfers come from all over the state to test their skills. The expansive layout provides broad fairways and roughs. This means players need less than pin-point accuracy to stay in the game. Landing zones get nuanced definition from the rolling topography since specific target zones make green approaches easier. Architect Carter Moorish also added graceful, sculptured bunkers, to help define shot placement. Views from tee to fairway easily identify the driving lanes and what challenges will be faced. Long-ball hitters find more difficulty avoiding bunkers, because Moorish compensated for new golf equipment technology by placing bunkers 20 yards further out than normal.

Number six at Saddle Creek is called the Beast. It's a rather harmless looking 400-yard uphill par 4 but has a treacherous green.

But, scratch golfers usually like to be challenged, and avoiding bunkers just makes the game more exciting. They get their retribution on the aprons and the greens, where their short-game skills make a huge difference. Management recently decided to *stress* the greens, meaning keeping them firm and dry. The resulting lower water and chemical use, helps keep the environment clean and gives an advantage to the low handicappers they are trying to attract. They can hit the ball high and stop it with spin, whereas firm greens usually frustrate bogey players.

The course map shows many lakes near fairways, but water severely intimidates shots on only a few holes, including signature number fourteen. This long par-three offers a picturesque downhill shot, at distances ranging from 243-yards at the tips to 121 up front. Bunkers and a lake surround the green, unless one bounces the ball off the hill on the right so it will roll onto the surface. Most players use long woods or driver. Normally the left front lake wouldn't come into play, but at this length, just a little pull or hook puts the ball in the drink. Two-putt, consider bogey normal, and move on. *Review based on play twice, last in April '08.*

Saddle Creek Resort

1001 Saddle Creek Road	**Reservations:** 888 852-5787
Copperopolis, CA 95228	**Golf Shop:** 209 785-3700
	Resort 800 611-7722
	www.saddlecreek.com

Managed by:	Castle & Cooke Properties **Architect:** Carter Moorish
Location:	East of Stockton 35 miles. Take State Rt. 4 exit from State Rt. 99, east through Farmington. Turn right (south) on Olive Ranch Road towards the new town center. Make right turn before town onto Little John Road. Go 2.4 miles to Saddle Creek Road. Turn right (west) and follow signs to course.
Style:	Rolling oak covered hills. Well sculpted fairways with frequent scenic bunkers. Greens have multiple terraces, are very firm and can be fast. Good chipping and putting are important.
Other info:	Resort Golf Course. Greens fees vary by time of year. Winter rates are about $20 less than those shown below. Course is usually in excellent condition, but fairway lies can be tight.

Greens Fees as of 10/08:	Weekends	Weekdays	Twilight	Seniors	Carts/person
	$99	$69	$75/$45	No savings	$35

Course ratings:	Men	Par	Rating	Slope	Yardage	Women	Par	Rating	Slope	Yardage
	Black	72	72.9	136	6773	White	72	75.4	135	6015
Saddle Creek	Blue	72	70.9	131	6356	Red	72	71.3	128	5334
	White	72	69.4	126	6015	Gold	70	67.1	111	4491

No. 22: Apple Mountain

Algie Pullet, architect of the well-known Chardonnay Golf Club in Napa, designed Apple Mountain in 1997. Originally named Gold Creek, new 2002 ownership wanted a name related to the vicinity where it's located, Apple Hill. Someone else already owned that trademark, so Apple Mountain became the new moniker.

The course sits five miles east of Placerville, towards Lake Tahoe on U.S. 50, at 2700 feet of elevation. Profuse pines, firs and spruce co-mingle with the oaks; and spectacular red-barked madrone trees frame views of ridgelines looking east.

Even at this moderate altitude, golfers find the topography quite steep. Shot elevations drop or increase more severely than on other highly ranked mountain courses such as Sierra Star in Mammoth, Coyote Moon in Truckee or Whitehawk Ranch near Graeagle. Only Mt. Shasta Resort comes close to matching the sizable alpine undulations faced at Apple Mountain. Scenery compares to that of Poppy Hills on the Monterey Peninsula: Rather than finding a plethora of panoramic vistas, nearby trees lines and hills block the longer views, forcing golfers to concentrate on their game. The beauty of the course lies in the design of the holes themselves and in the often striking trees that envelop it.

The first hole—a medium-length steeply sloped downhill par-four—represents a prototype for what's coming. Its highly elevated tee aims to a landing area some 240-yards down a tree lined chute, towards a river crossing 100-yards from the green. The sloping fairway descends sharply, with several humps, like giant moguls, spotted every 70-yards or so. The bottom of the slope flattens out, but just fifteen-yards short of the hazard. Most drives end on a downhill lie, assuming one doesn't pull or push it into the woods. The fairway opening between the tree lines looks fearsomely narrow, making the first drive of the day very scary. The coming approach shot is no simpler. An elevated green, with a hill and forest behind, bunkers on the corners and creek in front, presents a tough target from a downhill lie. It's 120 to 170-yards to the green, and only the second shot of the day. However, if you do manage to hit the ball squarely and well up in the air, its trajectory against the deep emerald forest is quite striking. Number one at Apple Mountain presents a fearsome introduction to the course.

Those who hit the ball far and wide should avoid coming at all. Shots into the woods usually disappear because steep slopes to the sides find multitudes of poison oak, berry bushes and thick underbrush. Management rarely sponsors medal-play tournaments because players spend too much time searching for balls. In a *medal-play* tournament, total score at the end determines the winner, so every shot counts towards the final result. This makes players search long and hard for errant shots. The primary alterative format, called *match play*, looks at individual holes won, rather than total score. So, if one's opponent is on the green in two, and you are in the woods, wasting time looking for a ball is pointless, because you will lose the hole anyway. A *medal-play* tournament round can easily take over six hours at Apple Mountain; *match play* finishes much more quickly. On a normal busy non-tournament day, expect over five hours on the course.

Maximum length measures a short 6300-yards. Long-hitting low-handicappers often become frustrated because many holes require lay-up drives short of hazards or fairway turns. The high 138 slope, versus low course rating of only 69.7, means players who hit it short-and-straight get a maximum advantage. For instance, number five heads 531-yards, up-hill, from the white tees. It's a sharp double-dogleg where drives must stop at about 210-yards from the tee. Very tall trees protect both of the sharp bends at each corner and prevent long shots from cutting across. This means a three full shots are needed (or four for many) regardless of player's strength. One of the local pros said he thought it was the worst hole on the course. Another player, a ten-handicapper, said he thought it was the best because big guys were cut down to size. I think the second guy might be right.

Hole number one at Apple Mountain introduces golfers to what's coming. Narrow fairways, target landings, small greens and short yardage mean shots need to be well-controlled all day long.

Another plus comes from the course's excellent condition. Fairways stay extremely green, as do the roughs. Maintenance crews also keeps external perimeters lush and well-trimmed, their softness helping slow the roll of stray shots. Designer Pullet created nicely shaped greens, without needing extreme contours. Putts roll smoothly across consistent, moderately fast surfaces, which hold well. Wide aprons help keep errant approaches stay in play—important because many greens perch on side-hill slopes, where it's easy to pull or push a shot into oblivion.

The key to success here comes from following suggestions of the printed guide-sheet posted on the back of each cart. It recommends how far to hit drives and which side of greens to approach. If you follow the guide, you will have a great day. If not, bring an extra dozen balls and buy a couple of six-packs. *Review based on play and interview in October '08.*

Apple Mountain Golf Resort

3455 Carson Rd		**Golf Shop:**	530 647-7400
Camino, CA 95709		**Fax:**	530 647-7407
		www.applemountaingolfresort.net	
Managed by:	Private, local	**Architect:**	Algie Pullet
Location:	East of Placerville about three miles just off U.S. 50. Turn left at the Carson Road exit and follow it a half mile. Course is on the left.		
Style:	Very hilly mountain style course. Narrow tree lined fairways with steep drop-offs to trees and heavy brush at the sides. Several drives require lay-up shots. Greens are often elevated with steep aprons. Expect to lose a lot of balls.		
Other info:	Difficult course but in excellent condition. Carts are mandatory unless special arrangements are made. Course has many steep climbs from green to tee.		

Greens Fees as of 10/08:	Weekends	Weekdays	Twilight	Seniors	Carts/person
	$60	$40	$55/$35	No savings	Includd

Course ratings:	Men	Par	Rating	Slope	Yardage	Women	Par	Rating	Slope	Yardage
Apple	Blue	70	69.7	138	6123	White	71	73.0	128	5553
Mountain	White	69	67.7	127	5553	Gold	69	67.4	117	4638

No. 23: Whitehawk Ranch

This modern mountain course has great basic characteristics . . . few hills, moderate difficulty, good grooming and a pleasing blend of pines, meadows and streams. It's about 40 miles north of Truckee on State Rt. 89, just a few miles south of Graeagle. The property rests on the perimeter of an alpine meadow, where cattle and grasslands mingle between the mountain ridges and forests of Plumas County.

Few people, few roads, a laid-back life style, and gentle rolling landscape apparently inspire good golf architecture: Whitehawk molded these attributes into a spacious upscale real-estate/resort development where homes look big, lots look spacious, and buildings have little if no impact on golfers. Many homeowners belong to the golf club, but play also stays open to the public.

The course has decent, not overbearing length, though at 6900-yards from the tips, it challenges those who choose that route. The 4500-foot elevation gives players a little extra distance. Fairway bunkers stagger from side to side at wide distances so drives can usually be aimed opposite their position or in a few cases, head straight over the closest one. Doglegs mostly utilize gentle turns—except, the short par-fours force medium-distance hitters to lay-up on sharp corners. These shorter holes find considerably more trouble on their entire length, whereas longer holes usually offer more space and approaches can usually roll onto greens.

Great conditioning is a real course strength. Lush green fairways predominate, even at the end of the long dry season. They make the straight shot requirements, long native grasses, and occasional hillside lies, a lot more enjoyable. Reaching the green does not assure victory either. Putting surfaces stay in excellent shape and hold well; but speed on chips and putts is hard to judge, even at standard pin placements. Greens generally run quick, so expect a few three-putts.

A small brook meanders peacefully through the course and designer Dick Bailey used it as a superb, but understated architectural element. Although only six to ten feet wide and just a few inches below the plane of the fairway, it provides a dangerous obstacle at key landing spots on holes number nine, eleven and eighteen. It adds signature definition, displaying the calm beauty of a mountain meadow on course marketing brochures.

Bottom line, Whitehawk Ranch is a fine course in excellent condition, but plays sneaky tough. Greens fees are high for the Graeagle area, but it is the top-ranked **Best 100** public course in town with tough competition. *Played in September '07.*

Whitehawk Ranch Golf Club

768 Whitehawk Drive	**Resort:**	800 332-4294
P. O. Box 300	**Golf Shop:**	530 836-0394
Clio, CA 96106	**Fax**	530 836-4504
	www.golfwhitehawk.com	

Managed by:	Highlands Mgmt. Group	**Architect:**	Dick Bailey
Location:	About an hour north of Truckee in the Sierras north of Lake Tahoe. Take Exit 188A off Interstate-80 and head north via Rt. 89. Course entrance is in 40 miles. Turn left on Whitehawk Drive and follow signs to the course.		
Style:	Gently rolling pine forest at the edge of mountain meadows. Fairways are mostly tree-lined but not too tightly. Brooks and streams meander the property. A level walk, but can be long from green to tee. Bunkers are strewn thoughout the course.		
Other info:	Resort Course in excellent condition. Lodging can be tricky to find so call their 800 number. Rates below are for the summer season. Savings in the Spring and Fall.		

Greens Fees as of 10/08:	Weekends	Weekdays	Twilight	Seniors	Carts/person
	$140	$125	$100/$85	No savings	Included

Course ratings:	Men	Par	Rating	Slope	Yardage	Women	Par	Rating	Slope	Yardage
Whitehawk Ranch	4 Hawks	71	71.7	129	6738	3 Hawks	73	74.2	142	6216
	3 Hawks	71	69.3	121	6216	2 Hawks	72	70.5	133	5490
	2 Hawks	68	65.8	113	5500	1 Hawk	71	65.4	123	4580

NO. 24: Diablo Grande: Legends

Diablo Grande, the huge 33,000-acre development between Patterson, apricot capital of the country, and Mt. Hamilton, the tallest peak around the San

Francisco Bay Area, opened in 1996. It started with two golf courses and the attitude, *build it and they will come.* Jack Nicklaus and Gene Sarazan designed the Legends West, which opened in 1998. Its variety and lower difficulty ratings (at non-Championship tees distances) make it the more popular than the complex's Ranch Course located across the street.

Like many big modern California courses built since 1990, it sits on ranch land with rolling topography, green/golden hillsides, mature oak trees and meandering creeks. Both nines utilize a similar style, though the backside perches a bit higher up the slopes of the local hills. Designers made driving friendly due to spacious fairways off the tee. Not so for the approach club repertoire. Bunkers, elevations, or water of some sort closely protect most of the greens.

Two interesting holes on the front side show these features and the kind of fun to be had at The Legends: Number three, a moderate length par-four, is the favorite of many, due in part to its risk/reward drive. The risky drive cuts through the dogleg by bouncing across a waste riverbed, and avoiding a huge oak. If successful, you have a simple wedge to an unprotected green. The safer route, up one dogleg and down the next, adds 35-yards to the hole and brings more bunkers into play. Number six presents a short par-five that initially appears rather ordinary, with a dogleg over a creek and up a hill. The driving zone appears wide, and tempts you to aim safely away from the creek; however, the next shot then needs to carry a 180-yard expanse of swamp and rock. Experienced players minimize overall risk by driving closer to the creek, yielding an easier second shot or even a chance at the green in two.

Another joy at the Legends comes from course condition that's excellent most of the year. Greens stay a bit softer and slower than on the nearby Ranch, which is another reason for the Legends' popularity. Why not take advantage of the two-for-one greens fee, play both courses, and make the decision yourself as to which is best? *Review based on play several times, last with interview in September '07.*

Diablo Grande Winery and Resort, Legends West Course:

9521 Morton Davis Drive	Golf Shop:	209 892-4653
Patterson, CA 95363	Fax	209 892-4136
	www.diablogrande.com	
Managed by: Sierra Golf Management	**Architect:**	Nicklaus/Sarazan

Location: Drive south from Tracy on Interstate-5 about 25 miles to Diablo Grande Exit. Head west seven miles, thru gate, and turn right onto Morton Davis Drive. Then turn left onto Morton Davis Circle.

Style: Rolling oak covered foothills. Some trees come into play, but most shots are open. Greens are moderate size, some with terracing. Greens well protected by bunkers and slopes.

Other info: Course has just come out of bankruptcy and changed ownership. Special price available to play both courses in one day.

Greens Fees	Weekends	Weekdays	Twilight	Seniors	Carts/person
as of 11/08:	$65	$49	none	none	included

Course ratings:	Men	Par	Rating	Slope	Yardage	Women	Par	Rating	Slope	Yardage
Diablo Grande Legends	Gold	72	74.8	147	7112	White	72	75.6	138	6057
	Blue	72	72.7	137	6680	Red Long	72	72.3	131	5461
	White	72	69.3	131	6057	Red	72	69.3	123	4930

No. 25: Presidio

Rarely does the U.S. government throw a bone to the golfing public. But they got a big one when the U.S. Army shut down its San Francisco Presidio Army Base in 1995, and transferred title to the Presidio National Trust. A combination of National Park, local, city and private interests oversee the Trust, so new development has been a slow process. Fortunately, they awarded a contract straight off to Arnold Palmer Golf Management, and Presidio Golf Course has been nurtured ever since.

This golf venue owns a long and illustrious history, starting with its founding in 1895. For the first 100 years it was the exclusive domain of the military and private Presidio Golf Club (which still exists), plus multitudes of guests. Presidents, pros, celebrities, and the best of amateurs frequently walked its hillside fairways. Now, anyone can play, and residents of the Bay Area get discounted fees. San Franciscans get even better deals.

Number eleven green at Presidio in San Francisco. Cypress trees, hilly terrain and lush fairways are hallmarks of this vintage 110 year old course.

Ask locals about the course and you will find two opinions. One group loves it, enjoying the serene, fog-shrouded trees, and classic seaside wetness that keeps drives from bouncing far down fairways. The other group only sees wintertime drainage problems, which cause drives to plug and shoes and pants to get messy. Certainly a bit of truth applies to both sides, though the course has a ten-year program to fix the drainage issues. It still bogs down in winter, and management often enforces cart-path-only rules. But, playing this course in its routine summer condition is such a treat, and so beautiful, that I come down on the positive side of the debate. Its ranking is based on summertime play.

Why is it special? Start with the majestic cypress trees that line the fairways, and then look at the lush, verdant fairways. Presidio offers an appearance and feel similar to that at the Olympic Club, four miles southwest, where pros come from around the world to play in the U.S. Open. Harding Park also comes to mind. All three have similar luxuriant grasses, uniquely picturesque cypresses, cloaking fog wisps, and the coolness and wind of the nearby Pacific Ocean. Presidio's layout comes with less acreage than these big tournament venues, so holes run closer together, with shorter yardages. Even bunkers, greens, and fairway-widths seem smaller. But this somewhat compressed appearance does not diminish its elegance, as everything fits together beautifully, like an inlayed mahogany puzzle.

Another difference from Harding and Olympic comes from its hillier landscape. Walking is not easy, though it was done for years by the rich and famous before carts replaced caddies. Elevation differences, normal on most holes, make up for some of the shorter yardages, and certainly add challenge and interest to approach shots. Greens are often quite small, adding to the course's complexity. A couple of short par-fours on the back side measure only 340-yards, but play well over 400, even down-wind.

The Palmer Management organization works hard to keep the course in year-round championship appearance. Many tees have been re-built by leveling them and some have been enlarged. Recently, a major tree restoration program finished, trimming thousands of dead branches and planting many young cypresses. Anyone seeking to shoot a low score should play soon, before the new trees mature. This trimming and grooming and extra care keeps Presidio one of the top choices for public summertime play in the San Francisco area. *Review based on play in August '08.*

Presidio Golf Course and Clubhouse

300 Finley Road @ Arguello Gate	**Golf Shop:**	415 561-4661
San Francisco, CA 94129	**Fax:**	415 561-4667
	www.presidiogolf.com	

Managed by:	Arnold Palmer Golf
Location:	From Park Presidio Blvd. (State Rt. 1) take Geary Blvd. east to Arguello Blvd. Turn north and drive 1/2 mile. Go through Arguello Gates. Course entrance is to the left, 50 yards past the gates.
Style:	Hilly green terrain where fairways are lined with large cypress and eucalyptus trees. Lush fairways yeild little roll. Greens can be very small. Short yardage is made longer by the terrain.

Architect: Robert Johnstone

Other info:	Course is maintained in excellent condition, except in winter it can get wet. Weather changes all through the day due to proximity to the Bay and ocean. SF and Bay Area residents get big discounts.

Greens Fees 10	Weekends	Weekdays	Twilight	Seniors	Carts
Non-NCGA	$132	$112	$92/$72	No Savings	$12

Course ratings:	Men	Par	Rating	Slope	Yardage	Women	Par	Rating	Slope	Yardage
Presidio	Blue	72	72.1	137	6477	White	73	76.1	136	6141
	White	72	70.8	133	6141	Red	73	74.2	131	5785

No. 26: Catta Verdera

Catta Verdera, roughly translated from Portuguese as "magical green place," began as Twelve Bridges Golf Course in 1996. It formed the anchor of a master plan community until the name change in 2003, and now heads towards becoming a private golf course. As of mid-2009, the public can still play, but availability will become more restricted if the membership fills.

Number fifteen tee at Catta Verdera. Trees and creeks beautifully frame this short par-four. The stone bridge pictured joins twelve others on a course originally named Twelve Bridges.

Membership status and course name represent just a few of the ongoing changes. Brad Bell renovated the young course in 2004; and players now report scoring to be easier. Another program of fairway and rough renewal began in 2006, bringing a new hybrid Riviera Bermuda grass to its second California location. This new blend may be the best all-round grass ever formulated. It presumably stays green down to 28 degrees F, needs very little water, grows on poor soil and is supposed to have the look and feel of bent grass.

Even though the current course plays fine, more bunker re-builds and re-designs will happen in 2009. The current greens need no extra work because they putt at the top level of any public course in the Sacramento area.

Catta Verdera's undeniably excellent design creates several photogenic holes. Fairways wind through mature stands of live, valley and white oak, with occasional small rock outcroppings. Landing areas appear rather narrow, and shots at the green require real precision. Widely spaced mansion-sized homes sit well back from fairways and many holes find no homes in sight. The most unusual feature comes from the flatness—or lack of contours—at fairway edges. The style is a throwback to days when golf terrain stayed natural, with little bulldozing, and saw wide expanses of space between the holes. Of course, without contours to stop them, drives hit to the side of the fairway or in the rough, usually bounce farther off-line, into the widely spaced oaks and hard dirt.

The back nine requires particularly straight shots, except for the three par-fives, which have wider drive landing zones. Number twelve, illustrated on the prior page provides an especially picturesque short 309-yard par-four. As one approaches the tee, the view of bridge and layout raises expectations about the precision needed for a good score. The drive-landing zone appears tiny because a bunker and creek on the left hide a seemingly narrow landing zone. Large trees on both sides and a steep hill on the right carefully protect the short approach to a narrow slightly elevated green. Play this hole successfully and at least one of Catta Verdera's many beauties could bring a little joy to your game. *Review based on play and interview in October '07.*

Catta Verdera Country Club

1111 Catta Verdera		**Golf Shop:**	916 645-7200
Lincoln, CA 95648		**Fax**	916 645-6729
		www.cattaverdera.com	
Managed by:	Private, local	**Architect:**	Brad Bell
Location:	Fifteen miles northeast of Sacramento. Take Interstate-80 to State Rt. 65 and go north towards Lincoln. Exit at Twelve Bridges Rd. and go 3 miles east to Catta Verdera Drive, then follow signs.		
Style:	Gently rolling terrain with creeks sprinkled throughout the layout. Oak forest lines most holes. Greens well protected by bunkers. Fairly easy walk. Very well maintained course.		
Other info:	Non-members only allowed after 11:00 am. Used to be named Twelve Bridges.		

Greens Fees	Weekends	Weekdays	Twilight	Seniors	Carts/person
as of 11/08:	$125	$125	No savings	No savings	Included

Course ratings:	Men	Par	Rating	Slope	Yardage	Women	Par	Rating	Slope	Yardage
	Black	72	73.9	137	7021	Combo	73	71.6	126	5352
Catta Verdera	Orange	72	71.6	134	6632	Yellow	72	69.5	124	5040
	Purple	72	69.0	127	6033					

No. 27: San Juan Oaks

Driving down from the San Francisco Bay Area to Monterey, this great Freddy Couples course sits just ten minutes off U.S. 101 between San Juan Batista and Hollister. It possesses every bit the quality seen at courses down in Carmel Valley, with the same bonus of warm summer weather. The relatively low greens fees, beautiful views, nice clubhouse, good practice area, and shorter drive from the bay area, make it a reasonable alternative for a weekend day-trip.

Many people describe San Juan Oaks as two courses in one, with a front nine on the valley floor and the second steeply sloped in the hills. The description is reasonably accurate, except that the front side is not flat, but also has nice, small elevation changes and mild undulations on every hole.

The second nine is not steep, but each hole climbs up or down enough to add or subtract 10 to 20 yards in distance. The exception comes at thirteen, a 440-yard par-four that plays an extra 60 yards, due to a prevailing afternoon 15-20 mph breeze directly into the face. The wind has a wearing effect on scores if you are not used to it. Another toughie, number fifteen, makes our list as one of the most difficult par-fives in the **Best 100**. Not only does it slowly climb about 60 feet in elevation, but also the second shot landing-area narrows to less than 30-yards on a crowned hill between two creeks. Figure an extra stroke for your second rolling into one of the two creeks, and just continue on. Later, the final two long, downhill par-fours make a tough finish. The seventeenth tee, which starts the drop to the lower valley, offers a full view of the Santa Clara Valley's southern reaches. Number eighteen requires an extremely long approach over a creek, trees and bunkers and also makes the **Best 100** list of toughest holes, this time a par-four.

The truth is that San Juan Oaks offers one of the better values for high quality golf within 45 minutes of San Jose. Special rye/*poa anna* turf sits the ball high off fairways making it easier to hit. The first cuts of rough also show care and consistent grooming. However, the secondary watered roughs grow long and show extensive matting, so try to avoid them. And the third tier grows longer yet, with natural grasses full of stickers and critters; forget even looking for the ball that far off track. The greens are large, moderately undulating, and well groomed, with many subtle hidden breaks. The aprons vary from steep slopes to narrow collars; so missed approaches rarely roll straight and often find bunkers. The five levels of tee boxes give as much as a 150-yard break per hole to those playing up front, and plenty of distance, at 7100-yards, from the tips.

A warning . . . like Apple Mountain (No. 22), this course does not set-up well for long, wild hitters. Do not expect to lower your handicap here, nor find a relaxed walk on a flat, straight, hit-chip-putt golf course. San Juan Oaks' design fits the adventurer who likes the flora and fauna of the rolling California landscape, who wants a fair challenge, who likes to climb hills, and who wants to face a variety of different shot-making situations. *Review based on play in July '07.*

Number ten, a par-five at San Juan Oaks, is the start of a gentle climb up into the local foothills. Later holes on the back nine are among the Best 100's toughest.

San Juan Oaks Golf Club:

3825 Union Road	**Golf Shop:** 800 453-8337
Hollister, CA 95023	**Golf Shop:** 831 636-6115
	Fax: 831 636-6114
	www.sanjuanoaks.com

Managed by:	Private, local **Architect:** Fred Couples
Location:	Between Hollister and San Juan Batista. Take U.S. 101 south ten miles from Gilroy to State Rt. 156. Go south 7 miles on Rt 156 to Union Rd. Turn right and go 300 yards. Turn right again onto Nothing Road; go about 2 miles to the clubhouse.
Style:	Front nine is gently rolling with nicely graded fairways and heavily textured rough. Back nine slowly climbs the foothills and then decends quickly on the last three holes. Has panoramic views. Greens are undulating and very well protected by bunkers and sloped aprons.
Other info:	Course is moderate walking challenge.

Greens Fees	Weekends	Weekdays	Twilight	Seniors	Carts/person
as of 10/08:	$80	$55	$55/$30	$45	$16

Course ratings:		Men	Par	Rating	Slope	Yardage	Women	Par	Rating	Slope	Yardage
San Juan Oaks	Black		72	74.6	140	7133	White	75	76.7	137	6342
	Blue		72	72.6	134	6712	Gold	72	73.8	135	5785
	White		72	70.9	130	6342	Red	72	86.1	120	4770

No. 28: Cinnabar Hills

Morgan Hill, about fifteen miles south of downtown San Jose, forms the epicenter for a group of the best quality golf courses in all of Northern

California. Cinnabar Hills Golf Club, on the west side of the Santa Clara Valley, lies five miles north of town and should be at the top of every golfers list. The course boasts a great combination of good fun, tough challenges and spectacular scenery. Completed in 1998, it includes a series of three nines: the Mountain, the Lake, and the Canyon.

The clubhouse houses a unique feature, called the Brandenburg Historical Golf Museum. Display cases contain hundreds of golf artifacts and memorabilia. They feature what may be the world's only collection of full sized, up-to-date replicas of trophies from the world's Major golf tournaments . . . including The Masters, U.S. Open, British Open, and Ryder Cup, among others. These are quite something for golf aficionados to see close-up.

The course itself also offers something special. It gets heavy play, but stays well maintained, and has many unique golf holes. Most believe the Lake/Canyon combination is the best grouping with the Lake being the most difficult nine. An especially challenging confrontation takes place on Lake number four. As an uphill 382-yard (back tee) par-four, the drive must carry over both a creek and a high cliff up to a blind landing on a narrow fairway. The second shot then needs to clear deep bunkers to land on a very long, well-elevated green. Take par or bogey here and breathe easily again.

Next, the Canyon-nine makes itself proud with several unusual holes, and ends with spectacular views of the Santa Clara Valley on the seventh green, the eighth tee and the entire ninth hole. Number-seven lists at only 341-yards long, but goes so steeply up the hill that it plays more like 420. It qualifies as one of the **Best 100's** toughest par-fours. Number eight, on the top of the ridge, plays 200-plus-yards and has often required me to hit an easy driver to carry a ravine and bunker when the pin is set back left. And then number nine, a moderate par-five, drops 130-feet over its 540-yard length, and bunkers dot the fairway at every jog.

The Mountain-nine also finds a good combination of holes. All are scenic, often down the heart of a canyon, but, like Poppy Ridge (reviewed later), none stands out as being particularly unique. Each of Cinnabar's three nine-hole groups provides interest, quality, and course conditions above most other courses in the **Best 100.**

Power carts come with the greens fee, but Cinnabar can be walked. Since it's very hilly, carrying a bag is probably preferable to pulling a cart. Tees stand not too far from greens. The Canyon nine give players the steepest climbs.

Other than the hilly lies, the biggest complaint at Cinnabar comes from the deep third-cut of rough. In spring and early summer, grasses grow wild and long. The wavy three-foot high grainy stalks certainly appear scenic when wind rustles through them, but finding balls is another story and hitting from them nigh impossible. Due to the difficulty of mowing or plowing on the steep slopes, they will probably stay a permanent feature of Cinnabar's style. Other features, such as fairways, greens, short roughs, bunkers and hazard borders all stay in great shape; so just eliminate those big hooks or slices and all should be well. *Review based on play several times, last with interview in August '07.*

Cinnabar Hills Golf Course

23600 McKean Road	**Golf Shop:**	408 323-7815
San Jose, CA 95141	**Fax**	408 323-9512
	www.cinnabarhills.com	

Managed by:	Private, local	**Architect:**	John Harbottle
Location:	Southern San Jose. Take U.S. 101 south to Bailey Rd. Turn west and go 3 miles to McKean Rd. Turn left and go one mile to course entrance on the left.
Style:	Hilly oak and grass covered foothills and canyons. Big views from many hilltops. Lots of up and down shots to elevated greens. Bunkers used liberally. Greens have slopes and terraces.
Other info:	Course is busy but in good shape. Many special greens fees and mini-memberships available. Savings available on weekdays for walkers, though walking is not easy.

Greens Fees	Weekends	Weekdays	Twilight	Seniors	Carts/person
as of 10/08:	$105	$82	$85/$62	No savings	Included

Course ratings:	Men	Par	Rating	Slope	Yardage	Women	Par	Rating	Slope	Yardage
Cinnebar Lake/Canyon	Hawk	72	72.7	138	6688	Quicksilver	72	73.3	135	5736
	Cinnabar	72	71.2	132	6318	Oak	72	69.1	120	4959
	Quicksilver	72	68.7	129	5827					

No. 29: Sierra Star

Most Northern Californians consider golf courses on the eastern side of the Sierras to be outside their playing territory. So it may come as a big surprise that Mammoth Lake's Sierra Star, about 100 miles south of Lake Tahoe, qualifies a **Best 100** top 30 course. Two others, Bishop Country Club in Bishop, and Furnace Creek in Death Valley also have quality worth playing if passing through, but Sierra Star deserves a special trip.

Some day the Northern and Southern California Golf Associations (NCGA and SCGA, respectively) will come to their senses and put these three into the SCGA. All find more access to LA Basin travelers than those from Northern California. I believe the organizations should swap them for Central Coast courses Avila Beach, Cypress Ridge, Monarch Dunes and Blacklake in southern San Luis Obispo County, because the latter group has more logistics in common with the North than the South. Then the stars will be aligned, and outlying courses in each Association will be in logical geographic groupings. Until then, it's a six to seven hour drive from almost everywhere in Northern California, except the Tahoe region, to play golf (or ski) at Mammoth Lakes. It takes a very special effort to experience one of our top courses.

Sierra Star's quality and style reminds me of the revamped Incline Village Champion course, with a bit of Coyote Moon thrown in. Sierra Star's fairways play better than those at Incline; in fact, its fairways are as good as any in the

Best 100 because the ball sits up and the turf underneath is soft. But, the course uses a small pre-fab clubhouse; and, like Coyote Moon, players need to warm up in nets rather than on a driving range. If one can get past these detractors, it is one fine track. Furnace Creek, further south, offers the lowest elevation in the state, indeed the world, and Sierra Star the highest in California at 8000 feet. This extra high altitude really makes a difference with lofted shots. Plan on using one and a half to two irons less to hit required distances.

Number eight at Sierra Star in Mammoth Mountain makes an excellent par-five, and shows an example of the scenic backdrops flaunted on most holes.

Beginners and players who cannot hit straight shots will struggle on this course. To remind us we are playing in a forest, designer Cal Olsen made roughs narrow, lined very closely by pines and firs; occasionally a conifer or two even protrudes into the fairway. Bunkers find strategic placement that provides beautiful sight lines and pushes players to favor one side of many fairways. Masterful contour work makes fairway slopes appear a natural part of the landscape. Greens undulate freely, and often find severe breaks and multiple terraces. The course guide-sheet even admits that the multiple tiered seventeenth green, at the end of a short par-four, is "maniacal" in its design. Play in June and greens will be slow, about 8 on the StimpMeter, but as the summer progresses, speeds can increase.

A special feature comes from the spectacular beauty of the high mountain setting just below Mammoth Mountain ski resort. Nearly every hole displays beautifully composed views of the surrounding ridges. Even the ball washers show artistry; superintendent Jon Cook hand-sculpted each one into unique large wooden bears.

The town of Mammoth appears to be newly constructed, and modern mountain architecture predominates. Local infrastructure such as roads, schools, shopping centers, and the many condominiums use a coordinated style, so town zoning must be strict. Course managers also report tough environmental rules for use of fertilizers, pesticides and tree maintenance. Motto of the town and the course is "we came for the winters, stayed for the summers."

The two par-fives, number eight and ten are wonderful holes, though their layouts are similar. Both play as uphill gentle doglegs where the entire design of the hole can be seen from the tee. Drives need to be straight, but have enough leeway to be hit hard. Second shots narrow a bit, with landing zones protected by bunkers and/or water. The final approaches go over hazards, to well sculpted elevated greens. Big hitters have the opportunity take a risky chance and make it in two, but shorter hitters will be hitting 125 to 175-yard approaches.

Toughest hole comes at number, six, and makes the **Best 100** list of toughest par-fours. Not only is it long, but the approach shot, to an elevated green, must clear a bevy of bunkers beneath the green. This hole, at 469-yards from the tips, down to 371-yards for the ladies, may be overly long for resort golf.

Nice as the course is, it does have a serious design flaw on the very first hole. The pro, staff, and everyone else fess-up and warn new players in advance. Still, the flaw needs to be fixed. This slightly uphill 375-yard par-four has the narrowest tree-lined fairway on the course. That's tough for players warming up in a net. Then, the approach shot must negotiate a very narrow tree-opening to the green, *and* clear a ten-yard wide ditch flowing immediately in front of the green. Please, cover the ditch! Talk about a wake-up call.

Fortunately, sixteen wonderful and varied holes follow (number two also has some issues), so by the end of the round that starting double-bogey, if not forgotten, finds itself overshadowed by other double bogeys. And fun double bogeys they are, in a very relaxing, well-manicured setting. *Review based on play and interview in June '08.*

Sierra Star Golf Course:

2001 Sierra Star Parkway	**Resort:**	800 MAMMOTH
P. O. Box 1942	**Golf Shop:**	760 924-2200
Mammoth Lakes, CA 93546	**Fax**	760 934-8600
	www.sierrastargolf.com	

Managed by:	Mammoth Mountain	**Architect:**	Cal Olson
Location:	South of Lake Tahoe about 150 miles. Take U.S. 395 23 miles south of Lee Vining to State Rt. 203. Turn right (west) and go 3.7 miles to Minaret Rd. Turn left and go about 1/3 mile to Sierra Star. Turn right and course lot is on the right.		
Style:	Gently rolling pine and fir forest. Fairways are mostly tree-lined and some are narrow. Greens can be multi-tiered. Course condition is excellent and greens speed up as summer progresses.		
Other info:	Altitude of 8000 feet can add over 10-15% distance to shots hit high. Rates vary throughout seasons. Minimal clubhouse facility and nets for driving range.		

Greens Fees	Weekends	Weekdays	Twilight	Seniors	Carts/person
as of 10/08:	$129	$104	$20	$94	Included

Course ratings:	Men	Par	Rating	Slope	Yardage	Women	Par	Rating	Slope	Yardage
	Black	70	71.1	138	6613	White	70	71.0	134	5430
Sierra Star	Blue	69	68.6	131	5972	Red	70	68.7	128	4912
	White	68	66.4	126	5430					

No. 30: Incline Village Championship Course

Golf Digest ranks Incline Village's Championship Course as the eighth best course in Nevada. Because of its immediate proximity to Lake Tahoe's north shore, I decided to incorporate it into in the **Best 100.** It ranks number three in the region from North Lake Tahoe to Truckee, and, given the tough competition from Coyote Moon and Old Greenwood, that's a very good ranking.

Incline Village actually operates two eighteen-hole courses, one a less challenging but very fun par-58 Mountain Course; the other, our subject, the full-sized Championship Course. Robert Trent Jones, Sr. originally designed the Championship layout in 1966, about the same time that he completed Spyglass Hill, our No. 2 course. After years of operation and some decline, the course closed in '04 and '05 for major renovations. Since re-opening in late '06, tuned up by Robert Trent Jones, Jr., the bells have been clamoring and for good reason.

Jones Sr. called it "the perfect mountain course." Its routing through the forest and fine homes of the Incline Village area follow a casual flow of golfing vistas that truly capture the beauty of the surroundings. Not only do the Ponderosa pine, the silvertip firs, and sumptuous homes provide a scenic backdrop, but also lake views and ridge scenes emanate from many a spot. And then there is the golf course itself . . .

All holes offer independent designs and blend together well, yet none appear particularly unique. The front nine, newly switched from the back, sits slightly higher on the slopes, creating a very gentle climb and offering good views of the Lake from tee-boxes on numbers six and seven. It also presents more doglegs, better-trapped greens, and more bunker-strewn fairways. The new beautiful white bunker-sand contrasts nicely with the greens and dark colored conifer backdrop. Bunker positions provide wide enough landing zones that players know they are on a relaxing mountain resort, rather than a brutal test of skill.

Late afternoon shadows cover the (now) eighteenth fairway on Incline Villages' Championship Course. Robt. T. Jones, Jr. updated the design in '05, and nines were reversed in '08.

The back side finds a couple of small brooks impacting nearly every hole. These rivulets have borders of heavy grassy vegetation or rocks and can easily be seen from hitting zones. The cart navigation system offers distance measurements to streams and bunkers, etc, making play a little easier for first-timers. Number eleven, a modest downhill par-five, tempts even medium length hitters to try for the green in two—over a boulder-laden creek-bed just in front of the green. Need extra ammunition? I found lots of balls down in these rocks, including my own.

If this rebuilt course's fairways and greens can mature properly, which had not happened by the end of '07, it may indeed end up meeting Jones's prophecy as "the perfect mountain course." *Review based on play and interview in September*

The Golf Courses at Incline Village, Championship Course

955 Fairway Blvd	**Reservations**	866 925-4653
Incline Village, NV 89451	**Golf Shop:**	775 832-1146
	Fax	775 832-1141
	www.golfincline.com	

Managed by:	Incline Village GID	**Architect:** Robt. T. Jones Sr.
Location:	North Shore of Lake Tahoe. Take Interstate-80 to State Rt. 267. Go south 17 miles to the lake and turn left on State Rt. 28. (Obey speed limits around the lake.) Go 6 miles and turn left on Northwoods, then right on Fairway.	
Style:	Gently rolling pine and fir forests line fairways. Back nine has more elevation change than front. Many elevated or well bunkered greens are usually firm. Fairway grass a bit thin.	
Other info:	Resort Golf Course, remodeled in 2006. Save $10 from fees in off season.	

Greens Fees	Weekends	Weekdays	Twilight	Seniors	Carts/person
as of 8/08:	$174	$174	$99	No savings	Included

Course ratings:	Men	Par	Rating	Slope	Yardage	Women	Par	Rating	Slope	Yardage
Incline Village	Black	71	74.1	144	7096	White	72	73.7	144	6004
Championship	Blue	71	71.8	138	6592	Combo	72	71.7	137	5603
Course	White	71	69.0	127	6004	Green	72	69.7	128	5208

No. 31: Hiddenbrooke

Just north of Vallejo, concealed in the hills south of Interstate-80, hides a real estate development and golf course that has made a big name in the past few years. The Arnold Palmer designed course opened in 2000, and Hiddenbrooke Golf Club has already played host to many tournaments. The 2002 Lady's Professional Golf Assn (LPGA) *Samsung World Championships* tops the list, and provided Annika Sorenstam one of her 89 career titles.

Tailored holes fit into the natural hilly topography in a very original fashion. They head around to the left, back to the right, with some short and tight, others long and open. Both nine's use routes with significant elevation gain and loss, while the fairways wind through rural grasslands and an expansive housing development.

Water comes into play on several holes, with many of the hazards environmentally protected. Players cannot retrieve their stray shots in these areas. Literally hundreds of hazard-bound golf-balls sit within 30-feet of one footbridge, just out of ball retriever range. Not being able to retrieve these brand-new-looking shiny white spheres frustrates many a golfer, including me!

The course offers a good mixture of target holes and those where you just hit-away. Two holes measure quite short, reachable in less than regulation; and none seem overly long. A few tight fairways demand good driver control, and approaches must always be accurate. Large greens have moderate undulation, and normally stay in excellent condition.

The downside comes from the location, just east of Vallejo, which can be extremely windy; and the hills provide few level lies. The nearby Carquinez Straight houses power generating windmills driven by the coastal breezes rushing towards the Sacramento Valley. The par-three third, only 135-yards long, can easily play 180 when the gusts blow down the steep grass covered canyon behind the green.

While both nines offer good challenges, the back side has the bigger elevation changes. Sixteen is a jewel, a downhill par-five double dogleg, bordered first on the right and then the left by the same creek. The drive usually heads down-wind, a big ego boost from any elevated tee. It must be hit long enough to clear the rough and close enough to the right-hand creek that it doesn't wander up the opposite hill into the high weeds. A good drive sets up a possible try for the green, but even a bailout second needs to be straight, due the narrow target zone across the creek in front of the green. The soft green mildly tiered green gets protection by water and traps all around, but for a small opening in front. No room for error here, but the patient straight shooter has a chance for easy par or even birdie.

Another good hole follows immediately. Par three seventeen measures 185-yards from the blue tees, but much longer from the tips. The approach shot, into a prevailing wind, aims over a lake that abuts the front edge. A pin in the front position is very dangerous. The pin in back isn't much fun either because the approach becomes 25-yards longer and the green narrows considerably, protected by bunkers and a creek at the sides. Finish up quickly and run to the easy eighteenth! *Review based on play many times, last in May '07.*

Hiddenbrooke Golf Club			
1095 Hiddenbrooke Parkway		**Golf Shop:**	707 558-1140
Vallejo, CA 94591		**Fax**	707 558-1144
		www.hiddenbrookegolf.com	
Managed by:	Kemper Sports	**Architect:**	Arnold Palmer
Location:	Between Vallejo and Fairfield just south of Interstate-80. Take I-80 to American Canyon Exit. Turn south on Hiddenbrooke Parkway. Drive 1.4 miles to club entrance on the left.		
Style:	Rolling grassy hills, some steep and some gentle. Surrounded by homes, creeks and lakes. Many greens bordered by slopes and bunkers. Straight shots important.		
Other info:	Course in good condition. Can be very windy in local hills just north of the Delta.		

Greens Fees as of 10/08:	Weekends	Weekdays	Twilight	Seniors	Carts/person
	$95	$65	$65/$45	No savings	Included

Course ratings:	Men	Par	Rating	Slope	Yardage	Women	Par	Rating	Slope	Yardage
	Palmer	72	73.8	142	6762	Gray	72	73.8	134	5773
Hiddenbrooke	Champ.	72	70.8	139	6205	Gold	72	71.1	128	5268
	Member	71	68.8	132	5727	Red	70	67.6	121	4557

No. 32: Harding Park

High-level members of San Francisco's golf community want to move the city back in the spotlight of big time PGA tournament golf. The city has four first-rate courses surrounding Lake Merced in the southwestern corner of the city, plus Presidio near the Golden Gate Bridge, to consider as candidates for play. Private clubs control three of the sites and their own destiny. These include (1) the private Olympic Club's Lake and Ocean courses, both host to many tournaments, and (2) the exclusive San Francisco Golf Club, which many rank as one of the best courses in the world, but doesn't open its gates to the public very often. The fourth candidate, Presidio, is a terrific course, ranked number 25 in the **Best 100,** but yardage runs too short for modern PGA competition, and the property size appears too small for big crowds.

Harding Park Municipal Golf Course, the final venue, becomes the logical choice. Its name may include the word "Municipal," but it's definitely not your typical muni. Why? First of all, like its neighboring courses around Lake Merced, huge old Monterey cypress trees soar over the fairways. This species, native to Cypress Point and Point Lobos near Pebble Beach, came to San Francisco years ago to add a truly majestic element to Golden Gate Park and various recreational arenas. They stand tall with imposing thick trunks, and dense dark green tops that seem to swallow golf balls at every chance. Second, the basic layout of the course, while constrained in spots by city streets, allows for good length, some elevation change, a variety of doglegs and large crowds can wander the ample space between the holes. It suits the pros well because fairways, roughs and greens can be toughened up for special events.

In 2002 the city decided it would invest nearly $20 million to renovate Harding Park in hopes of bringing back its '50's and '60's status as a perennial tour stop. The investment bought good deep bunkers, newly sculpted fairways, large and rebuilt multi-pin-placement greens, new tees, and a modern clubhouse. To inaugurate the refurbished course, city managers entered a contract with the PGA to host its year-end, biggest purse, *American Express Championship* tournament. Fortunately for all involved, the event was a great success. Not only did the pros love having a tournament back in the city limits of a major metropolis, but also the two biggest name long-ball hitters on the tour, Tiger Woods and John Daly, joined in a fabulous duel for the winning spot. Due to the timing of the tournament and popularity of the protagonists, many TV viewers tuned in to witness how those large cypresses could bring excitement to the game. Too bad John Daly's spectacular wedge approach, over one of these behemoths, had to be followed by a three-putt on the third playoff hole (number sixteen) to end the drama. Even Tiger wanted the match to go on.

Back to reality, the course and its future have yet to be finalized. Being a city owned course, other pressures come to bear to determine how much money can be spent on maintenance. The PGA looks to *increase* charitable contributions from tournaments revenues every year, something Harding and San Francisco may need to guarantee for future tournaments. The next scheduled event comes as the President's Cup of 2009.

The eighteenth at Harding Park started a climactic playoff duel between John Daly and Tiger Woods in the 2005 WGC American Express Championships.

In order to keep even a modicum of good maintenance, greens fees have been increased significantly, perhaps not to the level of Monterey Peninsula resort competition, but enough to make *non*-San Francisco residents pay a pretty penny. Daily local players are affected too . . . average Joes do not play those hard, tightly cut, beautifully manicured fairways and greens the pros always see. Rather, they often find a course well worn from volumes of play and slow grass growth. Even for their lower hometown greens fees, locals want more, especially in years when the course is not preparing for a major event.

Finally the weather keeps popularity low for those high paying visitors. Mark Twain's comment about "the coldest winter he ever spent was a summer in San Francisco" certainly rings true out near Lake Merced and Harding Park. A foggy, moist, 55-degree temperature and 20-mile-per-hour wind makes hands pretty numb after four and a half hours. My games at Harding have usually been in this cool weather. Natives love these conditions because they keep tourists—anyone who doesn't live in the Western neighborhoods of the city— away from the course. But, when the weather warms, the winds calm, and the course rounds into good condition, it definitely becomes a winner. *Review based on play several times, last in June '09.*

Harding Park Golf Course

99 Harding Road at Skyline Blvd.		Golf Shop:	415 664-4690
San Francisco, CA 94132		Fax	415 661-9512
		www.harding-park.com	
Managed by:	Kemper Sports	**Architect:**	Willie Watson
Location:	In Southwestern San Francisco. Take Interstate-280 to John Daly Blvd. Turn west, drive one mile to State Rt. 35/Skyline Blvd. Turn right, go two miles and turn right on Harding Drive.		
Style:	Very gently rolling terrain, bordered by giant cypress trees. Well bunkered throughout. Modern rolling greens.		
Other info:	Busy city course. Discounts available to Northern CA residents and bigger ones to SF residents. Can be foggy and windy. Fairway and green condition erratic. Nice Restaurant.		

Greens Fees	Weekends	Weekdays	Twilight	Seniors	Carts/person
as of 10/08:	$155	$135	$125/$105	SF only	$13

Course ratings:	Men	Par	Rating	Slope	Yardage	Women	Par	Rating	Slope	Yardage
	Blue	72	73.1	125	6829	Red	72	73.2	123	5866
Harding Park	White	72	71.1	122	6390	Gold	72	70.4	116	5374
	Red	72	68.7	116	5873					

No. 33: Tahoe Donner

Six thousand home sites and condominiums fill the Tahoe Donner real estate development on the northwest edge of Truckee's Interstate-80 corridor. During construction, most of the forest and trees were spared, so the landscape still maintains its natural wooded appearance. Homes and public structures blend nicely with the local mountain environment.

To stay consistent with this prescient sensitivity for the environment, architect Bob Williams designed Tahoe Donner Golf Course to follow a conservative, even classic mold. He moved a minimum amount of dirt, at least in the initial design, and found a way the holes could follow natural terrain through the pines and firs. Fairways run narrow, so few trees needed to be cut. Only four holes use adjacent fairways; in fact, the overall plan appears novel if viewed from the air: Its heart-shaped appearance, with nines heading in opposite directions around the two halves of the outline, provides a balanced design. Holes favoring fades equal about the same number as those needing a draw. Yardages vary extensively from hole to hole, so most players need to use all their clubs.

For those who haven't played it recently, Tahoe Donner underwent extensive maintenance the last five years. Starting in 2002 the Board of Directors saw local golf competition improving, with several new facilities built in the North Shore/Truckee area. To maintain parity, for both their own members and the paying public, they began significant renovations. A four-year program updated the course and facilities:

1. A new clubhouse replaced one about to be condemned.
2. Short distance tee boxes were added to reduce the 6000-yard distance for women. Ladies now play a manageable 5000 to 5500 yards. In addition, longer championship men's tees, some located in angled positions deep in the trees, increased length to 7003-yards.
3. Removal of several trees opened the fairways slightly. This process is standard on most courses, since new growth often clutters the original design concept.
4. Extensive bunker renovation, mostly around the greens but also in some fairways, preened the look. One of the country's renowned bunker shapers, Ed Krikorian, working for Cary Bickler Inc., came in for the job. He wanted to create patterns in the style of McKenzie and Tillinghast, designers of Cypress Point and San Francisco Golf Clubs respectively. The result keeps the classic feel of the original course, yet adds significant subtle drama and interest to most holes.
5. Putting and chipping practice-areas were rebuilt to match the feel, speed and style of the new green complexes. The driving range, 500 yards down the hill from the pro shop, also received a facelift.
6. A drastic modification to par-five number nine, created some controversy. Its long straight steeply angled fairway had followed the natural terrain. However, the slope allowed shots to bounce/roll out-of-bounds, because of the fairway's narrow width. The remodel leveled the fairway by adding hundreds of tons of dirt on the lower side. Currently the immature condition of the renovation appears unnatural and out-of-place from the rest of the course.
7. Men's course rating increased from 72.4 to 74.2 on the back tees, and from 71.2 to 72.4 at the regular tees. Women's rating decreased to 68.9 at the new front tees.

All this work seems to have paid-off, since most players believe Tahoe-Donner to be one of the tougher, but fairer tests in the Tahoe area. Even straight hitters, who can negotiate the rather narrow channels between the trees, need to deal with angled crossing creeks and well-placed fairway bunkers. The greens, which did not need change in the renovation, remain subtly undulating, but hold shots reasonably well. Putting remains straightforward, but getting there can be a challenge to wayward hitters.

The eighteenth at Tahoe Donner highlights four years of remodeling and updating. The new green complex uses bunkers shaped by Ed Krikorian, one of the game's premier specialists.

The eighteenth presents a good example of the result, as a fabulously picturesque finishing hole. The tee-shot aims steeply down hill, dropping about 50 feet, and long hitters must lay-up short of a stream/lake complex. Past the trouble lies the beautifully framed green, surrounded by new, large, well-shaped bunkers and a diagonal putting surface where the pin can be tucked tightly in corners when needed. Both the stunning view from the tee, and the shot to the green, make players eagerly anticipate the experience. It's a really fun, rewarding hole if you execute the shots properly. But as I know personally, that's a big "if." *Review based on play and interview in July '08.*

Tahoe Donner Golf Course

12850 Northwoods Blvd.		**Golf Shop:**	530 587-9443
Truckee, CA 96161		**Fax**	530 587-9496
		www.tahoedonner.com	
Managed by:	Private, local	**Architect:**	Bob Williams
Location:	In Truckee. Take I-80 exit 184 and go north to Donner Pass Rd. Then turn left and go 1/2 mile and turn right on Northwoods Blvd. Course is on the left about 2.8 miles up the hill, past Coyote Moon.		
Style:	Set on the side of a moderately sloped Sierra mountain ridge. Fairways are tightly lined with natural forest. Has some fairway bunkers and many nicely protected greens. Dogleg rights are balanced by doglegs left.		
Other info:	Semi-private course in excellent condition. Greens fee savings for members and guests. Course renovated over last 5 years.		

Greens Fees	Weekends	Weekdays	Twilight	Seniors	Carts/person
as of 10/08:	$150	$150	$70	None	Included

Course ratings:	Men	Par	Rating	Slope	Yardage	Women	Par	Rating	Slope	Yardage
	Blue	72	74.2	137	7002	Red	74	72.3	138	5588
Tahoe Donner	White	71	72.4	130	6562	Gold	74	68.9	127	4997
	Red	70	68.6	122	5588					

No. 34: Carmel Valley Ranch

Any golf course located within fifteen miles of the Monterey Peninsula faces a lot of strong competition. This beautiful area creates such a magnet for discerning golfers that courses trying to survive need to be special. Not all can have the scenic beauty of Pebble Beach, Spyglass Hill and Spanish Bay, so they need to find a different niche. Usually this means creating country club playing conditions comparable to local private courses such as Cypress Point, The Preserve, Tehama, Pasadera and Monterey Peninsula Country Club.

Carmel Valley Ranch (CV Ranch) operates a resort located ten miles inland and southeast of the Monterey Peninsula. It works hard to succeed in this highly competitive environment and has one big advantage. When the fog and cold of July and August shroud the Monterey Peninsula and Carmel-By-the-Sea, the Carmel Valley and its three public course complexes escape most of the cool weather. Being the easternmost setting in this little group, which includes Rancho Cañada's two courses and the Quail Lodge Resort, CV Ranch has the sunniest skies in the Monterey area, all summer long.

But it takes more than warm weather to compete, so the resort planned other distinguishing features. First, the design by famous architect Pete Dye offers his only course in Northern California. He used a shorter 6117-yard layout to make it friendly for resort golfers, while showcasing his famous sculpting talents on the greens and surrounding bunkers. Next, the course just finished a $4 million golfing facelift, with all fairways and tees renovated. Management rebuilt and re-shaped greens too because customers criticized the severity of their tiers and slopes. In addition, the resort's hotel just completed a $20 million renovation of the main lobby and restaurant. The revamped facility presents a modern, refined atmosphere, and strives to fill aspirations of the most discerning clientele.

Carmel Valley Ranch's back nine climbs high into the Santa Lucia Range foothills before a 100-foot drop back down from the back tee to the eleventh fairway.

The intent of CV Ranch's management, handled by Luxury Resorts, is to maintain the top-conditioned resort course in the area. In August of 2008, this was certainly the case. Beautiful manicuring matched firm, smooth greens, uniform and easy-to-hit-from fairways, well-groomed aprons and tees, nicely trimmed trees/shrubbery, and excellently maintained bunkers.

Finally, holes ten through fourteen give golfers as steep and dramatic an experience as any in the state. Whereas the front side and holes fifteen thru eighteen lie down in the valley along the Carmel River, number ten starts a long climb uphill. It's a mere 450-yard par-five but plays more like 510, with a double dogleg marching inexorably higher on each shot. Next comes one of the most spectacular holes you will ever encounter. Players start by motoring their carts up a steep group of switchbacks to tee boxes cut like notches into the hillside. Drives then head back down to a rolling fairway 100-feet below. The broad vista gazes on oak and villa covered hills across the valley, with ridges bordering the Salinas Valley in the distance. Down below, the fairway splits into two narrow strips, divided by a long bunker. Fortunately the lips are shallow, because most drives end up somewhere in its sand. And once at the bottom plan on at least another 180-yards back up again to an elevated green, where a flock of wild turkeys often meanders the aprons.

The next three holes continue wandering down to more normal golf terrain. One of them, a 150-yard par-three number thirteen, has another superb view, this time looking west through the valley. In the distance players often see a high gray bank of fog and clouds, reminding them of one good reason they should enjoy their day of warmth at Carmel Valley Ranch. *Review based on play and interview in September '08.*

Carmel Valley Ranch Golf Course

One Old Ranch Road		**Resort:**	866 282-4745
Carmel, CA 93923		**Golf Shop:**	831 620-6406
		Fax	831 626-2561
		www.carmelvalleyranch.com	
Managed by:	Luxury Resorts	**Architect:**	Pete Dye
Location:	About 25 minutes south of Monterey. Take State Rt. 1 south to Carmel Valley Rd. Turn left (south) and drive 6 miles. Turn right on Robinson Canyon road an go 1/4 mile to Old Ranch Rd. Turn left, and clubhouse is 1/2 mile on the left.		
Style:	Most holes are level, built in the Carmel Valley. Holes 10 thru 15 are steeply up and steeply down, with panoramic views. All are fairly tight, with some homes and trees bordering fairways. Greens are moderate sized and were made less extreme in a 2007 renovation.		
Other info:	Resort Golf Course in great condition. Guests and guest family members get big discounts. Greens fees lower from Nov thru May.		

Greens Fees	Weekends	Weekdays	Twilight	Seniors	Carts/person
as of 10/08:	$215	$195	$130/$110	No savings	Included

Course ratings:	Men	Par	Rating	Slope	Yardage	Women	Par	Rating	Slope	Yardage
Carmel Valley Ranch	Blue	70	70.1	131	6117	White	70	72.9	132	5664
	White	70	67.9	126	5664	Red	70	70.8	129	5230
	Red	68	65.7	121	5169	Gold	70	66.2	114	4433

No. 35: Yocha-de-he

Cache Creek Casino Resort advertises extensively in San Francisco. Although located only 45 minutes from Sacramento, they work hard to bring gamblers from the Bay Area because theirs is the closest casino to its huge population. The casino and new golf course stand together about a half hour north of Vacaville, in the tiny town of Brooks, fifteen minutes west of Interstate-505. With the 2007 opening of Brad Bell designed Yocha-De-He Golf Club, non-gamblers now have a reason to visit too. (Bell also designed highly acclaimed Coyote Moon in Truckee.) The clubhouse finally opened in early 2009.

The casino sits adjacent to the Capay Valley's main road, State Rt. 16, but the course lies about a mile east over a ridge of low hills. It rests in a cozy valley, once the "spring home," (translated "yocha-de-he,") to the Rumsey Band of Wintun Indians. The course nestles nicely between oak covered hills, though the layout seems compact compared to others built recently in Northern

California. It boasts an attractive bowl-shaped practice area/driving range, and the clubhouse overlooks the start and finish of the back nine.

Flooded with cross bunkers, the approach on par five number six at Yocha-de-he must hit the green or its back down into rough or sand or Indian burial grounds.

Perhaps the most dramatic shot on this very new venue comes on the first drive at number one. Players steer carts up a steep hill, overlooking the entire valley, and then tee-off down a 90 foot precipice to the flat wide fairway below. Unlike a similar tee shot on number fifteen at nearby Hidden Valley Lake (close to Clear Lake), the edge of the tee is not so steep as to cause vertigo; but the drop still appears quite spectacular. Bell's layout then proceeds around the valley floor with significant variation in designs and photogenic scenes. A concern would be that holes sometimes fit too closely together, with manufactured mounds separating them from each other. Such features—rather commonplace these days—detract from the originality that shows in other parts of the design. Respect for burial grounds and Indian archeology restricted some of the flow that would otherwise have been possible.

Some other features of the course prove quite memorable. The sixth hole makes a flowing par-five, double dogleg, where an uphill approach over extensively layered cross-bunkers challenges even short 125-yard shots. Other par-fives prove equally interesting and are a consistent strength of the course. Another outstanding hole comes at long par-three number thirteen. It's set within a vineyard on the north perimeter of the property and requires a wood or driver for most players. Swells, hollows and hidden bunkers protect the green approach and send short tee shots bounding in weird directions. The 234-yard length, from the gold tees, makes it one of the **Best 100** toughest par-threes.

The final hole, a 423-yard par four, also provides a beauty. The fairway curves around a lake on the right, a design becoming common on sophisticated courses. Yet it's fun to play, and complements the drama of the starting hole, this time with two shots near water, set against the backdrop of the new clubhouse-on-the-hill.

Yocha-de-he typifies the growing number of casino-related golf courses in the West. Future years may see may see this trend continue, because casinos seem too be the only organizations that can justify the sophisticated course designs now in fashion. Affluent golfers look for venues where fairways see few homes, where topography fits the game, and where designs compete aesthetically with top courses in the **Best 100**. Such venues cost $10-20 million to build, and who but casinos have that kind of money? *Review based on play and interview in June '08.*

Yocha-de-he Golf Course at Cache Creek Casino

14455 Highway 16		**Resort:**	888 772-2243
P. O. Box 65		**Golf Shop:**	530 796-4653
Brooks, CA 95606		**Fax**	530 796-5101
		www.cachecreek.com	
Managed by:	Troon Golf	**Architect:**	Brad Bell
Location:	Forty-five minutes north of Vacaville. Take Interstate 505 to State Rt. 16 exit and drive west fourteen miles. The Casino is on the right. Drive to main entrance door and valet arranges trip to course.		
Style:	Rolling terrain through graded fairways, oaks and vineyard. Many elevated greens, often with terracing and deep surrounding bunkers.		
Other info:	Clubhouse currently under construction; completion scheduled January '09.		

Greens Fees	Weekends	Weekdays	Twilight	Seniors	Carts/person
as of 10/08:	$85	$85	No savings	No savings	Included

Course ratings:	Men	Par	Rating	Slope	Yardage	Women	Par	Rating	Slope	Yardage
	Black	72	74.9	136	7222	Red	74	76.3	134	6277
Yocha-de-he	Gold	72	72.4	132	6775	Green	72	74.4	129	5937
	Red	72	70.2	129	6277	White	72	70.8	122	5331

No. 36: Bodega Harbour

Robert Trent Jones Jr. had his hand in the design of many fine courses ranked in the **Best 100**. One of them, the Links at Bodega Harbour, is especially familiar to residents of San Francisco's North Bay. It's a northern complement his Poppy Hills and Spanish Bay designs on the Monterey Peninsula to the south, but takes less than half the time to drive to from the City. Reasonably priced greens fees make it a wonderful getaway for urban adventurers from anywhere.

San Francisco may be well accustomed to Bodega's foggy weather, but outlanders wilting from the heat of July and August in other California valleys will relish the relief of a cool day on this distinctive course. Several fine lodges and lesser accommodations situate nearby, and stay-and-play packages come in many varieties. The low, dense, gray vapor virtually vanishes at other times of the year, making Bodega Harbour a pleasant retreat, out-of-season, for those averse to cooling misty moisture.

The drive from the course to the ocean is worth the trip even if you don't play golf. A picturesque combination of golden hills, thickets of oak and redwood, grazing cattle, and wisps of fog make the scenery both dramatic and distinctive. Add gently twisting roadways, small ocean-side communities, plentiful wine tasting, and beautiful coastal flora, and the trip to Bodega Bay becomes a nice way to spend almost any day.

However, the golf course alone more than justifies the drive, which takes an hour or less from the north tower of the Golden Gate Bridge (in light traffic). Bodega Harbour's front nine, built in 1985, starts with a steep climb through an area of high-end homes on the first four holes, followed by a long drop back down on the final five. Along the way, golfers viewed from a distance will appear to be riding the twists and turns of a roller-coaster among sheer hillside roughs, large fairway mounds, strategically placed fairway bunkers, and isolated target greens. When the fog lifts, an expansive view reveals Bodega Bay's beaches, compromised by encroaching development, and the Pacific Ocean beyond. Most mornings fog shrouds the hill, making it hard to see the ball—and reminding film fans why Hitchcock made this the setting for his horror classic, *The Birds.*

If playing the front side is a like a carnival ride, the back nine, built lower and closer to the bay, provides a very different ambiance. Constructed some years earlier in 1977, it has few if any fairway contours and less bunkering. While it does travel up and down a hillside, the grade is gentle and easy to walk, and the surrounding homes sit well off the fairway.

The course's distinctive glory comes on the last three holes. Number sixteen runs a short 300 yards, starting with a 150-yard forced-carry over a grass-filled salt marsh. Women get a big break and tee off on the other side; long hitters can choose to go for the green, about 300 yards away, but using two shots may result in a better score. If the prevailing crosswind blows right-to-left, the shots seem easy, but if it's blowing the other way, watch out! Likewise, hole seventeen heads back across the marsh on a 180-yard par-three in the opposite direction. Power carts can't be used on these two ocean-side holes, so the course maintains a nearby supply of hand-carts for players until they return to make the steep drive back up to the eighteenth tee.

The final long par-four requires a straight drive across a wide barranca (from the blue tees) to a peninsula-like fairway, set on a steep slope. No error to the right, left, short or long can be made. Then a 170-yard approach goes back down to the ocean, where bunkers and natural dunes surround the green. Here, too, stunning ocean views prevail.

Number fifteen is a relaxing par-five with a great view of Bodega Bay when the fog finally lifts.

Under the management of Kemper Sports, Bodega Harbour is kept in carefully manicured condition. Because the supply of water decreases in summer, imperfections may appear, almost imperceptibly, as the wind dries out knolls and knobs. But generally speaking, both fairways and roughs stay in good shape . . . much greener than at Sea Ranch, a hundred miles to the north. Excellent greens, rebuilt in 2008 using bent grass, are an oddity along the California coast where *poa anna* usually thrives. Management has leveled the greens a bit to make their tricky layouts friendlier for the out-of-town visitors Bodega Harbour tries diligently to attract.

A fun layout, good course conditions, relatively low prices, a nice drive over to the coast, and changeable weather . . . all combine to make Bodega Harbour an experience *not* for the birds! *Review based on play and interview in August '08.*

The Links at Bodega Harbour

21301 Heron Drive	**Resort:**	800 503-8158
P. O. Box 368	**Golf Shop:**	707 875-3538
Bodega Bay, CA 93923	**Fax**	707 875-3256
	www.bodegaharborgolf.com	
Managed by: Kemper Sports	**Architect:**	Robt. T. Jones, Jr.

Location:	An hour and a half north of the Golden Gate Bridge. Take U.S. 101 to Cotati and State Rt. 116 or to Santa Rosa and State Rt. 12. Go west to Sebastopol on either route. Once there, follow Bodega Ave. eleven miles to State Rt. 1. Turn right and go another 3.5 miles. Turn left on Harbor Way and a quick right on Heron. Go 1/2 mile to clubhouse. See Google Maps for a quicker route from SF.
Style:	Front nine is steeply up for 4 holes and then down for the rest. Very few level lies on this side. Back nine shows more gently rolling terrain, but with forced carries on last 3 holes. New greens throughout.
Other info:	Semi-private resort course. Can be very foggy and windy in summer, especially in the a.m. Spring and fall have best weather. Call proshop about stay-and-play options. Walking allowed but challenging.

Greens Fees as of 10/08:	Weekends	Weekdays	Twilight	Seniors	Carts/person
	$90	$60	$70/$40	No savings	Included

Course ratings:	Men	Par	Rating	Slope	Yardage	Women	Par	Rating	Slope	Yardage
Bodega Harbour	Black	70	71.5	129	6284	White	70	73.1	130	5489
	Blue	70	69.8	122	5907	Gold	70	68.6	118	4801
	White	70	67.9	119	5489					

No. 37: Callippe

Golfers in San Francisco's southern Bay Area received a terrific gift in the latter months of 2005. The city of Pleasanton opened a wonderful golf course. It sits well hidden from the freeways, is worth the effort to search out, and offers one of the best values in the South Bay. The small valley where Callippe has its home shares the area with an endangered species, the Callippe Silverspot butterfly. When opened, several publications ranked it as one of the best new municipal courses in the nation. That certainly remains the case in late 2008, since it makes a better play better than many California resorts.

Similar to recent layouts built in the rolling topography of Northern California, Callippe shows two different style nines. The front side fits neatly on the floor of the small valley, while the back nine covers the lower slopes of the hills blocking it from Interstate-680 to the west. The result becomes a fulfilling combination of varying hole designs.

The beginning group plays more open, with many doglegs well guarded by strategically placed bunkers. These sandy hazards force drives to be carefully aimed. In fact, medium length hitters may prefer the longer blue tees than shorter whites, in order to stay safely short of trouble.

The back nine is more unusual. It goes up, down and all around, including creeks, lakes, deep ravines, big elevation changes, narrow peninsulas and a few trees just to keep players from becoming reckless. You will find the greens especially challenging, not only because of sharp terracing, but also from long slopes and humps. Pins placed in awkward locations, only reachable from drive landing zones next to hazards. A good example comes at fourteen—a short par-four, slightly uphill dogleg, around a creek and large bunker. You will be tempted and even well advised to aim your driver or long iron away from the trouble. But the resulting position forces the 125-yard incoming approach to clear an elevated greenside trap *and* land on a firm down-slope heading away from the shot. A drive up the other side brings both a bunker and creek into play on the drive but makes the pin an easier target.

Rolling grasslands and pastoral views mark many back nine holes at Callippe reserve. By this eighteenth green players just concentrate on keeping the ball in play and praying putts go down.

Par-fives at Callippe fit in a special class, some of the best and most tantalizing in the **Best 100**. They all offer a high risk/reward benefit. Want to take a chance of placing your drive to go for the green in two? Have at it, but beware of multiple obstacles and very small target zones. Even if one plays short on the second shot, approaches to all four par-five greens can be tricky because tough pin locations—and no easy putts—seem to be the norm.

Course conditions, despite being a municipal course, usually appear excellent. Nearly perfect fairways use rye grass to sit the ball up, and also allow decent roll. Crews rake bunkers regularly and cut roughs evenly, allowing few bare spots. Greens unfortunately get more erratic maintenance. In June '06 they were gorgeous, but by March '07 they had lost much of their grass. A month later they were back in excellent condition and in May '08 the grass was disappearing again. However, even with occasional poor conditions, they are kept smoothly rolled so that the impact of bareness becomes minimal and putts still roll true. *Review based on play many times, last in May '08.*

Callippe Preserve Golf Course

8500 Clubhouse Drive	**Golf Shop:** 925 426-6666
Pleasanton, CA 94566	**Fax:** 925 426-6618
	www.playcallippe.com

Managed by:	CourseCo	**Architect:**	Brian Costello
Location:	Take exit 25 (Sunol Blvd) from Interstate-580 east towards Pleasanton. Go to second light, turn right on Sycamore Dr. Take first right to stay on Sycamore Rd., which turns into Alisal. Go 1.1 miles and turn left onto Westridge Ln. Follow around clubhouse.		
Style:	Rolling hills. Front nine has less elevation change than the back. Few trees but several holes require well placed drives, and greens are well guarded by hills and bunkers.		
Other info:	Pleasanton residents have priority for morning times and get decent greens fee savings.		

Greens Fees	Weekends	Weekdays	Twilight	Seniors	Carts/person
as of 10/08:	$63	$43	$53/$33	-$12 weekdays	$15

Course ratings:	Men	Par	Rating	Slope	Yardage	Women	Par	Rating	Slope	Yardage
Callippe Resreve	Black	72	73	133	6748	Yellow	72	72.4	127	5560
	Blue	72	71.5	130	6409	Red	72	68.4	114	4788
	White	72	69.8	125	6024					

No. 38: Castle Oaks

The Preston School of Industry occupied a large brick structure built in the 1890's as a reform school for children. It stands empty today but still dominates town skyline in Ione, and has become known as Preston Castle. Thus, the name Castle Oaks honors the history of its locale plus the local tree covered hillsides. It's situated half way between Stockton and Sacramento in the low hills east of State Rt. 99.

Like neighbors La Contenta, Saddle Creek and Greenhorn Creek to the south, Castle Oaks Golf Course forms the centerpiece for a large Central Valley foothill home development project. Here, the holes sit well away from homesites, but are often sandwiched between rows of lots and accessed only by walkways between them. To counteract the suburban feel of the immediate surroundings, extra care has been taken to create enjoyable designs on each hole. Thousands of tons of dirt seem to have been moved to carefully sculpt the fairways, lakes and green complexes. In addition, the plan completed by Brad Benz in 1994, adds many vistas of surrounding foothills and includes some highly distinctive golf holes.

Foremost among these is 440-yard number eighteen. This capstone hole, usually directed into a prevailing wind, needs to be played several times to understand a successful plan of attack. A par-four, and one of the most confounding for mid-distance hitters, it sits solidly in the **Best 100** toughest group. Three lakes come into play if one tries a frontal attack. The shortest route starts with a 210-yard carry over the first lake, on the left (from the blue tees). If that is too long for you, especially into the breeze, then the next shortest route is a bit to the right, near a large oak, but short of lake number two, which sits about 230-yards from the tee. If either of these drives prove successful, the approach needs to carry 160 to 200 more yards, into the wind, over lake number three, to a slightly elevated green. Bunkers dead ahead at the green must also be avoided. The safest but longest route heads far to the right, away from lakes one and two. This direction adds over 50 yards to the hole making it a par-five in distance. Most of us then need a lay-up second shot, still into the wind, followed by a short approach directed away from lake number three. No problems on this hole!

Eighteen represents just one example of how design brings character to the course. Other holes are much less treacherous, but use obstacles and distances that necessitate thought, experience and skill. The course is only measures 6750-yards at the tips, to 4950 all the way up; so distance only becomes a serious issue on number eighteen. Rather, understanding where to hit drives, so the next shot will be easy, is the key to success. Just hitting shots as far as possible usually leads to failure. The first hole, a downwind 550-yard par-five, offers a case-in-point. The tee shot must be fairly straight, to avoid OB right and a lake left, but the fairway is wide. The second shot, if hit at the green, leaves a very difficult third, over trees. Therefore, the correct second is to lay-up down the left side to a small landing area, where the next shot can go straight at the open green.

Three ponds block access to the eighteenth at Castle Oaks, another of the several tough finishing holes in the Best 100. It may be a par-four but playing it as a five usually generates the lowest scores.

Another plus at this privately owned but very popular public course comes from its good condition. Fairways offer well-clipped rye grass, so that the ball

sits up nicely. Wide roughs stay evenly cut and look green throughout. As is customary in California, dry, bare dirt prevails under oaks for fear of oak root fungus disease; however, poplars and other trees show plenty of grass under them. Greens display moderate, not extreme contours, and putting speeds of about 10 on the StimpMeter, which is fast and competitive for their junior and county tournaments. Due to heavy play, plan on over five hours for a full round.
Review based on play and interview in April '08

Castle Oaks Golf Course

1000 Castle Oaks Drive	**Golf Shop:**	209 274-0167
P. O. Box 1368	www.castleoaksgolf.com	
Ione, CA 95640		

Managed by:	Private, local	**Architect:**	Brad Benz
Location:	Between Stockton and Sacramento, 22 miles east of State Rt. 99. Take State Rt. 104 east towards Ione to Castle Oaks Dr; this junction is 1 mile northwest of downtown Ione. Turn left (south) and follow signs to course.		
Style:	Gently rolling terrain. Wetlands throughout, but trees sparsely line the fairways. Greens are well bunkered and many have separate terrace levels. Several paths between homes from greens to next tee.		
Other info:	Course usually in good condition. Busy due to local tournaments and general popularity.		

Greens Fees as of 3/09:	Weekends	Weekdays	Twilight	Seniors	Carts/person
	$47	$31	$25/$20	$38	$11

Course ratings:	Men	Par	Rating	Slope	Yardage	Women	Par	Rating	Slope	Yardage
	Black	71	72.2	131	6739	White	71	73.3	127	5948
Castle Oaks	Blue	71	70.3	126	6356	Gold	71	71.6	119	5447
	White	71	68.4	124	5948	Red	71	69.3	114	4953

No. 39: Quail Lodge

Nestled beneath steep bramble covered cliffs of the Carmel River, just south of Monterey, lies the Carmel Valley's original resort golf course. It opened in 1963, and remains one of California golf architect Robert Muir Graves' better-known designs.

The course history runs deep, not only because of its popularity as the first built in Carmel Valley away from notorious ocean-side summer fog, but also for the many tournaments played there. The PGA 1977 Seniors Championship, the California State Women's Amateur qualifying rounds, and the Spaulding Series were popular years ago. To this day, W. Lawson Little III, son of 1940 U.S. Open and 1935 Sullivan Award winner W. Lawson Little Jr., presides as President of Quail Lodge. Doris Day's home overlooks the eighteenth tee, and for years she was a prominent lunch guest.

The tenth at Quail Lodge provides one of the more memorable settings. After driving through a long chute and missing the large tree, the approach requires a medium iron from a rolling fairway to a tiny green. (This illustration replicates our Best 100 Cover Photo.)

Unlike several older public courses in Northern California, Quail Lodge has not seen serious renovation because the original layout has stood the test of time. Varieties of beautiful mature trees adorn edges of the fairways. These include alders, willows, and Chinese plum, in addition to the live oaks, white oaks, and various pines common to the area. This wide assortment adds to the calm beauty of multi-million dollar homes nuzzling perimeters of fairways, especially on the front nine. Gracefully cut bunkers, both around greens and in several fairways, create a crisp appearance from the tee boxes. They serve as guideposts revealing how holes should or should not be played.

Quail Lodge offers a player-friendly golf course. It's not long, stays in excellent condition, has a host of pleasantly designed golf holes, and provides an easy walk. It's also the only **Best 100** course to be advertised as "dog friendly;" that is, players can bring along their leashed pooches as they walk the course. Two housedogs, a border collie named Belle, and a standard poodle named Max, currently roam the course to keep waterfowl at bay.

Strengths of the layout come mostly on the front nine, where rolling terrain appears more elevated and undulating than on the back. Number four, a 400-yard par-four (back tees), offers the most difficult hole, partly due to its length, but mostly because of a steep hill, bunkers and trees in front of the small green. Use at least two extra clubs on the approach shot; anything short may roll back down to the bottom of a 30-foot hill. Next comes a wonderful par-three, with a 190-yard downhill shot, over a lake, to a well-bunkered green. Its tee-view looks west, up the Carmel Valley towards the ocean. Other par-threes also offer good challenges, especially at number twelve. There the back tee sits about 80-yards behind the regular men's blocks, stretching the hole to 221-yards. This drive must carry about 100 yards over the Carmel River, through a narrow opening, and then find a small slot between bunkers to hit the green. That's tough enough with a medium iron, let alone driver.

You can relax on the rest of the course, which has minor fairway contours, gentle doglegs, and good, smooth, mildly sloped greens. In tournaments putts can roll up to a very fast 12 Stimp speed; but normally they run 9 to 10, a good semi-fast pace. Par-fives measure moderate to short in length, so big hitters have a good chance to reaching them in two. Trees, cliffs, lakes, and the river add serenity and enough challenge, to make rounds very enjoyable. My only real criticism is that some holes can be soggy in winter, especially those in heavy shade.

For car buffs among readers, come to the Concours d'Elegance in early August. Quail Lodge provides the headquarters for display of vintage sports cars at the annual conclave. Other locations, including Pebble Beach's 18th fairway, feature all kinds of premier, antique and rare automobiles. Own a restored Maserati? Enter it in Lawson Little's 150-mile rally and see how you fare against one of the Shelby Cobras. *Review based on play several times, last with interview in September '08.*

Quail Lodge Resort and Golf Club

8000 Valley Greens Drive		**Resort:**	888 828-8787
Carmel, CA 93923		**Golf Shop:**	831 620-8808
		Fax	831 625-5848
		www.quaillodge.com	

Managed by:	Private, local	**Architect:**	Robt Muir Graves
Location:	Five miles south of Monterey Airport. Follow State Rt. 1 south to Carmel Valley Road. Turn left (south) and go 3.4 miles to Valley Greens Dr. Turn right, public parking is on the left, in .4 miles.		
Style:	Resort Course. Flat and gently rolling terrain, surrounded by expensive homes. Fairways, roughs and greens well groomed. Nice bunkering but not too difficult. Treelined fairways leave leave room for error.		
Other info:	Pet friendly: walkers allowed to bring a dog on a leash.		

Greens Fees	Weekends	Weekdays	Twilight	Seniors	Carts/person
as of 10/08:	$200	$175	$100/$75	No savings	Included

Course ratings:	Men	Par	Rating	Slope	Yardage	Women	Par	Rating	Slope	Yardage
	Blue	71	71.4	129	6449	Red	71	72.4	127	5509
Quail Lodge	Gold	71	69.6	126	6091					
	Red	71	66.3	118	5363					

No. 40: Whitney Oaks

The northeastern Sacramento area, between Roseville and Auburn, stands as a burgeoning golf Mecca. **Best 100** courses include The Ridge (No. 8), Darkhorse (No. 13), Catta Verdera (No. 26), Whitney Oaks, Turkey Creek (No. 42), Timber Creek (No. 94) and Woodcreek (No. 97). In addition, private Granite Bay, Winchester Country Club, Morgan Creek and Auburn Country Club occasionally open doors to some non-member play.

Johnny Miller's design for Whitney Oaks probably creates the most controversy of any in this group, because it has more detractors than the others. Players complain that too many environmental zones intrude on the field of play. Others say fairways have not been in good shape for years. Troon Golf managed the course until 2005, but a new team has since arrived on scene. They changed fairway turf to Bermuda grass in order to better withstand summer heat, and switched roughs from pure rye to a combination of rye and bluegrass. This work attempts to put the course back in the condition originally envisioned at its opening in 1998.

A distinctive par-five, number eleven at Whitney Oaks negotiates several rocky outcroppings. It's a scenic prelude to hilly holes coming on the way to No. 18.

Despite the transition and sometimes-mediocre hitting surfaces, the basic Miller layout remains a well-designed, difficult track. Most players who know Miller expect narrow (or at least the appearance of being narrow) fairways, greens with big undulations, long expanses of waste or hazards to carry on drives, and holes which make twists and turns mimicking Laguna Seca's race course. The pleasure at Whitney Oaks is that, except for undulating greens, features have been tamed enough for players who hit the ball short and straight to have a chance at success and a lot of fun.

If one were to look at this course as an art book, with one photo allowed per hole, several of the pages would have beautiful vignettes. Numbers one through six provide gorgeously framed views from the tee; and, including number eleven can be quite photogenic. Each requires drives be aimed at a landing areas closely bordered by hills, bunkers, creeks, trees, rock-outcroppings or textured heavy vegetation. Modern hillside homes, many with turrets, porticos, balconies and slate roofs, form the backdrop for wonderful settings. Fairways—rarely straight—weave back and forth in a relaxed manner. Greens nearly always stay visible so players can keep an eye on the objective. Miller's makes extensive use of huge native boulders, and golfers may actually find themselves wishing their shot would hit one of these obstacles to ricochet it back on line.

Whitney Oaks is not for the faint of heart, but changes in the past few years have dropped the slope somewhat, and make it more forgiving than the course of the early '00's. Some of the berry bogs have diminished or been eliminated. Now the charm of the location and the artistic design of the layout, make it a good play for those willing to give it another chance. *Played in October '07.*

Whitney Oaks Golf Club

2305 Clubhouse Drive	**Golf Shop:**	916 632-8333
Rocklin, CA 95765	**Fax**	916 630-0972
	www.whitneyoaksgolf.com	

Managed by:	BrightStar Golf Group, LLC	**Architect:**	Johnny Miller
Location:	Twenty-five miles northeast of downtown Sacramento. Take Interstate-80 to State Rt. 65. Go north towards Lincoln. Take exit for Pleasant Grove Rd and drive east 3.5 miles. (Becomes Park St.) Turn left on Whitney Oaks and right at the second Clubhouse Drive. Go 1 mile to Club.		
Style:	Moderately rolling terrain, with oaks and homes protecting fairways on some holes. Environmental areas are common and encroach into fairways. Undulating greens well guarded by bunkers.		
Other info:	Walking allowed but is difficult due to long stretches and hills from green to tee.		

Greens Fees	Weekends	Weekdays	Twilight	Seniors	Carts/person
as of 10/08:	$69	$49	$44/$34	$44 weekdays	Included

Course ratings:	Men	Par	Rating	Slope	Yardage	Women	Par	Rating	Slope	Yardage
	Black	71	74.2	141	6794	Gold	71	72.8	131	5478
Whitney Oaks	Gray	71	71.7	130	6383	Red	71	70.9	127	5118
	Tan	71	69.7	123	5950	Green	71	70.0	125	4980

No. 41: Bailey Creek

Is anyone looking for a get-away vacation with great boating, good fishing and wonderful golf . . . all at a reasonable cost? Consider Lake Almanor. It's two hours east of Red Bluff, two hours northwest of Lake Tahoe, or an hour from Graeagle. At 4500 feet, leave behind the heat of the Sacramento Valley and arrive at daytime summer temperatures usually in the high 70's. Unlike Lake Tahoe, its major competitor for mountain lakeside holidays, summer rain comes rarely; and the lake—actually a very large Feather River reservoir—offers good bass fishing and warm water-skiing and swimming.

As for golf, the area proffers a couple of 9-hole courses and a country club, but the best public golfing venue comes at beautiful Bailey Creek. It's situated on a large north shore peninsula, about four miles east of the area's primary town, Chester. The course opened only 10 years ago, in 1999, designed by Homer Flint, so it meets modern construction standards. Fairways see large conifers dotting strategic locations, but the sparseness of the local forests keep the trees from being too daunting. Large bunkers form the primary defense, giving the layout an open feel. Its airy environment allows scenic views of surrounding hills, including glimpses of local Mt. Dyer and distant Mt. Lassen.

On the north shore of Lake Almanor, Bailey Creek's twelfth hole presents a tough par three. The diagonally angled green causes many misses, and steep sand in the front traps makes recoveries difficult.

Outstanding features include deep emerald colored fairways, great weather, in addition to the abundant vistas. Hole designs, especially on par-threes, provide picturesque challenges; but just strolling along on plush blue/rye grasses, and hitting from their soft texture is a real treat. Wide landing zones come with most holes, and the layout flows gracefully around and through the broad property and light forest. Everything appears manicured like at a fine country club. Greens putt smoothly, though a little slow, about an eight on the StimpMeter. Surrounding bunkers, especially on shorter holes, form graceful protection from incoming shots, but are not so difficult to foil small errors. Longer par-fours offer more room than the short ones.

As is common on many modern courses, the second nine plays more interesting and challenging than the first. Most designers recognize that tougher holes require more warm-up, therefore place them further into the round. At Bailey Creek, the heart of the course starts at number eleven and culminates on fourteen. Eleven and twelve both compete as long par-fours, bordered by up-slopes on either side of the fairway and Mt. Dyer in the background. Then, comes a killer par-three. It measures only 179-yards from the back tee, but heads into the prevailing western breeze. The slightly elevated tee, points golfers over heavy rough, brambles, a grassy ravine, and two large face bunkers protecting the hillside green. The trap closest to the green has a severe slope. Balls landing along its upper edge require an awkward stance, and usually lie in someone's footprint because no one can rake the trap well. The diagonal green makes shot distance tough to judge, because pin position placements can be easily disguised.

The next hole, number fourteen, makes the **Best 100** list of toughest par-fours. To start, it measures a long 428-yards from the regular tees. A dogleg heads around a grassy hillside, but the wide fairway is easy to hit. Good length helps on the drive because the uphill second requires an extra club or two. A long green with the pin on an upper terrace requires even more club. The real difficulty comes from a bank of deep bunkers that front the twenty-foot high green elevation. Hit short and plan on an odyssey of sandy shots to get back in play. Those landing in lower bunkers should probably hit out sideways, rather than try for the green or they usually end up in the steeper bunkers near the top of the bank.

In fact, bunkers throughout the course create problems. Their lips, or top edges, may not be particularly elevated above the sand; but the steepness of soft sand causes unstable stances and footing. For instance, number-eighteen, a 400-yard par four, sharp dogleg left, finds a monster trap planted in the middle of the landing area. Big hitters can clear it with a draw, but lesser golfers must hit short, to the right, leaving a 220-yard shot to the elevated green. That hardly seems fair, so most many people aim near the sand, and end up in it faced with a fluffy lie and uphill/side-hill stance. After blasting out of the bunker, they still need another 160-yards left to the green. I was fortunate and one-putted for a miracle par. Oh well, the big hitters usually win on this hole, but the other seventeen are great to play. *Review based on play and interviews in July '08.*

Bailey Creek Golf Club

433 Durkin Drive		**Golf Shop:**	530 259-4653
Lake Almanor, CA 96137		**Fax**	530 259-4218
		www.baileycreek.com	
Managed by:	Private, local	**Architect:**	Homer Flint
Location:	75 miles east of Red Bluff; 65 miles northwest of Graeagle. Take State Rt. 36, 32 or 89 to Chester. Head east on Rt. 36 to County A13. Turn south and drive 1 mile to Red River. Turn right and follow signs to the clubhouse.		
Style:	Mostly gently rolling landscape with outstanding fairways. Many treelines but usually wide-set, open drive landing areas. Greens well protected and terraced. Lots of bunkers.		
Other info:	Seasonal savings of $10-$25 per round. Monthly rates available for huge savings. Season from May 1 to Oct 30. Elevation 5000 feet.		

Greens Fees	Weekends	Weekdays	Twilight	Seniors	Carts/person
as of 10/08:	$98	$98	$78	No savings	$15

Course ratings:	Men	Par	Rating	Slope	Yardage	Women	Par	Rating	Slope	Yardage
	Black	72	72.9	129	7043	Blue	76	74.1	133	6457
Bailey Creek	Blue	71	70.1	122	6484	White	72	71.3	127	5883
	White	70	67.5	115	5883	Red	72	68.7	121	5381

No. 42: Turkey Creek

Turkey Creek presents the best of four high quality ClubCorp golf venues in Metropolitan Sacramento. Teal Bend and Empire Ranch mark the company's other public options, and the terrific Granite Bay, reviewed in Chapter 4, is a private course. ClubCorp once again upholds its reputation for managing nice courses, and offers its members inexpensive reciprocal playing rights at hundreds of locations around the U.S.

Like Teal Bend, which is 40 minutes southwest towards San Francisco, Turkey Creek sits in park-like surroundings. It's located on State Rt. 193 about ten minutes north of Interstate-80, just east of Lincoln. Architect Brad Bell fashioned fairways from dense oak forest and left large expanses of land and trees between the holes to give a feeling of spaciousness. The area sees abundant wild life such as turkey, deer and waterfowl, yet the nearby highways offer easy access from all over northeastern Sacramento.

The course itself plays tough. Straight drives are needed all day long, after the uncharacteristically simple hole number one. A couple of 400-plus-yard dogleg par-fours, numbers five and nine, need drives hit long too, in order to have clear shots at the greens. An especially creative challenge comes at signature par-three number fourteen. The short hole, only 143-yards from the blue tees, has a comma shaped green, with a wide circular back and narrow curving front. In the hollow of the comma stands a steep mound, and to the right lies a lake. When the pin is on the front, and the rough on the hill is allowed to grow long, a ball hit just a couple of yards to the left of the pin, hits into and stays on the steep slope. The resulting chip usually rolls across the narrow green into water. This means your original tee shot may as well be aimed close to the lake or the larger back of the green. Even if you go in, you save a shot. Such are the subtle challenges of Turkey Creek.

The clubhouse overlooks an old stone quarry, now a lake. This unusual rocky hazard creates photogenic settings for holes number three and eighteen. Both require long approach shots over water; so the cliffs/banks in front, and nicely landscaped clubhouse architecture behind, make a stimulating backdrop for some challenging shots.

Another tough, scenic, but short par three at Turkey Creek, number fourteen is a signature hole. Come in early morning and feast on views of the big birds in full feather.

The disappointment at Turkey Creek, if you can call it that, is that grooming does not quite meet the standard of the design. While not bad, competitive neighbors at The Ridge, Catta Verdera, Lincoln Hills and even Woodcreek find better playing conditions. The chipping areas, especially on par-fives twelve and sixteen, were thinly cut and soggy the day I played. In fact the sixteenth hole seems as though it should be on another lesser course. It lacks contouring or other subtle grading seen on all other holes, almost as like the contractors ran out of money when they built it. But it is only one ordinary hole, on a group of otherwise good ones, so Turkey Creek deserves its top 50 rating. *Review based on play and interview in October '07.*

Turkey Creek Golf Club

1525 State Highway 193		**Golf Shop:**	916 434-9100
Lincoln, CA 95648		**Fax**	916 434-9477
		www.turkeycreekgc.com	

Managed by:	ClubCorp
Architect:	Brad Bell
Location:	Thirty miles northeast of Sacramento. Take Interstate-80 to State Rt. 65. Go north about ten miles to State Rt. 193. Turn Right (east) and drive 1 1/2 mies to Turkey Creek Dr. Turn left to parking lot.
Style:	Mostly flat terrain, easy to walk. Classic oak tree lined design, but with relatively broad fairways. Some rock outcroppings and well bunkered greens. Two holes surround a lake-filled quarry.
Other info:	Lots of wildlife.

Greens Fees as of 10/08:	Weekends	Weekdays	Twilight	Seniors	Carts/person
	$68	$44/$34	$34	$41 weekdays	Included

Course ratings:	Men	Par	Rating	Slope	Yardage	Women	Par	Rating	Slope	Yardage
	Black	72	73.6	138	6929	White	72	73.9	134	5858
Turkey Creek	Blue	72	71.3	135	6498	Gold	72	67.8	121	4897
	White	71	68.8	124	5858					

No. 43: The Ranch

The Ranch lies hidden in hills just above U.S. 101 in southern San Jose. On a clear day, downtown San Jose appears so close to the number five tee box, one can see jets gliding close to the Fairmont Hotel. Few people even know that this high quality, difficult course sits just above the Hellyer Avenue exit ramp.

By one key measure, The Ranch classifies as the most difficult course in Northern California. Its slope rating of 150, from the black 6656-yard tees, cannot be topped. *Slope* measures how hazards, greens difficulty, weather and terrain impact players of differing handicaps. It allows skill level adjustments to be fairer, depending on course features. The high slope at The Ranch comes because shots need to cross multiple deep canyons to exceedingly undulating greens. The ravines act like vacuums . . . once a ball goes in, steep slopes and nasty vegetation keep it there forever, and add many strokes to the score and ball purchases to the pro shop.

But, management knows the high slope rating scares people away and has been working to ease up the difficulty. Trees have been removed and roughs shortened since 2007. The back tee '09 slope of 150 came down from 152 a year before. The blue tee slope dropped from 147 to 142. The white tee slope dropped from 139 to 129. They are listening.

All the while, course condition remains superb, even in winter. Fairways drain beautifully, giving country club members on the Peninsula and the South Bay an alternative to slogging through water-saturated clay-based fairways at their home course.

Green designs remain extremely unusual, probably the most severe in the **Best 100**. Some show 5-foot elevation changes between tiers and multiple unique pin positions. Most people need to play a second or third round to begin appreciating a safe way to improve scores. When players finally realize they should not take tempting short cuts, but rather, try to keep the ball in play, scores plummet and spirits soar.

Two holes in particular combine panoramic and canyon views with good tests of skill. Number four, a par-five that starts high on a hillside, offers a clear look at downtown San Jose. The design tempts short cuts on both the drive and second shot, yet plays easy enough for an average hitter who just shoots down the middle. Number twelve is a beauty too, with views in an opposite direction of the mountain ridges and Mt. Hamilton the east. The elevation drop on the long par-four adds 30-40 yards roll to the drive. The approach, however, raises a few hairs on the neck because the flag often sits towards the rear, where a terrace lies lower than the front, and causes good-looking shots to bound behind the green.

Number four, a target style par-five, teases golfers to go for the green in two. Miss short and the ball is gone. Views in this drawing are typical of canyon/city vistas throughout The Ranch, in southern San Jose.

A different hole, 420-yard par-four number two, is the Ranch's toughest. It starts innocuously enough, with a blind drive over a low hill. The next shot gets real serious attention. The small two-level green, sits elevated above a rock wall, a creek, and a deep bunker. Native tall grasses, brush and steep slopes surround the rest. The second tier rises about four feet above the front, to a small plateau tucked behind the bunker. Any shot missing the green goes into a hazard or unplayable rough, and even hitting the green on the wrong level leaves a very difficult putt. Tough, tough, tough.

The first eleven holes were built several years before the final seven, with completion coming in 2004. The older ones are more difficult, and be prepared for a half-mile cart-ride between numbers eleven and twelve. The long path protects many rare shrubs, and golfers cannot enter these or other protected environmental zones. Power carts (or *buggies* as they call them in the Far East) must be used at The Ranch. Walking up the many canyons takes a long time and would be quite grueling.

The Ranch is an arduous steady diet for most golfers, but its outstanding condition and challenge make it a must to experience. Enjoy the views if you can, because another tough shot awaits! *Review based on play many times, last in February '08.*

The Ranch Golf Club

4601 Hilltop View Lane		Golf Shop:	408 270-0557
San Jose, CA 95138		Fax	408 270-2099
		www.theranchgc.com	
Managed by:	Private, local	**Architect:**	Casey O' Callaghan
Location:	In the hills of southern San Jose. Take U.S. 101 to Hellyer Ave exit. Follow Hellyer south a short distance to Dove Hill Rd. Turn left and go .3 miles to Hassler Pkwy. Turn Right and drive one mile up to Hill Top View Ave. Turn right into course lot.		
Style:	Very hilly course, few trees, lots of canyons to cross. Greens are extremely terraced. Target golf to the extreme. In excellent condition, good drainage even in winter.		
Other info:	Highest Slope rating in the **Best 100**. Walking not allowed.		

Greens Fees	Weekends	Weekdays	Twilight	Seniors	Carts/person
as of 10/08:	$100	$80	$70/$50	$40 weekdays	Included

Course ratings:	Men	Par	Rating	Slope	Yardage	Women	Par	Rating	Slope	Yardage
	Black	72	72.8	150	6747	White	73	73.9	142	5391
The Ranch	Blue	72	70.4	142	6389	Red Long	72	69.4	125	4516
	White	70	68.5	129	5808	Red Short	71	68.6	123	4399

No. 44: The Bridges

San Francisco Bay Area's western Livermore Valley provides home to several **Best 100** courses. The Bridges (San Ramon), Wente (Livermore), and Callippe (Pleasanton), rank towards the top of the **Best 100** and make a formidable threesome located within 20 miles of each other. In addition, Wente and The Bridges step up as two of the toughest courses reviewed herein. The Bridges, with Slope Ratings of 147 from the tips, 141 from the blues and 139 from the whites, presents an extreme challenge for all levels of player.

Johnny Miller designed this true test of high golfing skill, with the course opening in 1999. The location in the hills two miles east of Interstate-680 and Bishop Ranch Business Park, traverses ravines once grazed by cattle on the slopes south of Mt Diablo. The extreme difficulty comes from narrow fairways, where drives must often carry 120 to 200-yards, just to clear the hazards or waste areas in front of them. These *forced carries* measure very long from the rear tees but even exceed 100-yards from the white tees.

Second shots also require a good degree of finesse, both in direction and distance: The Bridges is *target golf* (i.e. distance control golf) to the extreme. For instance, par-five number six requires a drive to the left side of the fairway, short of a bunker; then a second shot hit to a small plateau well left of the green. The final approach comes from a short iron over a deep ravine to a steep back-to-front sloped green. The long hitter who hits inaccurately will have a very frustrating round. On the other hand, the straight shooter who has a good short game will have an awful lot of fun.

Johnny Miller's design at Bridges is well maintained but about as unforgiving as courses come. The view at number four shows how hillsides and heavy foliage await errant shots.

The entire facility appears in good shape, well trimmed and well-watered, including fairways, roughs, greens, aprons, tees and bunkers. The large greens use moderate undulations, often elevated and can be sped-up to meet whatever tournament situation arises. Normal speed runs about 10 on the StimpMeter. The roughs are wide enough in most instances, to catch balls heading towards ravines. And where they aren't, huge bunkers take their place to prevent the same penalizing fate. Normally golfers hate such traps, but here they can be a blessing.

A couple of suggestions for the new player at The Bridges: Make sure to consult and follow the advice of the course guide; it's very accurate, though mainly applicable to longer hitters. Expect to have a significant amount of side-hill lies. Also, steep hills and long distances prevail on walks from green to tee, so beware if you walk. Plan for six and a half to seven-miles, way up, way down, then way up again. *Review based on play in August '07.*

The Bridges

9000 South Gale Ridge Road		**Golf Shop:**	925 735-4253
San Ramon, CA 94582		**Fax**	925 735-4256
		www.thebridgesgolf.com	
Managed by:	KemperSports	**Architect:**	Johnny Miller
Location:	About 45 minutes southeast of Oakland. Take Interstate-680 to Bollinger Canyon Rd. Head east three miles and turn right at South Gate Road; then follow signs.		
Style:	Hilly course with canyons and forced carries off many tees. Narrow, sloped fairways, deep bunkers, well protected greens with slopes and terraces. Heavy vegetation off fairways. Difficult walking due to long uphill distances from green to tee.		
Other info:	Course is usually in very good condition.		

Greens Fees as of 10/08:	Weekends	Weekdays	Twilight	Seniors	Carts/person
	$85	$65	$65/$45	-$10 weekdays	Included

Course ratings:		Men	Par	Rating	Slope	Yardage	Women	Par	Rating	Slope	Yardage
	Black	72	74.5	147	6860	White	74	77.4	136	6229
The Bridges	Blue	72	73.4	141	6514	Gold	73	74.0	130	5730
	White	72	71.1	139	6123	Green	73	70.9	125	5229

No. 45: StoneTree

Many golfers drive up State Rt. 37, from Novato towards Napa, and wonder, "what are those lush green fairways cascading down the hill just south of the freeway?" The hill, less than a mile from U.S. 101, sits where the Renaissance Faire held court years ago, and is now houses StoneTree Golf Club. The course opened in 2000, designed by Jim Summers, assisted by Johnny Miller and Fred Bliss. Even though a public course, its set-up provides an aura of exclusivity and high quality service. The clubhouse size and modern use of rustic materials offer an impressive edifice for first-time players. Its combination of style and materials style well suit the contrasting experiences players are about to face, as they move from elegance to exuberance and then frustration on varying types of golf holes.

The first six holes at Stonetree sit low on the flats, in an area once covered by marsh and pasture. Number one begins the round auspiciously, because the fairway extends down an unusually narrow slot. No driving range (they do have nets) means the first few shots can easily be off track, in this case across a road on one side, or into a creek on the other. But after the strange start, the following holes widen and give more leeway. Summers and Miller keep your attention by adding undulations to the flat meadow. They created target landing-zones that make big hitters consider laying-up short of trouble. Heavy rough, meandering creeks, strategic bunkers and growing young trees all seem readily available to harass misguided shots.

The par-five fourteenth at StoneTree requires an accurate drive and two more good shots. Land on the right-hand hill and your shot may bound sharply sideways and roll halfway back to its starting point.

Then comes the first of two forays up the hillsides seen from the freeway. Number seven brings a short very steep dogleg, only about 330-yards long, but up about 5 extra club-lengths between the drive and approach. Next, number eight heads 150-yards across a deep gully to a green set on the side of a hill. Then nine goes back down to the clubhouse in challenging fashion . . . with a gully and trees to right, a hill to the left, and a distant lake all surrounding the drive target zone. After a sharp 90-degree dogleg, the mid-length approach must land on a narrow green, also protected by hills and the lake. Putting even presents a challenge, but at least players are back on the flats for a few holes, before heading up to some really narrow fairways.

The three-hole respite ends at thirteen, which begins the heart of the course. The hole looks so simple, at only 300-yards. Drives must hit safely to a narrow partially blind landing area; if missed, the green approach will require a lot more swings. The green deceives too, because its 40-yards length—split by a deep depression and apron on the lower side—is not easy to hit or to putt. Next, par-five fourteen, pictured on the prior page, first goes downhill and then steeply up. Fifteen goes down again on a long par-four, probably the toughest hole on the course. Its green banks so steeply that, even if reached in two, par becomes difficult. And finally, sixteen completes the hilly travel, with a par-five green at the end of a skinny fairway isthmus, where anything hit left sinks unceremoniously into another lake. The final two holes, even though flat, find swamp grass and creeks waiting to catch stray excursions.

Stonetree is neither for the faint of heart, nor for players afraid to climb steep hills, even though they ride in carts. It can be walked, but most walkers choose to use a complementary cart for the hillside holes. Conscientious maintenance crews keep the course in excellent condition. But, as with Miller's Bridges in San Ramon, the course is not designed for beginners or long, crooked hitters. It's a place where straight down the middle provides just the ticket. *Review based on play in September '08.*

StoneTree Golf Club

9 StoneTree Lane	**Golf Shop:**	415 209-6090
Novato, CA 94945	**Fax**	415 209-6925
	www.stonetreegolf.com	

Managed by:	CourseCo	**Architect:**	Summers/Miller/Tatum/Bliss
Location:	About 25 miles north of golden Gate Bridge. Take U.S. 101 to State Rt. 37. Head east 2.5 miles. Take Atherton Exit south to main entrance.		
Style:	Half gently rolling; half very hilly; mixed on each nine. Well sculpted and graded throughout. Greens can be terraced or sloped, and are protected by some bunkers and mildly sloped aprons. Young trees on lower, flatter holes, mature trees on the hills. Course is in good condition.		
Other info:	OK to take cart on hilly holes and walk the rest of the course.		

Greens Fees	Weekends	Weekdays	Twilight	Seniors	Carts/person
as of 10/08:	$120	$85	$65 weekdays	No savings	Included

Course ratings:	Men	Par	Rating	Slope	Yardage	Women	Par	Rating	Slope	Yardage
	Champ	72	73.1	138	6762	Blue	74	74.6	135	5818
StoneTree	Black	72	70.9	135	6318	White	72	70.2	125	5083
	White	70	68.6	123	5820					

No. 46: Ridge Creek

July 11, 2008 saw a squadron of F-15 fighters buzzing the clubhouse to signal the shotgun-start of a new venture. The growing city of Dinuba, located between Visalia and Fresno, bet the farm that their new top-flight links-style facility will pull in enough visitors for the new venture to succeed.

As the story goes, the city had a big water problem. Too much ground water was accumulating directly underneath its large sewer treatment plant. The water pressure bulged underlying soils, and would damage the plant unless two million gallons per day were pumped to another location. Options to solve the problem included: (1) sprinkling it on alfalfa croplands, or (2) building a golf course to use the excess. Golf advocates won the debate so they hired architect John Fought and project manager Kemper Sports to build a 300-plus acre golf complex. The question remains, can a good course, located in a warm summer climate zone with low population, attract enough players to thrive during the California and U.S. economic crises of the late '00's? Sand Hills Golf Club succeeded in Nebraska, Bandon Dunes succeeded in Oregon . . . can it be done again in Dinuba, California?

The course design meets a couple of basic objectives. Most importantly, as a city owned operation, the base clientele from the surrounding area needs to be satisfied. This means average golfers—in decent quantities—must play regularly. But also, management wanted to create "the best golf course within 100 miles," to bring golfing elite from all over the San Joaquin Valley.

Despite seemingly disparate ambitions, the new course may actually accomplish both. Designer Fought installed five sets of tees, ranging from 5400-yards for the women to 7350 for the big boomers. Fairways were sown with a hybrid small leaf Bermuda grass that allows easy lies for all, and lots of roll for short hitters. Fairway bunkers were positioned to affect the longest hitters, rather the rest of us, at least from the 6500-yard tees. The traps are so deep that long irons can rarely be hit to the greens.

No question Ridge Creek will get good reviews, but links and Heathlands-style courses are an acquired taste. When built on flat land away from the beach, they often find holes designed with the appearance of bland commonality. Courses like Ridge Creek have few cliffs or deep gullies to offset natural native terrain. Fought did a good job making each hole a challenge, and molding character and contour, but views from each tee do seem to meld together.

To counter this concern, a couple of distinctive holes on the back nine provide memorable experiences. Number fifteen, at 648-yards from the tips, is advertised as "the longest par-five in the state." (Not true, see Sevillano Links, ranked number ten in the **Best 100**, hole number 18 at 686 yards). But distance alone is not what makes it a distinct memory. After a good drive the second shot leaves players a decision to make, no matter which tee blocks are used: At 200-yards from the green sits a wide expanse of swale and manmade wetlands. (Fought uses sunken hollows filled with deep wet rough to attract native species of animals.) The second shot can either be laid up, leaving a 210-plus-yard approach shot straight to the pin or be hit to the right of the wetlands. However, this right side is well protected by a series of bunkers, and the green slopes steeply away from any incoming shot. The approach choice is tough on a monster-length hole.

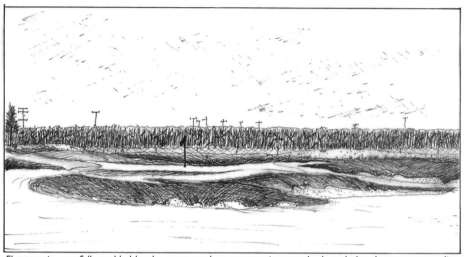

Flat terrain, carefully molded by the most modern construction standards and abundant water supplies, combine to make Dinuba's new 2008 Ridge Creek links layout a good challenge.

The next hole also offers an unusual, but a much shorter experience. It measures only 141-yards from the back tees, with a wide, fifteen-foot deep face-bunker blocking the steeply elevated green. Hitting to a front pin position can be quite nerve wracking.

Perhaps the best part of this intriguing layout is not the manicured fairways, the treeless links-style, the penalizing bunkers, or the unique wetlands. Rather it's the outstanding greens. They are maintained in excellent condition with moderate undulations throughout. Few have terraces or separate levels, but all have plenty of minor slopes with moderate breaks going every-which-way, and opportunities for dozens of pin positions.

The final verdict on Ridge Creek is out and only time will tell whether it matures as planned, or can be financially successful. I highly recommend taking the hour detour from I-5 over to State 99 on your next trip to Southern California. Greens fees are low by Bay Area and Palm Springs standards, and the layout has the potential to be a great play. *Review based on play and interviews in April '08.*

Ridge Creek Dinuba Golf Club

3018 W. El Monte Way,
Dinuba, CA 93618

Golf Shop:	559 591-2254
Fax	559 591-7070

www.golfridgecreek.com

Managed by: KemperSports

Architect: John Fought

Location:	25 miles southeast of Fresno. Take State Rt. 99 to County J40/E Mountain View Way, east towards Dinuba. Go 8.7 miles, course is on the right.
Style:	Flat terrain with graded contours. Wide hybrid-Bermuda grass fairways. Manufactured wetlands, with very few trees. Sophisticated deep bunkering. Huge mildly undulating greens. Called a Heathland style course. Long yardage but good rolls.
Other info:	Opened in July '08. Residents and Rewards members get significant discounts.

Greens Fees as of 10/08:	Weekends	Weekdays	Twilight	Seniors	Carts/person
	$61	$51	$40/$30	$41 weekdays	$14

Course ratings:	Men	Par	Rating	Slope	Yardage	Women	Par	Rating	Slope	Yardage
Ridge Creek	Silver	72	74.3	126	7368	White	72	72.3	118	5804
	Black	72	72.1	121	6880	Sand	72	69.7	112	5348
	Blue	72	69.5	119	6375					
	White	72	67.2	111	5804					

No. 47: Indian Valley

Players, who live outside Marin or southern Sonoma County, may not know of Indian Valley Golf Club. Its obscure location, about three miles west of downtown Novato, borders the south side of Lake Stafford. Cars need to enter through a water district gated access road, around the east end of the reservoir. But the confusing drive is short and worth the effort, because this is a very good course.

Built in 1958, it's Marin and Sonoma County's oldest continuously operating public eighteen-hole facility. The local hills once provided shelter to the Coastal Subgroup of Miwok Indians, but North Marin County Water District now manages the watershed. Stafford Reservoir, which dams up Novato Creek, dominates the landscape and can be seen from several holes on the back nine.

Indian Valley gets its quality from several subtle attributes:

1. Scenic and pastoral views abound. Nary a home or building, other than golf structures or roads, can be seen. Several elevated tees and greens give good viewing vantage points. Even gullies and canyon fairways offer pleasing backdrops of oak, bay and madrone forests.
2. No two holes look alike. Hills, narrow driving chutes, doglegs, trees in the fairway, tight target areas and wide fairways give something for everyone.
3. Course condition, at least in the summer, is good. Fairways stay green, with few dry or wet spots. Roughs find brown grass and dirt only at the outside edges, or where needed to protect oaks from too much water.
4. Greens' maintenance also meets modern standards. Several recent re-builds enlarged their dimensions to provide more pin placements, and

some were moved to sunnier spots for better for healthier growing conditions. Surrounding bunker complexes also got updates.

5. Interesting fairway layouts create good challenge, without overwhelming less skilled players. Several offer dramatic elevation drops, climbs, or obstacles to spice-up driving angst.

6. Hole length varies considerably, especially on par-fours and par-threes, forcing use of nearly every club in the bag.

This course, unknown to outsiders, is a real sleeper. Rebuilt greens, rolling fairways and good summer playing conditions make Indian Valley a favorite for those in the know.

If it's so good, why isn't it a great course? The prime reason comes from their management's philosophy. They don't want to compete with posh edifices such as nearby StoneTree or the new upscale Peacock Gap. Indian Valley likes its down-home image just fine. The small older clubhouse, plus narrow access roads and self-service for carts and other amenities, work well, so why change? Manicuring is good, not great, but they keep upgrading the course. Costs stay down so volume stays up. They also go out of their way to attract women, and recently added on-course restrooms to both nines.

More serious critiques also come into play. When the lake fills in winter, the ninth fairway floods, and storm-drains back-up in other places too. Carts must then stay on paths, sometimes for weeks at a time. The back nine wanders over many hills, so power carts really help on these holes. One green-to-tee walk even offers a rail-tram to help walkers climb the long hill to the fourteenth tee. Tournament days, even for normal weekday normal men's or women's groups, seriously bog down play, partly due to the 60,000 round annual volume. While that's good for owners, players behind the tournaments can have a slow round.

As with almost all good, popular courses, try to play early in the morning. Rounds go faster and you will enjoy more local fauna. But regardless of when you play, Indian Valley provides the best value at one of the top courses in its region. *Review based on play and interview in September '08.*

Indian Valley Golf Course

3035 Novato Blvd.		**Golf Shop:**	415 897-1118
Novato, CA 94947		**Fax**	415 892-3934
		www.ivgc.com	
Managed by:	Private, local	**Architect:**	Unknown

Location: 30 miles north of Golden Gate Bridge. Take Highway 101 towards Novato. Exit at San Marin Drive and head west 3 miles to Novato Blvd. Turn right and go one mile to course sign on the the left. Go through Water Co. gate and follow road l/2 mile to the clubhouse.

Style: Hilly, especially on the back nine. Mature oaks and bay trees line many holes and protrude into some fairways. Good condition, though some holes flood in the winter. Undergoing a continuing program of green enlargement.

Other info: Front nine easy to walk, back much more difficult. Busy, popular course.

Greens Fees	Weekends	Weekdays	Twilight	Seniors	Carts/person
as of 10/08:	$61	$36	$35	$29 weekdays	$15

Course ratings:	Men	Par	Rating	Slope	Yardage	Women	Par	Rating	Slope	Yardage
	Black	72	70.6	126	6228	White	73	73.4	128	5913
Indian Valley	Blue	72	69.1	124	5952	Red	72	69.4	120	5218
	White	70	67.7	122	5913					

No. 48: Rancho Solano and No. 49: Paradise Valley

Most travelers know the city of Fairfield as home to Travis Air Force Base, or perhaps the Anheuser Busch brewery visible from Interstate-80. The city has been one of the Sacramento River Delta's most successful for years: Its prime location, halfway between San Francisco and Sacramento rests near the junction of several freeways. And having big steady employers certainly doesn't hurt.

Needless to say, such a prosperous community needs a good recreational infrastructure. Consequently, back in the early 1990's the city invested in two excellent golf facilities. They aren't muni's in the classic sense, because a private firm runs them; but the city oversees contracts and provides for capital improvements. Rancho Solano, named for the local county, opened in 1990, followed by Paradise Valley in 1993. Kemper Sports, one of the premier sports property management companies in the country, took over operations of both courses in 2003, and has steadily nurtured improvements ever since.

The courses share a common bond with their top-notch course conditions. Paradise Valley has always been maintained well, and over the past few years, Rancho Solano added drainage lines, bringing it up to snuff. Today, many players say Rancho is now the better course, because it's in country-club-condition. Both have superb fairways and roughs nearly year-round, and allow carts on fairways in the winter, as soon as any daily rain stops. Players have dissimilar opinions about which is their favorite because terrains are totally different; however, rounds played per year run about the same. Despite recent doldrums in the golf business, Rancho Solano and Paradise Valley maintained their '07 and '08 play volume within five percent of peaks reached earlier this decade. That's good performance, especially considering Rancho Solano's elimination of a popular annual membership plan, in lieu of more costly monthly greens-fee schedules.

Short par-four number fourteen is a respite from a series of long narrow holes at Paradise Valley. This one is wide open—if you clear the tree on the left—and then follow with a short iron to a deep, well-bunkered green.

Paradise Valley, the flatter of the two designs, finds its outside perimeters surrounded by housing developments. Despite the homes, nearby rolling grass covered hills give the feel of being in a pastoral valley. Tree-covered creeks wander throughout and lakes encroach close to the line of play. Bunkers often appear extremely picturesque—and dangerous—since architects sought to create a medium-to-difficult test. A particularly scenic and well-designed series of holes starts at number nine, continuing through number fourteen. These demand even more accuracy on drives and approaches, because trees in the middle of the fairways—and bunkers at greens—force players to aim at tiny targets rather than the middle of broad open spaces. They are fun to play and require good course management.

Rancho Solano's par-three number four well represents the style of this top-50 course. Putting on its huge green surfaces can be very difficult.

Hills and rolling topography dominate the other course, Rancho Solano, especially on the back nine. Doglegs prevail, but with fairly wide landing areas, where 200 to 220-yard hitters wear out seven and eight irons on green approach shots. Balls landing in the fairway usually find reasonably level lies. Most of the gentle uphill approaches require an extra club, often two. Greens often slope steeply toward the front, so, it's usually better to hit short and chip up than miss long and chip back.

Each course flaunts wonderful greens. At Paradise Valley, they are neither particularly large, nor undulating, but wind in long narrow shapes among sculptured mounds surrounding them. A back pin position often appears to be a front pin position, because sections of green can be hidden from sight. This causes unsuspecting players to hit the wrong club to the pin and results in long first-putts or extra chips. Green speed at Paradise is moderate to fast, about 9-10 on the StimpMeter, so don't be surprised by a few three-putts.

Solano's greens are mammoth, the course's main defense against good golfers shooting low scores. They use multiple subtle terraces, and a few flat-topped mounds in the middle, just to add uniqueness. They putt much slower than at Paradise, because of summer hand watering in the middle of the day.

Normal speed runs a medium 8 to 9. Lower speeds on highly sloped greens means pins can be put in more positions, because putts don't run-by so easily. However, for tournaments, they will speed up to 10 to 10.5 and become treacherous.

Both courses are good ones; Paradise Valley is flatter and more traditional, and Rancho Solano shorter, rolling, with fewer trees and huge greens. Choose you own poison; they are equally fun for all levels of golf. *Played in early 2008.*

Rancho Solano Golf Club

3250 Rancho Solano Parkway	**Golf Shop:** 707 429-4653
Fairfield, CA 94533	**Fax** 707 427-8944
	www.fairfieldgolf.com

Managed by:	KemperSports **Architect:** G. R. Baird
Location:	Midway between San Francisco and Sacramento. From Interstate-80 take Waterman/Air Base Exit,; head west on Waterman. Follow it two miles to Rancho Solano Pkwy. Turn right and head another two miles to the round-about at the golf course.
Style:	Rolling and mildly hilly terrain, with wide fairways tapering to well protected greens. Homes on several holes. Greens are big and some have distinct undulations. A putter's course.
Other info:	Course is usually in great shape. Local residents get $10 discounts on prime greens fees.

Greens Fees as of 10/08:	Weekends	Weekdays	Twilight	Seniors	Carts/person
	$53	$38	$41/$26	-$10	$14

Course ratings:	Men	Par	Rating	Slope	Yardage	Women	Par	Rating	Slope	Yardage
	Blue	72	71.3	128	6598	White	72	73.5	127	6129
Rancho Solano	White	72	69.4	123	6179	Gold	72	71.7	118	5677
	Gold	69	67.2	119	5677	Red	72	69.5	117	5260

Paradise Valley Golf Course

3950 Paradise Valley Road	**Golf Shop:** 707 426-1600
Fairfield, CA 94533	**Fax** 707 426-1745
	www.fairfieldgolf.com

Managed by:	KemperSports **Architect:** Robt. Muir Graves
Location:	Midway between San Francisco and Sacramento. From Interstate-80 take N. Texas St. exit. Turn right (south) on N. Texas and go .3 miles. Turn left on Dickson Hill Rd and head .5 miles to Dover Ave. Turn left again. This becomes Paradise Valley Rd. Go .5 miles and follow signs to clubhouse on the right.
Style:	Flat terrain with well groomed fairways and greens. Some holes tree lined and a creek flows though much of the course. Greens are long and rolling, protected by mounds & traps.
Other info:	Course is usually in great shape. Local residents get $10 discounts on prime greens fees.

Greens Fees as of 10/08:	Weekends	Weekdays	Twilight	Seniors	Carts/person
	$53	$38	$41/$26	$28 weekdays	$14

Course ratings:	Men	Par	Rating	Slope	Yardage	Women	Par	Rating	Slope	Yardage
	Black	72	74.1	133	6993	White	72	75.3	127	6128
Paradise Valley	Blue	72	72.9	129	6704	Red	72	71.3	119	5413
	White	72	70.6	124	6128					

No. 50: Coyote Creek
Tournament Course

Coyote Creek, managed by David Murdock's Castle & Cook Golf Properties, operates two adjacent courses located on U.S. 101 south of San Jose. The Valley Course is ranked number 76 in the **Best 100** and is reviewed later in this chapter. The better-known Tournament Course opened in 1999, when it hosted the PGA Champion's Tour *Siebel Open*. Jack Nicklaus designed the course and made sure it got a proper christening by playing as a star participant. The tournament ran for three consecutive years through 2001.

Straddling a major highway, as Coyote Creek does, is both a blessing and a curse for a golf course: the venue gets visibility and becomes well known, but it also acquires the unwanted label of *freeway course*. Those who play Coyote Creek know that noise is a non-issue because it's almost non-existent. Although it's unlikely at 70 mph, the only danger of playing so close to the freeway may be a little paranoia: will the boss see me having fun as he whizzes by?

Coyote Creek Tournament Course offers a variety of terrain, from foothills to flatlands, with rolling grades and mounding throughout. Environmentally protected creeks cross several holes, and lakes affect almost every shot on the final two. This variation makes for a myriad of challenges. Fortunately, Nicklaus gave golfers who play to the correct side of the fairway a real break by providing wide landing areas away from bunkers. Sand traps only create big problems around the greens.

Key factors for success are (1) putting well on the fast, subtle breaking greens, and (2) handling the ever-present winds. The greens are hard to read. Regulars complain that maintenance crews place pins on knobs or at top edges of major breaking slopes. Hit it a few inches too hard and the ball will roll an extra eight feet. As for the wind, the last time I played it started blowing at 6:00 am and continued all day. But be patient. Shots going into the wind on one hole will go downwind on others, setting up some glorious long shots with a strong breeze at the your back.

Although creative hole designs can be found everywhere on the course, the most interesting may be found at numbers two through eight, on the east side of the freeway, and numbers seventeen and eighteen near the clubhouse. The eastern section, hillier and more protected, has holes that feature curious twists, along with well-contoured, well-bunkered greens. The challenge comes not from hitting booming drives, but from accurate shot-making.

Water surrounds the seventeenth green and eighteenth fairway on Coyote Creek's Tournament Course. This Jack Nicklaus design hosted the Senior Tour Siebel Open in the early '00's. Illustration modeled from photo supplied by Coyote Creek.

The last two holes have a totally different look. Seventeen, a 510-yard par-five, gives a chance for glory to the long-ball hitter. Its peninsular green protrudes into the far side of a lake, tempting some to try to reach it in two over the water. Even the safer lay-up and short-iron route, demands good shots because water and wind surround the entire putting surface,. The final hole lives up to the Nicklaus nickname, The Bear. The drive on this 400-yard par-four has to clear one lake and the second shot another. Pray to have the prevailing north wind behind your back, because hitting into one that blows from the south is very, very dangerous. From experience, I know that such conditions can cause several shots to land in water. Fortunately, I had no money on the line . . . and that's my advice to you too, at least on your initial adventure there. *Review based on play many times, most recently with interviews in August '07.*

Coyote Creek Golf Club, Tournament Course

1 Coyote Creek Golf Drive		**Golf Shop:**	408 463-1400
San Jose, CA 95037		**Fax**	408 463-8318
Mail to:	P.O. Box 2527	www.coyotecreekgolf.com	
	Morgan Hill, CA 95038		

Managed by:	Castle & Cook Properties	**Architect:**	Jack Nicklaus
Location:	In southern San Jose, along U.S. 101. Take 101 to Coyote Creek Exit. Turn west and follow signs to the course.		

Style:	Gently rolling terrain on eleven holes west of the freeway, hillier on the other seven. Criss-crossed by environmentally protected creeks. Wide fairways but tighly protected, sloped greens.
Other info:	Adjacent to Valley Course, managed out of same clubhouse. Walking relatively easy. Often windy, even in the early mornings.

Greens Fees as of 10/08:	Weekends	Weekdays	Twilight	Seniors	Carts/person
	$102	$80	$75/$68	$60 weekdays	$17

Course ratings:	Men	Par	Rating	Slope	Yardage	Women	Par	Rating	Slope	Yardage
Coyote Creek Tournament	Black	72	74.8	144	7027	Gold	72	74.4	132	5907
	Blue	72	73.2	137	6633	Red	71	70.4	124	5184
	White	72	72.2	134	6420					

No. 51: Riverbend

Twenty miles north of downtown Fresno, near grazing country on the east end of Avenue 12, sits Riverbend Golf Club. The site may sound a bit remote, but not really. Its proximity to the northern end of State Rt. 41 freeway makes it a very easy drive from town.

The quick trip will prove well worth the effort. Riverbend is a quality course, right up with Ridge Creek and Brighton Crest as the best public access courses in the Fresno area. This one really has it all, including amateur tournaments for Fresno County, Fresno State, the NCAA Central Region, the Central Valley, and multitudes of junior age groups. Tee blocks can be set back to 7400 yards, a test for anyone. On the other end of the scale, short hitters and new players will have great fun too, as the ball rolls far on firm hybrid Bermuda fairways. Then, everyone gets the same challenge on very fast, firm, well-protected greens.

The course's style mixes treeless Heathland-style holes with a group of six adjacent to a pastoral Audubon Cooperative Sanctuary. The nature preserve grouping finds artistic designs, where large oaks and classic bunkers define tight landing areas. Creative bunker placement around greens allows peninsula shaped putting areas and pin-placements near the traps.

Number twelve in the Audubon section is a wonderfully distinctive par-three. Its short yardage—150 from the tips, to 101-yards from the front tees—belies the nuanced difficulty. The elevated green has multiple tiers, with a small protruding front section about one to two feet higher than the larger back. A series of deep pot bunkers, some filled with sand and some with extremely heavy rough, protect the left front. A tall oak protects the right front, and bunkers circle the back. Success here usually comes with a shot high enough to stop after clearing the bunkers, and it better be straight. God help anyone who finds one of those deep rye filled pots. If you do, they are not hazards so just take an unplayable lie and drop out.

Links-style holes form the rest of the course, displaying a distinctive trait: Unusual long, flat, groomed waste bunkers border many of the fairways. These waste-areas use shallow lips with small clumps of deer grass interspersed within. They are mechanically raked on a regular basis, but signs advise golfers to merely use their feet and clubs to smooth them after a shot. Lies usually end up firm and level, so recovery shots play easier than from classic hazard-style bunkers. That's a good thing, because the rest of the each hole requires good accuracy, good putting touch, and well thought-out strategy. Normal bunkers, water hazards, and an occasional tree in the fairway, wait to grab shots.

Management maintains the course well; that is, if you don't mind the hybrid Bermuda grass used in fairways and roughs. Balls get good roll all year long, but the hybrid grass has a tough wiry texture, so be careful . . . any time the club head catches extra turf, especially on irons hit from the fairway, your wrists can feel a sharp twinge. Greens putt particularly nicely, and usually stay firm and *very* fast. Target Stimp speeds range from 10 to 14, with 14 used for big tournaments. Greens this fast require significant adjustment to player's strokes, making them a lot of fun, or a nightmare, depending on one's skill and attitude. *Review based on play and interview in May '08.*

Riverbend Golf Course

43369 Avenue 12   **Golf Shop:**   559 432-3020
Madera, CA 93636   **Fax**   559 822-4653
                          www.riverbendgolfclub.com

Managed by:	Sierra Foothills Public Utility District **Architect:** G. R. Baird
Location:	About 10 miles north of Fresno. Take State Rt. 41 from the south or Avenue 12 from Madera to the Rt. 41 junction, 8 miles east of Madera. Go east on Ave. 12 from that junction.
Style:	Mostly flat with gentle rolling slopes near the San Joaquin River. Hybrid Bermuda grass fairways give good roll. Huge sandy waste areas sit to the side of many fairways. Greens well guarded and have interesting contours. A few trees in strategic spots.
Other info:	Course is well maintained and very popular. Used for many amateur tournaments. Certified Audubon Cooperative Sanctuary.

Greens Fees as of 10/08:	Weekends	Weekdays	Twilight	Seniors	Carts/person
	$75	$45	$50/$30	No savings	Included

Course ratings:	Men	Par	Rating	Slope	Yardage	Women	Par	Rating	Slope	Yardage
	Black	72	74.7	139	7250	White	74	75.5	128	6261
Riverbend	Blue	72	72.1	135	6788	Gold	72	72.1	121	5679
	White	69	69.8	120	6261	Red	72	68.3	111	5074

No. 52: Windsor

The drive up to the clubhouse at Windsor Golf Club makes players wonder if they are on the right road. Condos and fences surround the access lane, making the entrance look more like a timeshare resort or housing development than a golf course. Even the pro shop sits in an unusual location, away from the restaurant and banquet rooms, across a bridge, distant from the parking area and a putting green. What's going on?

The answer is that, like at a few of our other courses, Windsor was built before the housing boom of the 90's caught up with neighboring open fields. Consequently, development surrounded the course before it could respond to the growth. Fortunately, the layout remains well-respected and enjoyable experience.

When first opened in 1989, the venue hosted several pro-wannabe events. Back then, instead of the Nike Tour, aspiring pros prowled the Hogan Tour. Young John Daly and other up-and-comers trained in these events, and helped promote the reputation of various courses. Today the pro tournaments are long gone from Windsor, but the quality of the course remains. It is very popular and busy; well known for reasonable greens fees and high quality-for-the-dollar.

Windsor's eighth hole is just one in a long series of moderate length holes that force good position on drives and accurate approaches.

In fact, this layout was one of the surprisingly positive experiences during my Northern California research. The design seems to suit the sensibilities of a golfer raised by depression era parents . . . waste is bad, conserve for a rainy day, keep the ball in play. The facility seems compact, wasting little space, yet broad enough to keep balls away from players in adjacent fairways. The bunkers, trees, thicket infested creeks, and silos (forming a backdrop for signature hole number three), seem to fit together appropriately, in a good visual proportion to the fairways and greens.

Fairways are cut relatively wide, but use artfully placed bunkers. Long hitters need to be careful of target-like endings to drive landing areas, but shorter hitters have the freedom to bang away. Windsor suits players who hit moderate length straight shots; and it handsomely rewards those with accurate medium irons and good touch around the green.

Each hole has a different challenge, with highly distinctive greens forming their foundation. Putting surfaces rarely show round or shapeless features. Some are wide and shallow, with the entire front covered by traps, and the back protected by more sand and hollowed aprons. Others appear long and tiered, or highly elevated. They usually sit diagonal to the fairway, with excellent protection for tucked-away pin positions. Tiers sometimes show elevation variance of over three feet. Two or three use raised pads in the middle of bigger surfaces to create small dome-like pin positions. Like Rancho Solano, speeds run moderate, to allow more pin placements on the multi-sloped surfaces.

The other distinction comes from architect Fred Bliss's crafty use of hazards and hills to make interesting and often difficult approach shots. Creeks seldom run next to greens, but force drives to be aimed at spots where approaches become longer or narrower. A moderate sized hill, sitting in the middle of the course, allowed him to place greens at the edge of precipices or behind rock and tree outcroppings

The only real drawback here is the irregular condition of bunkers. Most around greens were filled with extremely fluffy deep sand. Others had only a thin layer of sand above hardpan. Sometimes I had difficulty determining which was firm and which was not before hitting a shot. Afterwards I sure knew.

Windsor is located in the wine country, about seven miles north of Santa Rosa, one mile west of U.S. 101. That is a long way from Sacramento or the Bay Area, our prime population centers, but if ever traveling or visiting in this area, be sure to make it a stop. *Review based on play in July '08.*

Windsor Golf Club

1340 19th Hole Drive		**Golf Shop:**	707 838-7888
Windsor, CA 95492		**Fax**	707 838-7940
		www.windsorgolf.com	

Managed by:	Private, local
Location:	Ten minutes north of Santa Rosa. Take U.S. 101 to Shiloh Exit and go west one mile. Turn right on Golf Course Drive and then immediate left on 19th Hole Drive. Park in lot and cross footbridge to proshop.
Style:	Flat terrain except for a hill in the center of the course. Well graded and contoured to add interest. Creek crossed several times. Greens are small, elevated and often terraced.
Other info:	Busy course, can take over 5 hours, even on weekday mornings.

Greens Fees as of 10/08:	Weekends	Weekdays	Twilight	Seniors	Carts/person
	$56	$37	$39/$26	$19 weekdays	$14

Course ratings:	Men	Par	Rating	Slope	Yardage	Women	Par	Rating	Slope	Yardage
	Black	72	72.0	134	6621	Blue	72	75.6	141	6143
Windsor	Blue	72	70.0	126	6143	White	72	71.8	127	5591
	White	69	67.6	122	5591	Red	72	68.6	120	5026

No. 53: Graeagle Meadows

Graeagle is known as the course that brought top-notch golf to Plumas County. Back in 1966, owner Harvey West Jr., recognized that a first class golf course, built in the middle of the rural Sierras, could lure people to the area. *Build it and they will come.* Forty years later, the area has four ranked **Best 100** facilities and developers bet big money on their success. Graeagle was first, followed by Plumas Pines, Whitehawk Ranch and Nakoma (The Dragon), all within ten miles or each other. Grizzly Ranch, another excellent local course, is trying to make it as a private venue, but has also opened its doors to some non-member play. (See Chapter 4 for more info on Grizzly Ranch.)

View from one of the few elevated tee boxes at Graeagle Meadows. Par-four number six aims drives directly at Mt. Eureka, California's state symbol.

Graeagle bills itself as "golf friendly" and a good value, but it is more than that. Its design represents a throw back to a different way of building. Most modern courses use prominent elevated tee boxes, mounding/long grasses at edges of fairways, and elevated, sophisticated green complexes. This course remains an older style and does not intend to change. A few tee boxes sit high, but only due to natural terrain; most get just one to two feet of grade above the plane of the fairway. Few unnatural contours appear anywhere, and most green elevations also sit near the level of the meadow. As a result, the fairways barely interrupt the topography of the natural meadow or forest surrounding them.

Despite its lack of modern style, Graeagle remains a good test and good golf experience. Soft fairways prevent long roll. Water hazards add plenty of difficulty and interest to approach shots. Many long par-fours put a premium on good chipping to small greens. The beauty of hitting long shots to the few forest-surrounded greens is a real pleasure.

Primary attributes come from two distinctions: First, greens are terrific, as good as any in Northern California. This may not have been the case several years ago, but it certainly was in the fall of '07. Their speed stays moderate, about nine on the StimpMeter, but their texture, smoothness, and color are near perfect. The green maintenance when I played ranked with Cypress Point, one of the better-conditioned private courses anywhere.

Secondly, the course offers an excellent contrast between meadow and forest. The first fourteen holes wind through grassy flatlands bordering the Feather River. Fairways are wide, but the river, and a pond or two, add definition to several holes. The final four go well into the forest, with graceful doglegs and tight, pine-lined fairways. Combine these attributes with beautiful views of mountain ridges, including California's state symbol, Mt. Eureka, and you understand why Graeagle, though old in style, still garners great respect. *Review based on play and interviews in September '07.*

Graeagle Meadows Golf Course

6984 Highway 89	**Golf Shop:**	530 836-2323
Graeagle, CA 96103	**Fax**	530 836-1874
	www.playgraeagle.com	

Managed by:	Private, local
Location:	North of Truckee about an hour. From Interstate-80, exit north on State Rt. 89. Drive 44 miles. Course is on the right, five miles past exit for Whitewawk Ranch.
Style:	Gently rolling terrain. First thirteen holes wander through a large meadow, bordered by the Feather River and surrounding forest. The last five holes are in the woods. Course has wide fairways, little unnatural grading and few elevated greens or tees. Greens are beautiful.
Other info:	Lodging is difficult to find in motels. Most people rent condos at Graeagle or Plumas Pines.

Architect: Ellis Van Gorder

Greens Fees as of 10/08:	Weekends	Weekdays	Twilight	Seniors	Carts/person
	$60	$50	$50/$40	No savings	$20

Course ratings:	Men	Par	Rating	Slope	Yardage	Women	Par	Rating	Slope	Yardage
Graeagle Meadows	Blue	72	71.2	124	6725	White	74	75.5	136	6345
	White	72	69.3	123	6345	Red	72	71.3	125	5589
	Red	69	65.9	115	5589					

No. 54: Empire Ranch

Empire Ranch qualifies as the newest of three Club Corp managed public courses in metropolitan Sacramento. All three, Turkey Creek in Lincoln, Empire Ranch in Folsom, and Teal Bend in northwestern Sacramento have **Best 100** rankings, at numbers 43, 54 and 91 respectively. Each presents its own distinctive style: Turkey Creek is in a rural, almost rustic area, where wildlife abounds. Teal Bend shows a flatter river-plain environment, where tall reeds and bull rushes border many fairways, and each hole stays visually separated from the others. Our subject here, Empire Ranch, sits in a real-estate development, partially elevated on the lower slopes of Sacramento foothills, and uses natural contoured terrain to highlight its qualities. Judging from such a fine grouping, Club Corp seems to manage some of the nicest moderate-to-upscale courses around.

Another unusual par-three-on-the-eighteenth, Empire Ranch's clubhouse and the low foothills of southeastern Sacramento form a picturesque backdrop for a challenging closing shot.

Empire Ranch, built in 2002, and designed by Brad Bell, already makes a good course, though it's only six years old. Success comes through superb maintenance and excellent grooming. Except for neatly bordered hazards or well-defined waste areas, the entire layout appears covered in the deep lush green of fine eastern courses. Young trees aren't mature, but other details make up for their youth . . . grass clippings have been whisked away, fallen leaves vacuumed, bunkers raked and trimmed, and fairways borders cut distinctly with nice shaping. The overall visual impact is one of neatness, good organization, and a club that cares intensely about giving a good impression.

But this is just the start. Graceful mounding gives pleasing bends to fairway shapes, without appearing abrupt or un-natural. Lakes, especially on the low-lying front nine, create small fairway landing areas on shorter holes. Artistry abounds in subtle fashion . . . with numbers one and nine the bookends of a rolling nine holes. They both measure the same distance, about 385-yards from the blue tees. Number one offers players a spacious drive to the top of a dogleg, where the second shot then heads sharply left, downhill towards a very well bunkered, low-set green. Number nine requires a similar drive to the corner of another sharp dogleg; but this time it heads to the right and up a slope, instead of down, to an elevated green. Together these reverse twins punctuate the sophisticated architecture of the course.

The back side also includes a couple of distinguished holes. Number thirteen sends players up a brutal par-four, 469-yards, into the wind. Its runs straight, without doglegs, but brushy waste areas border the left, waiting to catch shots from anyone trying to hit the ball too hard. This hole argues for a separate set of moderate distance tee blocks that would reduce the overly punishing length. The other special hole, comes at par-three number eighteen. Tees vary from 190 to 211-yards for men, to a shorter 113-yards for women, so include a lady on your scramble team. The shot heads downhill, from a precipice on a hillside, over a large pond, to a well-contoured green complex. The main buildings of the clubhouse and local housing developments sit beyond, behind the green, buffered by practice areas and plenty of extra room. It's a pretty setting at the end of a very tailored course. *Review based on play and interview in September '08.*

Empire Ranch Golf Course

1620 East Natoma Street		**Golf Shop:**	916 817-8100
Folsom, CA 95630		**Fax**	916 817-8110
		www.empireranchgolfclub.com	
Managed by:	ClubCorp	**Architect:**	Brad Bell
Location:	About 30 miles east of Sacramento. Take U.S. 50 to exit 27/E, Bidwell St. Go north 1.3 miles to Broadstone. Turn right, then after 1 mile, turn left on Golflinks Rd. Go another 1.4 miles to E. Natoma. Turn left (north) and course is on the right in 1/2 mile.		
Style:	Front nine is gently rolling terrain, back nine is a bit hillier. Lots of nicely graded contours, bunkers and sophisticated green complexes. Entire layout is green and well maintained.		
Other info:	Heavy private tournament play, so rounds can be slow. Play early.		

Greens Fees as of 10/08:	Weekends	Weekdays	Twilight	Seniors	Carts/person
	$67	$47	$47/$35	$40 weekdays	Included

Course ratings:	Men	Par	Rating	Slope	Yardage	Women	Par	Rating	Slope	Yardage
Empire Ranch	Blue	72	71.1	127	6530	White	71	73.6	124	5959
	White	71	68.3	121	5959	Red	71	68.0	110	4977

No. 55: Gold Hills

A century and a half ago, hopeful prospectors thought the hills north of Redding were filled with gold, and the area became known as Gold Hills. Iron turned out to be the only ore worth mining, but the glittery name stuck, a legacy of the Gold Rush, when hope drove people from every country and state to seek their fortune in California, America's last frontier.

Today, Redding is a growing community, located at the northern reach of the Sacramento Valley and features a rich array of recreational pursuits. These include water-sports on Lake Shasta and Wiskeytown Reservoir, as well as land-exploration from Trinity Alps to the west or Mt. Lassen and Fall River Valley to the east. Fishing is the region's mainstay, but Redding also provides a popular rest stop for travelers driving Interstate-5 north to Oregon. What better respite than a game of golf on the best eighteen-hole public course anywhere in the northern third of California? (If your timing isn't quite right for Redding, drive north for another hour to Mount Shasta Resort or Lake Shastina, also ranked among the **Best 100.**)

Par-five number fifteen is the new signature green at Gold Hills. Stone has been added to enhance the ambiance views, and typifies upgrades made over the past several years.

Walter Wentz designed Gold Hills as a semi-private golf course in 1979, but new management recently upgraded the facilities. Improved drainage now allows good year-round play, and re-routed holes steer away from the low spots, lengthening yardage and adding difficulty and character. Upgraded bunkers have eliminated the old heavy lips and contain new sand and drains: they still protect the greens, but play much more easily for most players. Extensive decorative-rock walls now beautify and stabilize several slopes around greens, including new signature hole number fifteen. The re-designed clubhouse completes the facility makeover, providing a pleasant space for both the public and club members.

As in 1849, the word is out, and Gold Hills has become known as a fun, challenging golf course, kept in above-average condition. Golf style varies tremendously from hole to hole. For example, difficult number two, a newly lengthened 542-yard par-five, looks like marshland, with reed-filled lakes protecting its right flank. By contrast, at 518-yard number eighteen, houses border a steep, hilly drive on one side, and long drop to the driving range on the other. One hole looks lush, set within marshes and lakes; the other seems sparse, up and down a nearly treeless hill.

These two disparate scenes are bound together by a series of adventures that move back and forth from flat terrain to hilly fairways. Each one requires a different strategy. Par-threes go from 125 to 205-yards, for example, so most players end up using every club in the bag. They also have in common the same standard of maintenance. Bent grass greens have consistent speeds and can be made very fast for tournament play. Bermuda grass tees are trimmed long because that's what the members like. Fairways also feature longer-than-normal grass, but generally yield good lies despite the mixture of grass varieties. Management plans to phase out preponderance of Bermuda grass, and replace it with a Bent variety. How they will kill the Bermuda without destroying everything else remains an unanswered question.

Wherever it ends, the evolution of Gold Hills into a fine golf course is well underway. More will happen when the current economy improves. Meanwhile, the prospects for golfers in gold-turned-iron country are better than ever. *Review based on play and interviews in July '08.*

Gold Hills Country Club

1950 Gold Hills Drive	**Golf Shop:** 530 246-7867
Redding, CA 96003	**Fax** 530 246-4607
	www.goldhillsgolf.com

Managed by:	Local, private **Architect:** Walter Wentz
Location:	On north side of Redding. From Interstate-5, take exit 682/Oasis Rd. Head east 1/2 mile to Gold Hills Drive. Turn right (south) and go another 1/2 mile to the clubhouse.
Style:	Combination of hilly and gently rolling holes. Some hidden landing areas for drives. A few lakes and creeks. Moderately difficult to walk. Good greens and above average conditioning.
Other info:	Semi-private course, where Shasta County residents save on greens fees.

Greens Fees	Weekends	Weekdays	Twilight	Seniors	Carts/person
as of 10/08:	$60	$60	$35	No savings	$16

Course ratings:	Men	Par	Rating	Slope	Yardage	Women	Par	Rating	Slope	Yardage
	Black	72	72.9	140	6622	Blue	73	76.4	135	6208
Gold Hills	Blue	71	70.8	135	6208	Green	72	72.5	127	5538
	Green	69	67.8	128	5538	Orange	72	69.3	121	5005

No. 56: Half Moon Bay, Old Course

The Old Course at Half Moon Bay Golf Links is the original of two eighteen-hole courses. Located on the ocean, just south of downtown Half Moon Bay, the Old Course opened in 1974. Original neighbors included a mobile home park and fields of brambles and sea grasses. One could often find Joltin' Joe DiMaggio in the club's small breakfast nook, drinking coffee and reading the paper, a famous fixture back in those early days.

The 1990's brought expensive housing and exclusive lodgings to this rural seaside environment. Course yardages became shorter and grounds better manicured to fit the new local image. Close proximity to major destinations, such as San Francisco, the SF airport and the Ritz Carlton hotel next door, make Half Moon Bay a convenient spot for conventioneers, business meetings and tourists.

The eighteenth at Half Moon Bay's Old Course bestows one California's most distinctive finishing holes. With the Ritz Carlton and Pacific Ocean framing the tiny green, its stage is ready for high drama.

To the purest, the current course is not the rugged challenge it once was, but for today's clientele it has developed into an enjoyable golfing experience. Careful maintenance and cool moist weather combine to make excellent course conditions. The large greens, average in speed, stay naturally moist and beautiful. Fairways and bunkers meet high grooming standards, though morning dew traps plenty of fresh cut grass clippings on shoes and balls. Roughs are less pristine, since they're somewhat lumpy and can vary in depth; after all, they are *roughs*.

The front nine winds lazily through homes now surrounding it. Fairways measure shorter than on the back side, and stay firm enough in the summer to give long friendly rolls. Doglegs change direction just enough to create interesting approach shots, despite their abbreviated length. Need for straight tee shots, landed just at the corners, makes long hitters stow their drivers if they want to score well.

The back nine is much more difficult. Its layout has larger elevation changes, longer distances, and more lakes and gullies. Bunkers come closer to the playing area. Number fifteen's design well demonstrates the style: A long par-five has a lake guarding the entire 550-yard length on one side plus conifers or eucalyptus tight on the others. The green is close to the lake, protruding somewhat into it, and demands accuracy and risk to land close to the pin.

Then, the eighteenth gives us one of Northern California's most dramatic settings. It starts from tee blocks high on bluffs overlooking a long drop to the Pacific Ocean. Players aim southerly drives down an undulating fairway directed slightly away from the coastline. A shot close to the cliffs appears to save distance, but that's an illusion, just aim safely down the left side. Next, approaches need to be launched across a barranca, up a hill, to a green tucked directly beneath the towering terraces of the Ritz Carlton Hotel. Both the bunker-protected green, and castle-looking hotel, perch precariously above the ocean. Rocks and concrete pillars protect structures from battering waves and storms. When the pin sits in the back right corner, just above the ocean, the shot appears quite intimidating. Can you imagine cheers from hotel balconies and promenades as your approach lands on the back corner and spins one-foot below the hole? Only in your dreams! *Review based on play many times, last in August '07.*

Half Moon Bay Golf Links, Old Course

2 Miramontes Point Road	Golf Shop:	650 712-2200
Half Moon Bay, CA 94019	Fax	650 726-9039
	www.hmbgolflinks.com	

Managed by:	Kenmark Real Eastate Group **Architect:** F. Duane and A. Palmer
Location:	Just south of Half Moon Bay (HMB). Take State Rt. 92 west to HMB. Turn south on State Rt. 1 and drive 2 miles to Miramontes Point Rd. Turn right and then turn right again at Ritz Carlton hotel circle, to the proshop.
Style:	Gently rolling hills, front nine is short and easier, back nine is difficult. Many doglegs, well trapped greens. Some water holes. Homes line many fairways. Course is in excellent condition.
Other info:	Resort golf course adjacent to Ritz Carlton. 36 holes. Ocean Course is is the tournament venue, Old Course is more resort in style. Cheaper greens fees if you book less than 14 days in advance or play in mid-afternoon.

Greens Fees	Weekends	Weekdays	Twilight	Seniors	Carts/person
as of 10/08:	$205	$180	50%	No savings	Included

Course ratings:	Men	Par	Rating	Slope	Yardage	Women	Par	Rating	Slope	Yardage
Half Moon Bay Olod Course	Black	72	75.2	135	7003	Gold	72	75.8	138	6023
	Blue	72	73.4	131	6610	Red	72	73.0	126	5535
	White	72	72.0	130	6332	Red short	72	72.1	120	5292

No. 57: Haggin Oaks, MacKenzie Course

Haggin Oaks in Sacramento houses Northern California's premier Golf Academy. No other public golf complex has as many assistant pro teachers, as many underprivileged or specialized teaching programs, as many golf teaching stations, as much teaching equipment, as large a golf shop, as many participants, and as much measurable success as this facility.

Programs cater to everyone from youth, to stroke victims, Special Olympics players, the First Tee (inner city youth), even beginning retirees. Instructors aim to move players quickly from the range to real playing conditions . . . so newcomers will understand how to plan on the course and use proper golf etiquette. Morton Golf manages operations at this and other courses for the City of Sacramento, and does everything it can to bring new players into the game. Goodness knows the U.S. golf industry needs new golfers, since rounds played-per-year are down thirteen percent, since peaking in 2000. *

Two eighteen-hole courses, a large driving-range, a pitching practice facility, an indoor/outdoor swing analysis/club-fitting studio, and a three-hole on-course teaching area make up the playing areas at Haggin Oaks. The MacKenzie Course represents the primary eighteen and is their tournament venue. Arcade Creek, the other eighteen, offers a pair of nine hole practice courses built to the same length and condition standards as the MacKenzie course. (See Chapter 3, for detailed information on Haggin Oaks' Arcade Creek.)

Sacramento purchased the 400-acre facility from the Haggin family, which had used it as an airstrip and Morgan horse-breeding farm until 1932. Alister MacKenzie, designer of Cypress Point and Pasatiempo in California, and co-designer of famous Augusta National in Georgia, hired-on to design the original eighteen. MacKenzie also worked as a camouflage designer for the U.S. Army. He used those skills to create unusual fairway contouring, bunkers and greens, attempting to confuse golfers about distance as they attacked. His original greens at Haggin sloped so severely that, when modern era short-grass putting surfaces became standard, all were reconstructed to speed up play.

Other alterations resulted from two major civic construction projects—Interstate-80 on the north perimeter of the course, and the Capital City Expressway on the south. Today, only nine holes remain from the original MacKenzie layout . . . numbers 2, 5, 6, 7, 8, 14, 15, 16, 17, (and greens have been altered on all).

Current characteristics of the MacKenzie Course include broad, flat Bermuda grass fairways where the challenge only comes on green approaches. By utilizing wide driving areas between broad-set tree lines, learning golfers have a chance to get started on each hole. Tee shots require no forced carries, making play much easier for short hitters. They also offer four varying distance tee-options to suit all levels of ability. For tournament play the roughs grow longer and become trimmed narrower to increase difficulty. By today's standards, the 6991-yard Championship distance seems moderate, but offers a good test when maintenance crews firm and roll the greens. The designer's touch definitely shows in greenside bunkering. Multiple sand traps, many sitting well short of putting surfaces, tempt players to hit less club than needed. Players should trust yardage markers and in-ground distance gauges, rather than the eye, when judging club selection.

Course condition is spotty. Balls sit up nicely on fairways but dry patches show up in late summer, and also affect roughs and aprons. Grounds crews keep greens in good shape at moderate speed. Well off the fairways, hardpan dirt becomes the norm. Bunkers receive good care, in keeping with their importance to Mr. MacKenzie.

Open amateur tournaments frequently use the MacKenzie Course . . . The Sacramento City Championships, State Fair Championship Flight, and National Public Links Qualifiers top the current list; but back in the 1930's the PGA tour regularly stopped here. Today, company and charity tournaments are common due to easy access from central Sacramento, and an on-property 400-person tent/pavilion.

With all these capabilities and the great history, Haggin Oaks remains a popular and influential golf venue for the entire Sacramento area. *Review based on play and interviews in October '08.*

*Percentage decline reported in *The Independent*, article by Stephen Foley, 2/22/08.

Haggin Oaks, McKenzie Golf Course

3645 Fulton Ave.	**Golf Shop:** 916 808-2525
Sacramento, CA 95821	**Fax** 916 808-2523
	www.hagginoaks.com

Managed by:	Morton Golf **Architect:** MacKenzie/Asmundsen
Location:	Eastern Central Sacramento. Take I-80, U.S. 50, I-5 or SR. 99 to Capital City Freeway. From it, exit onto Fulton Ave. Course entrance is adjacent to northwest side of the freeway.
Style:	Flat terrain, easy to walk. Wide fairways narrow down close to greens. McKenzie's famous styling mostly appears in bunkers around greens. Course condition erratic in summer.
Other info:	Haggin Oaks Golf Academy has one of the best teaching facilities in the state, with a huge golf equipment store. The restaurant is a mini-museum of Sacramento golf history. Players get good discounts at Morton Golf managed Sacramento courses by purchasing Capital City Golf discount card.

Greens Fees	Weekends	Weekdays	Twilight		Seniors	Carts/person
as of 10/08:	$54	$44	$46/$36		No savings	Included

Course ratings:	Men	Par	Rating	Slope	Yardage	Women	Par	Rating	Slope	Yardage
Haggin Oaks MacKenzie	Black	72	72.5	122	6991	Crème	72	73.5	126	6057
	Burgundy	72	70.4	120	6542	Green	72	70.5	117	5452
	Crème	72	68.0	116	6057					

No. 58: Northstar

All winter long skiers and snowboarders fill Northstar-At-Tahoe Resort, located just south of Truckee. Come springtime, snowy meadows change to fields of high desert flowers, and golf begins in late May. At its 6000-foot elevation the season runs short, lasting only to mid-October. But with Interstate-80 only four miles north, Northstar still gets plenty of play.

*The first hole at Northstar heads out into a high desert meadow south of Truckee. State Rt. 287 angles towards to King's Beach on the eastern perimeter of the front nine. The back nine boasts the narrowest fairways in the **Best 100**.*

Robert Muir Graves designed the course, completing the first nine in 1975, and the balance in 1984. The two nines present as drastic a difference in style as on any **Best 100** course. Over the years, each has been used as the

135

front side, and then switched the back. Currently, players go out on the Meadows, and come back on the Mountain, which makes sense, because the mountainous back nine is probably the tightest, narrowest set of nine holes to be found in Northern California. A nice warm-up on wider Meadow holes helps prepare players for the upcoming difficulties.

Drivers traveling from Truckee to Kings Beach on State Rt. 267, head right by the beginning holes. From the road, distant green patches of fairway appear miss-placed amidst the natural high desert meadow terrain. Fairways sit up on the slightly-raised inclines of the resort's hills, so their greenery shows even more contrast to the arid meadow. Planted trees, placed along some fairways, differ from natural sagebrush and are, in my judgment, also out-of-place. However, once on the course, as a golfer, these holes play very nicely and do not seem contrived, only a little mundane. They cross the landscape fluidly and create interesting shots and allow a relaxing experience.

The second nine brings the character. Decent elevation gains and drops prevail among canyons filled with forest and resort homes. The pines bordering fairways certainly come into play, but not the houses—they just create viewing platforms for spectators to smirk at the troubles arising below.

The ayout on this nine is a target feast, where long hitters can use driver on only two par-fives. The challenge begins on number eleven, a short 350-yard par-four. A maximum 220-yard tee shot must find a small landing zone between bunkers and a tree filled gully. The 130-yard approach then flies high over a sunken creek, and squeezes into a tiny, cliff-protected green where no level spot exists for the pin. Next comes the first of two double fairway holes, twelve and seventeen. On the first, a creek splits landing areas into separate 15-20 yard wide targets. Tall pines reach in from four sides, trying to grab slightly errant shots. Thankfully, the short approach is more standard.

Then comes a very tight, wonderfully flowing, downhill, side-hill, dogleg par-five, where big hitters can try to blast their second over a 100-yard wide hazard in front of the small hillside green. (Suggestion . . . be sensible and lay-up short, then wedge it home for birdie.) Number seventeen has the other split fairway, where one option is to fly your drive over a river, 210-yards away. The other is to lay-up on the short side of the river to a very small, well-defended fairway, surrounded by a creek, out-of-bounds, trees, deep rough and houses. The second option leaves a longer 160-yard approach, but one straight at an open pin, versus a tiny opening from the first. Neither shot choice is easy, but typical of the unique and interesting challenges faced throughout this back nine.

Management keeps the entire course in good shape, though greens in the forest are slower than those in the meadow. Fairways, roughs, bunkers and aprons are all a pleasure, and help make Northstar the best value for eighteen holes on the North Shore. *Review based on play and interview in July '08.*

Northstar at Tahoe Golf Course

168 Basque Drive		Resort:	800 466-6784
P. O. Box 129		Golf Shop:	530 562-3290
Truckee, CA 96160		Fax	530 562-2035
		www.northstarattahoe.com	
Managed by:	Northstar at Tahoe	Architect:	Robt Muir Graves
Location:	Just south of Truckee. Take Interstate-80 to exit #188/State Rt. 267. Head south six miles to Northstar Drive. Turn right and follow signs to golf course.		
Style:	Two styles on one course. Front side is gently rolling mountain meadow/high desert terrain with nicely graded fairways and contoured greens. Back nine is unique, with extremely tight fairways in a thick, hilly forest. Expect elevated small greens guarded by steep aprons and hazards. Note high women's slope ratings.		
Other info:	Three-day golf pass saves substantially on greens fees. Altitude is 6000 feet.		

Greens Fees as of 10/08:	Weekends	Weekdays	Twilight	Seniors	Carts/person
	$80	$80	$60	No savings	Included

Course ratings:		Men	Par	Rating	Slope	Yardage	Women	Par	Rating	Slope	Yardage
	Gold	72	721	138	6615	White	72	73.8	142	5818
Northstar	Blue	72	69.9	135	6193	Red	72	70.8	136	5470
	White	72	68.3	129	5818					

No. 59: Plumas Pines

Here is another of the Graeagle region's four **Best 100** courses. It is not the toughest, the best designed, nor the one with the most history, but may be the one that best fits the image of a mountain resort getaway.

This impression begins when you drive into the hillside clubhouse lot, and the view shows what's coming . . . Fifty feet below sits a resort environment with practice areas, an abundance of green well-defined fairways, and a layout snaking through ponds, homes, condos and cart bridges crossing the Feather River. The condominiums probably provided your lodging the night before, and the dinner at Longboards, above the pro shop, served surprisingly good gourmet food. Now you anticipate a good relaxing day on the course. What you find will meet most of these hopes, but also a bit of controversy.

The first tee looks great, near this same elevated position high above the fairway, and begs players to cut the corner of a medium length par-five. But high ambitions are short-lived, because once down on the river-plain below, golf quickly becomes challenging. Number two may be fair, but it's a tough hole near the start of a round. It requires a very straight drive, with the river close on the left and trees tight on the right. The approach to this middle length par-four is long and extremely chancy, because the fairway becomes a skinny isthmus leading to narrow aprons separating the green from both the Feather River and several bunkers.

Number four, is not just difficult, it is a bad hole, one of the two worst designs in the ranked **Best 100**. (See Number 64: Brighton Crest for the other poor design.) Drives must negotiate a 150-yard long, 30-yard wide chute between tall trees on the left and condominiums immediately on the right. The condos are so close to the ball flight, they would be in-harm's-way but for fences and nets. Most golfers can't even hit short irons straight enough to negotiate the narrow alley from the blue tees. The second shot opens up a bit, but still contends with condos and trees, and the final shot is back to normal, towards a green set on the river's edge. Thank goodness number four's narrowness is an aberration, since the rest of the nine opens up to fun, interesting holes. To many players, however, the damage is done and they claim to dislike the entire course, not just one hole. Guess it's too late to re-locate those condos.

While a meadow environment envelopes the entire front side, the back cuts through local forest. Pine-lined holes meander in a relaxing fashion, with nicely graded contours giving good definition and safe playing conditions. Vacation homes sit far off line, protected from stray shots by trees set wide off the fairways. One hole, 150-yard number fifteen, is unique, with a tall cedar tree blocking most of the green. As the card instructions suggest, just hit it right over the 75-foot tree, and it plays easy! Surprisingly, I was able to do this with a decent seven iron.

Both nines receive wonderful maintenance, their lush appearance being a highlight of my experience and a strength of the course. Greens look fabulous, perhaps because their small size makes them easier to maintain. However, wide expanses of rough between holes also look perfect, and tees, fairways and bunkers are top notch.

If you can block out the one bad hole, and accept the quirks that come from shooting over trees and close to rivers, you should end up enjoying Plumas Pines. I did. *Played in September '07.*

Plumas Pines Golf Resort

402 Poplar Valley Road	**Golf Shop:** 530 836-1420
P. O. Box 1210	**Fax** 530 836-0801
Graeagle, CA 96103	www.plumaspinesgolf.com

Managed by:	Celtic Golf Management	**Architect:**	Homer Flint
Location:	An hour north of Truckee and two miles south of the junction of State Rts. 89 and 70. Take Rt. 89 to County A14. Go west 2 miles to Poplar Valley Road. Turn right, course is on the right.		
Style:	Front nine is relatively flat along the Feather River, with small creeks wandering along many holes. Second nine is in the forest, where homes and trees line the fairways; also relatively flat terrain.		
Other info:	Excellent gormet restaurant in clubhouse. Plumas Pines has best condo selection in area.		

Greens Fees	Weekends	Weekdays	Twilight	Seniors	Carts/person
as of 10/08:	$95	$80	$60/$45	No savings	Included

Course ratings:	Men	Par	Rating	Slope	Yardage	Women	Par	Rating	Slope	Yardage
Plumas Pines	Blue	71	71.1	134	6421	White	72	74.0	137	5946
	White	71	69.3	127	5946	Red	72	70.5	125	5297

No. 60: Wildhorse

The University of California Davis lady's golf team made the Top 25 at the 2008 NCAA Women's Golf Championships. After playing Wildhorse, their home course, it's easy to understand why their games can stand up under national pressure. Wildhorse toughens them up.

Gibson Golf Management Co. owns and operates this facility, which opened in 1999 but came to Gibson in 2004. Their new motto, " . . . a golf course for golfers, run by golfers, to take care of golfers," states their objective pretty clearly. They neither rent the clubhouse for weddings, like the prior owners, nor jack up greens fees to prices locals can't afford. They stress competition, by hosting multitudes of tournaments, including five local high schools' competitive matches. The rangers, the pro shop clerks, the cook and the bartender all must be golfers . . . at least these *were* the employment rules in mid-2008.

As for the course, the set-up and condition match this goal. Fairways, tees, greens, aprons and even the bunkers appear well maintained. A few grassy areas may see dry spots in the middle of summer, after all Davis often feels temperatures above 100 degrees F during July and August. Greens run moderately fast, around 9 on the StimpMeter, and use 95% Bent grass. *Poa anna* grass creeps in here and there, but is not an issue that hurts the quality of putts.

The heart and charm of Wildhorse come from special design features: First, the topography and local flora surprise unknowledgeable newcomers. I thought a layout in the middle of the flat Sacramento Valley would be routine and un-interesting. Not here. Years ago the land may have been level, but now it is molded beautifully into a continuous series of natural appearing ridges and undulations intertwined by lakes and depressions. Stands of black walnut and other full sized trees, which seem to have been integral to the landscape for years, augment the aura. The result is a preserve-type setting, private, concealed from surrounding homes and farmland. It's an oasis in the middle of the valley.

Next, a bushy variety of tall grass adds a common accent throughout the course. It rims various water hazards and bunkers, and matching strains dot the roughs. Together these tufts form a tapestry of soft borders, reminding golfers that they better hit it straight, or big trouble will gobble them up.

Dramatic bunker designs, especially those in the fairway, add to the ambience. Many elevated jagged lips protrude six to eight feet high, appearing like a diminutive version of craggy designs one might see on seaside links courses.

Finally, and perhaps most important to Davis residents, the city requires wildlife to be an active part of the course. Roped-off areas of rough protect burrowing owls and ground squirrels. The squirrels have grown extremely large due to good feedings from players, and constantly scurry between groups. The owls are harder to find, but pop up from their burrows now and then, even during the middle of the day. Other environmental zones protect waterfowl from golfer's intrusion into wetlands.

The course layout fits nicely into this unusual setting, with trees closely protecting fairways, and bunkers or lakes protecting the rest. Wide landing zones predominate, though a few demand good precision. Numbers seventeen and eighteen provide the most scenic and distinctive tests on the course. Seventeen, a short par-five, aims the tee-shot across a lake where players can cut off as much as they risk. Direction usually heads downwind, so a good drive means a reasonable but daring chance at the green in two. Number eighteen, a long par-four, heads back into the Delta breeze, and needs a long second shot over a wide marsh. Go for this last green at your peril, but if you don't, the third shot still needs a 150-yard carry into the wind. These final holes provide a character-building climax to a refreshing golf experience. *Review based on play and interview in June '08.*

Wildhorse Golf Course

2323 Rockwell Drive	**Golf Shop:**	530 753-4900
Davis, CA 95616	**Fax**	530 753-9879
	www.wildhorsegolfclub.com	

Managed by:	Gibson Golf Management	**Architect:** Jeffrey Brauer
Location:	On the north edge of Davis. From Interstate-80 take State Rt. 113 north. At Covell Exit turn east and go 2 miles. At Pole Line Road turn left (north) and go to Moore St. Turn right here and then left on Rockwell Drive.	
Style:	Relatively flat terrain but extensive grading creates hollows and wetlands amongst the black walnut groves. Distinctive bunker systems in fairways and around greens.	
Other info:	Course maintained very well and harbours extensive wildlife.	

Greens Fees	Weekends	Weekdays	Twilight	Seniors	Carts/person
as of 10/08:	$44	$30	$33/$26	$28	$5/$8

Course ratings:	Men	Par	Rating	Slope	Yardage	Women	Par	Rating	Slope	Yardage
	Black	72	73.0	135	6880	Gold	72	70.2	120	5300
Wildhorse	Blue	72	70.4	128	6335	Red	72	66.8	115	4565
	White	70	68.6	122	5935					

No. 61: Ancil Hoffman

Traditional is a good label for the Ancil Hoffman Golf Course. It's situated in unincorporated Carmichael, about eight miles east of downtown Sacramento. Ancil Hoffman, the individual, promoted boxing in the early 20th century. He donated the land as a park, in the best spirit of philanthropy, and later helped fund improvements to the golf course.

The setting, at the end of a narrow suburban street, looks like one would expect in an old-fashioned neighborhood park. Recreation trails surround the course and providing open access for joggers, dog walkers, picnickers, *etc.* Thick groves of large, full-grown oaks surround the fairways, just like elms, maples, pines and sycamores would on established courses in other parts of the country. Older, rustic style homes, same as might be found in any well-established California community, overlook several perimeter fairways. A flood plain dominates the topography, with banks and berms built up after millennia of overflows and droughts on the American River. Very few changes have been made over the course's 44-year life span, since the original William Bell design has stood well the test of time.

The third hole at Ancil Hoffman typifies the gentle bends and tree-lined fairways common to every hole. Beware of bunkers; they can be huge with high lips.

This is a ball striker's course rather than a putter's course, because of small greens and tree-lined fairways. Putts may be shorter than elsewhere, but narrow fairways force good accuracy and skill from the tee box. Large trees create narrow alleys, and give little leeway for hooks and slices. Once off the fairway, thick trunks block shots from coming back into play. Green approaches offer slender openings, especially when drives land on the wrong side of the fairway.

Designer Bell used terrain changes effectively. Although built on relatively flat land, undulations and swales create awkward stances at the most inopportune times. They force players to think, not just hit, because shots need positioning to avoid such slopes. Greenside bunkers are dangerous because the course's few traps are tall and broad. These monsters commonly force difficult mid-length 30 to 50 yard recovery blasts.

Many people ask which of Sacramento's premier downtown courses, Ancil Hoffman or Haggin Oak's MacKenzie, is the better track? Most locals prefer Hoffman; indeed I feel the same. Course conditions and course layout both beat MacKenzie. The greener, softer environment at Hoffman makes for a more relaxed game. However, when tallying points for overall course ranking, Mackenzie wins the day due to its myriad of extra features. Their teaching facility, catering tent, superb golf shop and interesting mini-museum, eek out enough extra points to win the overall comparison.

Want to bang long drives and then win around the greens go to McKenzie. Want to hit them straight and stay in the shade, go to Hoffman. *Review based on play and interview in October '08.*

Ancil Hoffman Golf Course

6700 Tarshes Drive		Golf Shop:	916 482-3813
Carmichael, CA 95608		Fax	916 482-3089
		www.empiregolf.com	

Managed by:	Empire Golf	Architect:	William Bell
Location:	Course is hidden away, just east of Sacramento. Take U.S.50 to S. Watt exit. Take S. Watt north 1.6 miles to Fair Oaks. Then turn left and head about 4.5 miles to Van Alstine. Turn right to California, turn left to Tarshes and then turn right and head through park to clubhouse.		
Style:	Mostly flat terrain, with minor undulations and fairways bordered by mature oaks. Need to keep ball straight. Greens guarded by very large bunkers. In a park-like setting, with easy walking.		

Greens Fees as of 10/08:	Weekends	Weekdays	Twilight	Seniors	Carts/person
	$37	$28	$20	23	$15

Course ratings:	Men	Par	Rating	Slope	Yardage	Women	Par	Rating	Slope	Yardage
Ancil Hoffman	Blue	72	72.6	128	6794	White	75	76.7	135	6434
	White	72	70.8	127	6434	Red	73	74.2	126	5954

No. 62: Poppy Ridge

Poppy Ridge, near Lawrence-Livermore Labs, opened in 1996, as the second of two Northern California Golf Association (NCGA) owned courses. It provides East Bay and Central Valley golfers easy access to a championship NCGA facility. Their other course, Poppy Hills on the Monterey Peninsula, ranks No. 4 in the **Best 100**. The NCGA has over 165,000 members, and sponsors many tournaments throughout the year.

Rees Jones, brother of Robert Trent Jones, Jr., designed this Livermore location. Junior designed Poppy Hills; and their father, Robert Trent Jones, Sr. designed the original NCGA headquarters course, Spyglass Hill, about two miles from Poppy Hills.

Number nine on the Merlot Nine at Poppy Ridge is a fun downhill par-five where a good drive earns a risky shot at the green in two.

In this location, Jones chose a Heathland style design. Heathland courses, in Scotland as well as other European countries, use terrain similar to links courses, but locate inland rather than on the coast. Their landscapes usually appear relatively flat, with arid vegetation. Sand dunes and waste areas, covered in gorse and heather, typify examples in Europe and Great Brittan. They use such locales because commercial crops would not grow well on the loamy soils and owners could buy the land cheaply. The same soils can prove perfect for golf courses, which need excellent drainage. In the U.S., we substitute mesquite, sage, and similar low shrubs for the indigenous British Isles heather and gorse. Poppy Ridge took a slightly different track, using tall grasses, vineyards, scrub oak and rolling hillsides to create their Heathland vision. Strong afternoon Delta breezes certainly add to the Scottish experience.

Depending on the time of year, players find Poppy Ridge course conditions either excellent or, at the end of a long, hot, windy summer, somewhat parched. Toughest months come in July and August, though management hopes to improve late summer dry/wet spots. The course drains extremely well, even after multiple storms, so in winter, leave your local Bay Area clay quagmires and come to Livermore.

Primary design features include large, well-maintained greens with moderate undulations and some large terraces. The course sits on a lower section of local rolling hills, but a few high vantage points give great views of the surrounding topography and vineyards. Picturesque fairways, often shaped to run between the hills, use bunkers to define where *not* to drive the ball. Steep sand traps also protect the many elevated greens. Players who enjoy interesting and challenging approach shots from side-hill lies really love Poppy Ridge.

Since the course has three nines, named Zinfandel, Chardonnay and Merlot, many individual holes qualify as the best. Fun par-threes sit in picturesque amphitheatres, requiring hits to cross lakes or canyons, with short enough shots for players at all levels. Number nine on the Merlot group provides a particularly good finishing hole. (See the drawing on prior page.) Its 525-yard downhill dogleg uses the clubhouse as a backdrop. A really good downwind drive, landing very near a lake on the left, gives a chance for even moderate-length hitters to go for the green in two. The hole shows how risk/reward can be made an interesting part of the game at a critical time in competition.

The NCGA tries hard to keep quality golf affordable. Players who want a lot of good golf for a reasonable greens fee should find Poppy Ridge a bargain, especially during the week. In 2008 they offered year-end specials that drastically reduced cost per round. *Review based on play many times, last in October '08.*

Poppy Ridge Golf Course

4280 Greenville Rd.		Golf Shop:	925 455-2035
Livermore, CA 94550		Fax	925 455-2020
		www.poppyridgegolf.com	

Managed by:	NCGA
	Architect: Rees Jones
Location:	Southern Livermore hills. From Interstate-580, head south from N. Greenville Rd. exit. Drive 4.5 miles and the course entrance is on the left, between rolling vineyards.
Style:	Very hilly course, can be windy in the afternoon. Lots of climbing between holes and side hill lies are common. Very few trees but great close-up views of vineyards. Big medium speed greens. Great drainage in winter, but patchy dry spots in late summer.
Other info:	27 holes with nines named Merlot, Chardonnay, and Zinfandel.

Greens Fees, 10/08	Weekends	Weekdays	Twilight	Seniors	Carts/person
General Public	$110	$100	$46/$32	No savings	$17
NCGA Members	$60	$45	$46/$32	No savings	$17

Course ratings:	Men	Par	Rating	Slope	Yardage *	Women	Par	Rating	Slope	Yardage *
	Black	72	75.0	138	7088	White	74	75.8	131	6214
Poppy Ridge	Blue	72	73.0	135	6676	Gold	72	70.4	120	5200
	White	72	70.8	130	6224					

* Averages per the NCGA Bluebook, Winter 2009

No. 63: Lake Tahoe

Lake Tahoe's South Shore houses the most highly developed section of the Tahoe Basin. Across the border in Nevada sits the thriving city of Stateline, with large hotels, casinos, Heavenly Valley ski resort, and a host of waterside amenities. This small city probably provides the most picturesque and relaxed setting for gaming entertainment in the world. On the California side, life slows down some, with a myriad of small motels, lodges, strip malls, vacation homes, beaches, two eighteen-hole golf courses and the airport. It is a sprawling area where forests hides much of the development, and provides a laid-back mountain vacation environment.

Back in 1959, before the south really started booming, Lake Tahoe Golf Course became the area's first such facility. It sits on property owned by El Dorado County, managed by American Golf Co. The severity and length of winter seasons often dictates whether summer playing conditions are poor or good. At 6500-feet, elevation can have a harsh impact on fairways and greens, but the winters of '08 and '09 were especially mild, and put the course in peak shape.

Mt Tallac, towering above Lake Tahoe's western shore, dominates the views on many holes at Lake Tahoe Golf Course. Number six, a par three, requires 175 yards to clear the creek from the back tee.

In fact, this course provides one of my biggest personal discoveries in the writing of the **Best 100** . . . Courses on the North Shore such as Incline Village, Coyote Moon, Old Greenwood, North Star, Tahoe Donner, and Squaw Creek, plus Nevada's Edgewood in the south, get most of the notoriety and press. Most golfers consider the south, at least on the California side of the border, a backwater for quality golf, and leave it out of their minds. Tahoe's wide, level fairways with little mounding or dramatic fairway bunkering definitely appear old school. But, those who play there know this course is no slouch. It is, indeed the best value in the Tahoe/Truckee basins.

The high quality comes from several factors: First, an open view of surrounding Tahoe mountains dominates nearly every hole. Mt. Tallac, the rim's highest peak at 9739 feet (2968 meters), rises high in the west. In the foreground, low granite-dotted hillocks remind players they are just a few hundred yards from camping and hiking. A nearby 2007 fire devastated south shore forests and homes, but local hills obscure most damage from visibility on the course.

Next, the course design appeals to both learning golfers and experts alike. Wide fairways, especially on the front side, and unguarded front tee positions make shots easier for players of lesser skill. Many greens are relatively flat and wide, allowing forgiveness on miss-hit approaches. However, the 6741-yard back tees, offer challenges from obscure starting points, 50-60 yards into the woods. They cause long forced carries and more difficult approach angles.

Excellent course maintenance and flat topography make the course a relaxing stroll. Its meadow location places tees fairly close to greens. Evenly watered fairways and roughs make the layout a nice green color, yet firm fairways allow balls to roll well. Trees line many fairways, sometimes closely, sometimes with a wide berth, and provide good shade from the high-altitude summer sun. Bent grass greens prevail, though *poa anna* is creeping in, becoming more prevalent every year. They roll true, have no bare spots, and hold good shots, offering a fair test for all. Back nine greens were built later than those on the front, and make smaller, more undulating, tightly protected targets.

Don't discount Lake Tahoe Golf Course. It's priced right, often shows good condition, has gorgeous scenery, and suits every ability. Try to play early though, before crowds arrive, or in the early afternoon before the twilight rates bring in the bargain hunters. Otherwise its popularity can cause a long day. *Review based on play twice, last with interview in July '08.*

Lake Tahoe Golf Course

2500 Emerald Bay Road	**Golf Shop:**	530 577-0788
South Lake Tahoe, CA 96150	**Fax**	530 577-4469
	www.laketahoegc.com	

Managed by:	American Golf	**Architect:** W. Bell, Jr.
Location:	Near Tahoe's south shore, on U.S. 50, one mile north of Meyers, on the west side of the highway.	
Style:	Flat terrain; wide fairways on the front nine, and tighter driving areas on the back. Tree lined in places. Greens often well protected, and can be small targets on the back nine. Altitude about 6400 feet.	
Other info:	Gorgeous views of surrounding mountains. Generally in good shape starting in mid July.	

Greens Fees	Weekends	Weekdays	Twilight	Seniors	Carts/person
as of 10/08:	$55	$55	$45	No savings	$25/$15

Course ratings:	Men	Par	Rating	Slope	Yardage	Women	Par	Rating	Slope	Yardage
	Gold	71	70.6	127	6651	Black	72	74.1	126	6201
Lake Tahoe	Black	71	68.7	119	6201	Silver	72	71.2	117	5696
	Silver	69	66.4	114	5696					

No. 64: Brighton Crest

Number four on Brighton Crest, a short par four has a great view of Sierra foothills just south of the San Joaquin River's Friant Dam.

Twenty miles north of Fresno, at the base of the Sierra foothills, sits Friant Dam. Its reservoir, Millerton Lake, provides flood protection, irrigation water and recreational facilities to the Madera/Fresno area. By 1990 local housing developments reached out to this sixty-year-old picturesque rural area. Brighton Crest Country Club, designed by Johnny Miller, became a lure, attracting affluent golfers seeking refuge from the city. It enticed buyers to investigate rural real estate, and even attracted construction of a small casino across the street. Recently the state and county widened Friant Road, the main access road, and thereby confirmed that county managers planned continued growth to these particularSan Joaquin Valley foothills.

Fresno golfers heaped praised on Brighton Crest for over a decade. Many believed it to be the premier NCGA public access course south of Stevinson Ranch. Other candidates fit into that group too, including Pheasant Run (Chowchilla), Sierra Meadows (near Oakhurst), and Riverbend (Madera). But the most recent addition, new Ridge Creek (Dinuba) has, in my opinion, leaped-frog the others to become the top of course within a half hour of Fresno.

Never-the-less, Brighton Crest's layout remains a good one, distinguished by rolling hillsides and local foothill topography. Designer Miller created many artistic tee shot vistas. Two perch on steeply elevated positions, giving excellent photo opportunities at numbers three and thirteen. Backdrops include expansive views of the local hills and/or the Valley beyond. The steep drops force big hitters to lay-up, while shorter hitters bask in the glory of extra long drives. Other starting shots may not be so dramatic, but valleys or hollows form nice settings, where side-hills slopes often ricochet balls back onto flatter fairway lies.

Greens throughout show lots of character. Many use two tiers with steep elevation changes between. Sometimes these plateaus are small enough that landing on the right level makes one-putting a realistic expectation. Balls on the wrong plane are very difficult to putt close to the cup, creating lots of three-putts. And even straight looking putts follow subtle breaks. Putting well challenges the best here, so bless the green's softness; at least they hold chips and approaches.

Overall course condition is excellent. Fairways contain hybrid Bermuda turf, with small, thin blades of grass. Unfortunately, the thin grass plus tight mowing create tight lies, but soft sub-soil eases the difficulty of hitting through shots. Roughs find a fescue variety grass, so are soft, fluffy, thick, and green, but evenly cut. Their heavy texture stops the balls from rolling wildly into gullies or more serious trouble. Maintenance crews keep cart paths edged, mind colorful flowerbeds, and nurture many wildflowers. Even though houses line one side of several fairways, pastoral scenery dominates the design.

A few problems do appear in the general layout. Miller creates extreme distances between green and tee on many courses. Brighton Crest's distances are so extreme that that players must use carts . . . walkers need not apply. Even the driving range sits more than a half-mile cart drive from the clubhouse, out on the perimeter of the property.

The design of hole number eighteen is one of the worst in the **Best 100**. This dogleg par-five requires a drive that can easily land on cars in the clubhouse lot, and a second shot that can bounce balls off roofs of homes on the other side of the fairway. Its design seems totally out-of-place with the rest of the spacious plan. Management realizes the problem on this closing hole, and plans a redesign, but until then, it's a disappointing end an otherwise excellent round of golf. *Review based on play and interview in April '08.*

Brighton Crest Golf & Country Club

21722 Fairway Oaks Lane	**Golf Shop:**	559 325-8900
Friant, CA 93626	**Fax**	559 299-8565
	www.brightoncrest.com	

Managed by:	Private, local	**Architect:**	Johnny Miller
Location:	About a half hour north of Fresno. Take State Rt. 41 from the south or State Rt. 145 to Rt. 206 from Madera. At Friant Road turn east, pass the dam and first views of Millerton Lake. Turn right on Brighton Crest Road and follow signs.		
Style:	Hilly terrain. Very well manicured fairways, greens and flowerbeds. Course winds through twisty canyons and hills. Many well protected greens surrounded by bunkers, trees and steep aprons. Drives need to be moderately straight on most holes.		

Other info:	Semi-private. Walking allowed but not easy. Has some gorgeous elevated views.

Greens Fees as of 10/08:	Weekends	Weekdays	Twilight	Seniors	Carts/person
	$60	$45	$50/$35	No savings	Included

Course ratings:	Men	Par	Rating	Slope	Yardage	Women	Par	Rating	Slope	Yardage
Brighton Crest	Blue	72	72.8	136	6788	White	72	76.5	134	6298
	White	72	70.7	127	6298	Red	72	70.6	122	5195

No. 65: Nakoma, (The Dragon)

The last few years have been a roller coaster ride for Nakoma Golf Resort, which opened originally as The Dragon in 2000. Located about 50 miles north of Truckee, competition from neighboring Whitehawk, Graeagle and Plumas Pines courses has never been easy. From the beginning, golfers found the 147 slope-rated course very difficult. Also, normal new course issues such as rock-hard greens and wild roughs didn't help. For these and many other reasons, including the building of an expensive, non-functional Frank Lloyd Wright designed clubhouse, owners declared bankruptcy in 2004 and the grounds became a park for two years.

Then, in May 2007, under supervision of the court, the operation re-opened as Nakoma Golf Resort. Modifications eased course difficulty: New management removed trees, eliminated the longest tees, softened greens, and altered or removed several bunkers. Slope dropped to 139 and Nakoma became a better place to play. It now deserves to be ranked with other Graeagle region courses.

In fact, the exceptional back nine would rank in the **Best 100's** top five, if taken as a separate unit. This outstanding grouping of holes challenges players with plenty of well placed bunkers, sharp doglegs, unique greens, and terrific course conditioning. Par-threes and fives illustrate particularly good design. Number thirteen heads 190-yards up a narrow stream bed where surrounding sage brush, sand, rock and sparse pine trees remind me of pioneer wagons rolling up a gentle gulch. Number fifteen, another good par-three shows more typical golf-like character. The approach goes steeply up a grassy hill over deep bunkers to an elevated double level green with sharp breaks and a huge false front. Number eighteen, an uphill double dogleg par-five, begins through a minefield of bunkers, almost like a links setting in Ireland. The sand contrasts sharply with the ultra-green fairway. Big hitters try to launch their second uphill at the 45-degree turn, over another large set of bunkers to an elevated green. The rest of us, who cannot cut the long corner, settle for normal play and longer distances over many of the same hazards.

The front nine is another story. Its greens have been softened since re-opening, and trees have been removed from some severely punishing positions. But poorly maintained fairways, roughs and bunkers make it a tough go. Fairways display many dry spots, bunkers edges are lined with weeds, and the greens show bare spots and uneven mowing. Apparently different water systems supply each of the two nines, causing some of the disparity. Also, its northwest ridge location faces more extreme weather than the back nine, making winter recovery more difficult. Plan a higher score at the start, and wait patiently because a luscious dessert comes at the end.

Once a frighteningly difficult course, Nakoma has been toned down significantly. Number eighteen remains an excellent closing double-dogleg with bunkers everywhere.

Due to its difficult financial history and past style of play, Nakoma came up with an inventive way to ease difficulty and increase rounds per year. They created a guidance stake system that not only advises direction for players to aim, but also the distances to hit the ball. Target stakes are placed at the center of recommended landing zones. Players use a pro-shop provided guide that lists the distances from each tee box to the landing stakes. Some are set well short of normal driving distance and create much longer green approach shots. Result: In 2008, management said players using the system--trying to hit within 20 yards of each stake--cut 10 strokes off their score. That seems like an exaggeration, but any such system makes play a lot easier for newcomers. What do you suppose would happen if the USGA allowed such an idea to be used in tournament play? Perhaps a whole new group of less experienced players would be encouraged. *Review based on play and interviews in September '07.*

Nakoma Golf Resort (The Dragon)

348 Bear Run	Resort:	877 462-5662
Clio, CA 96106	Golf Shop:	530 832-5067
	Fax	530 832-4356
	www.nakomagolfresort.com	

Managed by:	Private, local	**Architect:**	Robin Nelson
Location:	North of Truckee about an hour. From Interstate-80, exit north on State Rt. 89. After driving 42 miles, turn right on A15/Portola-McLears Rd. Go 3.5 miles to Bear Run. Turn right and follow signs to the course.		
Style:	Very hilly terrain. Narrow driving areas, normally needing lay-up shots off the tee to stay out of trouble. Greens very guarded and with big undulations. Difficult walking. Back nine is much better maintained than the front and is a terrific group of holes.		
Other info:	Ask proshop for guide sheet and explanation of target stakes. Altitude 4650 feet.		

Greens Fees	Weekends	Weekdays	Twilight	Seniors	Carts/person
as of 10/08:	$65	$55	$55/$45	No savings	Included

Course ratings:	Men	Par	Rating	Slope	Yardage	Women	Par	Rating	Slope	Yardage
	Black	71	72.0	139	6791	White	72	74.4	144	5961
Nakoma	Blue	71	71.0	135	6454	Red	71	70.9	136	5289
	White	71	68.9	129	5961	Gold	70	66.6	128	4611

No. 66: Greenhorn Creek

The low foothills of the Sierra Nevada offer many promising sites for new golf courses and real estate development. Its gently rolling topography allowed architects Don Boos (original) and Robert Trent Jones, Jr. (re-design) to loosen their imaginations on Greenhorn Creek, one of the earliest projects. The course is located near downtown Angel's Camp in the heart of Gold Country, where players can still feel the pull of future riches . . . now in real estate, rather than gold. Today, fully developed lots surround the property and Trend West operates a large time-share condominium just down the street. Together, homeowners and vacationers guarantee a consistent flow of golfing customers throughout the year.

The course design takes advantage of several structures left over from the Gold Rush era. For example, the fourth hole, a par-five illustrated on the next page, features a weathered stone fence crossing the fairway about 225 yards from the green. An abandoned kiln still stands in the left hand rough of the same hole; Indian grinding bowls, set in granite stones appear on the right. The artifacts add a special charm, which should be particularly appreciated by tourists taking a day off from the Angel's Camp frog jumping festival. That jubilant event, chronicled by Mark Twain in *The Famous Jumping Frog of Calaveras County,* is held on the third weekend of May every year.

Unique relics, colorful history, and great topography are magnetic, but the golf course provides its own attraction. Its design provides plenty of challenge, including unique holes and good grooming. Length caps out at only 6,750 yards for top players, but even club pros find breaking par difficult in their annual tournament. Two out of three drives on par fours require precise accuracy, and all the par-three greens are well protected. The big greens run fast and are kept in top shape, although difficult reads and firm surfaces make putting difficult. Pro Darryl Pief notes that the subtle breaks fall toward nearby Tulloch Lake, about five miles to the southeast.

A group of unusual par-fours will appeal to many medium handicappers because, while they aren't too long, their unique layout can be overcome with good, straight shots. Number five requires drives to skirt a lake protected by willows on one side and a hillside, protected by oaks, on the other. The approach shot has to travel 140 to 150 yards through a narrow opening, over a swampy creek, to an elevated, well-bunkered double-level green. Number eleven presents another large oak tree set in the middle of the fairway, too far out to clear with a driver. This forces the tee shot through a narrow space on one or the other side of the tree, followed by a 200-yard-plus approach to another well-guarded, two-tiered green slightly elevated on a hill. The dogleg seventeenth demands a precision drive through a small gap 180 yards out, to a hidden landing area over a rise, just short of a creek. The approach still requires between 150 and 200 yards, through another gap to a green partially obscured by trees.

A gold country museum piece, the fourth at Greenhorn Creek features an old mill on one side, Indian grinding stones on the other, and a Gettysburg-style stonewall crossing in between.

But don't be frightened. Enjoyable adventure awaits on the easier holes, the course setting is very attractive, and good scores can be had to balance out the bad ones. Be sure to follow your round with a meal at the clubhouse; my wife Jess (our illustrator) says it offers equally great food at lunch and dinner. *Review based on play many times, most recently with interviews in June '07.*

Greenhorn Creek Resort			
711 McCauley Ranch Road	**Golf Shop:**	209 736-8111	
Angels Camp, CA 95222	**Fax**	209 736-8264	
	www.greenhorncreek.com		
Managed by: Private, local	**Architect:**	Don Boos/R. T. Jones Jr.	

Location:	50 miles east of Stockton. Take State Rt. 4 to Angels Camp. Just before arriving in town, 1/4 mile west of State Rt. 49, turn south on Angel Oaks Drive. Follow signs the last .8 mile to the course.
Style:	Rolling terrain with some oak lined fairways. Many doglegs and tricky narrow drives. Some small greens, others much more open; lots of variation in hole design.
Other info:	Watch for Gold Country artifacts, especially on hole number 4.

Greens Fees as of 10/08:	Weekends	Weekdays	Twilight	Seniors	Carts/person
	$90	$70	$50/$40	No savings	Included

Course ratings:	Men	Par	Rating	Slope	Yardage	Women	Par	Rating	Slope	Yardage
Greenhorn Creek	Gold	72	72.9	137	6694	White	72	73.4	133	5708
	Blue	71	70.4	134	6166	Red	72	70.7	125	5192
	White	70	68.2	123	5666	Green	72	69.5	122	4882

No. 67: Fall River Valley

The town of Fall River Mills sits in the center of California wild rice country. How can a town in the mountains, 70 miles northeast of Redding, be a farming Mecca? Answer: Spring run-off from the Little Tule and Fall Rivers nurture the pastoral Fall River Valley. With Mt. Shasta at one end and ridges of the Cascade Mountains surrounding others, the 50-square-mile valley provides a seldom seen jewel in the northern part of the state. About two miles from the nearby wild rice capital, these two rivers join the Pitt River, and flow onward as a major feed into Lake Shasta.

But back in the mountains, just west of town, pumps push several hundred thousand gallons of water per day up a hundred feet or so, to the lowest reaches of steppes above the valley floor. Here, Fall River Valley Golf Course opened in 1977. Gentle slopes combine with widely spaced pines, firs, sagebrush and a few homes nestled near the clubhouse. Broad fairways and spacious roughs allow players to imagine they trod the same paths as settlers immigrating years ago thru this high desert wilderness.

The golf course beckons long hitter's from far and wide . . . fairway bunkers are rare, and the back tees can be set to over 7400 yards. Pull out the big dog, let it eat, and don't worry about a few degrees of misdirection. Oh, you do have to keep it between the widely spaced tree lines, but at 3200 ft. elevation, a nice high hard one flies quite a way. Shorter hitters will enjoy the layout too, but come time for competition, better accuracy means little when the big guns clear the trees and cut the corners. We lesser types have to settle for the beautiful high desert scenery, and compete amongst ourselves. Ladies who are strong hitters will like it too. Their tees are at almost 5900-yards, a pretty healthy distance. The greens lie fairly flat, and only a few holes require approaches over protective front bunkers.

Number one at Fall River Valley. This course is a gem, especially in the spring when snow tops the nearby ridgelines. Mt. Lassen and Mt. Shasta loom over the nearby valley.

High desert environs surround most of the front nine. Unlike the Arizona desert, which is full of rocks and cactus, Northern California's high-desert rough finds sparse vegetation and lots of sand and dust. Walking and hitting form our deserts is less treacherous than from those in the Southwest.

The back nine exhibits much more variation in both vegetation and landscape. Six holes on the upper steppe require players negotiate around lakes and their environs; and three others sit on a lower plateau, nearer natural water. This lower stretch winds through dense forest and related shrubs, bringing more need for shot finesse.

Number eighteen offers the most memorable hole on the course. It is a par-five, only 500-yards by the card, but the yardage measurement assumes shots go around a lake, not over it. The lake has an island in the middle, which looks like a nice target for an accurate iron . . . a stepping-stone for another iron to the green. But without a bridge to get there, forget the island approach. Rather, the water and its protective trees can be cleared with a high 210-yard flight (blue tees), leaving a 180-yard approach. If you can hit farther and want to cut around more trees, aim to chop off a greater portion of the lake and end up with a wedge to the green. Eighteen is the one tricky hole on a course that elsewhere is what-you-see-is-what-you-get, and an off-the-beaten-track beauty. The course is one of my *top value* personal favorites. *Review based on play and interview in April '08.*

Fall River Valley Golf Course

42889 Highway 299 East	Golf Shop:	530 336-5555
Fall River Mills, CA 96028	Fax	530 336-6005
	www.fallrivergolf.com	

Managed by:	Private, local	Architect:	Clark Glasson
Location:	East of Redding about 70 miles. Use State Rt. 299 to Fall River Mills. About one mile west of town is the golf course, on the south side of the highway. Rt. 299 has great scenery, east of the course on the way to Alturas.		
Style:	Gently rolling terrain, with mountain ridges close on the south side. Lightly forested with high desert vegetation in the deep rough. Wide fairways . . . A real big hitter's feast. Challenging approach shots to scenic green settings.		
Other info:	Nice stay-and-play package and restaurant at the Fall River Hotel.		

Greens Fees	Weekends	Weekdays	Twilight	Seniors	Carts/person
as of 10/08:	$35	$30	$30/$25	$19 Mondays	$15

Course ratings:	Men	Par	Rating	Slope	Yardage	Women	Par	Rating	Slope	Yardage
Fall River Valley	Black	72	74.7	134	7391	White	72	76	132	6539
	Blue	72	72.7	132	6988	Red	72	72.6	124	5842
	White	72	70.9	122	6539					

No. 68: Deer Ridge

The town of Brentwood is home to two co-managed golf courses located just southeast of Antioch. Extensive housing developments surround each, but unlike its cousin Shadow Lakes across the street, Deer Ridge has fewer homes along its fairways. Lying toward the back of development, the course features several holes adjacent to rural ranch-land, providing a casual, pastoral setting for the final holes.

Deer Ridge is one of the most enjoyable moderately short courses in the **Best 100**. Although the card shows a low 71.2 course rating and maximum distance of 6,300 yards, the high 138 slope means plenty of obstacles and a need for precise shots. Difficulties include creeks, lakes, strategic bunkers (especially near greens), wind blown canyons, a few hilly lies, and hard-to-read putts. Soft aprons help mitigate the dangers, and trees are rare.

Subtlety rather than harshness characterizes the shape and pattern of greens. Gentle breaks may prevent one-putts, but they won't cause balls to roll 10 feet past. Canyon breezes help more than hinder, since their prevailing direction is down-wind on long holes and upwind on short ones.

The nines at Deer Ridge differ significantly from one another. Here, the front side, reversed from the back in 2007, is the milder, easier, and less dramatic of the two. The first hole looks out-of-place---short, open, and easy to the point of being boring. But don't let it lull you to sleep. The remainders are well designed, with good contouring and a nice balance of level and sloped lies; they offer green approach shots that aren't too difficult but can still be interesting. Be careful though: a couple of lay-ups (see the free yardage book) are needed to keep drives short of trouble. Greens, fairways, bunkers, and roughs are well maintained, so poor performance can't be blamed on the course.

The real fun and beauty begin on the back nine. As before, drives need smart play to avoid trouble. Don't take any risks: hit away from or short of the bunkers and lakes, and all will be well. For example, number ten aims at an angled bunker 210-yards down the left edge, with a lake way to the right. Choose a club from the tee that hits 220 yards or less and most of the bunker will be out of reach. So what if your next shot has to travel an extra 20 yards?

Deer Ridge may have originally been a real estate venture, but you sure can't tell it on the back nine. Beautifully designed holes, like the par-five sixteenth, are found at every corner.

Bunkers add artistry and force strategic decisions at holes eleven and twelve, both beauties. Eleven appears to require a solid uphill carry, over one bunker and short of another to reach the landing zone. However, the bale-out (or safe) position to the right actually provides a better view of the green and leaves a shot of 150 yards or less. Number twelve is the prettiest hole, heading up a wide canyon, over another creek and bunker, and toward an oak tree framing the fairway in the opposite rough. The second shot requires another 195 yards up, over a long diagonal bunker short of the green. Clearing the bunker can be a thrill, but hitting too far means a very difficult downhill-sliding putt.

The remaining holes provide even more drama, created by the hills they climb and chutes that cascade back to the canyon floor. Par-five number sixteen, with its multiple descending tee boxes and five ponds closely protecting the side of the fairway, crowns the hilly stretch. With holes like these, it's no wonder that low handicappers—who may have lost a little yardage to age—love Deer Ridge. *Review based on play and interview in March '08.*

Deer Ridge Country Club

801 Foothill Drive		Golf Shop:	925 516-6600
Brentwood, CA 94513		Fax	925 516-6769
		www.deerridgecc.com	

Managed by:	SunCoast Golf, Inc.	**Architect:**	Andy Raugust
Location:	From Livermore and I-580, take Vasco Road north 17 miles (becomes Walnut St. in city of Brentwood) to Balfour. Turn left (west) and head two miles to Foothill Drive. Turn Left and follow signs. From Concord and I-680, take State Rt. 4 east to the Brentwood/Rt. 4 Bypass. Go another five miles to Balfour. Turn right (west) and go to Foothill Dr. Turn left and follow signs.		
Style:	Some holes relatively flat, others climb up into the hills. Well contoured fairways, with few trees. Homes surround bordering hillsides. Mostly wide driving areas, but tight approaches to good, big greens. Can be windy in afternoons, especially when the bay is foggy.		
Other info:	Walking OK, but some climbs. Driving range is across Balfour Rd. at Shadow Lakes.		

Greens Fees	Weekends	Weekdays	Twilight	Seniors	Carts/person
as of 10/08:	$63	$36	$35/$25	$28 weekdays	$12

Course ratings:	Men	Par	Rating	Slope	Yardage	Women	Par	Rating	Slope	Yardage
	Black	72	71.1	137	6302	White	71	71.5	130	5344
Deer Ridge	Blue	72	69.2	132	5866	Gold	71	68.5	120	4775
	White	72	66.2	122	5344	Green	70	67.3	116	4539

No. 69: Peacock Gap

Real estate costs in Marin County have been breaking the bank for years. Scarcity and expense make local golf courses few but usually very good. Located in eastern San Rafael near Point San Pedro, Peacock Gap is the southernmost eighteen-hole public course in the county. Because of its longevity and proximity to San Francisco, it's well known. It joins San Geronimo, Indian Valley, StoneTree, Adobe Creek, and Rooster Run as the highest-quality public courses, serving northern San Francisco, Marin and southern Sonoma counties.

The Peacock family once owned property just north of the course and gave its name to a natural pass between the surrounding hills. The course lies in the valley below, land that was once marshland off northern San Rafael Bay.

Like an adjacent estuary, the course underwent a major modernization project and re-opened in late '07. Golf Solutions, the firm that owns the Wigwam and Biltmore Resorts in Arizona, purchased Peacock Gap in 2004. After extensive study they decided to (1) renovate the course; (2) re-build, upgrade, and expand the clubhouse; and (3) add new private members. With course re-construction complete, the rest of the plan awaits economic recovery. Current selling points include the completed construction on holes five through nine and new green complexes on the remaining thirteen. Additional fairway bunkers and re-planted fairways were added as a bonus. Tall rye grass now dominates certain focal points, further adding to the visual appeal. These improvements upgraded course quality and are reputed to have cost $6 million.

The distinctive appearance of the new greens highlights the updated course image. Number seven, a brand new 300-yard par four, boasts a two-level green where tiers are separated by a steep four-foot drop. You had better make sure to hit the right level! Number ten, a short 130-yard par-three, contains a whirlpool-shaped indentation in its middle, about a foot deep and 10 feet across. Pins placements around the edge of the vortex make for very interesting putts, especially across its depression. Number fourteen, the most extreme green in the **Best 100,** should probably be remodeled again. Not only did the designer subtly tier its large surface, but a three-foot trench runs diagonally from front left to back right. Putting across this trench reminds me more of miniature golf rather than the real game.

One of the Best 100's most unusual greens sits on Peacock Gap's short par-three number ten. The indentation in the middle is over a foot deep and makes for interesting putting challenges at pin placements around it.

The most distinctive hole comes at 435-yard number eleven. This dogleg requires a long drive be threaded between out-of-bounds hills on one side and a creek close by on the other. It then turns 30 degrees, 200 yards from the green. Tall bunkers guard both sides of the putting surface about 20 yards in front, but playing short of them leaves a 50-yard chip to the pin. The narrow green contains plenty of defenses, attributed to a slope on the right, bunkers and mounds on the left, and a hump in the middle. This very difficult hole definitely makes the **Best 100** list of toughest par-fours.

The next phase of the project planned by Golf Solutions—replacing the old clubhouse—received city approval in mid '08. Scheduled along with additional parking is a new private clubhouse complex with restaurants, a pool, locker rooms, and exercise rooms. The range will be renovated to include expanded putting, short-game practice, and teaching areas. A public pro shop and eating area near the range are also planned. The completion date wasn't available at the time of this printing. But at least we know that the course renovations are complete. *Review based on play and interview in September '08.*

Peacock Gap Country Club and Spa

333 Biscayne Drive		**Golf Shop:**	415 453-4940
San Rafael, CA 94901		**Fax**	415 485-0743
		www.peacockgapgc.com	
Managed by:	Golf Solutions	**Architect:**	William Bell

Location:	Take U.S. 101 or I-580 to San Rafael. Exit Central San Rafael and take 2nd St. south. Continue when it merges with 3rd and again when it becomes Point San Pedro Road. Drive on four miles from the 3rd St merge to Biscayne Dr. Turn left there and go .4 miles to clubhouse on the left.
Style:	Flat terrain with a small hill on the western perimeter. Several sloughs and drainage ditches criss-cross fairways. Landing areas are reasonably wide, but doglegs and bunkers add interest. New greens have unique terracing and slopes.
Other info:	Golf course remodel completed in late 2007.

Greens Fees	Weekends	Weekdays	Twilight	Seniors	Carts/person
as of 10/08:	$75	$65	$60/$50	$50 weekdays	$15

Course ratings:	Men	Par	Rating	Slope	Yardage	Women	Par	Rating	Slope	Yardage
	Champ.	71	70.6	127	6261	Blue	73	76.0	135	6355
Peacock Gap	Compet.	71	69.9	125	6101	White	73	74.0	131	6000
	Challenge	71	68.3	123	5792	Red	73	71.9	126	5621

No. 70: Shadow Lakes

The city of Brentwood, about 10 miles southeast of Antioch, contains more good courses in a new community than any I know. Four of them, all within five miles of each other, include Shadow Lakes, Deer Ridge, Roddy Ranch and Brentwood. Only the Monterey Peninsula comes close to having such a dense radius of quality courses—and these in Brentwood are priced-to-play.

Shadow Lakes sits near the top of this group, second only to Deer Ridge, across the street. The course construction finished in 2001, as the kick-off for a major housing development. Homes border some fairways, but only intrude into photos, not the actual game itself. SunCoast Golf Inc., took over management from Troon Corp in 2007, and now oversees both Deer Ridge and Shadow Lakes. Annual members pay for playing rights at both facilities.

Shadow Lakes offers a good test, made tougher after 1:00 pm by strong Delta breezes. The local topography features rolling grassy hills, with steep climbs and descents on some shots. Trees come into play too, but usually on holes near creeks at the base of gentle ravines. At first glance, the course appears a bit scruffy. However, on closer inspection, what seems to be blemishes are merely grasses and vegetation of a contrasting darker color, not dead spots. In fact course maintenance is quite good, if one understands the unusual grasses just represent the designer's personal style choice.

The hills may not be tall but can really impact strategy and difficulty. The first such encounter takes place on par-five, number six, locally named *Diablo Grande*. The 550-yard, uphill climb goes straight at Mount Diablo and into the prevailing wind. Add fairway bunkers that are so deep only a wedge can be used to get out, and this hole never seems to end. The second steep hole comes at number twelve. It's shorter, only 340-yards, but after an uphill drive—and avoiding a bunker at the dogleg—one still has a 125-yard approach up another 40 feet. The green's false front, sends many a short shot fifty yards back downhill for another try.

Up, up and away on par five number six at Shadow Lakes. After clearing the lake on your drive, beware of bunkers and steep lies chasing the ball uphill towards Mt. Diablo.

The final major hill encounter comes on another short par-four, number sixteen. This time the shot heads *down* to a landing area, then across a lake sitting about 225-yards from the tee, into the wind. After a lay-up drive comes a 150-yard approach along a narrow isthmus-like fairway to a peninsula green. The wind and narrow shank of land make a risky combination.

Shadow Lakes ends up a good experience because the hills give challenges, holes vary in design, and both fairways and greens are kept in good shape. Its weakness (unless you ride in carts), comes from long walks between green and tee, often uphill, Delta winds can also be harsh. Some holes have level fairways, but many do not, so if you hate side-hill lies, neighboring Deer Ridge may be your better choice. *Review based on play in March '08.*

Shadow Lakes Golf Course

401 West Country Club Drive	**Golf Shop:** 925 516-2837
Brentwood, CA 94513	**Fax** 925 516-2045
	www.golfinbrentwood.com

Managed by:	SunCoast Golf, Inc. **Architect:** G. R. Baird
Location:	From Livermore and I-580, take Vasco Road north 17 miles (becomes Walnut Rd. in city of Brentwood) to Balfour. Turn left (west) and head 2.5 miles to W. Country Club Drive. Turn right and follow signs. From Concord and I-680, take State Rt. 4 east to the Brentwood/Rt. 4 Bypass. Go another 5 miles to Balfour. Turn right (west) and go .3 miles to W. Country Club Dr. Turn right and follow signs.
Style:	Hilly terrain, with some steep downhill drives. Links type style due to lack of trees and firmness of fairways. Greens and fairways well guarded by bunkers. Lakes on several holes.
Other info:	Can be windy especially strong when SF has fog.

Greens Fees as of 10/08:	Weekends	Weekdays	Twilight	Seniors	Carts/person
	$75	$50	$45/$35	No savings	Included

Course ratings:	Men	Par	Rating	Slope	Yardage	Women	Par	Rating	Slope	Yardage
	Black	71	72	136	6577	Silver	71	74.2	134	5884
Shadow Lakes	Gold	71	70.5	134	6251	Jade	71	71.4	124	5250
	Silver	71	68.9	128	5884					

No. 71: Monarch Bay, Tony Lema course

Want a little touch of Scotland right here in our own backyard? The Tony Lema course, at San Leandro's Monarch Bay, gives an affordable way to experience links golf—American style. Just ten miles from downtown Oakland, Monarch Bay offers easy access, avoiding a costly ten-hour flight across the Atlantic.

Several features make this course special: The wind, the bunkers and tall thick grasses certainly associate it with the likes of Troon and Muirfield. Also gorgeous views of our own San Francisco Bay contain every bit the drama of those at St. Andrew's beach. On clear days, both the San Mateo Bridge and downtown San Francisco seem close enough to touch. And the bay just waits to catch extremely errant shots.

Tony Lema's links-like appearance comes on property that is as flat as a pancake. Builders moved a lot of dirt out of the estuary environment to create sculptured bunkers, elevated greens and above-sea-level fairways. More recently, management added heavy marsh grasses around tees and other visually prominent spots, to augment the British Isle texturing. In actual play, the long, tufted vegetation interferes little with normal shots; you'd need to dribble drives off the tee or hit well off line to be impacted.

Course maintenance is good. Firm, smooth fairways sit the ball up nicely for easy woods and irons. Short roughs look good too, not too heavy, but with variation in density depending on sprinkler coverage. Greens with consistent firmness have the shape and character one might expect on a links course.

San Francisco and the entire SF Peninsula sparkle brightly on clear days at Monarch Bay's well designed links-style course. Illustration based on photo courtesy of the golf course.

Number seven, a 200-yard par-three into the wind, flaunts a long, narrow multi-tiered, elevated green. Steep, deep bunkers flank the putting surface, so approaches just a little off line require difficult sand recoveries. Its tough, Scottish-like test makes the **Best 100** list of toughest par-threes.

Monarch Bay's greatest challenges come when approaching unusual pin positions, over deep, well-placed bunkers. To gain these experiences properly, players must choose the correct set of tees, at the outset of the game, so the approach shots are set at the right distance. Medium-hitting golfers usually find the white tees too short because success on a 145-yard seven iron gives more joy than success on another ordinary wedge. In addition, the front tees eliminate opportunities to hit drives over water and also bring too many distant bunkers into play. On the other hand, inexperienced golfers should definitely play the whites because they will want to clear the heavy grasses frequently located between tee and fairway.

Unless you want a truly windy challenge, schedule an early starting time or choose a very warm day. Otherwise, as one might expect on the bay, wind can create havoc. Under such conditions even a short course can turn into a beast. *Review based on play several times, last with interview in August '07.*

Monarch Bay, Tony Lema Golf Course

13800 Monarch Bay Drive		**Golf Shop:**	510 895-2162
San Leandro, CA 94577		**Fax**	510 895-0221
		www.monarchbay.americangolf.com	
Managed by:	American Golf	**Architect:**	John Harbottle
Location:	Take the Nimitz Freeway, *i.e.* Interstate 880, to Exit 33A/Marina Blvd. Follow Marina Blvd west two miles to merge with Monarch Bay Dr. Go south another .6 miles and make u-turn to the course.		
Style:	Flat terrain, modified to image of a links style design. Deep bunkers protect fairways and greens. Greens often elevated and can have extensive breaks. Few trees.		
Other info:	Beautiful panoramic views of San Francisco Bay. Location on the shoreline is often windy.		

Greens Fees	Weekends	Weekdays	Twilight	Seniors	Carts/person
as of 10/08:	$61	$39	$35/$25	$25 weekdays	$14

Course ratings:	Men	Par	Rating	Slope	Yardage	Women	Par	Rating	Slope	Yardage
	Tourn.	71	73.5	125	6937	Member	72	75.0	127	6061
Monarch Bay	Champ.	71	71.8	122	6567	Resort	71	71.8	121	5502
Tony Lema	Member	71	69.1	118	6061	Forward	70	69.8	117	5143
	Resort	68	66.6	112	5502					

No. 72: Rancho Cañada West

Rancho Canada's two courses, the East and the West, launched operations in 1970. They sit near the throat of Carmel Valley and provide players the closest of three public golf venues just east of the Monterey Peninsula. For the other two, Carmel Valley Ranch and Quail Lodge, head further inland. All three border the Carmel River, but don't expect a flowing torrent and swampy backwaters in this valley. The river sometimes fills in winter but usually dries to a trickle by May. The Cañada name (pronounced *can-ya-da*) originates from the 4366 acre Mexican land grant, Rancho Cañada de la Segunda, that covered hills and valleys south of the river.

Carmel Valley's climate suits golfers to a tee. Situated on an east-west axis, the farther east (inland) one travels, the warmer temperatures become, at least in summer months. At Pebble Beach, which is on the ocean, summer temperatures may read low 60's F, yet ten-miles east they can be in the 90's. Fortunately, humidity stays low year-round, both along the coast and inland. Rancho Cañada's location, near the western entrance to Carmel Valley, generally avoids the extreme readings mentioned above. In summer, fog dissipates between 10:00 am and noon to an average mid-70's temperature.

Those who want real warmth must drive farther east and pay higher prices at the more expensive resorts.

Rancho Cañada caters to the high volume public crowd, specializing in low priced (for the area) individual play, plus business and convention tournaments. Of its two courses, the longer West Course shows more challenge and character than the East. Tournaments usually play on the West, though the East Course serves as back up for large groups and multiple round events.

Both courses show similarities: The same gracious grooming provides good quality greens, fairways, bunkers and roughs, and each makes multiple crossings of the 50-yard wide Carmel River. However, the West uses more tree-lined fairways, more bunkers, and longer yardages, increasing Slope and Course Ratings by one to three points.

For years number fifteen on Rancho Cañada's West Course has been its most memorable hole. Recently limbs were trimmed from the tree on the left front of the green, finally opening an easier approach shot.

Because of the more interesting challenges, plus a few unique holes, the West Course gets more play. In late spring, summer and early fall the Sycamore and Cottonwood flaunt their leaves, and the course plays at peak quality. Pines, cedars, live oaks and other non-deciduous trees cover most California courses, but Rancho Cañada offers one of the few **Best 100** courses where seasonal foliage shows its color. Tree with leaves, right in the heart of Monterey Pine country . . . how unique!

The West course's style appears traditional, with medium-width fairways and only minor graded contours. Par-fours vary in length from 300-yards to 440-yards. Longer ones have broad fairways, but watch out because

164

overhanging trees do catch crooked drives. Short 300-yard number thirteen looks simple on the card, and can be birdied easily if you hit the 20-yard wide landing area off the tee. But miss it and nasty bunkers portend an easy double bogey.

Big hitters usually reach the fairly easy par-fives in two. Their sculpted doglegs may be nicely designed, but trees and bunkers at the corners only keep short hitters honest.

Most players remember the West for its ultra narrow fifteenth hole. A few years back, the approach shot on this 370-yard par-four was so tight, the opening between tall trees was only five to ten-yards wide. Going under or over limbs was the only practical shot. Nowadays, the gap has been widened to 25-yards, still narrow by most measures. This hole has been has been a symbol for the good quality thousands have found at Rancho Cañada over the years. New players, looking for a good, traditional style course, should enjoy it too. *Played last in September '08.*

Rancho Cañada Golf Club, West Course

4860 Carmel Valley Road		**Resort:**	800 536-9459
P. O. Box 22590		**Golf Shop:**	831 624-0111
Carmel, CA 93922		**Fax**	831 624-6635
		www.ranchocanada.com	

Managed by:	Private, local · **Architect:** Robt. D. Putnam
Location:	Drive south from Monterey on State Rt. 1 to Carmel Valley Road. Turn left (east) and go one mile to course entrance on the left.
Style:	Flat terrain. Fairways are closely bordered by asorted varieties of fully grown trees and cross the Carmel River several times. Greens are well trapped and course is in good condition. Best to play here when leaves are on the trees in late Spring and Summer.
Other info:	Fog usually lifts by 10:00 or 11:00 am in summer. Try on-line specials for savings.

Greens Fees as of 10/08:	Weekends	Weekdays	Twilight	Seniors	Carts/person
	$70	$70	$40	No savings	$18

Course ratings:	Men	Par	Rating	Slope	Yardage	Women	Par	Rating	Slope	Yardage
Rancho Cañada	Bleu	71	70.6	124	6349	White	72	75.0	127	6116
West	White	71	69.2	119	6116	Red	72	72.1	121	5600

No. 73: Pheasant Run

Back in 1999, real estate development was hot and heavy in the San Joaquin Valley. Pheasant Run Golf Course is situated at the center of housing tracts on the north side of Chowchilla and became a draw for buyers considering a move. Its location, just north of the junction of State Rt. 152 and State Rt. 99, is convenient from any direction in the region. Unfortunately, vast housing tracts now sit partially foreclosed, devalued by the '08 recession. A year later, one can only hope that the homes and the course survive in the same fine condition I observed in early '08.

The houses may look commonplace to anyone driving by, but the course behind the gates off Avenue 26 certainly isn't. Fine playing conditions are the result of a long nurturing process, and on that April day I played, Pheasant Run offered the most lush springtime fairways and roughs of any central valley **Best 100** course south of Merced. Fairways sown with a mixture of ryegrass and *poa anna* were cut just right. Balls sat up well, yet the turf's soft texture allowed club heads to swing easily through the ball. Wide rye roughs were evenly cut and had few bare spots. Hitting out may not have been easy, but thickness and consistency made the course both tough and ready for serious golf. Nine years after its completion, the course has finally matured sufficiently, in the minds of its developers, to qualify for open tournament play.

The back tees stretch 7,350 yards, far enough for almost anyone. However, even at this enormous distance, the Slope rating runs a low 129. The contrast between long distance and low slope says a lot about the style of the course. Only three fairways have bunkers that could affect drives, and few trees stand close enough to make big hitters nervous. But this doesn't mean boomers have free reign: the thick rough stops long rolls and makes for heavy recovery shots. Sparkling lakes and ponds can cause havoc as well, but overall, par-fours and par-fives require less finesse than on many shorter courses.

The par-threes are different, building character while creating difficulties due to water, length, elevated greens and roller-coaster putts. Number four, for example, is one of the prettiest, toughest over-the-water shots around. Driving distance ranges from 200 yards at the back tees to only 90 for women, and shots have to carry the full distance to stay dry. The green sits on a peninsula surrounded on three sides by lakes, with a large bunker in front. The prevailing 20 mph headwind can easily ruin a good shot. But too much club, and you're over, in the water behind. Despite a relatively flat putting surface, this hole makes our list of toughest par-threes.

While Pheasant Run certainly looks lush, its holes nonetheless display a certain sameness. Long, straight par-fives start each nine; short, tricky par-fives end each side. Par-fours, except for the number fourteen around a lake, have long, unmemorable designs. The biggest difference between them seems to be whether a hole heads into the wind, across it, or back down the other way. Walkers should be prepared for long hikes from green to tee, adding over a mile to the usual five-mile stroll.

Players who want the freedom to hit their drives hard, who swing strongly enough to escape from the rough, who appreciate good greens and like the variation caused by changing winds, should definitely place Pheasant Run on their play list. *Review based on play and interview in April '08.*

Pheasant Run Golf Club		
19 Clubhouse Drive	**Golf Shop:**	559 665-3411
P. O. Box 788	**Fax**	559 665-1970
Chowchilla, CA 93610		
	www.pheasantrungolfclub.com	
Managed by: Sierra Golf Management	**Architect:**	Richard Bigler

Location:	37 miles northwest of Fresno, just off State Rt. 99. Take Ave 26 exit, just north of Chowchilla, and head east one mile to course entrance on the right.
Style:	Flat terrain graded to provide contours and slopes for fairway perimeters and greens. Wide laidng areas and several water holes with big greens. Long walks, often on paths between homes, to find the next tee. Trees provide decent shade in summer.
Other info:	Very green course, kept well watered and in nice condition.

Greens Fees as of 10/08:	Weekends	Weekdays	Twilight	Seniors	Carts/person
	$49	$32	$39/$22	$22 weekdays	$13

Course ratings:		Men	Par	Rating	Slope	Yardage	Women	Par	Rating	Slope	Yardage
	Black	73	75.1	129	7322	White	74	76.7	132	6247
Pheasant Run	Blue	72	73.3	123	6851	Gold	73	74.2	126	5864
	White	70	70.9	117	6289					

No. 74: Rooster Run

Years ago Petaluma boasted the label *Chicken Capital of California*. But growers and processors moved off to lower cost fowling grounds in the Central Valley or Arkansas, as land values soared in the Bay Area. The name Rooster Run is one of the few remains, an acknowledgement to those good old days. It's also one of two Petaluma public golf courses, both located in the southeastern part of town.

Back in 1998 bulldozers and heavy grading equipment transformed flat farmland into a golf sanctuary, full of lakes, trees and undulating hillocks. After only 10 years it has matured into one of Sonoma County's best courses.

Rooster Run possesses a bit of a split personality. Its pastoral section flourishes with reeds, cattails and water fauna such as geese, ducks, turtles, frogs and the occasional skunk. However, megalopolis also shows its face, especially if judged by commute traffic on U.S. 101, about a mile away. The city environment impinges the course itself, with busy East Washington Street splitting the layout in half. The back nine contains a long narrow stretch of fairways, with the western set bordering the Petaluma Municipal Airport, and the eastern set against local vineyards. Fortunately, designer Fred Bliss camouflaged the airport well, as extensive tree-cover provides wide screens for playing areas. Besides, golfers don't pay much heed to the quiet small planes; rather, their minds are busy trying to remember the idea some buddy gave them on how to hit the ball straight or win a bet on the final few holes.

Rooster Run is a good test for those who like its 7000-yard maximum length, or just want a nice walk in the park from shorter tees. Reasonably wide fairways find minor mounding in adjacent roughs and follow a seemingly natural flow through curves on each hole. Good course maintenance provides soft fairway lies, at least in the summer. Close-cut roughs make finding balls easy, and long rough-recovery shots can be easily managed despite the longer grass. Management boasts that the fairways drain better here than anywhere else in the area, so winter play is popular. The course range offers real turf-grass, making warm-ups and practice more realistic than on mats.

The real interest at Rooster Run is the extensive system of water hazards. Lakes line many of the holes, but few find normal clean-cut edges. Rather most are bordered and even filled with various styles of vegetation: Marsh grasses provide a soft texture, around the perimeters. Lily pads, and other flowering plants often extend far into the water. Finding balls in these grasses may be neigh impossible, but the bucolic design element seems to make local fauna happy. Long rye grasses also surround some bunkers, complementing the feathery texture of the lakes.

One hole, short par-three number six typifies the style. Water surrounds the green, almost making an island. Website www.hookedongolf offers a very nice description with photos of the short 130-yard venture. Fortunately, the hosts' antics about how tough the hole plays are highly exaggerated.

Poplars define just one shot, to the eighteenth green–on Rooster Run. The rest of the course is chock full of reeds, cattails and ponds, and ten year-old trees need more time to mature.

A word of caution . . . calm air usually prevails in the morning, but winds whip-up in afternoons, especially during summer. The layout directs the last four finishing holes straight north, into the breeze; and they become very difficult in these conditions. Some local golfers suggest that Windsor Golf Club, fifteen miles north might be a less windy choice on summer afternoons, whereas Rooster Run would be preferable the rest of the year. The same private company manages both **Best 100** courses. *Review based on play and interview in August '08.*

Rooster Run Golf Course

2301 East Washington Street	**Golf Shop:**	707 778-1211
Petaluma, CA 94954	**Fax**	707 778-8072
	www.roosterrun.com	

Managed by:	Private, local		**Architect:**		Fred Bliss	
Location:	15 miles south of Santa Rosa. Take U.S. 101 to Petaluma's East Washington St. exit. Head east one mile to the course. Clubhouse is on the north side of the street.					
Style:	Flat terrain between local airport and vineyards. Lakes and marshes added for a wonderland of wetlands. Bull-rushes everywhere. Medium width fairways and nicely mounded greens.					
Other info:	Sister course to Windsor, 25 miles north. Can be windy on summer afternoons.					

Greens Fees	Weekends	Weekdays	Twilight	Seniors	Carts/person
as of 10/08:	$58	$38	$39/$27	$27 weekdays	$14

Course ratings:	Men	Par	Rating	Slope	Yardage	Women	Par	Rating	Slope	Yardage
	Tournament	72	73.8	136	7001	Regular	72	73.5	127	5855
Rooster Run	Champ	72	71.3	129	6462	Forward	71	70.1	118	5139
	Regular	72	69.0	120	5889					

No. 75: Metropolitan

Salt-flats south of Oakland Airport have long been used to entertain golfers in the East Bay. Originally, the course adjacent to the airport access road was named Galbraith, but in the early nineties, a couple of major infrastructure projects necessitated big changes. The airport needed a new runway, and the seaport needed new shipping channels. The two huge construction ventures needed a place to store acres of excess bay bottom fill. Galbraith's fairways were sinking into an old garbage dump anyway, so its property provided a logical spot. Besides, any new course would need better sub-soils to stabilize the old landfill. When the channel and runways were finally completed, Johnny Miller hired on to design a brand new venue. Earthmovers went to work sculpting the landscape and created an excellent foundation. Oakland even got a bonus from the new material. It was mostly sand, perfect for draining rainwater off a wet golf course. Today the course operates one of the better all-weather golf locations in the Bay Area.

Metropolitan, as it was renamed, gives players a good test. Miller and the builders created links-style mounds, strategically placed lakes, a couple of drainage creeks, and well-graded greens. Except for the views, players feel they are playing a flat course in the British Isles. Add decent maintenance, and plenty of ball grabbing bunkers near tee shots landing zones, and one ends up with a challenging yet playable venue. When the afternoon bay breeze picks up, as it almost always does, a true links experience ensues.

Johnny Miller has designed several other courses throughout Northern California including some of our toughest. The Bridges, Eagle Ridge, Brighton Crest and StoneTree come to mind; but Metropolitan does *not* fit the same style. Rather, it's flat terrain, with only moderate mounding, make it much easier than his hilly cousins. As a municipal course, it's intended to suit all levels of golfer at a reasonable price. The length can extend to 7000-yards, plenty for most. The

6500-yard blue tees also present a good challenge, depending on wind speed and direction.

One hole in particular, plays very tough when a storm wind blows from the south. Par-four number fourteen, a 400-yard-plus dogleg, starts with a series of bunkers on the bend in its dogleg. A good drive still leaves a long iron or fairway wood, over a deep creek located just in front of the elevated green. Only the best of approach shots will make this distance into the wind. Even those who choose a lay-up second, must work carefully to hit the third far enough to carry the sharp slope that falls back into the creek. Bunkers and mounds protect the rest of the steeply breaking green, making par an extremely satisfying score.

Management at Metropolitan seems to control maintenance wisely. They try to concentrate water, fertilizer and handwork on tees, drive landing zones, aprons, bunkers and greens. This process yields the occasional dry spot in-between, but is a good trade-off.

Unusual grasses force players to be careful in certain spots. In the rough these tufts look relatively harmless, but that's an illusion, especially on par-fives. Balls can easily be lost under rye-grass adjoining various landing zones. Even when coming to rest on top of the mats, spongy, intertwined grass blades usually grab club heads, twist their swing angle and ruin shots. It's frustrating to end up with double bogey when par appeared so attainable.

A bonus is the pictorial beauty and convenience of the course location. It borders the airport, but not so closely that the buildings or roads distract. Rather they act as a visual focus for the activity of an energized and bustling metropolis—hence, the name Metropolitan? San Francisco and Oakland skylines also appear close at hand from a few vantage points, adding to the theme.

This combination of attributes creates an extremely popular venue. UC Berkeley uses the course to tune up their golf teams; alumni have even built a private practice area. Amateur tournaments also use the links. This creates one serious problem; play can be onerously slow, despite the best-stated intentions of the pro-shop. So prepare yourself for a long day even starting as early as 9:00 am. *Review based on play and interviews in November '07.*

Metropolitan Golf Links

10051 Doolittle Drive	**Golf Shop:**	510 569-5555
Oakland, CA 94603	**Fax**	510 562-6129
	www.playmetro.com	
Managed by: CourseCo	**Architect:**	Johnny Miller

Location:	Adjacent to Oakland airport. Take I-880 to Hegenburger or 98th St. Head west towards airport. Turn left at Airport Access Rd. Then, at Doolittle Drive turn left again and course entrance is on the right in 1/4 mile.
Style:	Flat terrain along the Bay with sloughs, lakes and a few trees. Long matted grass at edges of several roughs. Wide fairways, lots of bunkers, nice big undulating greens.
Other info:	Can be windy along the bay. Busy course so it can play slowly. Nice views of Oakland, its airport, and even San Francisco.

Greens Fees as of 10/08:	Weekends	Weekdays	Twilight	Seniors	Carts/person
	$62	$40	$37/$25	$35 weekdays	$16

Course ratings:	Men	Par	Rating	Slope	Yardage	Women	Par	Rating	Slope	Yardage
	Black	72	73.8	131	6959	White	73	73.8	124	6069
Metropolitan	Blue	72	71.8	128	6529	Red	72	71.0	118	5565
	White	72	69.8	121	6069	Gold	72	68.5	114	5099

No. 76: Coyote Creek, Valley Course

The Valley Course at Coyote Creek is a classic tree-lined design. Jack Nicklaus updated the layout in the early '00's by adding shallow fairway contouring, new bunkers and modern-style greens.

Coyote Creek operates a modern two-course golf complex, located adjacent to U.S. 101 in southern San Jose. It's probably best known for easy visibility from the freeway, or because the Tournament Course hosted a stop on the PGA Champions Tour. But in fact, it offers a lot more. The excellent clubhouse works well for banquets and post tournament celebrations, and the practice facility is one Northern California's best.

More importantly, the Valley Course is now open and fully operational. It offers something unique to public golfers in the south bay . . . an old fashioned, flat terrain, heavily tree lined golf course. No other Santa Clara County venue really comes close to this classic style of play. Years ago known as Riverside Golf Course, the older grounds were completely renovated, re-routed and upgraded. The renamed Valley Course offers the feel of bang-em-down-the-middle golf. Want fewer doglegs, mature oaks and pines, level lies, an occasional creek, tiny changes in elevation, and a course that has good, fair greens? This could be your choice.

The lakes and rolling hills prevalent at the Tournament Course may be missing, but your experience on the Valley will not be dull. Nicklaus & Company took the old Riverside Course, added minor contouring to fairways, put in a few strategic, visually aesthetic bunkers, and modernized the greens. They also added a couple of brand new holes to lead the old course to and from the new common clubhouse. No buildings or homes line fairways or greens; and neighboring U.S. 101 has no impact on play.

Choosing the best holes on this track is not easy because wind-direction has such an impact on playability. Normally breezes come from the north and can average 10-25 mph, especially in the afternoon. In these conditions number two, a medium length par-three with a bunker in front middle of the giant green, creates a tough shot into a links-like setting. Number sixteen, one of the few long shots over a lake, and numbers one, three, and five, also offer scenic and imposing challenges into a down-valley north-wind. Tree-lined fairways are reasonably wide, but the wind amplifies any hook or slice. If breezes switch to the south, holes number seventeen and eighteen, both par fours, head straight into it, making the finish very difficult.

Except for the omnipresent air movement, playing conditions on the Valley course are excellent. Greens, bunkers, roughs and aprons all receive good manicuring. Walking used to be easier though, because the new hole sequences introduced long distances from green to tee.

The ambience and old-time style of the Valley Course are a treat. If you can afford the relatively high greens fees, put it on your list of places to try again in the Santa Clara Valley. *Review based on play and interviews in August '08.*

Coyote Creek Golf Club, Valley Course

1 Coyote Creek Golf Drive		Golf Shop:	408 463-1400
San Jose, CA 95037		Fax	408 463-8318
Mail to:	P.O. Box 2527	www.coyotecreekgolf.com	
	Morgan Hill, CA 95038		

Managed by:	Castle & Cook Properties	Architect:	Jack Nicklaus
Location:	Southern San Jose, along U.S. 101. Take 101 to Coyote Creek Exit. Turn west and follow signs to the course.		
Style:	Flat terrain. Classic style: Fairways are lined by mature trees of various varieties. Well maintained, Greens are terraced, sloped and well protected by nicely shaped bunkers.		
Other info:	Adjacent to Tournament Course, managed out of same clubhouse. Walking relatively easy except long distances from green to tee. Less crowded than Tournament Course.		

Greens Fees as of 10/08:	Weekends	Weekdays	Twilight	Seniors	Carts/person
	$102	$80	$75/$68	$60 weekdays	$17

Course ratings:	Men	Par	Rating	Slope	Yardage	Women	Par	Rating	Slope	Yardage
Coyote Creek Valley	Blue	72	74.6	129	7048	Gold	73	76.1	133	5863
	White	72	71.2	126	6431	Red	72	69.8	117	5187
	Gold	72	68.2	121	5863					

No. 77: Dairy Creek

Half way between San Luis Obispo and Morro Bay, just north of State Rt. 1, sits Dairy Creek, the southern-most course in the Northern California Golf Association (NCGA). It joins Hunter Ranch, Avila Beach, Monarch Dunes and Cypress Ridge as **Best 100** ranked courses along the Central Coast.

The eleventh at Dairy Creek in San Luis Obispo shows off the rolling terrain and park-like setting of the course. Aim towards the high side of each fairway to keep the ball in play.

Rolling grass-covered hills and a county park provide the backdrop for a course design that has plenty of interest and all the walking exercise a golfer could want. The layout starts down one hill, back up another, then across, around and up, on a continuing array of well conceived, circuitous adventures. Fairways sown with well-matted Bermuda grass create a very firm hitting-surface. Environmentally protected creeks or wetlands often border landing zones. Hit the ball into the rough and hard, hilly, dry ground causes balls to roll far off line into trouble. Fairways have few crowns, and usually slope sharply in one direction or the other. This means drives should be aimed towards the high side of the slope almost at the cart path, so balls roll to the center rather than the rough on the low side or down into a creek.

Back tees at Dairy Creek measure a short 6500-yards, so success comes from either strategic course management of the medium length hitter, or long blasts of the big guys, who can play it accurately with driver and wedge. Everyone needs to be careful, because several holes have creek-crossings that force lay-ups, unless you can hit the ball over 270-yards on the fly. For instance, number two requires a drive be aimed way left on the upper side of the fairway. Anything landing on the lower side of center rolls into the creek on the right. Even balls hit on the high side of center, roll down to the lower rough, and add significant elevation to the second shot; balls hit too long increase crooked rolls even further because of steeper drop-offs. Number eleven, another scenic but restricted driving hole, requires drives to stay short of a diagonal creek. Other creeks cross at awkward spots in front of greens on par-fives ten and thirteen—they force players to lay up, or risk shots across to tiny landing areas.

The ten-year-old course was built by modern standards, so drainage works well and greens stay in good, often fast condition. It is located about five miles from the coast, so winds are not quite as strong as at nearby Morro Bay, but can still whip up in the afternoon. All and all, it's good, fun, and very reasonably priced roller-coaster golf, worth playing if you're in the area. *Review based on play in June '09.*

Dairy Creek Golf Course

2990 Dairy Creek Road		Golf Shop:	805 782-8060
San Luis Obispo, CA 93405		Fax	805 782-8054
		www.centralcoastgolf.com	

Managed by:	Fairway Management	**Architect:**	John Harbottle

Location: Halfway between San Luis Obispo (SLO) and Morro Bay, on State Rt. 1. Take U.S. 101 to Rt. 1 (west) exit near downtown SLO. Follow signs to Rt. 1 west. Drive 5 miles to Dairy Creek Rd exit. Turn right and then quick left to stay on Dairy Creek. Clubhouse is 1/4 mile off Rt. 1.

Style: Hilly grasslands. Many fairways are slopedand firm that so shots need to be aimed at edge to roll back to middle. Greens well shaped and bunkered.

Other info: Many discount plans available.

Greens Fees	Weekends	Weekdays	Twilight	Seniors	Carts/person
as of 10/08:	$45	$36	$24/$20	$26 weekdays	$16

Course ratings:	Men	Par	Rating	Slope	Yardage	Women	Par	Rating	Slope	Yardage
	Gold	71	72.0	129	6548	White	71	73.6	128	5561
Dairy Creek	Blue	70	69.9	127	6103	Red	71	70.5	121	4965
	White	69	67.6	119	5561					

No. 78: Eagle Vines

Eagle Vines Golf Club, the newest of Napa's public golf courses, has received good press since opening in 2004. Its location sits adjacent to Chardonnay Golf Club, near the junctions of State Rts. 12 and 29, about 5 miles south of Napa. Ten of the holes should be familiar to those who played Chardonnay in the late 90's, since they formed part of its Shakespeare course.

Today, only a split rail fence separates holes between the two competing facilities.

Holes purchased from the prior landlord had been some of its best and now form the nucleus of the newer course. These include two excellent par-threes, both over water, one illustrated below to a peninsula style green. Other picturesque water holes include par-five eleven with two lakes and par-four number four.

The latter hole, played from either set of rear tees, presents another of the toughest par-fours in the **Best 100.** It's a dogleg left, around and over a lake to a green set on the side of a hill. The tee shot must steer right of the water, and the long approach reach up to a well-bunkered green. Even near the green, putting and chipping remain difficult because a long slope separates two narrow tiers. Putts on the correct level break sharply, cementing the challenge of each and every shot.

Number six at Eagle Vines is one of the Best 100's *most dramatic par threes, especially when the pin is placed on the back left peninsula position.*

Good and tough as these holes are, Eagle Vines cannot compare to the condition of holes next door at Chardonnay. Tees on the imported holes appear worn and some give un-even stances. P*oa anna* greens have a blotchy appearance, and show irregular grainy breaks in the afternoon. The deep primary rough grows wild. Whether a matter of style, environmentalism or money, this newer course appears less tailored than its neighbor.

Another peculiarity comes from the contrast between the newer holes and those purchased and integrated into the course. The newer fairways appear relatively flat, with little or no grading or undulation; few bunkers provide definition to fairways; and many greens have reasonably level surfaces with minimal mounding among the aprons. These features show stark contrast to the rich textures, undulations, folds and furrows of holes number 2, 3, 4, 5, 6, 7, 8, 9, 11, and 12, all purchased from next door.

That is not to say the newer holes play easy. They have length, bordering vineyards and water to make up for missing contours and bunkers. Some younger architects might even argue that the natural-look of the newer holes is the way of the future, whereas the embellishments of the older ones are *passé*. Such a minimalist style may work well if the natural terrain shows enough variation and character to give good shot making challenges. But the inconsistency seen at Eagle Vines, makes most of the newer set appear quite bland and ordinary. *Review based on play in August '08.*

Eagle Vines Vineyards and Golf Club

580 South Kelly Road		Golf Shop:	707 257-4470
Napa, CA 94558		Fax	707 257-4476
		www.eaglevinesgolfclub.com	
Managed by:	Private, local	Architect:	J.Miller/J. Barry
Location:	Next to Chardonnay GC, 8 miles north of Vallejo, near junction of State Rts. 29 and 12. From Rt. 29, go east on Rt. 12 to first light, S. Kelly Rd. Turn right (south) and course entrance is 1/4 mile on the left. From I-80, take Rt. 12 exit or Red Top Rd (to Rt. 12) and head west on Rt. 12 five miles. Turn left on S. Kelly Rd. and course is 1/4 mile on the left.		
Style:	Hilly terrain amongst the vineyards. Some holes are rather plain, open and long. Others are contoured, edged with deep rough and bordered by elegant landscaping or lakes. Greens have lots of character and terraces, usually well bunkered.		
Other info:	Can be very windy on days when the SF Bay is foggy.		

Greens Fees	Weekends	Weekdays	Twilight	Seniors	Carts/person
6/08	$90	$65	$75/$50	No savings	Included

Course ratings:	Men	Par	Rating	Slope	Yardage	Women	Par	Rating	Slope	Yardage
	Black	72	75.3	140	7250	White	72	76.8	135	6359
Eagle Vines	Blue	72	73.4	135	6819	Red	72	73.2	128	5652
	White	72	70.6	125	6359					

No. 79: Plumas Lake

Marysville and its twin city, Yuba City, sit across the Feather River from each other, about 45 miles north of Sacramento. Plumas Lake Country Club is about 10 miles south of town, in the midst of what used to be the Feather River flood plane. The original nine, built in 1928, sat near a lake, Plumas Lake, that no longer exists. Over the decades, flood abatement programs and levee construction have eliminated flooding and related features (unless a levee breaks). By 1960, another nine came on-stream to finish off the design. Hopefully the course name only reminds us of the old days.

Plumas Lake gets mixed commentary from local players, depending on the skill level of those playing it. Golfers will encounter some quite unique and controversial features. Chief among these are new greens built in late 2006, where breaks can be quite severe. Also, the locations of certain trees force players to make abnormal shots, either directly over or directly under large, fully mature oaks. Finally, some members complain about poor course maintenance. In the end, I liked the course and here is why . . .

First, the greens: The summer of 2006 contained a two-week stretch of 110+ degree F days, highly unusual for the Sacramento Valley. The heat severely stressed several golf courses and Plumas Lakes took some of the biggest hits. All of its greens died because their *poa anna* grass could not handle the heat. Even when wet, the roots cooked. Club members could not afford the estimated $50,000 plus to rebuild each green to USGA specs, and instead hired Greenway Golf to implement an alternative approach. For about half the replacement cost, the company re-mixed and augmented existing sub-soils of the old greens with a significant amount of new sand, and then re-contoured the surfaces. The new Bent grass requires steeper than normal slopes to promote fast drainage, since the subsoil was not up to spec. This approach created unusual greens, ones with smooth, reasonably fast surfaces that use less water than before. Maintenance crews needed extensive retraining to learn where— and where not—to place pins fairly on the undulating slopes, and players groused loudly until the learning process finished.

As for the trees: Golfers, usually those with higher skill levels and lower handicaps, like to face new and different challenges. Plumas Lakes tries to accommodate. The most notable challenge comes at hole number nine, a short par-four. About halfway down the middle of the 340-yard fairway sits a small grove of full-sized oaks. A lay-up drive doesn't work since the next shot cannot fly high enough or long enough to clear the trees and reach the green. The logical alternative is a low shot with a half-driver or long iron that skips *under* the oaks. Even then, the approach shot may also have to be hit low, if the drive doesn't land in precisely the right spot. Later, another hole, number eleven, presents a different challenge over full sized eucalyptus. It's a sweeping 370-yard down-then-up dogleg, where the drive must carry very long to have a clear, short approach. Most players can't do this, so the second shot must be hit directly over the eucalyptus. Fortunately, an uphill lie helps, and the green is big; so a good swing can succeed if it also clears a deep front greenside bunker. What a thrill when it does!

As to course condition: By June 2008, Greenway seemed to be doing a fine job. The course was in good shape when I played in the early summer. Many courses have had to make management changes when funding is not available, to bring maintenance conditions up to standards of the **Best 100**. Hopefully, the good results will continue at Plumas Lakes.

One final personal comment . . . Don't pre-judge the quality of this course by the beat-up road leading to it. Given the high quality of some nearby homes and the improved condition of the course, perhaps Yuba County can make an investment of their own and re-pave the ratty stretch starting at Feather River Road. *Played in June '08.*

Plumas Lake Golf and Country Club

1551 Country Club Road	**Golf Shop:**	530 742-3201
Olivehurst, CA 95961	**Fax**	530 742-4382
	www.plumaslake.com	
Managed by: Greenway Golf	**Architect:**	Bob Baldock

Location:	10 miles south of Marysville. From the north: take State Rt. 70 to Riverside exit. Follow it south, where it becomes Feather River Blvd. Continue 8 miles to Country Club Ln. Turn left to golf course. From the south, take State Rt. 99 to Rt. 70 (north). Go 9 miles to Feather River Road turnoff. Head left (west, then north) 6 miles to Country Club Rd. Turn right to the course.
Style:	Mostly flat terrain with a few swales and slopes. Tree lined fairways, including some severe doglegs. A couple of drives must be aimed over or under trees. Unusual highly sloped medium sized greens.
Other info:	Semi-private course. Can get soggy in the winter.

Greens Fees as of 10/08	Weekends	Weekdays	Twilight	Seniors	Carts/person
	$32	$25	$21/$18	$19 weekdays	$13

Course ratings:	Men	Par	Rating	Slope	Yardage	Women	Par	Rating	Slope	Yardage
Plumas Lake	Black	71	71.1	126	6422	White	72	74.2	131	5760
	Blue	71	70.2	123	6159	Red	72	69.8	122	5115

No. 80: Pine Mountain Lake

Pine Mountain Lake is a gated community on the way to Yosemite via State Rt. 120 out of Manteca. It's located a few miles east of Groveland, above lake Don Pedro and the infamous Priest Grade. This grade, a twisty five-mile uphill stretch of the highway, climbs 1,500 feet. It used to be considered a tough drive, but with modern vehicles the steep climb only takes about 12 minutes; and road improvements make it okay for most cars. The course sits in the center of the development, a drive of 50 minutes from Sonora and 90 minutes from Modesto or Manteca. That's not far for valley golfers trying to beat the heat at a true mountain-style venue.

Pine forests surround the 3,000+ homes behind the gates, but the oak trees down in the small valley are what really affect play on the course. White oaks, live oaks, and blue oaks seem to thrive on the flatter basin of the 2,400-foot elevation. While the layout requires walking up some hills, most climbs are found around the clubhouse, and walking out on the course is easier than I expected.

Hole number one gives Pine Mountain Lake its signature view. Beginning with a steeply elevated tee, this downhill dogleg heads to a lower plateau and lake, providing a nice photo-op along the way. Next, huge oaks dominate the dogleg right at number two, and number four offers a par-five I remember from playing 30 years ago. Its drive heads across a steep hillside and has to find a soft landing spot to keep from rolling down into the trees. The next shot continues farther around the hill, to a hollow in front of an amply bunkered green. In the past 10 years, irrigation upgrades have softened the fairways to keep them green year-round and those downhill bounces have been reduced. Now, if you aim towards the upper edge, the ball usually rolls safely into the middle.

Par-five number sixteen begins a climb back up from lower levels at Pine Mountain Lake. Oaks closely line the hole, which has views of the High Sierra ridges in the background.

Number eleven, a steep, downhill 489-yard par-four dogleg left deserves the designation *best hole* at Pine Mountain Lake. Prevailing winds come from behind and the drive descends nearly 100 feet from the back tee to the down-sloped landing zone, so just let'er rip! After the fun drive, the second isn't so easy. A spruce tree guards the dogleg's corner and hooking the 200-yard approach around the tree from your downhill stance is not easy. For this reason, most approaches end up in bunkers lining the right side, short of the green. The remaining 40-yard bunker shots have to land on the right level of a double-tiered green, another difficult task. The combination of a fun drive and the demand for a skilled approach shot(s) makes this hole an unusually good adventure.

Other designs are interesting because of the varied rolling terrain. Trees line most fairways but are set wide enough apart to keep balls in play. Greens and aprons can be tricky because of their firmness. Knowledgeable players use run-up shots to bounce on—a rare requirement of playing in Northern California.

Although Pine Mountain Lake is a public access course, with a gracious pro shop staff, the club has a large local private membership. Some members' attitudes are like those encountered at elite country clubs, *i.e. . . . . what's that stranger doing here?* Just bring your own friends, smile at the regulars, and remember . . . it's their course. *Review based on play twice, most recently with interview in April '08.*

Pine Mountain Lake Country Club

12765 Mueller Drive	Golf Shop:	209 962-8620
Groveland, CA 95321	Fax	209 962-5302
	www.pinemountainlake.com	

Managed by:	Private, local
Location:	In a Gated Community 50 minutes south of Sonora. Take State Rt. 120 southeast towards Groveland. Turn left on Ferretti Rd and go 1.3 miles to Mueller Drive. Turn right on Mueller and clubhouse is 1/3 mile down the road on a steep sidehill slope.
Style:	Hilly terrain at the base of a mountain canyon, with oak lined fairways. Greens are small with some well bunkered. Maintenance has improved in recent years. Several elevated tees. Greens can be firm, requiring chip and run or roll-up approaches.

Greens Fees	Weekends	Weekdays	Twilight	Seniors	Carts/person
as of 10/08:	$68	$41	$13 weekdays, late	No savings	Included

Course ratings:	Men	Par	Rating	Slope	Yardage	Women	Par	Rating	Slope	Yardage
Pine Mountain Lake	Blue	70	70.3	128	6314	White	73	74.4	133	6041
	White	70	69.1	126	6041	Red	72	72.7	129	5625
	Red	69	67.1	119	5625	Gold	72	68.5	120	4988

No. 81: Mare Island

Years ago wild horses lived on a Mexican land grant owned by General Marino G. Vallejo. Legend has it they used to swim across the Napa River seeking refuge on Mare Island to bear their foals. That quarter mile swim created quite a scene for early settlers and earned the long, narrow island, adjacent to the old California capital city of Vallejo, a name that sticks to this day.

When statehood came, Spanish land grants were transferred to U.S. government ownership, and eventually Mare Island went to the US Navy. In 1892, the first 18-hole golf course west of the Mississippi was built on the rocky bluffs at the southern end of the island, and it stayed in operation until WWII. At that point, the northern nine holes were bulldozed to make way for Marine barracks. Soon after the war, Mare Island became a repair and retrofit station for the Navy, and a submarine pen for both conventional and nuclear powered vessels. Then, defense cost cutting came along, catching the station in its web. The U.S. Navy left, and the golf course was sold to the civilian community. In 2000 owners deemed the remaining nine-hole layout insufficient for growing golf demand, so a second nine, designed by Nelson & Hayworth, came back into being. Once again Mare Island became a distinctive modern 18-hole golf course.

Except for its short 6150-yard length, the course acts as a good competition test, and is another of the real surprises I found in researching this book. The old holes are carefully crafted, with interesting fairway contours and an aura similar to that of Presidio Golf Course in San Francisco. Nicely placed mature trees and well-located greenside bunkers force drives to be accurately aimed for easier approaches to small greens.

Refined scenery dominates these older less elevated holes. Nearly every one has a differing vista of adjacent San Pablo Bay and many have subtly outlined views of old munitions assembly buildings, weathered much like barns on old farm homesteads. Good golfing conditions prevail too, with nice fairways and decent rough, unless shots are far off line onto hardpan. Greens are a little slow, but Touchstone Golf, LLC, is working to speed them up.

Number sixteen is just one of many picturesque scenes on this hilly back nine of Mare Island. What you can't see is the 20-30 mile an hour delta breeze that buffets balls on many afternoons.

The front side has two particularly special holes, both par-threes. Number three gives a wonderful, old style links-type design. A 190-yard shot heads downhill through a trough of stubby brush to a tiny green and backdrop of salt marshes and the East Bay waterfront. Then, number eight requires a 210-yard, uphill shot, to a highly elevated green. The drive must clear a broad pond, and climb about 50 feet to the top of a hill, beyond which sits a steep drop to out-of-bounds. Strong breezes coming off the bay make gauging distance for this long shot a real challenge.

On the back nine, San Pablo Bay breezes really start to take a toll. This newer side has steep hills and fewer trees. Greens and tees perch on top of undulating hillsides. The holes go across canyons, up steep fairways, or down precipitous drops. None measure ultra long, but all appear harrowing from their elevated tees, narrowing the appearance of fairways below. In actuality, landing areas are reasonably wide. The winds, however, blow much stronger on these hills than on lower tree protected slopes of the front nine. Keeping the ball on-line becomes very difficult. Add the distraction of spectacular panoramic views of the SF Bay, neighboring downtown Vallejo, the Napa River ship terminals (see the illustration on the prior page), and Benicia's refineries across the Carquinez Straight . . . and golf at the top of Mare Island is quite an experience.

The new holes on this course may not be for everyone. They are hilly, and approach shots need to be hit over steep, deep bunkers fronting every green. But for players who like to test their short and medium iron play, there is no better, more economical place to do it, and 2008 midweek play was quick. Its location, close to other popular challenging venues such as Hiddenbrooke, Eagle Vines and Chardonnay, is very convenient, so Mare Island would make a very good, less expensive change of pace. *Review based on play and interview in August '08.*

Mare Island Golf Club

1800 Club Drive	**Golf Shop:**	707 562-4653
Mare Island, Vallejo, CA 94592	**Fax**	707 562-8891
	www.mareislandgolfclub.com	

Managed by:	Touchstone	**Redesign Architect** Robin Nelson
Location:	On south end of old Navy Base near Vallejo. From the north: Take State Rt. 29 south to State Rt. 37. Head across bridge to Mare Island exit. Go South on Walnut St. for .7 miles. Turn right on G St. then immediate left on Azuar. Go another 1.2 miles to Club Drive. Turn right to clubhouse. From all other directions take Tennessee exit off I-80 and head west 3 miles. After crossing bridge, go to Azuar and turn left. Follow it 1.2 miles to Club Drive and turn right to clubhouse.	
Style:	Hilly terrain. Front nine is older style, short and tight with tree lined fairways. Back nine is new, extremely hilly, with few trees, lots of wind and steep shots both up and down.	
Other info:	Course has magnificent views of the Bay, the East Shore and Vallejo docks. Men's slope and rating are way understated.	

Greens Fees as of 10/08:	Weekends	Weekdays	Twilight	Seniors	Carts/person
	$44	$30	$22/$16	$20 weekdays	$14

Course ratings:	Men	Par	Rating	Slope	Yardage	Women	Par	Rating	Slope	Yardage
Mare Island	Blue	70	70.4	124	6150	White	70	76.0	126	5788
	White	70	68.7	122	5788	Red	70	71.4	117	5336

No. 82: Laguna Seca

Imagine two of the country's best golf architects, father and son, collaborating to build one course. Near the outskirts of Monterey, Robert Trent Jones Senior and Junior joined in 1970 to build on property next to the famous Laguna Seca racetrack. Jones Sr. finished Spyglass in 1966, and Junior was finally out on his own, re-designing Silverado (North) and creating Silverado (South). At Laguna Seca, Senior started the work and Junior finished it.

Monterey Peninsula and Carmel Valley are known for their famous but pricy golf venues. Pebble, Spyglass, Spanish Bay, Quail Lodge and Carmel Valley Ranch all cost well in the hundreds of dollars for a morning summer round. Laguna Seca Golf Ranch gives golfers a lower cost way to have a good game and enjoy a few days in one of the world's most picturesque vacation spots. Its pedigree includes hosting small, but well-known events, such as Spaulding and Callaway tournaments in the 1970's. The California Match Play Handicap Championships also used the course earlier this decade.

Its location offers a major weather advantage over courses located on the Monterey Peninsula or near the ocean. Deep fog banks often shroud coastal areas in the summertime, but when Pebble Beach is covered in low clouds, Laguna Seca is usually clear by 10:00 to 11:00 am.

Today, most amateur and professional tournaments have moved on, but Laguna Seca still features its original quality layout, plus upgrades and improvements. Recent bunkers rebuilds and green renovations keep the course in good shape. Drainage improvements added yearly help with winter play, and the large driving range/practice area is scheduled for a beautification effort in 2009. Kikuyu grass impinges on several fairways but an eradication experiment will be tried on a couple of fairways in the winter of '09. Management wants to research this new treatment before extending it to the entire facility.

Your first shot on Laguna Seca heads down a short par-four towards an oak covered ridge. Though not long, many holes have twists and hazards that keep the game interesting.

Fairway layout at Laguna Seca is well conceived, though rather twisted. The course sits on a low ridge of hills at the edge of a narrow valley. The clubhouse perches near the top, so the first hole heads down, and the ninth comes steeply back up. In between, front nine fairways aren't exactly flat, but flow gently through the moderately rolling oak covered terrain. They stay well maintained and each displays a different look. Some use sharp doglegs and elevated greens, others reveal long, mildly sculpted fairways that wind through hillocks or along a creek at the edge of the property. Course total yardage, even from the rear blue tees, runs only 6161-yards, so most players find it a relaxing encounter.

The back nine is hillier, more challenging, and players find several tricky/difficult holes. Number ten starts with a blind drive to a narrow, turning fairway, followed by a long approach over a tall oak and gully. It's an abrupt contrast to those meandering fairways on the prior nine. Five holes later comes another killer, this time a par-five, where drive and second shot are both tightly bounded by trees and creeks. Its last two shots negotiate hilly lies and cross a couple of lakes. Players hitting balls square and straight will be OK, but those heading crooked will have big problems. Other holes on this nine have lots of character in doglegs and elevation change, but are much more forgiving.

Except for the Kikuyu grass, the course is in good shape. Fairways have medium softness, so drives roll well, yet irons cut easily through the turf. Maintenance crews rake bunkers at least every other day and trim them neatly. Short roughs make finding errant shots easy. The perimeter of the property has some hardpan, but only to keep the oaks healthy from over-watering. Mounded aprons have been created to add extra challenge to the short yardages. Similarly, greens stay smooth and at moderate speed. However, if a big tournament needs them to be fast, double cutting can be arranged.

Overall, Laguna Seca is a decent value, in a convenient location, on a nicely maintained—if somewhat quirky—short course. *Review based on play many times, last with interview in September '08.*

Laguna Seca Golf Ranch

10520 York Road	**Toll free:** 888 524-8629
Monterey, CA 93940	**Golf Shop:** 831 373-3701
	Fax 831 373-3899
	www.lagunasecagolf.com

Managed by:	Private, local **Architect:** R. T. Jones Jr. & Sr.
Location:	Take State Rt. 68 from either State Rt. 1 in Monterey, or U.S. 101 in Salinas. Course is 5 miles east of Monterey Airport. Turn north on York Rd. and go to top of the hill. Veer right and follow it to the end. Clubhouse is 1.1 miles from Rt. 68 turnoff.
Style:	Some hills, but mostly rolling terrain. Nicely contoured fairways and well shaped greens. Trees, a couple of lakes, and OB stakes keep long hitters honest.
Other info:	Joins Rancho Canada program of big greens fee discounts to frequent players.

Greens Fees	Weekends	Weekdays	Twilight	Seniors	Carts/person
as of 10/08:	$65	$65	$35 weekdays	No savings	$18

Course ratings:	Men	Par	Rating	Slope	Yardage	Women	Par	Rating	Slope	Yardage
	Black	71	70.6	132	6174	White	72	72.6	127	5683
Laguna Seca	Blue	71	69.8	129	6007	Red	72	70.2	122	5190
	White	71	68.3	127	5683					

No. 83: Mount Shasta Resort

Set deep in the mountainous lower forests of Mt. Shasta, holes number four and eleven aim straight up at the mountain's peaks.

Planning a drive to Bandon Dunes for a cold, wet, windy, pure-links experience? Stop on the way to Oregon at Mount Shasta Resort, or on the way home at Lake Shastina. These courses will give you the opposite encounter—great weather in a glorious mountain setting.

Mount Shasta Resort is the southern-most of these two courses located near the base of iconic Mt. Shasta. It's on the southwestern slopes at an elevation of 3500 feet, about 2 miles from downtown Mount Shasta. The design of the fairly new course, built in 1993, comes from Jim Summers (who also helped design StoneTree in Novato) and Sandy Tatum (the San Francisco golf impresario who has been a part of several Northern California golf projects). Whereas Lake Shastina uses a meadow-oriented layout, Mount Shasta rightfully claims a mountain moniker. Forests line fairways all the way, with many holes going up or down the slopes. The trees may restrain views of Mt. Shasta and nearby mountain ranges, but when you do see them, fairways frame the peaks in spectacular fashion.

Except for Apple Mountain, Tahoe-Donner, and Northstar, all reviewed earlier, tree lines throughout are narrower than at any other course in Northern California. The short layout, at about 6000-yards from the tips, 5700 from the whites and 5100 for ladies, is as tight as they come. For example, the first hole, a 511-yard downhill sharp dogleg requires a 225-yard drive that, if hit too far, ends with a blocked second shot. Even with a perfect drive, the second scoots through a tunnel of pines only thirty yards wide, headed steeply downhill. A 200-yard shot can roll the 300 yards to the green, but hit five yards right, and you're in a greenside bunker; hit five yards left, and find a trap well short. Long hitters can try to cut the dogleg with a three-wood off the tee, but they need skill and experience to know exactly what they are doing. Their drive heads over the middle of the forest, praying its the right distance and headed at the right tall tree. And this is just the first hole!

The toughest and perhaps best hole on the course is number four, a very long par-five. Its tee box and fairway have one of those fabulous views of Mt. Shasta. The drive must be straight and very long, so the view is somewhat distracting. Even a strong straight shot can leave a long second, which must fly up-hill over 200-yards, with a fade, just to clear a deep ravine. A lay-up is possible instead, but that makes it four shots for most of us to reach the green. Even after clearing the ravine, another 160-yards remains, steeply uphill to the bunker protected green. Most pros can't reach the green with two very long, very straight shots, so this is another of the **Best 100's** toughest par-fives.

Mount Shasta Resort will be enjoyed immensely by golfers who hit the ball straight, even if they don't hit it far, despite difficulties on number four. It's in great shape starting around June 1. Long hitters can test risk/reward chances on certain holes, but need guidance before doing so. They also need to shorten up on many holes. The greens may be its biggest defense against attack by those who know it well. They have multiple minor terracing that wreaks havoc when rolled firm for tournament play.

Beginning players, who do not hit the ball consistently in the direction intended, will not have much fun. If that's you, head up Interstate-5 to Weed and play wider fairways at Lake Shastina. *Review based on play and interviews in April '08.*

Mount Shasta Resort

1000 Siskiyou Lake Blvd.	**Resort:**	800 958-3363
Mount Shasta City, CA 96067	**Golf Shop:**	530 926-3052
	Fax	530 926-0333
	www.mountshastaresort.com	
Managed by: Private, local	**Architect:**	Summers/Tatum

Location:	60 miles north of Redding at base of Mt Shasta. 3500 ft altitude. Take Central Mount Shasta Exit off I-5, and head west over the freeway. Turn left at Lake St and go to end. Turn left onto Old Stage Rd. It becomes W.A. Barr Rd. Go 1.2 miles and turn left on Siskiyou Lake Rd. Resort and clubhouse are on the right.
Style:	Very hilly course in the thick of the forest. Narrow fairways, often up or down a moderate slope. Trees force shots to be straight. Creeks and lakes also come into play. Not easy to walk.
Other info:	Fairways and greens in very good condition. A few outstanding views of Mt. Shasta.

Greens Fees	Weekends	Weekdays	Twilight	Seniors	Carts/person
as of 10/08:	$55	$45	$35/$25	No savings	$15

Course ratings:	Men	Par	Rating	Slope	Yardage	Women	Par	Rating	Slope	Yardage
Mount Shasta Resort	Blue	70	68.1	129	5721	White	71	70.1	130	5309
	White	70	66.0	126	5309	Green	70	67.9	122	4897
						Gold	70	66.6	118	4653

No. 84: Mountain Springs

Mountain Springs is an appropriate name. This Sonora course combines lakes, some of which are spring-fed, and lots of hilly topography, to create peaceful views of the surrounding foothills and ridges. Pine and fir forests may not adjoin the property, but enough oak and other trees, plus local ridgelines, make players know the true Sierras peak a few miles east up State Rt. 108.

Four years ago, Mountain Springs would not rank in the **Best 100** but a lot has changed. As with many other Northern California courses, owners recognized that dry, weedy, hilly venues no longer attracted the golfers they sought. The 1990's brought new concepts in golf course design, and renovation became a necessary competitive tool. Mountain Springs added a modern irrigation system and hired new maintenance management to put the course in good shape. These changes allowed big improvements. Fairways now contain pure grass, not a weedy combination; it's cut so the ball sits up nicely, yet rolls a decent distance. The watered roughs look good and the hills have been softened to prevent rolls that used to kick balls into hazards. Greens too, are in good condition, reasonably firm, and kept at a Stimp speed between 9 and 10. Some display double tiers, but with elevation changes of only a foot or so. Putting is easier and truer than on many newer courses around the state.

New tee boxes were added too, to eliminate blind drives and improve line-of-flight to diagonal fairways. Awkward shots that once aimed across hills instead of into them, such as on numbers one and four, were to be eliminated. Unfortunately, these new tees now sit weed covered, since funding for irrigation never materialized.

Regardless of the changes and plans, Mountain Springs remains a very hilly layout. Nearly every fairway on the front nine has a severe up-slope, making walkers work hard. Only one hole, number sixteen, presents a flat, straight 350-yard par four. Usually I would call such a hole dull, but here it's a godsend, a rare relaxing respite from the many bends, curls and un-level lies found elsewhere. Best advice for the newcomer--closely follow the layout guide printed on the scorecard. It gives correct guidance on how to play holes from the white tee-blocks. Without it, distance and direction on many drives would be quite confusing.

Par-fives on Sonora's Mountain Springs are the pride of the course. This one, number fourteen heads down a series of rolling side hill lies and then abruptly left around trees to the green.

Par-fives, especially from the black 6559-yard tees, are a special treat, and really make Mountain Springs a memorable and worthwhile venture. The drive at par-five number six must carry about 215-yards to cross a steep swale. If you don't make it, your uphill stance on the second shot will just go straight up in the air. Number fourteen looks at a beautiful 550-yard side-hill fairway, into the breeze, where the green hides behind a bend and creek at the end of a tree line (see illustration above). And number eighteen ends with an uphill stance for a medium/short iron to a green about 50 feet above the fairway. It serves a final reminder that you *are* climbing towards the high Sierra. *Review based on play several times, last with interviews in June '09.*

Mountain Springs Golf Club		
17566 Lime Kiln Road	Golf Shop:	209 532-1000
Sonora, CA 95370	Fax	209 532-0203
	www.mountainspringsgolf.com	
Managed by: Private, local	Architect:	Robt. Muir Graves
Location:	Sonora sits 1 1/2 hours due east of Stockton. Take State Rt. 120 east to State Rt. 108 and follow signs for Sonora. Once there, turn right (south) on Lime Kiln Rd. Take it back up the hill 3.2 miles to club entrance on the right.	

Style:	Hilly terrain at elevation of 1600 feet. Level lies are a rarity. Many dogleg fairways, usually reasonably wide. Course has a few trees, but they are widely spaced. Greens often elevated and some have mild terraces. Aprons usually mounded.
Other info:	Clubhouse on an open hill with nice views of pastoral gold country topography. See website for stay and play packages.

Greens Fees as of 10/08:	Weekends	Weekdays	Twilight	Seniors	Carts/person
	$40	$27	$22/$16	$17 Mon, Tues	$15

Course ratings:	Men	Par	Rating	Slope	Yardage	Women	Par	Rating	Slope	Yardage
Mountain Springs	Black	72	72.0	131	6529	Gold	73	72.5	127	5592
	White	72	70.1	125	6149	Red	71	70.0	122	5169
	Gold	71	67.6	119	5592					

No. 85: Avila Beach

The town of Avila Beach sits in a small valley tucked between old volcanic hills next to the Pacific Ocean. About five miles south of San Luis Obispo, and three miles north of Pismo Beach, the local turnoff from U.S. 101 is near southbound driver's first views of the Pacific Ocean, since crossing the Golden Gate Bridge 225 miles north. The delightful resort course offers many holes adjacent to the town's access road, so it's hard to miss. The tenth tee and practice green abut the town dog-beach between the Avila Beach piers.

Years ago known as San Luis Bay Golf Club, the course was at one time financially connected to resort condos perched above the entrance drive. It is now separately owned, and managed privately in tandem with Blacklake Golf Resort in Nipomo, 15 miles south. The adjacent condo's, called the San Luis Bay Inn, now affiliate with Interval International, a worldwide timeshare exchange organization. Their lodging provides an excellent hub for exploring surrounding San Luis Obispo County.

The course location is a real plus for golf too. Not only is it near the small local town, with nice lodging and good restaurants, but also nearby mountains create a wind block and a wonderful microclimate. It's said to have calmer winds, and a beach clearer of fog than others nearby. Downside is that it gets more rain, but since California's Central Coast is so arid, what are a few more inches per year?

Avila Beach Golf Resort is one of the five courses reviewed in the **Best 100** that, by rule, are not part of the Northern California Golf Association (NCGA). Monarch Dunes, Cypress Ridge, Blacklake, Rancho Maria and Avila Beach are all south of the latitude, which the NCGA and SCGA chose as their jurisdictional dividing line. In this book, we take the broader view that the City of Santa Maria, about 30 miles south of Avila Beach, is a more logical break point for the southern border of Northern California.

Avila Beach is a resort course, designed for all levels of player. Downhill par three, number seven, is one of the more scenic shots on a course nestled in a canyon bordering the Pacific Ocean.

The course is fun to play, with plenty of character and enough water hazards to keep players alert. Its moderate length allows good times and good scores for short/straight hitters. In the winter, when the fairways turn a dormant color, balls get good roll; but in the summer the dominating tough Kikuyu grass grows a healthy green and slows everything down. A few years back they tried to eradicate this grass variety, but even a foot of silt from a flood couldn't prevent it from regenerating. For the time being, they have given up and live with it.

The front nine has more hills than the back, and straight shots become especially important. Number two is probably the toughest hole for men, and makes our **Best 100** list of toughest par-threes. It's 200 to 230-yards long, depending on the tee, up a slope, to a green elevated even further. Drives must clear a bunker 40-yards short of the green, and then bounce up even further. (Such bounces are nearly impossible to find on the heavy Kikuyu grass.) Those capable of flying it to the flat green, often find balls roll over the back.

The next seven holes also have plenty of ups, downs and side hill lies; and numbers four and seven require lay-up drives to stay short of lurking trouble. Several greens find large, deep bunkers directly in front, and make distance control important too. The best hole on the course, or at least the most unusual, is number five. It is a 360-yard par-four that can easily play over 400-yards. The fairway doglegs around a hill where a tiny 20-yard wide plateau offers the landing area that shortens distance to its 360-yard published length. However, most drives bounce off-line down to the base of a hill, still in play but about 30 feet below green level. The elevation and crooked bounce add significantly to the approach distance and, if it's then hit a little short, the ball rolls halfway back to your feet.

The back nine exhibits level terrain, but four holes deal with a tidal estuary that dominates landscape on this side. Hole number eleven, a short par-five, is unusual because the fairway cuts through an excavated narrow gap in the middle of a small hillside, suggesting a two-lane road once followed the same route. The final hole on this side, though not long at 350-yards, requires a drive clear 150 to 200-yards of water. This can be a real challenge at the end of a long round when the sea breeze blows directly into your face.

Avila Beach is an enjoyable resort course, with excellent greens, and good maintenance. Like Laguna Seca up in Monterey, it's a bit quirky, with twisted holes, abrupt elevation changes and some difficult hazard placements, but keeps pace with the area's growing golf reputation. *Review based on play several times, last with interview in February '08.*

Avila Beach Golf Resort

6464 Ana Bay Drive		**Golf Shop:**	805 595-4000 ext. 1
Avila Beach, CA 93424		**Fax:**	805 594-4002
		www..avilabeachresort.com	

Managed by:	Private, local **Architect:** Desmond Muirhead
Location:	Just south of San Luis Obispo. Take U.S. 101 to Avila Beach Exit. Follow Avila Beach Dr. three miles to Ana Bay Dr. Turn right and signs point the way.
Style:	Front nine mildly hilly with a stream running throughout. Back nine mostly flat, alongside San Luis Creek; crosses wide expanses of water on several holes. Moderate size greens, not too many bunkers. Drives often required to be straight due to water hazards, hills or trees
Other info:	Partners with Blacklake Golf Resort in Nipomo (20 miles south) for lodging and greens fees.

Greens Fees	Weekends	Weekdays	Twilight	Seniors	Carts/person
as of 10/08:	$70	$56	$50/$40	$58/$48	$17

Course ratings:	Men	Par	Rating	Slope	Yardage	Women	Par	Rating	Slope	Yardage
Avila Beach	Blue	71	72.3	138	6580	White	71	75.8	135	6053
	White	71	69.6	130	6053	Red	71	70.3	121	5041

No. 86: River Island

River Island Country Club is located near Porterville, in the southern central valley Sierra foothills. Its riverside setting, about 60 miles due north of Bakersfield, features the NCGA San Joaquin Valley Area's southernmost course. Back in the '60s, when it was a private club, many holes occupied an island between two separate channels of the Tule River. But floods occurred and player growth stopped. Today, the island is gone and the course is semi-private. Almost 70 percent of play comes from the public-at-large.

In keeping with the trend to upgrade and modernize golf courses, River Island is in the midst of a major renovation project overhauling green complexes. After an eight-month hiatus, the front nine re-opened in May '08 with brand new putting surfaces, bunkers, and aprons. A couple of greens were moved to more challenging or scenic locations, and all underwent some reconstruction. The project was so well planned and implemented that I didn't realize it had just been finished, until the interview after my round. Firmnesses varied and the new bunker sand was fluffier; otherwise, the nines seem utterly unified in style and playability. Similar back nine renovations are scheduled for mid-'09.

Another of the Best 100's unusual par three eighteenth is framed by the Tule River for the 140-yard final shot at River Island in Porterville.

The course features two distinct hole styles, intermingled between the nines. Half of the holes, including those that start and finish each nine, are set along the river. Large cottonwoods, oaks, bay trees, and pines form a dense shield along the riverbank, protecting wildlife from ball-searching golfers. Fairways incorporate old berms and ancient riverbanks as an essential character in their layout. One of these banks sits at an angle halfway up number ten's fairway, so that an accurate draw or hook (from a right-hander) will bound around the corner of the dogleg, quite close to the green. On number eighteen, the same bank forms a steep down-slope about 220 yards from the blue tees. A decent drive rolls halfway down the slope to an awkward lie, so experienced players lay-up short and hit much longer approaches across the river.

The other half of the course, away from the river, has a different character. One stretch on the front nine comes following a cart tunnel under State Rt. 190 to the north quadrant of the property. Here, rolling, oak-covered hillsides provide classic foothill topography, with new greens strategically placed beyond ponds and canyons. Number seven, a 215-yard par-three at the end of the stretch, heads into the breeze from the rear tee. I needed a strong driver to reach the bunker-guarded green.

Yet other holes, such as thirteen and fourteen, lack personality. The trees are still immature and fairways are flat and shapeless. Perhaps the planned overhaul will correct this incongruity and bring lesser holes up to the standard set elsewhere at River Island. *Review based on play and interview in June '08.*

River Island Country Club

31989 River Island Drive
Porterville, CA 93257

Golf Shop:	559 784-9425
Fax	559 782-1735

www.riverislandcc.net

Managed by:	Private, local
Location:	Course is an hour north of Bakersfield. From State Rt. 99 take State Rt. 190 east 27 miles to River Island Dr./Rd 320. Turn right and follow signs. Course is 11 miles past junction with State Rt. 65.
Style:	Rolling riverside terrain with lots of oaks bordering the fairways. Greens protected by trees and new bunkers. Lots of shots played across the Tule River.
Other info:	Non-member play limited to afternoons on most days.

Architect: Robt. D. Putnam

Greens Fees	Weekends	Weekdays	Twilight	Seniors	Carts/person
as of 10/08:	$55	$55	$55	No savings	Included

Course ratings:	Men	Par	Rating	Slope	Yardage	Women	Par	Rating	Slope	Yardage
River Island	Blue	72	73.5	135	6910	Red	72	73.1	130	5665
	White	72	70.6	129	6364	Red-short	72	72.9	129	5632

No. 87: Dry Creek Ranch

Twenty miles north of Stockton, straddling State Rt. 99, lies the town of Galt. Readers may wonder if the name has anything to do with John Galt, the hero of Ayn Rand's *Atlas Shrugged*. The answer is "no." John McFarlane, an emigrant from Canada, named Galt after his hometown in Ontario.

But this small crossroads of 20,000 widely scattered citizens possesses other distinctions. It hosts well-known festivals throughout the year, and customers from all over the Central Valley attend Galt's semi-weekly flea market. The town seems to have more freeway exits per resident than any other municipality in the region (six on Rt. 99; another from I-5), and in 1982, readers of the *San Francisco Examiner* voted Dry Creek Ranch the Best Public Golf Course in Northern California.

A few things have changed since the poll. The *Examiner* merged with the *Chronicle*, millions of people moved into the state, and 85 additional eighteen-hole public golf courses were built in Northern California. In other words, both the competition got tougher and the character of the voters changed. That doesn't mean that the quality of golf at Dry Creek Ranch has declined. In fact, it remains a **Best 100**-ranked course and is still near the top of the list in the Stockton area. While it might not be up to the standard of newer Saddle Creek or Castle Oaks, its nicely designed holes and prolifically set trees more than offset its age (55) and its location (straddling the Rt. 99 freeway).

Dry Creek Ranch has an element of Silverado North in its make-up, with beautiful full-sized oaks and wide, well-conditioned fairways. Small greens have subtle breaks and putt very smoothly. Natural oaks, planted cedar (cedrus deodara), willows, and stone pine protrude into the fairways, forcing shots to be hit over, under, or around them. They also add variety to hole design and force golfers to think about strategy.

For example, number ten starts with a drive across a wide (dry) creek on a 540-yard par-five. Players must then decide whether to lay-up and hit well short of the oaks trees closely guarding the green, or roll it under or through a tiny opening. A lay-up second-shot leaves enough space to hit the third over the trees, whereas a longer, straight rolling shot can set up a short chip to the green. Years ago, when young lady pros held three-day mini-tour stops here, some complained about having to negotiate hole designs like these. But a lot of amateur, senior, and weekend players enjoy such tricky layouts. Narrow gaps and protruding trees give an advantage to short, accurate hitters—and a hindrance to those spoiled by courses catering to pros and scratch golfers.

The freeway, regrettably, is a distraction. A pair of long, low overpasses has split off a third of the course, as six back-nine holes head west of the divide; the rest, plus the clubhouse and the range, remain on the east. Trees and leaves absorb the sound of traffic in most places, but car whooshing creates a piercing annoyance on holes adjacent to the freeway. Another negative comes from a low, swampy area where a few holes can flood in winter. Tule fog typically settles in till noon in February. Visitors should plan their games when the river is low and the fog has disappeared. Then, they count a having a really good experience, just like those *Examiner* voters back in 1982. *Review based on play twice, last with interview in September '08.*

Dry Creek Ranch Golf Course

809 Crystal Way		Golf Shop:	209 745-2330
Galt, CA 95632		Fax	209 745-6658
		www.drycreekranchgolfcourse.com	
Managed by:	Private, local	Architect:	Jack Fleming
Location:	Half way between Sacramento and Stockton on State Rt. 99. From the north take exit 274B and make immediate left turn across the freeway to Crystal Way. Turn right and go 1/2 mile to the course. From the south take exit 274A/Crystal Way. Turn right to the course.		
Style:	Gently rolling riverside terrain. Oaks guard many fairways, making drive accuracy important. Greens protected by well designed bunkers and aprons. Course is split by a long State Rt. 99 overpass/bridge across river floodplains.		
Other info:	Can be wet and foggy in winter.		

Greens Fees as of 10/08:	Weekends	Weekdays	Twilight	Seniors	Carts/person
	$37	$25	$25/$18	$18 weekdays	$13

Course ratings:	Men	Par	Rating	Slope	Yardage	Women	Par	Rating	Slope	Yardage
Dry Creek Ranch	Black	72	72.4	132	6753	White	72	75.0	133	6094
	Blue	72	71.4	127	6521	Red	72	72.1	128	5647
	White	72	69.8	123	6161					

No. 88: Del Monte

Del Monte, one of the oldest golf courses east of the Mississippi, once advertised itself as the first 18-hole course "on the Coast." Its rich history began as the golf playground for society mavens who patronized the old Del Monte Hotel around 1900. Course quality was so respected that it hosted the original Northern California Open Championships as well as the first State Championships. Its legacy as a golf resort helped establish the Monterey Peninsula as one of the most famous golf venues in the world. Currently it is owned and operated by Pebble Beach Corp, and sits adjacent to the Hyatt Regency Hotel and Spa, just off State Rt. 1 near the Naval Postgraduate School.

The course lives in the shadow of its corporate sisters, Pebble Beach, Spyglass Hill and Spanish Bay, but remains a part of the package available for visitors of the Pebble Beach Co. hotels. A marketing organization named the Dukes Club was established to give savings for frequent players of all these courses except Pebble Beach. Further information about this Club can be obtained from the Del Monte golf shop number listed below.

Significant changes have occurred over the years. The original nine-hole layout used oil-sand greens, the norm on most courses at the turn of the 20th century. They consisted of a sand base, with oil sprinkled on top, then rolled to compact the surface. By 1910, real grass greens took over and the course lengthened to 4934-yards. By 1990 distance was up to 6350-yards and remains near that today. Few changes have taken place over the last 20 years, with one major exception. In 2005, a modern irrigation system was added for the entire facility. The result is a course now maintained in excellent condition, with beautifully manicured greens, aprons, fairways and roughs.

The climate in the city of Monterey is better than on the Monterey Peninsula. When fog rolls onto the major tournament courses, Del Monte often basks in the sun. Visitors, who have come to be challenged by the big names, often run to the warmer respite at Del Monte. In fact, the PGA Champion's Tour's *Wal-Mart First Tee Championships* are played annually at Pebble *and* Del Monte. Also the *Callaway Golf Pebble Beach Invitational,* a year-end tournament combining selected players from the PGA, LPGA, Champions and Nationwide Tours, uses Del Monte for one round.

Though owned by Pebble Beach Corp, Del Monte Golf Course sits adjacent to the Hyatt Regency Hotel, an unrelated property, in Monterey. The hotel lobby hides behind the green of par-five, number fourteen.

Most players find its layout a throwback to older styles, a relaxing break from the rigors of modern contoured course design. Flat fairways prevail, with wide landing areas, and trimmed hedges surrounding the tees. Although many shallow mounded fairway bunkers have been updated over the years, most tee shots can be aimed to stay out of trouble. Long hits are not really necessary, as only one par-four measures over 400-yards. Even approach shot length is modest, since six par-fours measure less than 335-yards from the regular men's tees. A couple of par-threes do extend nearly 200-yards, adding some spice to the course's challenge.

In addition to excellent course condition, Del Monte offers well-manicured greens. Their *poa anna* grass—grainy and easy to cut short—grows well in coastal environments. When used as alternating courses in tournament play, greens at Pebble, Spyglass and Del Monte can all be set up to play with similar speeds and firmness, due to their similar specifications. Except for the three-tiered seventh green, all are small. Subtle breaks often turn in directions opposite from what you'd expect. As summer afternoons lengthen, the grain of the fast growing *poa* becomes even more difficult to judge. Mornings definitely provides the best opportunity for good scoring.

All and all, Del Monte offers a nice, relaxing golf course, in excellent condition, with a superb and historic pedigree. However, to suit the needs of the next generation, additional modernization—in the form of landscaping or moderate sculpting—could add the touches necessary to bring it more in line with the image of its corporate partners. *Review based on play many times, last with interview in March '08.*

Del Monte Golf Course

1300 Sylvan Road		**Resort:**	800 654-9300
Monterey, CA 93940		**Golf Shop:**	831 373-2700
		Fax	831 655-8792
		www.pebblebeach.com	
Managed by:	Pebble Beach Co.	**Architect:**	Charles Maud

Location: Adjacent to Hyatt Regency, Monterey. From the north, take State Rt. 1 to Casa Verde Exit. Turn left and go to end at Fairgrounds Rd. Turn left and go 1/3 mile, across Rt. 68 to Josselyn Cyn Rd. turn left and clubhouse is on immediate right. From Carmel, take Rt. 1 to Aguajito Exit and continue straight onto Mark Thomas Rd. Go past the Hyatt and turn right onto Sylvan Rd. Clubhouse is on the immediate right.

Style: Mostly flat terrain, easy to walk. Beautifully manicured. Classic hedge-lined tees, wide fairways, small greens. Pines and oaks occasionally force accurate shots.

Other info: Home of the Dukes Club for discounts at many Pebble Beach Co. managed courses.

Greens Fees	Weekends	Weekdays	Twilight	Seniors	Carts/person
as of 10/08:	$110	$110	$110	No savings	$25

Course ratings:	Men	Par	Rating	Slope	Yardage	Women	Par	Rating	Slope	Yardage
	Blue	72	71.5	127	6357	White	74	74.3	122	6052
Del Monte	White	72	70.1	124	6052	Red	74	70.8	115	5429
	Red	69	67.3	117	5429					

No. 89: Teal Bend

Northwest of downtown Sacramento, near the International Airport and adjacent to the Sacramento River, lies the first built of local architect Brad Bell's six **Best 100** courses. It was completed in 1997 and local colleges and one of the pro mini-tours use it for competition. ClubCorp, who also oversees Empire Ranch, Granite Bay, and Turkey Creek in eastern metropolitan Sacramento, manages this course too, so it's popular with private tournaments and corporate outings.

Even though golfers cannot see the river, which is protected by a tall levee, the course feels like it's nearby. Reeds, lakes, creeks, trees, and twists of the fairways lend to this aura. Flat terrain has been marginally contoured to add interest. Large native oaks, plain trees and heavy river-brush border fairways so densely that players think each hole is its own private domain; they cannot see adjacent fairways. Thankfully, these barriers are far enough from fairways that only the most crooked shots get lost in the bull rushes. In fact the actual playing zones seem links-like on most holes. Trees rarely block shots, and fairway bunkers are so nicely spaced and contoured that one imagines ocean breezes could cool the afternoon summer heat.

Teal Bend's maintenance crews have been challenged the last few years. The summer of '06 had a record heat spell that dehydrated and burned-out many Sacramento Valley courses. Those which were known for good playing conditions, using *poa anna* grass, got a real wake-up call. With the addition of Bermuda grass seed to some of the fairways, plus a lot of nurturing and cooler weather in '07 and '08, the course recovered. Fairways again show an even green color with good texture. Roughs that had severe divot-worn areas are back to normal. Greens, saved during the hot spell, continue to be smooth, hold shots, and look beautiful. In fact, all areas surrounding the greens exhibit good grooming.

A disadvantage at Teal Bend is that the vegetation barriers make hole designs themselves look very similar. Elevation variations aren't present to give that feeling of space and texture found near the ocean or in the hills. The unchanging tree-filled backdrops add to the sameness and block views out into the surrounding countryside. Only the ninth hole, a three par over a reed filled lake, and the seventeenth, a par-five where the drives need to clear a lake and/or traps, have a significantly different appearance from the tee.

However, the course's good condition, its calm riverside appearance, the well designed greens, interesting fairway bunkering, and abundant local fauna, all combine to make Teal Bend an enjoyable and challenging experience. *Review based on play and interviews, last in July '08.*

Teal Bend Golf Course		
7200 Garden Highway	**Golf Shop:**	916 922-5209
Sacramento, CA 95837	**Fax**	916 646-8716
	www.tealbendgolf.com	
Managed by: ClubCorp	**Architect:**	Brad Bell
Location:	West of Sacramento Airport on the Sacramento River. Take I-5 to State Rt. 99. Exit here and go north 3.2 miles to Elverta Rd. Turn left (west) and go 3.6 miles to the end at Garden Highway. Turn left (south) and go 1 mile to the course entrance on the left.	

Style:	Flat terrain with many sloughs and lakes surrounded by cat-tails and grasses. Each hole is separated from others by trees and heavy vegetation. Broad fairways and well designed green complexes.
Other info:	Popular tournament course, usually in good condition.

Greens Fees as of 10/08:	Weekends	Weekdays	Twilight	Seniors	Carts/person
	$66	$46	$46/$36	$39 weekdays	Included

Course ratings:	Men	Par	Rating	Slope	Yardage	Women	Par	Rating	Slope	Yardage
	Black	72	73.9	131	7008	White	73	74.1	123	5944
Teal Bend	Blue	72	71.7	127	6532	Gold	72	68.8	112	5077
	White	72	69.2	120	5944					

No. 90: Sierra Meadows

Number five is one of four excellent 180 to 195-yard par threes at Sierra Meadows. Once known as Ahwahnee Golf Course, recent major investments have improved tees, greens and drainage throughout the course.

Located about half way from Fresno to Yosemite, just west of the thriving town of Oakhurst, lies one of Northern California's most unknown but charming mountain courses. It used to be known as Ahwanee, but name and ownership changed in 2003. New investment has since gone into irrigation, drainage, and hole re-routing to improve the course. With its new name, Sierra Meadows, it joins Apple Mountain (Placerville), Pine Mountain Lake (south of Sonora), Alta Sierra (Grass Valley), and Mace Meadows (east of Jackson) as one of our best mountain-style golf courses built down in the foothills.

Some other low-altitude competitors also claim to be mountain courses. However, they usually play through more meadow than forest. Consequently, their designs are flatter, often hotter (in the summer), and windier. The group of six above offers plenty of trees, lots of shade, clearer air, quality turf-grass, up-and-down lies, and opportunities for ingenious shot making. Except for Darkhorse, they also have shorter yardages than their less sheltered cousins, adding to the casual feel of the playing experience.

Improvements over the last few years make Sierra Meadows worth the effort to find in its relatively remote setting. It sits at the bottom of a shallow canyon, with a creek wandering casually along several fairways. No two holes are alike, ranging from rolling tree-lined par fives to twisted doglegs with elevated greens. Green approaches vary too, some over deep bunkers and water, others with wide aprons for easy roll-up shots. Every club in the bag should come into play.

Trees, usually oaks, guard strategic locations on most holes. They often impinge at corners of the doglegs, making drivers think twice about swinging-away, but forcing enough distance to clear the obstacles. Number ten illustrates this contradiction, as two monsters guard both the left and right of the drive landing area. Hit short of them, and the green is well over 200-yards away, with trees in the way. Hit straight through the small gap and the approach becomes much easier.

Par-threes offer the most striking designs, especially from the rear 6400-yard tees. One of these, number five, heads over a broad lake to a highly sloped, well trapped green illustrated on the prior page. The lady's tee perches on a small box-shaped artificial peninsula that extends out into the lake for a shorter crossing. Number fourteen also finds an extended tee, which provides a small opening around a slot in the trees, over a wide creek, 190-yards to the green. It's very easy to dump this approach into the woods or the creek.

Players from the Fresno area who think that Brighton Crest, Riverbend and Pheasant Run are the best courses north of town should definitely add Sierra back to their list. It's well worth the hour drive, or the two hours from Modesto. It's also great stop for other tourists on their way to Yosemite. *Review based on play in April '08.*

Sierra Meadows Country Club

46516 Opah Drive	**Toll Free:**	800 642-7448
Ahwahnee, CA 93601	**Golf Shop:**	559 642-1343
	Fax:	559 642-1346
	www.sierrameadows.com	

Managed by:	Private, local	**Architect:**	Alan Thomas
Location:	Fifty miles north of Fresno on the way to Yosemite. Take State Rt. 41 to Oakhurst and turn left (northwest) on State Rt. 49. Go 2.5 miles to Harmony Ln. Turn right, go about 1/3 mile to Opah and turn right. Go 2.7 miles down to the course. From the north: Take State Rt. 140 east from Merced to Rt. 49. Turn south 26 miles to the Harmony Ln turnoff. Turn left, go to Opah then turn right and go 2.7 miles to the course.

Style:	Moderately hilly terrain on some holes, meadow style layout on others. Trees come into play on most holes. Rivers, creeks and lakes add to need for accuracy. Tight shots into most greens.
Other info:	Drainage, condition and layout improved over days when course was named Ahwahnee.

Greens Fees as of 10/08:	Weekends	Weekdays	Twilight	Seniors	Carts/person
	$39	$34	$30 weekdays	$34/$29	$15

Course ratings:	Men	Par	Rating	Slope	Yardage	Women	Par	Rating	Slope	Yardage
Sierra	Blue	70	70.2	133	6389	White	72	73.5	131	5924
Meadows	White	70	68.4	124	5924	Red	72	68.9	122	5062

No. 91: San Geronimo

San Geronimo, currently managed by American Golf Corp, is in a special group of California golf courses built or renovated by the late Ken Hunter Jr. His philosophy was to create easily affordable public courses, hire designers who insured interesting layouts, and make sure they could be kept in good condition. His goal was to stimulate interest in the game across a broad spectrum of economic classes, and create arenas all golfers would enjoy together. Hunter Ranch on the Central Coast is the best of his Northern California courses and is ranked No. 12 herein. San Geronimo, his other **Best 100** course, is not to the standard of Hunter Ranch, but still gets a top 100 ranking and is fun to play.

The course dichotomy makes it interesting. The front nine, with seven holes south of Sir Francis Drake Blvd, looks flat, not nearly as challenging or difficult as the 136 Slope (blue tees) indicate it should be. The back nine is another story. One explanation as to why the nines differ so much comes from the pro shop: Since the course has no normal driving range, golfers need easier starting holes to tune up their games. True to form, the first six holes are rather mundane and can be used for that warm-up.

Instead of a range, San Geronimo has a practice hole. Again, the pro shop staff offers a creative explanation why this 105-yard area is better for warming-up than a traditional range: Normally, players spend a lot of time blasting drives on the practice tee, destroying any swing tempo. A short wedge shot, however, should be perfect for a relaxing warm-up, emphasizing smoothness and touch, both of which create good scores. A rationalization? Maybe, but it also holds an element of truth. A friend once told me of his trip to Augusta National. At the time, there was no driving range on the main property, so members and guests warmed up on a short par-three course. Holes ranged from 80 to 150-yards. After this nine-hole warm-up, he went out on the course, hit good drives all day long and shot a career-low score . . . with no big swing tune-up. Maybe the 105-yard practice shots really do work.

San Geronimo's toughest holes start at number ten on undulating terrain. Nearly every non-par-three on the backside finds a major dogleg and most fairways border creeks or out-of-bounds. Many have narrow landing areas for drives, and others long carries for approach shots. With a couple of exceptions, fairways still run fairly level, but the surrounding roughs certainly aren't. Most greens appear elevated, sloped, and extremely well protected by bunkers.

Unusual design elements show their face on this back side. Number twelve has a flowing two-piece fairway, first towards traps at the turn and then down over a lake protecting the right front of the green. Number fourteen, another par-four (and seen below) features a blind drive over a steep hill, then a narrow opening guards a green tucked between all kinds of hazards. Number sixteen's fairway flirts with a water hazard protruding nearly half way across its width, forcing a lay-up drive or risky shot to a narrow opening. Its highly elevated green sits behind deep bunkers, and the back tier tucks well into a grove of oak trees.

A flat front nine balances steeply rolling terrain on the back side. San Geronimo's fourteenth requires a blind drive over a hill to a fairway that narrows to nothing at the end of a long par-four.

The other holes on the back have just as much character, and make the 11-mile drive up from U.S. 101 worth the short trip. Reportedly San Geronimo's popularity has grown in the last two years, partly because competitor Peacock Gap increased greens fees after their major renovation, and pushed players elsewhere. San Geronimo also expended some capital, over $1 million on improved drainage, to make winter play much more pleasant. As of summer '08, greens fees were safely near the same low rates as in the recent past.

It is certainly a balanced layout, with several holes pleasing to the average golfer, and some serious challenges for the good ones. Unfortunately, while the greens, bunkers and tees are in good shape, fairways had several dry spots, due to a continuing drought. The course needs better-assured water sources to counteract our seemingly ever-increasing dry spells. *Review based on play and interview in May '08.*

San Geronimo Golf Course

5800 Sir Francis Drake Blvd.	**Golf Shop:** 415 488-4030
San Geronimo, CA 94963	**Fax:** 415 488-4385
	www.sangeronimogc.com

Managed by: American Golf   **Architect of redesign:** Robt. M. Graves

Location: In central Marin County. From the south, take U. S. 101 to Sir Francis Drake Blvd, and head west 11 miles to the course. From the north, take Central San Rafael Exit and head northwest towards San Anselmo on 3rd St. This becomes 2nd St. and then 4th St. and finally Red Hill Road. Once in downtown San Anselmo, veer right on Sir Francis Drake Blvd and head west 8 miles to the course.

Style: Front nine is flat terrain with wide fairways. Starting on number six, green approaches tighten. The back side is very hilly, with many doglegs and hazards to avoid. Greens throughout well protected by elevation, hazards or bunkers.

Greens Fees as of 10/08:	Weekends	Weekdays	Twilight	Seniors	Carts/person
	$64	$36	$40/$28	$40	$15

Course ratings:	Men	Par	Rating	Slope	Yardage	Women	Par	Rating	Slope	Yardage
	Black	72	73.5	137	6780	White	72	74.0	128	5982
San Geronimo	Gold	72	71.6	136	6439	Blue	72	69.2	120	5140
	White	72	69.3	132	5982					

No. 92: Sea Ranch

To most Californians, Sea Ranch is known as a remote get-away on the Sonoma County coast. It's a place to kick back, enjoy the beach, cycle, hike, and cuddle by an evening fire with family or friends. The Sea Ranch community includes a lodge and restaurants at the southern end of an eight-mile long coast-side development, plus homes stretching to the northern end. Zoning strictly controls development, so buildings see wide-spaces between them and tasteful architecture, suitable to the rural environment. The golf course, on the northern end of this same stretch, borders a few of these homes but is no longer officially part of the lodge or housing development. It operates independently, and, as May '09, is for sale.

The course's CC&R's (codes, covenants and restrictions) are said to strictly limit the use of land occupied by the golf course. It either remains a course, or becomes open space. Losing it would be a real shame, because the 1974 Robert Muir Graves design is a beauty.

For years, Sea Ranch operated with just nine-holes. This front nine lies on the western ocean side of State Rt. 1, slightly inland and high above the waves. It never reaches directly to any seaside cliff, but number eight has very nice views of the ocean. Its links-like look, with slightly rolling hills, broad fairways and stretches of low shrubbery and grasses, has plenty of wind. A few trees dot the landscape too, but seldom come into play. Fairways flow through the low native vegetation, and avoid small flat bunkers that Graves uses more as artistic statements than effective hazards.

Number eight on the older front nine at Sea Ranch is a tough par-three over a deep barranca. Tasteful seaside architecture flanks the double-tiered green.

It's a course where you need a good guide or experienced partner on your first game, otherwise newcomers easily hit through the landing zones, or in the wrong direction. Greens fees are relatively low, and the course is fun enough, to play two or three times and get the tricky layout figured properly. At only 15,000 rounds per year, starting times come easy, especially during the week, and play goes speedily.

The second nine, completed eighteen years later, was designed at the time of the original in 1976, also by Graves. It is on the eastern side of the Rt. 1, and is hillier because holes perch further up the coastal slopes. Most people consider it more difficult, though the length measures 100-yards shorter. The complexity comes from broader water hazards, bunkers closer to play, and winds stronger due to the higher elevation and lack of tree protection.

It showcases a couple of very well designed holes, like number fifteen. This simple-looking par-four length heads straightaway, up a modest slope, with only a few minor undulations. Far off to both sides are long deep golden grasses, and close on the right sits a series of bunkers designed to steer the drive to the left. A drive hit left certainly stays safe, but the approach becomes difficult because all the green's bunker protection lies on that side. The green is rock hard, so a short to medium iron approach, if hit at the pin, risks bouncing well over the green or landing in the traps. If you steer the approach safely right, putts or chips will be miles away. This type of deceptive design typifies a good links course; and Graves told local owners that Sea Ranch was among his best.

One caveat . . . Water supply is a often a big concern in this part of the state, and Sea Ranch has very little in years when Spring rains are light. In such periods fairways will be dry, often even brown. This is also a classic links trait, but one Americans usually like try avoid rather than enjoy. *Review based on play and interview in June '08.*

The Sea Ranch Golf Links

42000 Highway 1	**Golf Shop:**	707 785-2468
P. O. Box 749	**Fax:**	707 785-3042
Sea Ranch, CA 95495	www.searanchvillage.com	
Managed by: Private, local	**Architect:**	Robt. M. Graves

Location: About three hours north of San Francisco, overlooking the Pacific. Take U.S. 101 40 miles north of the Golden Gate to Railroad Ave. Turn left and go under freeway to Stoney Point Rd. Turn right 1.7 miles to Roblar Rd. Turn left and head west 7 miles to Valley Ford. Turn right for another 7 miles to State Rt. 1. Turn right (north) and travel 54 miles to the course.

Style: Gently rolling hills about a half mile from the ocean. Mixture of trees and grasses, with well cut fairways and artistically trapped greens. Several shots cross barrancas, but drives have room for a little error. Course can be very dry in the summer.

Other info: Weather varies by the hour from calm to wind, from fog to sun.

Greens Fees as of 10/08:	Weekends	Weekdays	Twilight	Seniors	Carts/person
	$70	$50	$40/$30	No savings	$13

Course ratings:	Men	Par	Rating	Slope	Yardage	Women	Par	Rating	Slope	Yardage
	Blue	72	72.5	134	6601	Gold	73	73.9	128	5526
Sea Ranch	White	72	71.0	125	6219	Red/Yellow	72	70.2	120	4867
	Gold	70	67.4	118	5526					

No. 93: Lake Shastina

Anyone who has driven north to Oregon on Interstate-5 knows the commanding presence of Mt. Shasta. About fifteen miles north of the mountain, nearly 12,000 feet below the summit, sits a low basin, filled with a large reservoir, forests, several meadows, and many small volcanic cinder cones. What better place for a broad-based community of homes, a resort and 27 holes of golf. The views are impressive, not just of Mt. Shasta, but of the Eddy Range to the southwest, the Siskiyous to the northwest, and the Cascades to the northeast. Nearly every view, whether from a golf hole, a back porch, a road curve or a camping tent, fills with mountain ridgelines.

From the start, the mountain overshadows golf at Lake Shastina. Your first drive on number one heads at towards center of the huge snow covered 14,162 ft. volcano. The next five holes thread through tall Ponderosa pines, so Mt. Shasta is obscured, but the other ranges can be seen in the open sky behind each green. Homes nestle unobtrusively on one side of the fairways, and pines occasionally protrude into the other. Bunkers are full of dark red pulverized lava, and give distinct sight lines for each shot. These woodsy holes are truly mountain golf at its best. They require good driving accuracy and well-controlled shots into moderate sized greens.

Then, at number seven, players emerge from the fragrant forest, back into an open meadow. Mountain peaks and ridges now form the backdrop for nearly every shot. Number eight and nine have the added texture of reed-edged lakes to complement vistas on the horizon. These large ponds must be cleared or avoided, and add extra adrenaline at the close of the front nine.

Views of Mt. Shasta and other prominent mountains abound on scenic Lake Shastina. Holes two through five wind through heavy forest . . . where deer (not antelope) play.

The back side is a story of open-appearing holes, with all but two in the meadows. Small hills closely surround these fairways but an unfortunate forest-fire burned most of their trees. The hills appear full of scrub-brush and rock and do not have the same pristine appearance of forest seen on the front nine. A highlight comes at number thirteen, one of the most beautiful par-threes you will ever play. Its tee-boxes, all well above the green, stair-step down a hill from the 190-yard tips to a short 111-yards for ladies. The longer the tee shot, the more interesting and dramatic it becomes. Your drive is directed out of a small chute, over a lake, where the tiny tree-framed green sits in front of a mini-cinder cone. Typical of most greens, this one is rather flat and slow, but the shot at it, with the close-up volcanic backdrop, is quite special.

After this treat, the remaining group seems of lesser design. Fairways spread broadly, are flat, and have bunkers so widely set that they rarely impact play. Green complexes on these latter holes aren't bad; they just aren't as special as when surrounded by forest and water. Nevertheless, Mt Shasta still looms up-close-and-personal, reminding golfers that Lake Shastina is a great place to spend an afternoon any time during the year. *Review based in play and interview in April '08.*

Lake Shastina Golf Resort

5925 Country Club Drive	**Golf Shop:**	530 938-3205
Weed, CA 96094	**Fax:**	531 938-4653
	www.lakeshastinagolf.com	

Managed by:	Private, local	**Architect:**	R. T. Jones Jr. and Sr.
Location:	10 miles north of Mt. Shasta. Take I-5 to exit 747/U.S. 97. Head northeast following U.S. 97 towards Klamath Falls for 5 miles. Turn left at Big Springs Rd. Go 2.8 miles north to the course.
Style:	Mostly flat terrain. Holes two thru five are in the forest, tightly bordered by trees and homes. Rest of the course is meadow-bound with fine views of surrounding mountains. Wide fairways on meadow holes. Greens are nicely bunkered and shaped. Bunkers filled with red lava sand.
Other info:	Altitude 2300 feet. Open all year long.

Greens Fees as of 10/08:	Weekends	Weekdays	Twilight	Seniors	Carts/person
	$53	$53	$29	No savings	$16

Course ratings:	Men	Par	Rating	Slope	Yardage	Women	Par	Rating	Slope	Yardage
	Blue	72	72.8	134	6910	White	74	74.4	129	6268
Lake Shastina	Gold	72	70.9	132	6529	Red	72	70.4	121	5530
	White	72	69.8	129	6268					

No. 94: Timber Creek

Northeast Sacramento suburbs offer many excellent golf courses. Darkhorse and The Ridge in Auburn top the list, but Cherry Island, Woodcreek, Catta Verdera, Whitney Oaks, Lincoln Hills, Turkey Creek, and Timber Creek, all provide good experiences too. What's a bit surprising is that a Dell Webb project, owned by the residents, makes the top 100 list. Just goes to show that an active adult community does not mean dull and uninteresting golf. It also means challenges and beauty amongst homes built for those 55-years and older.

The first thing one notices when arriving at Timber Creek's clubhouse is the enthusiasm and fitness of players climbing into their personally owned carts. Everyone looks tan, has good muscle tone, and appears lean and athletic looking, despite gray hair and crows feet around the eyes. Even the 90-year-old great grandmother, whose sons bought her a home where she could play golf for the rest of her years, maintains a 25 handicap. This is a group of fun-loving energetic souls we all hope to emulate someday.

Maybe the reason they all appear so enthusiastic and motivated is their well-designed course. True, Timber Creek winds through some homes, but it also has a series of holes on the back nine where houses are replaced by creeks, oaks and a nature preserve filled with wild turkey and other fauna. These features remind players that gulches and creek beds once occupied the nearby grass covered hills. And unlike Lincoln Hills, a newer and bigger Del Webb facility about five miles east, this course is very walk-able for those so inclined. (At Lincoln hills, carts must be used.)

The waterfall-graced eighteenth at Dell Webb's Timber Creek in Roseville, finishes a fine adventure through a back nine full of trees, wildlife and tightly bunkered greens.

Billy Casper and Steve Nash designed Timber Creek in 1996, and then Lincoln Hills four years later. Timber Creek offers 27 holes, with the Lakes/Oaks as the primary eighteen, and another 9-holes called Sierra Pines down the street. The Oaks back nine is the real gem, with most holes adjacent to the nature preserve. Here, two par-fives, number twelve and eighteen, dogleg through and around beautiful mature oaks, nicely positioned bunkers, sloped fairways, a man-made waterfall and a well-positioned creek crossing. All these features add the interest, texture, beauty and challenge that make this nine a real pleasure to play. Par-threes measure short, at 125 and 150-yards (back tees), but the shape and contouring of greens and green-surrounds require well-hit, accurate approach shots. Pin positions throughout the course can be set on multiple slopes or tiers, and vary by up to a foot and a half in elevation. (Such slopes seem mild compared to more extreme variance and size seen on greens up at Lincoln Hills.)

The other nine, called the Lakes, appears more typical of Del Webb courses, as it treks wide alleys between the home sites. It shows more water, less bunkers and more fairway contouring than the oak covered back nine.

As is true of most Del Webb courses, maintenance crews keep most everything in good shape, with green fairways, green roughs, medium speed putting surfaces and well-manicured bunkers. Beware though, some of the bunkers may look pretty and well raked, but contain only about a quarter inch of thin-packed sand and a hardpan base. Give your feet a good waggle to make sure you know whether the sand is fluffy or hard-packed. *Played in September '08.*

Timber Creek Golf Course

7050 Del Webb Blvd		Golf Shop:	919 774-3850
Roseville, CA 95747		Fax:	916 774-3889
		www.timbercreekgc.com	
Managed by:	Private, local	Architect:	Nash/Casper
Location:	30 miles northwest of Sacramento. Take I-80 to State Rt. 65. Go north 2.5 miles to Blue Oaks Exit. Turn left (west) and head 3.3 miles to Del Webb Blvd. Turn left again and the clubhouse is just over 1 mile on the left.		
Style:	Flat terrain, graded nicely to provide elevation changes. Homes surround many holes, but not all. The Oaks nine has many tight drives and distinctive greens and bunkers. Course is in good condition.		
Other info:	Three nine-hole courses, primarily using the Lakes/Oaks for 18-hole rounds.		

Greens Fees	Weekends	Weekdays	Twilight	Seniors	Carts/person
as of 10/08:	$64	$49	$44/$40	No savings	Included

Course ratings:	Men	Par	Rating	Slope	Yardage	Women	Par	Rating	Slope	Yardage
Timber Creek: Lakes/Oaks	Black	72	70.7	123	6401	Gold	72	72.7	127	5617
	Blue	71	69.0	119	6040	Red	72	70.4	119	5182
	Gold	71	67.2	115	5617					

No. 95: Roddy Ranch

Roddy Ranch is one of the four relatively new golf courses located in western Brentwood, ten miles south of Antioch. Its setting on grassy rolling hills overlooks eastern Contra Costa County. It's in an area south of State Rt. 4 freeway, just outside of suburbia, where cattle ranches still dominate the landscape.

Completed in 2000, the course opened to great critical acclaim and was a favorite of golfers trying to expand their experiences to new and different venues. Here they found a links/Heathland-style design, which had the best greens in the area—fast, true and full of character. Today, the course remains almost treeless; and plenty of bunkers, doglegs, hills and elevation changes continue to keep long ball strikers under control and normal players interested.

But as time progressed, the golfing boom of the late 90's finally met the financial busts of 2001 and 2008, so the course suffers from lack of play and lack of revenue. The local economy faltered, other new courses opened, business outings lessened, growth in the area slowed, houses went into default and people found they needed to work more and play less.

In addition, water usage became an issue. These arid hills, windy much of the summer, need even more moisture than courses down on the flats. Summer brings dry spots in fairways, just like the British seaside links that its design reflects. Unfortunately, most Americans do not like dry, hard fairways. They want good roll, but also want turf soft enough to keep the ball from bounding into never-never-land.

Despite various pressures and less maintenance, the course remains an attractive design, and provides a good test. However, the green conditions change frequently; in February they can be shabby and then great again by summer. The character of their mounds and slopes continue, but they lack the beautiful manicured surfaces of the opening years. Fairways remain green in winter, but are very firm. Roughs are spotty, with the first cuts in marginal shape, and the next level full of weeds and squirrel holes.

Roddy Ranch's starting hole is a good lead-in to what is coming on this hilly course at the perimeter of East Bay cattle country.

Local golfers often compare Roddy to Poppy Ridge, its competitor 30 miles south. Both offer good value, promote treeless terrain, and sit on similar style grassy hillsides. Roddy climbs somewhat lower slopes, so walking is easier; it also features more creative fairway bunkering. In fact, many holes on the front side are quite photogenic. Yet, Poppy's green complexes show more variation and character, and playing areas stay in better, more consistent condition. Also, Roddy's shallower hills bring a sameness to its tee-box views; whereas, higher elevations and surrounding vineyards at Poppy Ridge add more drama to vistas.

The middle stretch of holes, from numbers eight to sixteen, are those with the best character. They force more accurate drives, green-side bunkers have more personality, and pins can be placed in more interesting locations. One hole in particular, par-three number thirteen, is a notable challenge, and a **Best 100** toughest hole. Prevailing winds blow directly at the tee, so the uphill shot of 210-yards from the gold blocks is a big challenge. A steep slope in front and an even deeper bunker protect the huge green. For many that means driver is required from the tee, and then a chip or two, and at least two putts. Bogey may sound dull, but it's hard to do much better without sinking a long putt. *Review based on play in February '08.*

The Roddy Ranch Golf Club

1 Tour Way	**Golf Shop:**	925 978-4653
Antioch, CA 94531	**Fax:**	925 706-0222
	www.roddyranch.com	

Managed by:	Touchstone Golf LLC	**Architect:** J. M. Poutlet Design
Location:	Southeast of Antioch. From west, take State Rt. 4 to Lone Tree Way. Turn right (south) and head 3 miles to Deer Valley Road. Go right again, another 3 miles to Tour way. Turn right to clubhouse. From south, take Vasco Rd exit off I-580. Go north towards Brentwood, about 16 miles. At Balfour Rd, turn left and go 4.5 miles to its end. Turn right on Tour Way, the course entrance, is on the left.	
Style:	Hilly grasslands with few trees. A Heathlands style course. Lots of bunkers in fairways and around greens. Firm fairways, sometimes wide, sometimes not. Some long, tough par-threes. Many non-level lies. Condition varies throughout the seasons.	
Other info:	Can be windy is this unprotected Delta location.	

Greens Fees	Weekends	Weekdays	Twilight	Seniors	Carts/person
as of 10/08:	$70	$45	$45/$35	$35 weekdays	Included

Course ratings:	Men	Par	Rating	Slope	Yardage	Women	Par	Rating	Slope	Yardage
	Black	72	74.5	136	6945	Silver	72	75.4	129	5990
Roddy Ranch	Gold	72	72.6	134	6529	Rust	72	71.7	120	5390
	Silver	72	70.4	130	5990					

No. 96: De Laveaga

Looking for a shorter course, at only 6100 yards from the tips . . . one that's in good condition and has plenty of challenge? De Laveaga may fit the bill if you live in the South Bay or Santa Cruz County. What it lacks in yardage is certainly made up with hazards and hilly terrain. Years ago it was heavily criticized for firm fairways and crowned roughs. Together, they allowed well-hit balls to keep rolling until finding deep ravines or barrancas. Recently, better irrigation and improved maintenance have softened up the fairways. The result is a more playable layout that allows players to relax and enjoy the beautiful forested surroundings.

Don't worry, plenty of danger still lurks, but not from bad rolls . . . rather it comes from side hill lies and narrow fairways guarded by plenty of trees and gullies. For example, number ten is one of the toughest par-fives in the **Best**

100. Its 590-yards tees aim at a tiny landing-area bordered by trees, a creek and a road. Only the most accurate of drives will hit the target. The second shot must then clear a 150-yard wide ravine and stop quickly after landing before bouncing out-of-bounds. Bunkers and a creek protect the small elevated green, but most of the damage is done before arriving. Another example comes on long par-four number eighteen. The hole's shape tempts players to drive balls near a deep gully on the left and shorten the shot to the green. But that would be a mistake because the hazard protrudes unseen a third of way across the fairway, and catches the best of such daring attempts.

Santa Cruz's venerable De Laveaga holds its reputation as a short, tight course with plenty of slopes just angling to roll balls into trouble.

De Laveaga, named for the family that donated the land to Santa Cruz, opened in 1970. The city still manages operations of the park-like setting and, given water restrictions and low maintenance budgets, markets a good product. The greens hold shots, stay well groomed all year round, and have plenty of character. Course managers even relocated a couple into fairer positions over the past few years. However, despite recent improvements, fairways continue to show many dry spots; and their grasses are cut so closely that thinly hit shots become the norm for average players.

For decent quality and interesting play, De Laveaga remains an excellent experience for straight hitters. Because of its well-known high value, play is heavy; so, be ready for six-hour Saturday afternoon rounds. According to one of the marshals, "if its light outside, the course is crowded." Drown your sorrows with a drink and meal at the De Laveaga Golf Lodge (upstairs above the pro-shop). The food is great and portions gargantuan. *Review based on play several times, last in September '08.*

De Laveaga Golf Course			
401 Upper Park Road		**Golf Shop:**	831 423-7214
Santa Cruz, CA 95065		**Fax:**	831 458-1309
		www.delaveagagolf.com	
Managed by:	City of Santa Cruz	**Architect:**	Bert Stamps
Location:	Twenty miles south of San Jose. Between State Rts. 17 and 1, in the forest above Morrisey Ave. Due to recent road construction, see Google, MapQuest or call the proshop for precise directions.		
Style:	Mildly hilly terrain, with creeks and canyons at sides of most fairways. Short yardage but tight landing areas place a premium on accuracy. Not difficult to walk.		
Other info:	Volume discount cards available for frequent players. Very busy course, so play often slow.		

Greens Fees	Weekends	Weekdays	Twilight	Seniors	Carts/person
as of 10/08:	$68	$53	$42/$34	No savings	$18

Course ratings:	Men	Par	Rating	Slope	Yardage	Women	Par	Rating	Slope	Yardage
De Laveaga	Blue	70	70.0	136	6114	White	72	73.0	131	5708
	White	70	68.4	132	5708	Red	70	70.2	123	5265

No. 97: Woodcreek

Roseville, a suburb northeast of Sacramento, clearly cares about golf. Woodcreek, its newest municipal course, exemplifies the high quality that has spoiled its residents. Heavy competition nearby keeps local managers on their toes; and many retirees have moved to town, so proper facilities also seem to be important to local politicians.

As a result, muni golf here is very, very good. Architect Robert Muir Graves designed Woodcreek in 1995, and the town keeps it in excellent condition. Gentle swales, lakes, bull-rushes, attractive planting, and plenty of space all combine to minimize the distraction of houses clustered around the perimeter of the large development. Fairway maintenance is excellent, with over-seeding in winter, frequent mowing and fertilizing in summer, and sharply cut edges at the various depths of rough. Smooth greens hold well and putt about 8.5 on the StimpMeter; tees appear in good shape too. Regular sweeps of leaves and acorns keep the fairways and roughs clean and smooth. And, a real rarity for **Best 100** courses, Roseville thought to put good signage throughout the town directing drivers to both its courses, Woodcreek and Diamond Oaks.

From the tee-boxes at Woodcreek, each hole vista invites play. Fairway grading, dogleg shape, mature oak placement, and occasional creeks keep players coming. Although not a particularly difficult course, Woodcreek inspires golfer to take the game seriously and play to their full potential. Fairways have plenty of room and water rarely comes too close to greens, so every level of player can find something for their ability. Would a few deep bunkers and big mounds scare away those Roseville retirees? Apparently not!

A few par-fours, especially those less than 400 yards long, feature tightened-up drive landing-zones. Short number eleven demands good placement to avoid trees and a creek, before a short iron to the green. The thirteenth hole requires a lay-up for long hitters to keep from rolling into the brush and a fence at the end of the landing area—followed by another short iron to a small green surrounded by bunkers.

Par-fives number five and ten display good design that demands thought and accuracy on second shots. The tenth calls for pinpoint placement to a gap between two oak groves for a player who wants a short approach. On the fifth, the second shot forces players to choose between a medium iron lay-up zone and a full swing across a marsh to a tiny opening near giant utility towers. Then, from either landing spot, the approach must to cross a deep pot-bunker to a tiny green.

Interesting designs and good maintenance . . . not bad for a local muni!
Review based on play in October '07.

Woodcreek Golf Course

5880 Woodcreek Oaks Blvd.	**Golf Shop:** 916 771-4653
Roseville, CA 95747	**Fax:** 916 771-4651
	www.golfroseville.com

Managed by:	City of Roseville	**Architect:** Robt. M. Graves
Location:	Thirty miles northeast of Sacramento. Take State Rt. 65 north 2.5 miles to Blue Oaks Blvd. Turn left (west) and drive 2.2 miles to Woodcreek Dr. Turn left again (south) and go 1.7 miles. Course is on the left, after U-turn at Canevari Dr.	
Style:	Gently rolling terrain with a couple of creeks and lakes. Reasonalbly wide fairways and nice, modern green complexes. Course is kept very green except under the sporadically spaced oak groves. Large greens in good shape.	
Other info:	One of two muni courses in Roseville. The other is Diamond Oaks.	

Greens Fees	Weekends	Weekdays	Twilight	Seniors	Carts/person
as of 10/08:	$40	$28	$25/$18	$22 weekdays	$16

Course ratings:	Men	Par	Rating	Slope	Yardage	Women	Par	Rating	Slope	Yardage
	Gold	72	71.9	131	6518	Gold	72	71.2	126	5483
Woodcreek	Blue	72	69.9	123	6043	Red	70	66.2	112	4739
	White	71	67.1	117	5483					

No. 98: Lake Don Pedro

Hard to find? Yes. Worth finding? Absolutely. Lake Don Pedro Golf and Country Club is about forty miles due east of Modesto, off State Rt. 132, just past La Grange. The club originally opened in the late '60's and operated successfully for years. At one point the name changed to Hidden Hills, but when real estate boomed almost everywhere else in the 90's, values in La Grange stayed much lower. The old name came back but that didn't improve matters and financial difficulties finally shut down operations. New owners came in and completed a total facelift for a re-opening in February '08.

At 245-yards, slightly downhill into a breeze, this long par-three at Lake Don Pedro gives a good test. Reopened in early 2008, after years of renovation, course conditions have improved considerably.

Millions of dollars were invested, and the work really shows. Every green complex got a complete rebuild. The new greens, surrounding bunkers, and aprons now show top conditions. Most remained in the same location as before, but a few were moved to better sites. New tees came with the project too. Hole layout appears similar to the original design, but the entire course has been updated to current construction standards. Mud holes disappeared. Creeks and lakes—now lined with stone—give everything a tailored appearance. Added rock walls even bring a touch of elegance. Given a year or two of maturity and addition of a driving range Lake Don Pedro could be a higher rated **Best 100** course. New owners even built multi-story condos around the clubhouse to attract new members and vacation and conference rentals.

But conditioning as of early '08 had a ways to go. The fairways, were re-seeded with a modern Bermuda hybrid grass, and need more growth. They are green, nice looking in spring, and over-seeded in the winter, but weeds remain and it will take a year or two and lots of summer heat for the new grass to develop decent thatch. The clubhouse is finished and looks great, but land has not yet been purchased for a driving range.

As for style, the course is very hilly. Few tees aim at level fairways. Walking is so challenging that management usually requires players to use carts, (included in the greens fees). Fairways are moderately wide, forgiving some driver wildness. However, the front nine has a serious design flaw. Five of the holes cross a small creek or lake located at about 200 yards from the white tees. Their position forces players to either blast tee shots and try to clear the hazards, or lay-up and add 30-40 yards to the often-long approaches. Making such a choice two or three times in a round is understandable, but five times on one nine is overkill for the average golfer, and is an Achilles heel for the course design.

Still, I eagerly wait seeing how the new layout matures. *Review based on play and interview in March '08*

Lake Don Pedro Golf and Country Club

9643 Fachada Way	**Toll Free:**	888 525-5152	
La Grange,CA 95329	**Golf Shop:**	209 852-0404	
	Fax:	209 852-0405	
	www.deerwoodcorp.com		

Managed by:	Deerwood Corp.	**Architect:** William Bell/Ray Clavern
Location:	Forty miles east of Modesto. From State Rt. 99, take State Rt. 132/Yosemite Ave east, through La Grange to Hayward Rd. Follow signs to course: Right on Hayward, left on Hernandez then left on Fachada.	
Style:	Hilly terrain, few trees, with moderately tight fairways. Very nice new greens and bunkers. Front side has creek crossings, which impact drive distance, on several holes.	
Other info:	Renovation, including all new green complexes, completed in Feb '07.	

Greens Fees	Weekends	Weekdays	Twilight	Seniors	Carts/person
as of 10/08:	$55	$35	No Savings	No savings	Included

Course ratings:	Men	Par	Rating	Slope	Yardage	Women	Par	Rating	Slope	Yardage
Lake Don Pedro	Blue	72	72.7	122	6745	Red	71	72.7	126	5635
	White	72	70.6	121	6290					
	Gold	70	67.9	113	5635					

No. 99: La Contenta

This Sierra foothill course sits about thirty miles northeast of Stockton, on State Rt. 26, two miles south of the small town of Valley Springs. Three Sierra river reservoirs supply the main attractions for what used to be a small crossroads community. New Hogan on the Calaveras River and both Pardee and Camanche on the Mokelumne River, are favorites for water-sports. The area also provides homes to growing numbers of commuters, retirees and younger residents searching for a lower cost of living. Several housing developments have burgeoned over the years, with La Contenta Golf Club secluded in one of the more mature neighborhoods. Homes loosely line its fairways, and provide attractive backdrops and landscaping that make it appear like an affluent country club community.

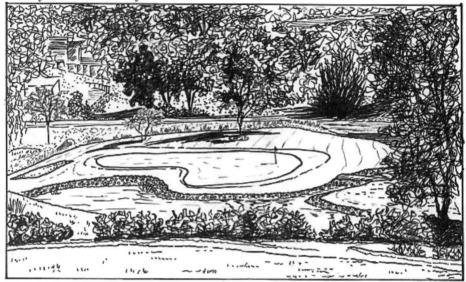

Number thirteen is a wonderful setting for one of La Contenta's excellent par-threes. The shot, about 190 yards from the back tees, must clear a creek and land on the correct putting tier for a chance at birdie.

The golf course condition matches the bill too, even though it's never been a private club. Outstanding maintenance keeps fairways beautiful, greens smooth, roughs cut, and the entire layout green. Because it was built in the 70's, the amount of land for golf is not as expansive as on modern courses. But, house's hillside locations sit well above most fairways, out of the line-of-fire, and only the wildest shots find their way into backyards. Played from the regular tees, yardage measures only 5800-yards for the men, and 5000 for the women. But the black men's tees card 6400-yards and play all of it. So, tighten your belt and play it back for a more serious challenge.

Although La Contenta's greatest asset is its fabulous condition, several holes demonstrate good design and prove quite photogenic. The par-threes have especially nice settings and require long shots to gracefully mounded green complexes. Designer Richard Bigler used the flat terrain around the clubhouse to good avail. He added nicely shaped tree lines, gentle contours and interesting bunkers to make these holes interesting.

However, the course also presents several weak holes with weird designs. They are kind of fun, but require intimate course knowledge because shots bounce off steep hills into illogical places. The most extreme example comes at number twelve, a 340-yard par-four with a sharp uphill dogleg to an extremely elevated green. A tree stands 100-yards in front of the back tee, forcing players to start with either a large hook or big slice to go around it. And when the drive lands, the steep hill bounces the ball down to the bottom of a banked fairway. Cart riders must walk about 40 feet down, and 100 yards across, to reach their ball. Another hole, the short par-five number three, requires a blind second shot from a severe uphill stance, to another hill and another severe side-hill stance. On the next hole, the approach up par-four number five aims at a green unseen atop the crown of a hill. These holes may be memorable but the drastic slopes taint the overall quality of their design.

The *coup-de-grace* comes at number eighteen, which could have been a normal, difficult, long 440-yard par-four dogleg into the wind. But that apparently wasn't enough. A wide pond sits in front of the green, about 20 yards short of the front fringe. Only really long hitters have a chance of clearing the water in two from the 6400-yard tees. And after a lay-up for most of us, the approach still needs a full swing, with 80 or more yards left to the pin. It might as well be a par-five. The lake positioning is a poor feature at the end of an often gorgeous, sometimes perplexing course design. *Review based on play and interview in April '08.*

La Contenta Golf Club

1653 Highway 26	**Golf Shop:** 209 772-1081
P. O. Box 249	**Fax:** 209 772-1085
Valley Springs, CA 95252	www.lacontentagolf.com

Managed by:	Empire Golf **Architect:** Richard Bigler
Location:	Thirty-five minutes northeast of Stockton. From State Rt. 99, take State Rt. 26 thirty miles north. Course is on the right side of the highway, two miles south of junction with State Rt. 12 in Valley Springs.
Style:	Hilly terrain on at least half the holes, some very steep. Course is beautifully manicured, like a private club, with nice homes lining many fairways. Greens are often small with steep breaks. Has several challenging par-threes.
Other info:	Discounts available on-line.

Greens Fees	Weekends	Weekdays	Twilight	Seniors	Carts/person
as of 10/08:	$34	$24	$22/$18	$20 weekdays	$16

Course ratings:	Men	Par	Rating	Slope	Yardage	Women	Par	Rating	Slope	Yardage
	Black	69	69.9	129	6103	White	72	73.7	136	5749
La Contenta	White	69	68.2	128	5758	Red	72	69.5	127	5084
	Red	69	65.1	121	5058					

No. 100: Micke Grove

William Micke grew up to be a vineyard owner and fruit packer in Lodi, during the first half of the 20th century. Successful in business and civic-minded, he began developing what became Micke Grove Regional Park in the '50's. It was eventually donated to San Joaquin County. Golf was always a part of the long-range plan, but it wasn't until 1991 that the Garrett Gill-designed course finally opened for play. When it did, it became the only 18-hole Northern

California course to be co-located with a zoo and a Japanese Garden, on the same property. Today, the 258-acre park, located south of town and west of State Rt. 99, is a center for county recreational life.

It may have taken a while, but when the county decided to begin, it built a good course, one that has a classical appearance but continues to stand well with contemporary expectations. Medium-width, tree-lined fairways use bunkers to catch moderate length 200-plus-yard drives. But the park setting, with graceful lakes and well-groomed fairways, remains enjoyable for golfers of every skill level. The grounds stay green and are well-maintained. Holes vary in design: some have good doglegs with gentle elevated mounding and slopes; others exploit trees and water hazards to please the eye and influence shot placement. The compact course fits the space available efficiently and with little impingement from adjacent holes.

Nicely shaped greens display varying sizes, with enough undulation to add interest, but not enough to overpower high handicappers. Pin placements typically present a challenge because they sit close to the edges of inclines where new breaks begin.

Par-threes comprise some of the most distinctive experiences. None is too short, and many require shots over water. Back tees add even more risk—their off-line rear settings force shots to clear extra water, toward more dangerous sections of greens. Golfers afraid of getting wet can easily bail out to the side and keep from losing extra strokes or golf balls.

Nothing is perfect, even at Micke Grove. The short overall yardage will send those who are looking for a more serious test up to Castle Oaks or Saddle Creek. The popularity of the course means that it is busy and play is slow, at least during summer afternoons. But a combination of attractive greens fees and good-quality, high-variety course design definitely qualifies it as one of our ranked **Best 100** courses. *Review based on play in August '08.*

Micke Grove Golf Links

11401 North Micke Grove Road		**Golf Shop:**	209 369-4410
Lodi, CA 95240		**Fax:**	209 339-8635
		www.mickegrove.com	

Managed by:	Eagle Golf	**Architect:**	Garrett Gill
Location:	Five miles north of Stockton. From State Rt. 99, exit at Eight Mile Road. Head west .6 miles. Turn right (north) on N. Micke Grove Dr. Course is on the left in .8 miles.		
Style:	Flat terrain, sculpted and graded for bunkers, lakes and some contouring. Shortish course, but has plenty of trees and traps positioned to catch slightly errant drives. Greens are well sloped and pins are often placed in challenging positions.		
Other info:	Part of Micke Grove Park, which includes a zoo and Japanese garden.		

Greens Fees as of 10/08:	Weekends	Weekdays	Twilight	Seniors	Carts/person
	$35	$25	$25/$19	$19	$12

Course ratings:	Men	Par	Rating	Slope	Yardage	Women	Par	Rating	Slope	Yardage
Micke Grove	Blue	72	71.6	124	6572	White	73	74.0	124	6020
	White	72	68.5	122	6020	Red	72	70.0	116	5296

Chapter 3:
The Rest of the Courses

Northern California boasts over 400 golf courses. About 90 are private eighteen-hole venues, and another 100 or so have only nine holes. The remaining 220 are public, semi-private and resort courses that the public can play, and are the subject of this book. The **Best 100** of these were reviewed and ranked in the prior chapter; Chapter 4 adds another five courses, which are private but accessible under limited circumstances to non-members; and this chapter reviews the remaining 115.

Several factors keep courses from being ranked in the **Best 100**. For some it is their less sophisticated designs, for others, their poorer condition, lack of updated facilities, or even prevailing foul weather. A few didn't make the cut because of incomplete construction projects. Some were impossible to walk and a few had substandard or remote practice facilities.

Despite their various shortcomings, many of "the rest of the courses" remain the most popular facilities in the state. Usually it's their convenient location, lower greens fees, or easier playing conditions that attract us; and all deserve a review in this book. Every reader wants to see a few honest words about the places they play every day.

This chapter's discussion will be much briefer and will be unranked. Most of these courses have fewer unusual traits, and no course should suffer the ignominy of being labeled the "worst."

Remember, there are at least three primary ways to rationalize a good day on the golf course: (1) Shoot a good score, (2) win money, or (3) play well. And if none of these pan out, maybe you still had a couple of good shots or your friend did, or you helped one of your fellow golfers and got some good exercise. If not, maybe *working* would truly have been a better way to spend the day.

Adobe Creek: This Robert Trent Jones Jr. course offers a good playing

opportunity in Petaluma. I was disappointed by the first few mundane holes, but then the course becomes much more interesting. Despite wandering through homes and condos, the Jones' architectural look takes over on the rest of the front nine . . . with distinctive bunkers, sophisticated greens, sculpted fairways, a well-wooded hazard, and two excellent par threes.

The back nine shows even more artistry. Hole number ten feels like playing in Florida, around a lake all the way to the green. Numbers twelve and fourteen require approaches over water to greens on opposite sides of the next pond. Fairways on the back offer more contours than the mild mounding on the front side. Tall knolls encircle many greens in order to dampen strong afternoon crosswinds.

Adobe Creek now strives to bring the course back to the excellent condition of its opening days in 1991. Fairways and roughs are generally OK, but several dry spots appear in late summer. Inconsistent bunker sand depth means plays must waggle their feet carefully to test sand underneath. Greens are a work in progress. Management says they will trim the deep thatch to have them faster and back in shape by '09. We'll see.

Owners want local regulars to know they strive for a balance between price, service, quality golf, a good practice range, nice golf shop and an excellent restaurant. They're also scheduling a special summer junior program, which offers unlimited late afternoon play at one low monthly cost. This is a good idea because U.S. golf needs all the new juniors it can find. *Based on play and interview in September '08.*

Adobe Creek Golf Club

1901 Frates Road	Golf Shop:	707 765-3000, ext. 100
Petaluma, CA 94954	Fax:	707 765-3022
	www.adobecreek.com	
Managed by: Golf Solutions	Architect:	Robt. T. Jones Jr.

Location: Southeastern Petaluma. From U.S. 101 take State Rt. 116 East exit. Head east on Rt.116/Lakeview Hwy for 1.5 miles. Turn left at Frates Rd and go northeast 1 mile. Course is on the left.

Style: Mostly flat terrain, with mounding at sides of fairways. Homes surround fairways on holes five thru nine. Several lakes or creeks. Greens are well designed and well protected, but need work to bring them back into good shape.

Greens Fees as of 10/08:	Weekends	Weekdays	Twilight	Seniors	Carts/person
	$61	$40	$42/$30	$29 weekdays	$15

Course ratings:	Men	Par	Rating	Slope	Yardage	Women	Par	Rating	Slope	Yardage
	Gold	72	73.1	129	6886	White	72	72.1	122	5743
Adobe Creek	Blue	72	70.0	121	6224	Red	72	68.2	115	5085
	White	70	67.6	116	5743					

Airways:
This short, 5300-yard course sits next to the Fresno Airport. ClubCorp manages it, in addition to four very good Sacramento courses: Teal Bend, Empire Ranch, Turkey Creek and Granite Bay (private).

Unfortunately, Airways falls well short of the ClubCorp quality seen in Sacramento. Its short yardage is unchallenging, and course condition mediocre at best. Carts find bumps all over the fairways, and turf varies in thickness. Most holes are flat, with wide landing areas; greens are decent but bunkering is uninspired. Although trees line most holes, rarely do the pines and eucalyptus come into play. The layout suits golfers who want a very easy round, not one where quality shot making is required. Miss the fairway and roll into very thin lies on hard-packed bare dirt.

Your drive on number one will be the most interesting shot of the day: Yardage of about 330-yards heads around a sharp dogleg. Down the middle, 190-220 yards from the tee, stand a series of trees, in varying sizes, spaced about 20 yards apart. Question is, where do I hit the drive? If played short, with a medium iron, a wedge could clear the trees but wouldn't reach the green. On the other hand, the trees are too far away to clear with a driver on the fly. My solution was to aim at the corner of the dogleg, hit a low drive, land short, and hope the ball would roll under the trees into the open. This almost worked, though I needed to hit a low approach under limbs to reach the green. Too bad some of this trickery and finesse isn't needed later to make the round more interesting. *Review based on play in April '08.*

Airways Municipal Golf Course			
5440 E. Shields Avenue		Golf Shop:	559 291-6254
Fresno, CA 93727		Fax:	559 291-8413
		www.airways-golf.com	
Managed by:	ClubCorp	Architect:	Bert Stamps
Location:	On the north side of Fresno airport. From State Rt. 99 and/or 41 take exit for State Rt. 180. At Clovis Ave turn left (north). Go 2 miles to Shields. Exit and turn left onto Shields. At first light turn left again on E. Airways and follow it west to the course entrance.		
Style:	Flat terrain, short course with tree-lined holes. Lots of hardpan off the fairway. Greens are in good shape. A very easy walk with very low greens fees.		

Greens Fees	Weekends	Weekdays	Twilight	Seniors	Carts/person
as of 10/08:	$20	$18	$14	11	$12

Course ratings:	Men	Par	Rating	Slope	Yardage	Women	Par	Rating	Slope	Yardage
Airways	White	68	64.9	112	5288	Red	71	69.9	120	5240

Alta Sierra: This semi-private golf course, in the low Sierra forests just

south of Grass Valley, opens for public play on most afternoons. Management advertises it as "a public access course in country club condition." That may be true, but Alta Sierra is prettier than it is challenging. For those trying to escape the severe heat or fog trapped in the nearby Sacramento Valley, it could really fit the bill.

Full-grown conifers line most of the fairways at an elevation of nearly 2000 feet. These trees give the feel of a true mountain course. The layout's lack of adjacent holes, adds a sense of spaciousness. Fairways get a good, even, regular trim, though cut longer than normal to suit the soft fluffy lies preferred by most members. Roughs are watered to stay green up to the tree lines, where they become dry and scruffy.

Success here comes from straight shooting rather than big length. The fairways may be wide, but out-of-bounds stakes stand immediately under the first tree line. This leaves no room for extra roll. The elevated, well-bunkered greens, place a premium on quality chip shots and good approaches. Most break from back to front, and are medium sized with moderate speed. They putt true and receive good maintenance.

Despite its site amidst a forested hilly housing development, the course is fairly easy to walk. Only a few holes show significant inclines. Plus, designer Bob Baldock found reasonably level terrain for most fairways making side-hill lies uncommon. So, if you want a quick get-away from metropolitan Sacramento, and desire forest scenery with a relatively open layout, Alta Sierra is a good choice. *Review based on play in July '08.*

Alta Sierra Country Club			
11897 Tammy Way		Golf Shop:	530 273-2010
Grass Valley, CA 95949		Fax:	530 273-2207
		www.altasierracc.com	
Managed by:	Private, local	Architect:	Bob Baldock

Location:	North of Auburn. Take I-80 towards Auburn and exit north on State Rt. 49. Drive 18 miles to Alta Sierra Dr. Turn right (east) and follow carefully for 1.3 miles. Turn right on Norlene and go .8 miles. Turn left on Tammy and clubhouse is 1/2 mile ahead.
Style:	Mildly rolling forested terrain where most fairways are reasonably level. Wide fairways, but OB stakes are close to tree lines. Course is in good shape, and greens nicely bunkered.

Greens Fees as of 10/08:	Weekends	Weekdays	Twilight	Seniors	Carts/person
	$76	$69	$60/$50	No savings	Included

Course ratings:	Men	Par	Rating	Slope	Yardage	Women	Par	Rating	Slope	Yardage
	Blue	72	71.1	128	6549	Red	73	73.6	133	5786
Alta Sierra	White	72	70.1	126	6336	Red	73	73.2	132	5701
	Silver	72	69.2	125	6170					

Antelope Greens:
Looking to shoot a career round or boost your golfing confidence? No question, Antelope Greens provides the opportunity. Most of its fourteen par-threes play short, with only four requiring shots of 170-yards or more. Par of 58, includes no par-fives, and par-fours all less than 350-yards. Trouble is minimal, except on the signature hole number five, where a TPC Sawgrass style green sits on what appears to be an island. Also be careful on the shortest hole, 85-yard long number four, because shots over the back bounce into a deep creek and those short find a deep bunker. The rest of the holes are fun, because all the fairways, roughs and greens stay in excellent condition, and traps only impact a few off-line shots. Greens are small but don't worry if you miss one, chipping from the soft aprons is a real pleasure. Bottom line . . . Antelope gives a wonderful opportunity to introduce new golfers to the game. Walking is a piece of cake, less than two miles on flat terrain. *Review based on play in September '07.*

Antelope Greens Golf Course

2721 Elverta Road		Golf Shop:	916 334-5764
Antelope, CA 95843		Fax:	916 334-9074

Managed by:	Private, local	Architect:	Don Reiner
Location:	10 miles northeast of Sacramento. Take I-80 to Watt Ave and go left (north) five miles to Elverta Road. Turn left (west) and course is 1/4 mile on the right.		
Style:	Flat terrain, executive course, with 14 par-threes and 4 short par-fours. Course is in good condition, with excellent, mildly bunkered greens. Trees rarely impact approaches. Very easy walk.		

Greens Fees as of 10/08:	Weekends	Weekdays	Twilight	Seniors	Carts/person
	$25	$20	$15/$13	$17	$10

Course ratings:	Men	Par	Rating	Slope	Yardage	Women	Par	Rating	Slope	Yardage
Antelope	Blue	58	56.8	86	3215	Blue	58	57.3	84	3215
Greens	White	58	56.3	85	3007	White	58	56.1	81	3007

Bartley Cavanaugh:
Named for a past Sacramento city manager, Bartley Cavanaugh markets itself as "Sacramento's number one course for fun." The short layout, about 6150-yards from the tips and 4700-yards up front, shows narrow fairways, lots of raised grading between holes, and a well maintained layout. Good

drainage brings out winter players, and in summer stays reasonably soft and very green. The course site, only 90-acres, is tiny for an eighteen-hole course. However, designer Perry Dye did a good job of shoehorning the holes and tee-boxes into various corners of the property. Players need be careful to watch for wayward shots hit from other fairways in a couple of spots. Cart paths were worn out when I played, but were scheduled for repair in '09.

Seniors, beginners, and ladies (it's home to the Sacramento State Fair Women's Championship) seem to be its core customers, though anyone who hits the ball straight should have success. Only four par-fours have lengths over 360-yards, so long hits are rare. The six shorter par-fours require accurate drives but leave very easy approaches to nicely shaped greens. Most distinctive holes are (1) the 445-yard par-four fifteenth, which requires by far the longest approach shot to a nicely designed sculpted green; and (2) number seventeen, a 100-yard short iron to a small island green. Many a good round ends in the pond surrounding this latter green.

At a time when most courses are experiencing a drop in play, Bartley Cavanaugh claims volume is growing. Whether that's because it offers good course conditioning or is just good for the ego, is a matter of conjecture, but the advertised "fun" experience is truly accurate. *Review based on play and interviews in June '08.*

Bartley Cavanaugh Golf Course

8301 Freeport Boulevard		Golf Shop:	916 665-2020
Sacramento, CA 95832		Fax:	916 665-9173
		www.bartleycavanaugh.com	
Managed by:	Morton Golf	Architect:	Perry Dye
Location:	Southern Sacramento. Take I-5 from north or south to Pocket Drive. Follow towards Meadowview (east). At first light turn right (south)on State Rt. 160/Freeport Drive. Course is ahead 1.8 miles on the left.		
Style:	Flat terrain with significant grading and sculpting. Young trees line fairways. Greens use terraces sand slopes to provide challenge on a fairly short, tight course. Kept in excellent condition, very green throughout.		

Greens Fees as of 10/08:	Weekends	Weekdays	Twilight	Seniors	Carts/person
	$35	$25	$19	$32/$20	$15

Course ratings:	Men	Par	Rating	Slope	Yardage	Women	Par	Rating	Slope	Yardage
Bartley Cavanaugh	Gold	71	68.9	122	6118	Blue	72	72.8	124	5734
	Blue	71	67.2	119	5734	White	71	70.6	119	5337
	White	71	65.5	113	5337	Black	71	66.3	107	4714

Bass Lake:
This course offers a short, hilly 5900-yard layout about ten miles west of Placerville. Local Sierra foothill terrain makes for several interesting, narrow holes. Greens can be tiny, especially on some short par-fours, with bunkers sitting directly in front of pin positions. Others have no dangers nearby and offer short, easy birdies. Putting surfaces stay in good condition, running smoothly and relatively fast. Just as the green setups vary, so do fairway landing-zones. Five use narrow alleys only 25-yards wide. Others are free of boundaries or trees within fifty yards, so tee-shots can be launched at will. Such a wide dichotomy is quite unusual.

Current management bought the course in 2002 and has made many improvements since then. New cart paths, a modern irrigation system, a couple of new greens, and a new clubhouse restaurant top the list. Now they need to eliminate weeds that permeate the fairways, roughs, tees and even some of the greens. With real efforts at better grooming on tees, fringes, and creek crossings, and more water in the roughs, this course would have much more appeal. It's in an area of great natural beauty, where the few adjacent homes hide out-of-sight, and the clubhouse has nice views of the distant Sacramento Valley. But lack of care around the periphery detracts so much from the native beauty, that its appeal can easily be missed. *Review based on play in September '08.*

Bass Lake Golf Course

3000 Alexandrite Drive		Golf Shop:	530 677-4653
Rescue, CA 95672		Fax:	530 677-5216
		www.basslakegolfcourse.com	
Managed by:	Private, local	Architect:	Gene Thorne
Location:	In the foothills, due east of Sacramento. Take Capital City Fwy or State Rt. 99 to U.S. 50. Head east 27 miles to Exit 32/Bass Lake Rd. Go left after exit (north) four miles to GreenValley Rd. Continue straight across to Alexandrite, then 200 yards to clubhouse.		
Style:	Rolling terrain with oaks bordering several fairways. Many very tight, short holes with small greens. Some very accurate approaches needed, others not-so-much. Course needs a lot more grooming to be in good shape.		

Greens Fees as of 10/08:	Weekends	Weekdays	Twilight	Seniors	Carts/person
	$38	$28	$28/$22	$30/$22	$12

Course ratings:	Men	Par	Rating	Slope	Yardage	Women	Par	Rating	Slope	Yardage
Bass Lake	Blue	70	69.4	124	5938	Yellow	72	68.1	122	5003
	White	69	67.4	121	5516	Red	72	66.2	116	4585

Beau Pre: "Beautiful Prairie" is the literal French translation for this

northernmost coastal Northern California public eighteen. As a semi-private facility in McKinleyville, twenty miles north of Eureka, Beau Pre sits ten minutes from Arcata's Humbolt State University. Wet winters, summer fog and an off-the-beaten-track location, keep play down to 15,000 rounds each year. This means that when fairways dry out, rounds can be quick, and starting times are easy to get. Summer temperatures usually hover in the low 60's F, which is very pleasant when the wind is calm. But pack extra layers in your bag, because wind and fog can change quickly.

Built in 1967, Beau Pre's property was originally rolling grassland, like its prairie name. Owner and designer Don Harling added hundreds of Monterey and other pines to the few native firs, giving it the current forested appearance. Yardage may be short, but, as local journalist Ken Dalton wrote years ago, "the challenge is greater than the yardage." Water hazards, bunkers, tiny elevated greens, and tight fairways usually eradicate hopes for low scores. Most of the course is maintained well, but many fairways have very thin grass.

A special challenge comes on six holes, three each nine, which climb a naturally forested hill at the eastern perimeter of the property. The first of these, number five, offers a 430-yard uphill par-five double-dogleg, which can be a nightmare for anyone trying to reach the short hole in two. Drives need a long accurate fade, around a tree on the right, and then a hook back the other way on the second shot, around another set of trees. Add a small forest-surrounded green, with a ditch protecting one side, and you have a real test. The next hole, a short par-three, finds its green perched on a ledge, where any miss-direction means serious tree trouble. Even shots on target can bounce off the broad vertical spine down the middle of the putting surface. Other holes in this group have similar challenges, so enjoy the ride on their hilly adventures.

Shorter hitters, who are not trying to break the course record, can have a lot of fun and success too, because the 5750-yard length allows them to play-it-safe and avoid the risks. Long hitters have the option to take risks and get glorious results (which are rare). This variation in options of play make Beau Pre a course for players of all skill levels. *Review based on play and interviews in June '08.*

Beau Pre Golf Club

1777 Norton Road		Golf Shop:	707 839-3412	
McKinleyville, CA 95519		Fax:	707 839-5037	
		www.beaupregc.com		
Managed by:	Private, local	Architect:	Don Harling	
Location:	North of Eureka 15 miles. Take U.S. 101 north past Arcata to Airport Rd., Exit 722. Turn right & drive one mile. At Central Ave. stop sign turn right and then an immediate left onto Norton. Clubhouse is about 1/4 mile up on the right.			
Style:	Mostly flat terrain with six hilly holes. All fairways are tree-lined, some requiring very accurate drives, others giving open shots. Lakes, creeks and slopes make for several interesting holes. Greens are small, some with undulating breaks. Fairway grass can be thin, making irons and woods hard to hit.			

Greens Fees	Weekends	Weekdays	Twilight	Seniors	Carts/person
as of 10/08:	$38	$28	$22/$19	No savings	$13

Course ratings:	Men	Par	Rating	Slope	Yardage	Women	Par	Rating	Slope	Yardage
Beau Pre	Blue	67	68.2	120	5748	White	72	71.8	128	5417
	White	67	66.7	118	5417	Red	68	70.0	124	4869

Bennett Valley: The City of Santa Rosa Department of Recreation and

Parks operates Bennett Valley, located southeast of town. In some ways it's just another muni course, especially on the back nine where holes march back and forth like a drill team trying to optimize use of the parade grounds. However, the front-nine layout shows much more creativity, flowing organically through the trees. Fairways follow contours of local hills, with a densely thicketed creek intersecting many. Greens often sit off the centerline of the fairway, almost around a corner, forcing approach shots to cut across trees or bunkers.

Fairways throughout appear narrow and in decent condition. But roughs, though green in color, can be hard as a rock, allowing crooked shots to bound way off-line or into the omnipresent creek. Greens putt smoothly, at least in the summer, and old-fashioned bunkers sit at the front left and right corners of most.

The course gives a relaxing, if uninspired stroll through a rustic landscape on a mid-week summer afternoon, but has questionable conditions in winter. The clay soil underneath apparently drains poorly, and my playing partners reported soft and mushy conditions persist after rains. Green fees are low, so take advantage when you can. *Review based on play in August '08.*

Bennet Valley Golf Course

3330 Yalupa Avenue		Golf Shop:	707 528-3673
Santa Rosa, CA 95405		Fax:	707 528-1762
		www.bvgolf.org	
Managed by:	Santa Rosa Parks & Rec	Architect:	Ben Harmon

Location:	Eastern Santa Rosa. Take U.S. 101 to State Rt. 12. Head east I.3 miles to Hoen Frontage Rd. Continue straight another .6 miles to Yulupa Ave. Turn right (south) and go 1.6 miles to golf course on the left.
Style:	Front side offers gently rolling hills but back side is flat with uninspired design. Fairways are tree lined. Smallish greens usually have bunkers on the front corners. Rough are very firm, so crooked shots roll into trouble.

Greens Fees as of 10/08:	Weekends $39	Weekdays $25	Twilight $21/$15	Seniors $18 weekdays	Carts/person $13

Course ratings:	Men	Par	Rating	Slope	Yardage	Women	Par	Rating	Slope	Yardage
Bennet Valley	Blue	72	71.3	120	6548	White	75	74.5	123	6207
	White	72	69.5	117	6207	Red	75	71.8	118	5788

Bethel Island:
Years ago, before real estate boomed in nearby Brentwood, Bethel Island opened the second 18-hole golf course in the western Delta. (Lone Tree, p.272, was the first.) Built in 1964, it flourished for years. However, over the past two decades five new courses sprouted in Brentwood and Rio Vista, creating significant competition, and the course now struggles to find players. New owners hired fresh management in 2007, with a plan to renovate greens, bunkers, sprinklers, and eradicate fairway weeds. To date changes include trimming trees, installing a new grass practice tee, and opening a chipping/putting practice area.

Until the more extensive renovation plans become reality, maintenance conditions hold at what I would call mediocre. Greens have an inconsistent mixture of Bermuda and Bent grasses, with some harder and faster than others, and a few even shaggy. Fairways show a mix of many grasses, and are cut longer than at other courses. However, the extra length means the ball sits higher off the ground, so hitting off them is usually okay. Similarly, the roughs are a mix of dense weeds and grasses, but cut so evenly the ball sits up. Bunkers look ratty, with grass growing in at the edges.

As one might expect from a '60's Delta course, course layout was designed more for boaters needing a break from fishing or water-skiing, than for avid golfers. Fairways have average width, and widely spaced trees are set far off the sides of the rough, taking them out of play on most holes. Bunkers sit few and far between, seldom affecting approaches. Back nine fairways exhibit a bit more contouring than the front, and contain a short string of interesting holes at ten, eleven and twelve. Trees on these are closer to the line-of-play, and bunkers or doglegs add some beauty and character.

The biggest challenge at Bethel Island comes from the Delta breeze. Finish your game before 9:00 am or after 5:00 pm unless, like Lee Trevino, you are an expert at hitting the ball low, below the wind. *Review based on play and interviews in June '08.*

Bethel Island Golf Course			
3303 Gateway Drive		Golf Shop:	925 684-2654
Bethel Island, CA 94511		Fax:	925 684-0720
		www.bethelislandgolf.com	
Managed by:	Private, local	Architect:	Bob Baldock
Location:	In the heart of the Delta, east of Antioch. Take State Rt. 4/160 to exit for Brentwood/Stockton. Head east on Rt. 4, through town of Oakley on twisty Main St. for 3.5 miles. Turn left on East Cypress Rd. and head east another 3.1 miles. Turn left on Bethel Island Rd and go 2 miles, across the bridge. Turn right on Gateway; course is on left.		

Style:	Mostly flat terrain, with trees well away from play. Very windy location. Bunkers have been added to increase interest, but are in poor shape. Greens putt well. Good drainage.

Greens Fees	Weekends	Weekdays	Twilight	Seniors	Carts/person
1/1/09	$35	$22	$15/$8 late	$28/$18	$13

Course ratings:	Men	Par	Rating	Slope	Yardage	Women	Par	Rating	Slope	Yardage
Bethel Island	Blue	72	70.7	119	6592	White	76	75.3	129	6292
	White	72	69.3	117	6292	Red	74	72.8	124	5839

Bidwell Park:

The town of Chico, at the north end of the Sacramento Valley, is best known for Chico State University. But it holds another distinction: Bidwell Park, home of the golf course, is one of the largest metropolitan parks in the U.S. Over eleven miles long, and 3760 acres, it stretches from the center of town east into the foothills. About halfway through its width, their golf course started operations in the '20's, and underwent extensive renovation in the '90's.

Terrain here is grassland, rolling hills, creeks, and oak forest, typical of California foothills. The first ten holes present a nice, fluid design where many fairways roll like mild swells on a calm ocean. Others are flat, and tree lines give the character. Greens heave slightly above ground level, adding visual depth to approach shots. Par-five number nine displays a unique feature with a pine tree sitting directly in front of the green at the end of a well-shaped double dogleg. Hitting a wedge high enough to clear it and stop on the green is not easy.

Then at hole eleven, the course changes complexion and difficulty, waking players from the lulling effect of their gentle ocean drift on the front nine. Slopes become more angular, trees bigger, fairways narrower, and distances longer. Greens exhibit more shape, some with mounds in front, so miss-hit approaches bounce off in weird directions. Putting surfaces become longer and narrower, giving more options for unusual pin locations between the bunkers and slopes.

Were it not for the spotty wet and dry condition of fairways, this could well have been a **Best 100** ranked course. If managers from American Golf can get the water and the irrigation system up to snuff, it will be a very fine venue. Even now, it's a good test at a decent price. *Review based on play in July '08.*

Bidwell Park Golf Course

3199 Golf Course Road
Chico, CA 95973

Golf Shop:	530 891-8417
Fax:	530 891-5623

www.bidwellpark.americangolf.com

Managed by:	American Golf	Architect:	Jim Summers
Location:	In Chico's Bidwell Park. From State Rt. 99 take Exit 387B for East Ave. Head east about 2.5 miles, past fire station on left and turn left on Wildwood Ave. Follow it 1.5 miles to the end. Turn right and course is through a park gate about 1/2 mile ahead.		
Style:	Rolling terrain, with tree lined fairways. Front side has less contour than the back. Course is in a large park, so environment is very pastoral. Fairways can have dry spots but are generally good for hitting. Greens have moderate speed, usually well protected by bunkers.		

Greens Fees	Weekends	Weekdays	Twilight	Seniors	Carts/person
as of 10/08:	$33	$25	$21/$17	$19 weekdays	$13

Course ratings:	Men	Par	Rating	Slope	Yardage	Women	Par	Rating	Slope	Yardage
Bidwell Park	Blue	72	70.4	127	6366	White	73	74.7	131	5991
	White	70	68.8	121	6019	Gold	72	70.7	121	5440

Bing Maloney:
Just four miles up Freeport Boulevard from Bartley Cavanaugh sits another of Sacramento's municipal layouts. Bing Maloney, with an older design built in 1952, occupies a much larger property. Consequently, it's longer, flatter, and more classically styled. While Cavanaugh may be the host of State Fair tournaments for ladies, and Haggin Oaks (see No: 57, p.133)) runs the championship flight events for men, Bing Maloney sits in between, managing the middle handicap competition. Its placement in this hierarchy accurately represents the quality and difficulty of a popular, well-priced course.

The design is neither extreme nor difficult, especially with its moderate 6500-yard back-tee length. It has just enough length, trees, and variation around the greens to make interest for players of all abilities. Good conditioning prevails, with *poa anna* greens, wide, flat fairways, and fairly short roughs. Trees usually sit back from the fairway, but not always. Fairways are a combination of well cut Bermuda grass and clover, allowing the ball to sit-up. Bunkers locations lie wide enough of the greens, that approaches have some room for error. The big, mature oaks give good cover from sun on hot summer days.

One hole offers an interesting twist. At number twelve, a long par-four dogleg left, a huge eucalyptus tree sits square in front of the tee box. To its left is a tempting opening between tall redwoods, standing just out-of-bounds, and the big tree. To the right is a small slice of fairway and expanses of open rough. Hit it right and you are safe, but well out of range of the green. Hit left and you risk thumping the big tree or going OB. With the tree about 150 yards out, hitting high drives over it can be done, but require a squarely hit, very high draw to have a chance at the green in two. Anyone knows how to control that high draw? Please advise. *Review based on play and interviews in July '08.*

Bing Maloney Golf Course

6801 Freeport Boulevard		Golf Shop:	916 433-2283
Sacramento, CA 95822		Fax:	916 433-6389
		www.bingmaloney.com	
Managed by:	Morton Golf	Architect:	Mac MacDonaugh
Location:	Southern Sacramento. Take I-5 from north or south to Florin Road. Turn east and follow for .8 miles. Turn left on Freeport Rd and go north .4 miles. Course is on the right.		
Style:	Flat terrain with mature trees. Good *poa anna* greens, which are well bunkered. Fairways are nicely shaped to wind through the oaks, but lave little contouring.		

Greens Fees as of 10/08:	Weekends	Weekdays	Twilight	Seniors	Carts/person
	$35	$25	$19	No savings	$15

Course ratings:	Men	Par	Rating	Slope	Yardage	Women	Par	Rating	Slope	Yardage
	Champ	72	70.8	121	6536	White	74	75.3	127	6452
Bing Maloney	White	72	69.7	120	6289	Red	73	72.2	120	5912
	Red	72	67.9	116	5912					

Bishop:
The town of Bishop, located east of Sierra Mountain passes, is seven hours drive for most of us in Northern California. However, the trip is gorgeous, and

another course, nearby Sierra Star in Mammoth Mountain, ranks No. 29 in the **Best 100**, so here's a suggestion how golfers can experience the area . . .

Take a June drive over the Sierras via Carson or Ebbetts Pass; it's a spectacular month for scenery. Find your way to U.S. 395, either south from Minden, NV, or south from Monitor Pass. The 90-mile stretch of U.S. 395 from Minden to Mono Lake boasts special beauty this time of year. Streams and rivers run full, wildflowers bloom prolifically, and both shrubs and grasses show fresh green growth. Mountain ridges line the highway, traffic is light, and conditions are perfect for superb sightseeing. Both courses sit south of Mono Lake, but less than an hour away; and really ambitious adventurers can head another three hours farther to Furnace Creek Golf Course, in the depths of Death Valley.

Bishop Country Club sits adjacent to U.S. 395, just south of town, about 65 miles south of Mono Lake. Although 90 percent of play comes from local members, the course is public and wants to attract more outsiders and tournaments. In such a low-density population area, one might expect just another dusty valley track. Not so. Bishop presents a mature layout, in good condition, with many modern greens and bunkers. Fully-grown sycamores and cottonwoods create interesting drives and approach obstacles. Fairways mix *poa anna* grass with Bermuda varieties, and are well kept. The greens use nearly pure *poa* and shorter par-threes have huge surfaces.

Nearby 13,682-foot Mt. Tom dominates the western high Sierra ridgeline. While course elevation measures only 3300-feet, and is essentially flat, the commanding vigilance of mountain ranges both east and west, makes for good photos and dramatic scenery. Add a myriad of trees, doglegs, plus a few ditches, and you have a course worth pausing to play. It makes a good second stop, at a very reasonable price, after playing Sierra Star, just up the road. *Review based on play in June '08.*

Bishop Country Club			
1200 South U.S. Highway 395		Golf Shop:	760 873-5828
P. O. Box 1586		Fax:	760 873-5830
Bishop, CA 93515		www.bishopcountryclub.com	
Managed by:	Private, local	Architect:	Unknown
Location:	Eastern Sierras, 3 hours south of Lake Tahoe, on highway 395, just south of Bishop.		
Style:	Mostly flat terrain, with nice fairways and well placed trees. Greens remodeled, with modern contours and bunkers. Fairways in good condition. Great views of surrounding mountain ranges.		

Greens Fees as of 10/08:	Weekends	Weekdays	Twilight	Seniors	Carts/person
	$50	$40	$35	$30	$10

Course ratings:	Men	Par	Rating	Slope	Yardage	Women	Par	Rating	Slope	Yardage
Bishop	Blue	71	71	128	6576	White	71	74.5	131	6084
	White	71	68.9	123	6084	Red	71	70.3	123	5453

Black Horse:
Sharing property with Bayonet (see Chapter 2, p.45) is the Black Horse course. The venue was shut down for renovation and re-styling in 2007, with re-opening planned for mid-2009. At the time of publication, I had not reviewed the new layout.

Blacklake Golf Resort:
This is the fourth of the five Southern California Golf Association (SCGA) courses included in the **Best 100**. Blacklake, located

about fifteen miles south of San Luis Obispo, is managed by the same organization that handles the Avila Beach Golf Resort (see No. 85 in Chapter 2). Both facilities offer reciprocal golf fee packages. Despite the "Resort" label, neither location offers overnight hotel lodging. Rather, Blacklake provides access to extended condo rentals. Winters and summers bring the busiest condo seasons; and most people who rent, stay for at least a month. Spring and fall, which have the best weather, offer better flexibility for shorter stays and lower rents.

Blacklake's facility consists of three nines: The older groupings, named the Lakes and the Canyons, opened in 1962; the third nine, named the Oaks, followed in 1998. This latter option has modern fairways, greenside bunkers and sculpted holes, but is the shortest and narrowest of the three routes. Long hitters find the original two circuits more forgiving, in keeping with resort golf. Tee shots on all three seem fairly open, because fairway bunkers are rare. However, trees, slopes, gullies and industrial-looking concrete lined lakes can come into play. The Oaks requires a couple of precision lay-up drives, and several approaches on the Lakes/Canyon combo find large eucalyptus trees about 125-yards out, protecting both sides of the green.

Fairways play firm, allowing roll to extend 20 to 30 yards more than normal. Wiry Kikuyu grass has invaded, making iron play more difficult than it would be on softer rye grass. Other grass species cause multi colored patches throughout the layout. In fact, except for the greens, January—a peak season—showed lax grooming, perhaps because snowbirds from Chicago or northern Europe may not be to fussy at this time of year. Fairways were cut OK, but roughs had lumpy growth; and leaves and tree droppings cluttered fairways and roughs. Obviously the short-staffed winter greens-crew gave its priority to the greens, which were smooth, fast and held approach shots well. They were a real highlight of the course. *Review based on play in January '08.*

Blacklake Golf Resort

1490 Golf Course Lane		Golf Shop:	806 343-1214
Nipomo, CA 93444		Fax:	806 343-6317
		www.blacklake.com	
Managed by:	Partners with Avila Beach	Architect:	Ted Robinson, Jr
Location:	South of San Luis Obispo 20 miles. From U.S. 101 take Tefft St. exit and go west .8 miles. At Pomeroy Rd, turn right; it turns into Willow. After 2.5 miles turn left at Willow junction, then right on Black Lake Canyon. Follow signs to course.		
Style:	Hilly terrain on three separate nines. The Lakes/Canyon is the older primary course, with lakes and small, highly sloped, well protected greens. The Oaks is newer, with tighter drive landing areas on shorter holes. Oaks and eucalyptus trees prevail throughout.		

Greens Fees as of 10/08:	Weekends	Weekdays	Twilight	Seniors	Carts/person
	$70	$56	$50/$40	$58/$48	$17

Course ratings:	Men	Par	Rating	Slope	Yardage	Women	Par	Rating	Slope	Yardage
Blacklake: Lakes/Canyon	Back	71	71.2	125	6401	White	72	72.1	122	5743
	Middle	71	69.6	122	6056	Red	72	68.2	115	5085
	Forward	71	67.8	117	5628					

Blue Rock Springs, East and West Courses: In

1994, the city of Vallejo began developing large tracts of land on its northeast perimeter. Marine World/Africa USA moved from Redwood Shores in San Mateo County to a site north of Interstate-80's junction with State Rt. 37 in Solano County.

The Lake Chabot Golf Course (yes, there *were* two of them) was eliminated, replaced by a new course, about 2 miles south of the amusement park, which became Blue Rock Springs East. It joined the existing Joe Mortara Golf Course to form a new 36-hole golf complex. The huge project also opened expanses of undeveloped property for new homes, extending from Marine World (now known as Six Flags) south down to Interstate-380. A new expressway, named Columbus Parkway became the transportation axis and now splits the two courses. Joe Mortara was also renamed to Blue Rock Springs West, and one clubhouse now serves both facilities.

The name "Blue Rock" comes from the unusual stone found underneath soil on the property, a crumbly material that looses its color when exposed to the air. The older Joe Mortara Course, underwent many changes including adding and loosing some holes. The West now shows flatter terrain, shorter overall length, and has many more full sized trees lining fairways. These features make an easier, more walk-able and less windy course, popular to those looking for a relaxing park-like experience.

The East Course is quite different. Being newer and built in 1994, immature trees need more growth, and Delta breezes can be quite prominent on its steep hilly setting. Even summer mornings can be quite cool if winds are up. Hills and long distances from green to tee creates long climbs, making walking quite tedious. However, this same terrain adds lots of distinction and character to those seeking interesting and unusual shots.

Nine of the East Course holes, mixed between the front and back sides, are quite different and fun to play. All par-threes qualify to be in this group, with long shots to elevated greens over deep gullies. Number sixteen, at 190-yards (blue tees) is particularly beautiful, with the green set directly below a thirty-foot high vertical cliff dotted by unusual desert vegetation.

The other nine more-ordinary holes are not badly designed; they just don't have the same unusual bunkers, elevations and/or slopes as those in the first group. In fact, the course's blend of *the unique* with *the normal* make an uncommon combination, so players get a break from difficult shots.

The downside at Blue Rock Springs is irregularity in the texture and appearance of fairways and roughs. A mixture of differing grasses, including wiry Kikuyu, keep them from an even green appearance. The colors range from blotchy deep green to light chartreuse (yellow-green), plus plenty of bare dirt and brownish vegetation between fairways and open hillsides. With a more consistently lush appearance and continuity to the holes, the East Course would have been higher rated. *Review based on play and interviews in September '08.*

Blue Rock Springs Golf Course, East

655 Columbus Parkway		Golf Shop:	707 643-8476
Vallejo, CA 94591		Fax:	707 642-1065
		www.bluerockspringsgolf.com	
Managed by:	City of Vallejo	Architect:	Robt. M. Graves
Location:	Northeastern Vallejo. Take Exit 33/Auto Mall Parkway/Columbus Parkway. Drive east 1.7 miles. Clubhouse is on right (west) side of the expressway, as is parking.		
Style:	Very hilly terrain. Modern design bunkers and greens. Some fairways tree lined, others more links-like. Decent lies in fairways and roughs, but multiple varieties of grass gives blotchy appearance. Many side-hill lies. Walking is allowed but challenging.		

Greens Fees as of 1/09:	Weekends	Weekdays	Twilight	Seniors	Carts/person
	$37	$31	$23/$20	$23 weekdays	$16

Course ratings:	Men	Par	Rating	Slope	Yardage	Women	Par	Rating	Slope	Yardage
Blue Rock Springs: East	Blue	70	70.0	132	6133	White	73	73.4	126	5776
	White	70	68.3	125	5776	Gold	70	70.9	121	5332
	Gold	70	66.3	120	5332	Red	70	68.3	114	4851

Blue Rock Springs Golf Course, West (Formerly Joe Mortera GC)									
	Architect:			Joe Mortera					
Style:	Rolling terrain, with some hills on course perimeter. Nearly all fairways lined with mature trees. Nice small greens, well protected by bunkers and sloped aprons. Short course easily walkable.								

Course ratings:	Men	Par	Rating	Slope	Yardage	Women	Par	Rating	Slope	Yardage
Blue Rock Springs: West	Blue	71	68.7	128	5948	Gold	72	70.5	115	5400
	White	71	67.2	123	5701	Red	72	68.5	111	5164
	Gold	71	65.8	120	5400					

Boulder Creek:

The Santa Cruz Mountains, south of San Jose and just north of Santa Cruz, offer all variety of redwood groves, campgrounds and narrow twisty roads. Nestled among these backwoods, sits a rustic resort and wonderful little golf course that have been around since 1961. The compound sits fifteen miles west of the ocean near the entrance to Big Basin Redwoods State Park.

Course style fits nicely into the local scene. It is has the same tall redwoods, verdant grasses and dusty paths one would find in nearby parks. Fog shrouds the giant trees on many mornings, but by 10:00 am, bright sun usually streaks though lacy limbs, and a deep blue sky proves players are truly in the woods, not megalopolis. Contrasts between the dark greens of the tree foliage and the bright green of the well-tended *poa anna* grass is a joyous one, a primary reason many people enjoy the course.

The layout includes 9 par-threes, making it an executive style facility. It's hallmark redwoods provide more than just window-dressing, they create many very narrow fairways, and act as serious obstacles. Small greens, quirky twists, clover in fairways, and mild summer weather add to the mountain-type environment. Course grooming is just average, but the overall aura makes Boulder Creek a nice getaway from the hubbub of Silicon Valley. *Review based on play in August '08.*

Boulder Creek Golf & Country Club and Resort			
16901 Big Basin Highway		Golf Shop:	831 338-2121
Boulder Creek, CA 95006		Fax:	831 338-7862
		www.bouldercreekgolf.com	
Managed by:	Touchstone Golf, LLC	Architect:	Jack Fleming
Location:	Thirty minutes north of Santa Cruz near Big Basin State Park. From Santa Cruz, take State Rt. 9 north 13 miles to Boulder Creek. Turn left on Big Basin Hwy; course is 3.2 miles up the road. From the South Bay, take State Rt. 17 south to Lexington Reservoir. Turn right on Bear Creek Rd and head 13 miles to Boulder Creek. Turn left on Rt. 9 and right on Bear Creek Rd. Course is 3.2 miles up the road.		
Style:	Rolling terrain in a mature redwood grove. Tall trees line many fairways. Executive length course, with narrow fairways and small greens. Short and straight will win the money here.		

Greens Fees as of 10/08:	Weekends	Weekdays	Twilight	Seniors	Carts/person
	$45	$24	$30/$20	$19 weekdays	$11

Course ratings:	Men	Par	Rating	Slope	Yardage	Women	Par	Rating	Slope	Yardage
Boulder Creek	Blue	61	60.9	105	4136	Front	67	63.3	98	3699
	White	61	60.6	105	4079					

Boundary Oak: The name honors a huge old oak, still standing near the

eighth tee on the lowest reaches of Mt Diablo. Terrain, near Walnut Creek's city limits and Shell Ridge Open Space, has just enough rolling slope to give pleasing tee-vistas and distinctive fairways, but not too many side hill stances. Wildlife abounds because the course perimeter adjoins grazing land, creeks and roads, rather than housing. Boundary Oak is not quite rural, but close.

Originally designed by Robert Muir Graves, long-term pro/manager Bob Boldt (recently retired) kept course features relatively modern. The classic style offers tree-lined fairways augmented by steep breaking greens. The first few holes aren't difficult but serve notice that good concentration and precise iron play will be necessary all day. Number two, a 160-yard par-three, portends future putting difficulties with a shallow figure eight shaped green, bunkered in the front/middle, and a severe right-to-left slope. Hit to the wrong loop of the figure eight, and find a ten-foot break plus a putt hard to stop within 15 feet. By the ninth, a longish par-four, the challenge stiffens. Here drives head up-hill to a green mostly hidden from sight. Unseen lakes and culverts guard aprons both left and right. Will experienced local opponents warn you of these blind hazards?

The best hole, or at least the toughest, is par-five, number fourteen. It's a long 565-yard (blue tees) dogleg right, with trees bordering both sides, out-of-bounds (OB) to the far left, and a slight grade angled down towards the OB. Many drives end up in trees on the high side, because players try to cut the dog leg and also prevent rolls into the opposite rough. Recovery shots usually cross the hard fairway anyway, landing in low-side trees. After negotiating the constantly curving fairway, the steep two-tier green gives no rest to the weary.

Course maintenance is just OK, not great. Greens and aprons look good, but fairways contain multiple varieties of grass, including blue, rye, *poa anna*, Bermuda and the dreaded Kikuyu, making for a blotchy appearance. When crews cut the Kikuyu short, irons are tough to hit through its coarse thatch; and when the *poa anna* dies in summer, brown patches appear intermittently. Structures throughout the facility definitely show their age, especially at the old driving range. But for these flaws, Boundary Oaks course gives an enjoyable round, at a good price, offering a different adventure on each hole. It is a Best Value course in the East Bay Region. (See Chapter 5, Region 8.) *Review based on play in June '07 and January '09.*

Boundary Oak Golf Course

3800 Valley Vista Road		Golf Shop:	925 934-4775
Walnut Creek, CA 94598		Fax:	925 934-9128
		www.boundaryoak.com	
Managed by:	CourseCo, starting 7/1/09	Architect:	Robt. M. Graves/R. Boldt
Location:	Eastern Walnut Creek at foot of Mt. Diablo. From I-680 take Ygnacio Valley Road exit east. Drive 4 miles to Oak Grove. Turn right at the light and go to the third stop sign. Turn left onto Valley Vista. Course is 1/3 mile up the road.		
Style:	Rolling terrain, with mature trees lining many fairways. Generally broad driving areas, but hills and/or bunkers can narrow them down. Interesting greens with steep breaks and good bunkering. Course condition can be erratic, depending on water availability.		

Greens Fees as of 10/08:	Weekends	Weekdays	Twilight	Seniors	Carts/person
	$39	$30	$22/$20	$24 weekdays	$15

Course ratings:	Men	Par	Rating	Slope	Yardage	Women	Par	Rating	Slope	Yardage
	Black	72	74.1	130	7110	White	72	76.8	128	6381
Boundary Oak	Blue	72	72.7	126	6751	Red	72	72.3	122	5736
	White	71	71.2	122	6381					

Brentwood:

Twenty-seven holes, on nines named Diablo, Creekside and Hillside, are located within an active adult community built in the 90's. The Diablo nine is shorter, narrower, and more manicured than the others, suited for players who hit balls short and straight. The Creekside/Hillside combination is Brentwood's traditional championship/tournament course at 7000-yards from the rear tees. Its ninth green is located far from the clubhouse, so combining either of its nines with the Diablo grouping is rather inconvenient.

Despite a few dry spots in fairways and roughs, the Creekside/Hillside course is well maintained and can be quite challenging. Fairways flow around mounding to complement contouring of hills and slopes. Closely mown green roughs have fairway edges cut precisely and show good grooming. The roughs stop crooked shots from long rolls, but sit the ball up nicely for easy recovery swings. Greens maintain consistent firmness from hole to hole, usually putt at medium speed, and can be firmed-up for tournament play. A course highlight comes on par-threes, which show particularly good design. Two require 220-yard drives from the back tees, to small, well-protected greens. The others require approach shots over lakes or bunkers to greens where pins can be hidden in small corners or on terraced plateaus.

The ninth and eighteenth holes on the tournament course give tough challenges, handicapped at number one and number two. Each measures well over 400-yards from the middle (blue) tees, with creeks or lakes protecting drive landing zones. But the one and two handicap rankings cause problems for betting and tournament play: (1) If a player gets a one stroke advantage in match-play competition, that stroke advantage may come after the match is already lost. (2) In a common Nassau bet, players receiving a stroke often wait till the last hole of the nine to double-up (press), giving too much advantage on the one hole played in that extra bet. Most courses recognize these subtle difficulties and assign the number one and number two handicaps to earlier holes on each nine. *Review based on play in October '07.*

The Brentwood Golf Club

100 Summerset Drive		Golf Shop:	925 516-3400
Brentwood, CA 94513		Fax:	925 516-3405
		www.brentwoodgolf.com	
Managed by:	Trilogy	Architect:	Ted Robinson

Location: Just east of Antioch. From Livermore and I-580, take Vasco Road north 17 miles (becomes Walnut St, in Brentwood) to Balfour Rd. Turn left and head two miles. Course entrance is on the left, just past Fairview. From Concord and I-680, take State Rt. 4 east to the Brentwood bypass. Continue another 5 miles to Balfour Rd. Turn left (east) and course is immediately on the right.

Style: 27 hole complex. The Diablo section is a separate nine, among retirement homes. It is shorter, tighter, with refined design and well groomed. The Creekside/Hillside combination is the primary tournament venue, with the ninth green far from the clubhouse. Reasonably wide fair-ways, homes farther from play, plenty of length, well protected greens, trees mostly out-of-play. Carts are mandatory.

Greens Fees as of 10/08:	Weekends $70	Weekdays $53	Twilight $37/$29	Seniors See website	Carts/person Included

Course ratings:	Men	Par	Rating	Slope	Yardage	Women	Par	Rating	Slope	Yardage
Brentwood:	Black	72	73.5	133	6824	White	72	75.4	138	5992
Creekside/	Blue	72	71.7	127	6413	Red	72	71.9	130	5357
Hillside	White	72	69.5	124	5992					

Canyon Lakes: This fairly short, tight hillside course sits above Chevron
Corp's world headquarters, just east of Bishop Ranch Business Park in San Ramon.
Despite the gated communities backing up to fairways, the course has been public since
opening in the mid-60's. Originally easy to find, a small shopping mall now sits on land
in front of the clubhouse, so the pro-shop and restaurant hide out of sight from nearby
roads.

The course is lots of fun and is kept in good condition. Wonderful landscaping
augments narrow fairways, usually tree lined with lots of doglegs. Many drives must be
both distance-controlled and straight. Numerous par-fours need only short irons to the
greens, but these must be hit accurately or end up with tough chips. Throughout the
course, elevated greens have multiple tiers, good bunkering, and protection by water
hazards of some sort. The five par-threes offer a group of the **Best 100's** finest. Each
offers medium to long approaches, always over well placed traps, usually to the most
sophisticated green designs on the course.

Canyon Lakes would be a **Best 100** ranked course were it not for a couple of
shortfalls. Due to space constraints, they have no driving range, but just a couple of
warm-up nets. Also, no players are allowed on the course without a power cart. This
latter rule means an adult must accompany children under age eighteen. It keeps
tournaments, such as local amateurs and junior events, from choosing to play here. Deal
with these shortcomings and you should have a good experience. If they allowed
walkers, it would be one of my favorite Bay Area courses. *Review based on play in
November '07.*

Canyon Lakes Country Club

640 Bollinger Canyon Way		Golf Shop:	925 735-6511
San Ramon, CA 94582		Fax:	925 735-5114
		www.canyonlakesgolfclub.com	
Managed by:	Private, local	Architect:	Ted Robinson

Location: Fifteen miles south of Walnut Creek. Take I-680 to Bollinger Canyon Rd. exit. Head east
just over one mile, past Alcosta Blvd, to Canyon Lakes Drive. Turn left, go a couple
hundred yards, turn left again into Canyon Hills Place. This is a large strip mall. Proshop is
in the right rear, behind the shops.

Style: Hilly terrain with tight, tree lined fairways on most holes. Good accuracy needed on most
green approaches. Course is between homes, but they do not interfere with play. Carts are
mandatory, no walkers allowed.

Greens Fees as of 10/08:	Weekends $82	Weekdays $55	Twilight $52/$42	Seniors $42, Mon-Wed	Carts/person Included

Course ratings:	Men	Par	Rating	Slope	Yardage	Women	Par	Rating	Slope	Yardage
Canyon Lakes	Blue	71	71.9	131	6370	White	71	74.5	133	5966
	White	71	70.3	129	6066	Red	71	70.6	123	5191

Chalk Mountain: This very hilly track in Atascadero, just south of Paso
Robles on the Central Coast, provides lots of interesting shots. However, play with
someone who knows the course, or you will not understand the layout of the very first
hole. The starting par-five has so many twists, turns, and blind shots, that it cannot be
briefly described in this review. The general topography of the area includes sharply
contoured hills that create many challenging approach shots to elevated greens. However,
with the exception of uniquely designed and challenging par fives, most driving areas
offer plenty of landing area. Unfortunately, fairways are in erratic condition, with many
dry spots in summer and one smelly septic field. Work was underway in 2007 to
improve some of them. Most roughs show bare hardpan, where balls can easily roll 50-
yards in the wrong direction. Greens are consistent, hold well, are maintained in decent
shape, and putt slowly. Locals say the course gets soggy in winter, so check before
playing at that time of year. *Review based on play in October '07.*

Chalk Mountain Golf Course

10000 El Bordo Road		Golf Shop:	805 466-8848
Atascadero, CA 93422		Fax:	805 466-6238
		www.chalkmountaingolf.com	
Managed by:	Private, local	Architect:	Robt. M. Graves
Location:	Ten miles north of San Luis Obispo. Take U.S. 101 to Santa Rosa Rd. exit in Atascadero. Turn east and go 200 yards to El Camino Real. Turn left and go .3 miles north to La Linia Ave. Turn right and then right again in another .3 miles on El Bordo. Course is 1/3 mile on the right.		
Style:	Hilly terrain with a mixture of severe doglegs and straight hilly holes. Some lay-up drives needed. Elevated greens are common and often small. Fairways in erratic condition, and roughs can be good, or muddy or hardpan. Unusual mix of unorthodox holes.		

Greens Fees as of 10/08:	Weekends	Weekdays	Twilight	Seniors	Carts/person
	$37	$32	$21/$20	$23 weekdays	$16

Course ratings:	Men	Par	Rating	Slope	Yardage	Women	Par	Rating	Slope	Yardage
	Blue	71	70.9	125	6298	White	73	74.3	133	5927
Chalk Mountain	White	71	69.3	120	5927	Red	72	71.1	125	5341
	Red	69	67.0	115	5341					

Cherry Island: Golf architect Robert Muir Graves certainly made an
impact in Northern California, with more than 16 public courses, seven ranked in the
Best 100. One of these, Cherry Island, opened in 1990 and is located northeast of
downtown Sacramento about 10 miles, just a few miles west of Roseville.

Empire Golf took over management in 2006 and their new greens keeper turned a
run-down facility into a popular one. Without making changes to the layout itself, the
fairways, roughs and greens came up-to-standard. Crabgrass was eradicated. Greens
show excellent condition, hold shots consistently, and now run 9 on the Stimp-meter.
Fluffy aprons allow easy chipping. Fairways and roughs are fully green, grass properly
trimmed, and few, if any bare spots show in late summer. One of the few complaints . . .
in the fall, acorns under the oaks pile so deep that taking a firm stance is almost
impossible. (Of course the ball is not supposed to be under the oaks.) Also, watch out for

squirrel burrows near the acorns; they gobble up balls hit under the oaks, and can easily twist or break an ankle.

Holes have good shape, but perhaps the strangest hole is number one; so, do not be deterred if you think it sets the example for the rest. The par-four is 331-yards from blues, but only 295 from the whites, and 230 from the reds. It is has a 90-degree dogleg at about 75-yards from the green, so locals often just hit straight at the green, through or under the oaks, and the risk the perils of trees and bunkers blocking the way. With hardpan under the oaks, a 200-yard hit can almost roll to the apron. Of course some players just hit down the narrow slot of the traditional target line and approach with a wedge or short iron. What fun is that? Holes ten and sixteen are the toughest on the course. Ten forces a lay-up drive and then a 200-plus second across a wide creek. Later, sixteen gives us one of the few treeless holes but allows two opportunities—on the drive and the approach—to hit into a large lake.

Nice design, several interesting twists, and good condition make a good combination at Cherry Island. It came very close to a **Best 100** ranking. *Review based on play in October '07.*

Cherry Island Golf Course

2360 Elverta Road	Golf Shop:	916 991-7293
Elverta, CA 95626	Fax:	916 991-6512
	www.empiregolf.com	
Managed by: Empire Golf	Architect:	Robt. M. Graves
Location:	10 miles northeast of Sacramento. Take I-80 to Watt Ave and go left (north) 5 miles to Elverta Road. Turn left (west) and course is 1/2 mile on the left.	
Style:	Flat terrain graded nicely into mild contours and doglegs. Trees line most fairways, but not tightly. Fairway and roughs in good condition. Greens are well protected with multiple bunkers.	

Greens Fees	Weekends	Weekdays	Twilight	Seniors	Carts/person
as of 10/08:	$33	$25	$19/$16	$20	$15

Course ratings:	Men	Par	Rating	Slope	Yardage	Women	Par	Rating	Slope	Yardage
	Blue	72	71.6	123	6562	Gold	72	71.8	129	5556
Cherry Island	White	72	70.2	118	6201	Red	72	71.0	121	5158
	Gold	71	67.2	114	5556					

Chuck Corica: Earl Fry and Jack Clark Courses:

The city of Alameda operates two eighteen-hole muni's and one short nine-hole course. All lie at the extreme southern end of the Alameda peninsula, adjacent to northern runways of the Oakland Airport. The North Course, now called the Earl Fry Course, opened in 1928; the South Course, named after columnist Jack Clark, came in the mid-50's. Later, in 1992 the city honored Chuck Corica, mayor of Alameda during construction of the second course, by changing the complexes name from the original Alameda Golf Courses.

The older north venue gets more play. Though 250-yards shorter and narrower than the south course, full sized trees give a sense of maturity. Hazards tightly protect many landing zones, so its slope rating is two points higher than Jack Clark, despite lesser length. Fairway shapes can be very distinctive and unusual, with mowing crews leaving strategically placed patches of rough in areas normally at the center of fairways. These patches can be seen from the tee-box and force drives to be aimed off center, closer to tree lines. This unusual touch adds character to the North Course. Maintenance seems to keep a tighter reign on the North, as the greens speed is faster, and aprons are more evenly trimmed.

The south course, with its wider fairways and broader bunker spacing around greens, encourages the big hitters to let-it-loose. Even balls hit off-line into bordering tree lines usually find an opening for recovery shots. The greens putt slower, making short play easier for many players.

Although not very challenging, the maintenance and conditioning of both Chuck Corica courses (at least in the spring) make them a good experience. Roughs stay evenly cut, with dry-spots rare. Fairways roll well but the ball sits up nicely. I had no bad lies. Trees, usually pine or eucalyptus, line all fairways. Since eucalyptus trees routinely drop seedpods, leaves and bark, greens-keepers stay busy, cleaning up after them. A more serious problem is the severe encroachment of Kikuyu grass, especially around aprons on the greens. Players not experienced with this wiry type of chipping surface, should plan on several flubbed shots before getting used to it. *Review based on play and interviews in May '08.*

Chuck Corica Golf Courses: Earl Fry/North Course

1 Clubhouse Memorial Road		Golf Shop:	510 747-7824
Alameda, CA 94502		Fax:	510 522-0848
		www.golfinalameda.com	
Managed by:	KemperSports	Architect:	William P. Bell/D. Muirhead
Location:	Southern Alameda, just north of Oakland Airport. From 1-880, take High Street/Exit 38, towards Alameda. Go 1.5 miles to end at Otis Dr. Turn left, go across bridge and take immediate right on Island Dr. Go another .5 miles and turn left on Clubhouse Memorial Dr. into golf complex.		
Style:	Mostly flat terrain, with wide, treelined fairways. Some are cut so that rough protrudes and creates narrow landing areas. Greens have moderate slopes and bunkering, with Kikuyu aprons.		

Greens Fees as of 10/08:	Weekends	Weekdays	Twilight	Seniors	Carts/person
	$35	$28	$25/$23	$23 weekdays	$15

Course ratings:	Men	Par	Rating	Slope	Yardage	Women	Par	Rating	Slope	Yardage
Chuck Corica: Earl Fry	Black	70	70.4	121	6307	White	72	72.3	120	5708
	Blue	70	68.8	117	5985	Red	72	70.6	112	5286
	White	69	67.5	112	5651					

Chuck Corica Golf Courses: Jack Clark/South Course

		Architect:	William F. Bell/Robt. M. Graves
Style:	Flat terrain with some lakes and wide-set trees. Course is newer and not as mature as North Course. Wider landing areas and somewhat more wind.		

Course ratings:	Men	Par	Rating	Slope	Yardage	Women	Par	Rating	Slope	Yardage
Chuck Corica: Jack Clark	Black	71	71.6	119	6586	White	73	72.4	119	5743
	Blue	71	70.1	117	6296	Red	70	70.0	113	5310
	White	69	67.5	112	5743					

Cordova:
During the 90's, Cordova Golf Course saw more rounds played than any other metropolitan Sacramento golf venue, peaking at 120,000 rounds per year. Since then the number of competitive tracks has doubled, and number of rounds at Cordova cut in half. That's still not bad for a par-63, 4800-yard executive course.

The secret to keeping a 60,000 annual volume, has been to understand the strengths of the course, and then find customers that fit. First the course: It's very short, with trees set well back from fairways, but individual holes require full-length shots. Of the nine par-threes, three of them have 200-yard or longer approaches. The other six have varying lengths, from 150 to 195-yards, so players can use several different clubs. Par-fours mostly range from 380 to 400-yards, with some greens well bunkered, requiring good skills to hit them in regulation.

Now for the customers: Wide fairways make it easy for beginners, juniors and seniors to learn and practice real shots on full-sized holes. With decent fairways, slow greens, short rough, and few water hazards, play is relatively easy and quick. Three-hour rounds are common mid-week. Normal length par-fours and long par-threes mean good players still have fun and challenge. Put these features together, add super-low greens fees, plus a course that's flat and easy to walk, and you have popularity. Grandma, Grandpa and a couple of grandkids can afford to play together for less than the cost of one greens fee at a fancy course. Maintenance is not perfect, but irrigation improvements and a new, energized greens-keeper are moving things in the right direction. *Review based on play and interviews in October '08.*

Cordova Golf Course

9425 Jackson Road	Golf Shop:	916 362-1196
Sacramento, CA 95826	Fax:	916 362-6172
	www.cordovagc.com	

Managed by:	Private, local
Location:	Southeastern Sacramento. Take U.S. 50 to State Rt. 16 exit. Go southeast on Rt. 16, about 4 miles, past S. Watt Ave. to the course on the left.
Style:	Flat terrain, executive short course. Fairways and roughs are in playable but not great condition. Greens fees set for great deals on low cost family groups.

Greens Fees as of 10/08:	Weekends $19	Weekdays $13	Twilight $12/$9	Seniors ask proshop	Carts/person $11

Course ratings:	Men	Par	Rating	Slope	Yardage	Women	Par	Rating	Slope	Yardage
Cordova	White	63	61.9	95	4842	Red	66	65.8	99	4728

Coyote Run:
Beale Air Force Base, six miles east of Marysville, has operated a military golf course since 1968. In 1988, after the Air Force took over from the Army, the course opened to public play. Now, anyone can arrange a game, provided they call the pro shop to get advance approval, and then show up at one of the Base gates with a driver's license, car insurance papers and registration. Beware; this is a huge base with over 50 square miles of space, so the North Beale Drive gate, six miles due east of the Hamonton-Smartville Rd. junction, is the easiest place to cross onto the premises and find the course.

Since Coyote Run is owned and operated by the military, outside paid publicity is not authorized. As with most military and ex-military courses, maintenance crews keep the course in good shape. It has nice greens and roughs, and a traditional layout that extends to almost 6800-yards. Soft fairways prevent the long summer rolls experienced on other area courses. Mature trees line front-side fairways, but smaller trees on the newer back side give it a more links-like feel. Gently rolling terrain, with natural mounds and ridges, brings variation to hole designs. Beginners who don't hit the ball too far will find it a good place to learn or practice, but players who hit the ball really crooked will loose lots of balls, because the wide-set primary rough stays quite wild.

Speed of play at Coyote can be very fast unless you end up behind one of the frequent military leagues. The lack of open publicity keeps non-military away, so those who know the ropes can speed around in no time. I prefer it to Travis' Cypress Lakes. *Review based on play and interviews in June '08.*

Coyote Run Golf Course

17440 Warren Shingle Boulevard	Golf Shop: 530 788-0192
Beale AFB, CA 95903	Fax: 530 788-0199
	www.bealeservices.com

Managed by:	USAF
Location:	On Beale Air Force Base, east of Marysville. From Yuba City/Marysville, take State Rt. 70 to State Rt. 65 and continue south to S. Beale Drive. Turn left and go 4 miles to Beale AFB Gate. Ask there for further directions. Remember to ask pro-shop to advise Gate you will be coming. Have drivers license, registration and proof of insurance to get on the base.
Style:	Gently rolling terrain. Front nine has reasonably wide fairways, many bordered by trees. Back nine is more open with ponds, bull rushes and a links-link feel on most holes. Greens in good shape, usually fronted by traps on the corners.

Greens Fees as of 10/08:	Weekends	Weekdays	Twilight	Seniors	Carts/person
	$25	$25	$29 includes cart	$22 weekdays	$12

Course ratings:	Men	Par	Rating	Slope	Yardage	Women	Par	Rating	Slope	Yardage
	Gold	72	72.3	128	6814	White	72	71.8	126	5598
Coyote Run	Blue	72	70.0	123	6347	Red	69	66.8	112	4624
	White	69	66.6	114	5598					

Creekside:
Most visitors wouldn't know it, but the road to Modesto's Creekside Municipal Golf Course leads right past headquarters of E&J Gallo, largest wine maker in the world. No signs, no massive tanks, just lots of cars in a full parking lot. Gallo, it turns out, is one of the few successful agricultural businesses left on busy State Rt. 132. Lots of empty buildings remain on the south side of the thoroughfare, victims of California's manufacturing malaise. Now Modesto growth comes from transplanted commuters or retirees who have fled the Bay Area to find affordable and less crowded living.

Creekside offers the newer and more modern of two municipal courses in town, the other being Dryden Park. Grasses are green throughout; landscaping is attractive and the course is well maintained. By today's standards, length measures only a moderate 6610-yards. However, attractive bunkering surrounds large putting surfaces, and approach shots need plenty of shot-making skill. Greens seeded with bent grass often sport double-tiered designs with moderate slopes, so they can be fun to putt.

The course's two nines display somewhat different looks. The back nine plays longer and flatter, with mostly straight fairways. Because it lacks hills and hollows, holes seem undistinguished, though attractive. Number eighteen is the exception; its green is well defended by lakes on both sides and a tree on the corner of a dogleg blocks errant drives. The front side shows more interest, since several holes run through a recessed flood plain on the north boundary of the course. An elevated tee on number six aims drives downhill to a long left-curving par-five, where bunkers and out-of-bounds guard the left and a hill protects the right. Next, number seven turns back to the right, around the same hill and trees, with a sharp dogleg and an approach over bunkers to a long undulating green. If only the rest of the course had the character of these two, it would easily make the **Best 100** rankings. *Review based on play in March '08.*

Creekside Golf Course		
701 Lincoln Avenue	Golf Shop:	209 571-5123
Modesto, CA 95354	Fax:	209 578-1914
	http://www.modestogov.com/prnd/facilities/golf.asp	
Managed by: City of Modesto	Architect:	Halsey Daray Golf.
Location:	On State Rt. 132, in eastern Modesto, about 4 miles east of State Rt. 99. From State Rt. 132, take Lincoln Avenue turnoff and head north about 3/4 mile to the course.	
Style:	Mostly flat terrain with some mounded and sculpted roughs. Tree lined fairways. Nice modern greens with terraced putting and extensive bunkers. Some fairway bunkers.	

Greens Fees as of 10/08:	Weekends	Weekdays	Twilight	Seniors	Carts/person
	$30	$23	$21/$17	$19 weekdays	$15

Course ratings:	Men	Par	Rating	Slope	Yardage	Women	Par	Rating	Slope	Yardage
Creekside	Blue	72	70.9	121	6610	White	72	73.3	116	6021
	White	72	68.2	114	6021	Red	72	70.3	110	5496

Crystal Springs:
Renowned for its hilly terrain and views of Crystal Springs Reservoirs, this is one of the oldest public courses on the San Francisco Peninsula. Built in 1924 and designed by William Herbert Fowler, re-designer of Scotland's renowned Cruden Bay, it comes with an excellent pedigree.

The layout displays two contrasting environments, one low on the sloping hill that dominates the area, the other near its top, easily visible from nearby Interstate-280. On lower holes, the tranquil environment of tree-covered hills protecting San Francisco's water reservoirs dominate the atmosphere. Wildlife from protected watershed runs rampant. The sixth tee, at the start of this stretch, gives a great view of all three lakes and is so picturesque that nearby terracing has been landscaped for a pagoda and wedding ceremonies.

Back up top and to the north, many back nine holes run adjacent to or within easy earshot of the Interstate. To be fair, the highway was built in the 60's, well after the course, and unfairly intruded on an otherwise serene setting. Now, despite the cypress, eucalyptus and oaks shielding the eastern perimeter, freeway noise pervades and detracts from the visual beauty of the surroundings.

Maintenance conditions on greens, fairways and roughs are inconsistent. Drainage improvements were made in the last ten years, but minor wet spots remain.

Roughs are sparse a mere 10-yards off the fairway, fading quickly into weeds and hard dirt. Greens come with only medium speed; some show blotchy and dry patches, some look fine.

Despite these contrasts, the course contains five noteworthy holes: Number six has the great view mentioned above and its downhill slope can add an ego boosting 75-yards to drives. Nine demands a very straight drive; then a tight left side out-of-bounds catches many shots approaching the green. Twelve calls for a steep uphill approach, which adds three clubs to the final shot; and if overshot, a slope behind the green leads to purgatory. Fourteen, a flowing, long, dogleg left, through the trees to a well-bunkered green, is a classic tree lined hole. And finally, the clubhouse-on-the-hill, reminds me a little of the eighteenth green setting at nearby Olympic Club, up in San Francisco.

Course maintenance conditions may be a little erratic, but the ups and downs of the topography make Crystal Springs a fun game. *Review based on play and interviews in July '07.*

Crystal Springs Golf Course

6650 Golf Course Drive	Golf Shop:	650 342-0603
Burlingame, CA 94010	Fax:	650 342-1769
	www.playcrystalsprings.com	

Managed by:	CourseCo	Architect: Herbert Fowler
Location:	In the hills west of San Francisco Airport. Take I-380 west and then I-280 south to Black Mtn Rd/Hayne Rd. exit from I-280. Turn west towards the ocean. At dead end in 200 yards turn right (north) and drive 1/2 mile to the clubhouse on the left.	
Style:	Hilly terrain with many sidehill lies. Small greens and many doglegs. Fairways in good shape, greens can be slow and bumpy. Some excellent views of Crystal Springs Reservoirs. Several holes within earshot of I-280 freeway.	

Greens Fees as of 10/08:	Weekends	Weekdays	Twilight	Seniors	Carts/person
	$51	$36	$36/$25	$25 weekdays	$15

Course ratings:	Men	Par	Rating	Slope	Yardage	Women	Par	Rating	Slope	Yardage
	Blue	72	72.2	127	6590	White	72	76.0	134	6238
Crystal Springs	White	71	70.3	125	6201	Gold	72	72.5	126	5561
	Gold	69	67.1	118	5483					

Cypress Lakes:
Travis Air Force Base is one of only four military/U.S. Government installations that maintains eighteen-hole golf courses in Northern California. Located near Fairfield it runs the Cypress Lakes course, just off base. The other three include (1) Beale AFB, which manages Coyote Run Golf Course on the property, so their pro shop must arrange for a pass at the security gate; (2) the Golf Club at Moffet Field, which remains private, and is operated by NASA; and (3) Monterey Pines, run by the Dept. of Defense for the Naval Post Graduate School, in Monterey. Other ex-military installations such as the Presidio in San Francisco, the old Fort Ord near Monterey, Mare Island in Vallejo, and Mather AFB in Sacramento, have sold their courses either to cities, counties or private parties. Lemoore NAS has a course nearby, but it's always been a muni, not military.

Cypress Lakes (Travis) is not as interesting a design as Coyote Run (Beale), but it is a good place to get away for a quiet afternoon round. Only military personnel or members can play in the mornings, but the-public-at-large is invited on weekday afternoons. Call in advance to make sure. Course conditions are good, typical of the military, with nice greens, tees and bunkers. Fairways are especially well-trimmed, with sculpted edges on some holes. Old-fashioned amenities such as benches-under-trees and water coolers—rare in an era of carts—are located near almost every tee.

The course layout and design are a little mundane. Large mature eucalyptus and evergreens give a wide berth to the broad fairways. A few doglegs show up, but not many. Flat fairways prevail, and push-up greens get routine bunker protection on the front corners. Those so inclined can find plenty of length from the tees, and the layout does not yield low scores, even from the regular men's or lady's tees. Hole number eighteen is the whopper of the group, a doozie at 425-yards, around a sharp corner, over a creek fronting the green. Many a good round ends on the final approach. In summers, expect cooler Delta weather and Delta breezes. *Review based on play in August '08.*

Cypress Lakes Golf Course

5601 Meridian Road	Golf Shop:	707 448-7186
Vacaville, CA 95687	Fax:	707 452-9961
	www.60thservices.com/recreation/cypress	
Managed by: USAF	Architect:	USAF/unknown

Location: In southeastern Vacaville. From the west, take I-80 to Alamo Rd exit in Vacaville. Head east 5 miles (becomes Fry Road) to Meridian. Turn right (south) and course is one mile on the right. From Sacramento, take I-80 to Liesure Town Road. Head south 3.5 miles to Fry. Turn left for one mile then turn right on Meridian and go one mile to the course entrance.

Style: Flat terrain, with wide, well manicured fairways and good greens. Very good walking course with frequent water fountains and benches. Tree lined, mostly straight fairways with plenty of length, even from regular tees. Near Delta, so can be windy.

Greens Fees as of 10/08:	Weekends	Weekdays	Twilight	Seniors	Carts/person
	$29	$24	$24/$19	No savings	$15

Course ratings:	Men	Par	Rating	Slope	Yardage	Women	Par	Rating	Slope	Yardage
Cypress Lakes	Blue	72	72.5	120	6855	Red	73	72.0	121	5809
	White	72	70.6	115	6492					

Davis: Looking for an inexpensive round on a course where par is only 67? This

could be your choice. Built in 1964, its layout is very flat and outdated. Many holes have a similar appearance, so the view from the tee-box gets a little monotonous. Numerous par-fours require a repetition of drive/wedge, drive/wedge. Par-fives show a similar repetition of drive/fairway-wood/and maybe a chip; so, club selection repeats over and over. However, for golfers who want an ego boost or a learning opportunity, it's a simple decision to play here.

With the back tee course rating at 63.1, almost four points below par, the course is about as easy as anywhere. Want a lot of birdies or pars? This is the course to play. Most holes are short, with many 300-yard par-fours. One of these, number nine, measures only 220-yards and tempts even not-so-strong strong golfers to go for the green on the drive. Even at this extremely short distance, a huge bunker in front makes it fun. Clearing it is a thrill, but hard to accomplish.

Davis gets heavy usage, over 70,000 rounds per year, so weekend play is slower than I expected for a short course. But low cost and a high number of club outings, keep players—from retirees to beginners—coming back for more. *Review based on play and interviews in July '07.*

Davis Golf Course

24439 Fairway Drive		Golf Shop:	530 756-4010
P.O. Box 928		Fax:	530 756-0647
Davis, CA 95617		www.davisgolfcourse.com	

Managed by:	Private, local
Location:	Northwestern edge of Davis, 15 miles west of Sacramento. Take I-80 to State Rt. 113 North. Go five miles to Rd 29. Take the exit, turn left and head west 1/4 mile to Fairway Drive. Turn left (south) and go 1/2 mile to course.
Style:	Flat terrain, very short course, but more than executive length. Tree lined fairways with some bunkers protecting landings areas. Bermuda fairways and greens. Fairways in mediocre condition and very firm. Greens small, some protected by shallow bunkers.

Architect: Bob Baldock

Greens Fees as of 10/08:	Weekends	Weekdays	Twilight	Seniors	Carts/person
	$20	$16	$12/$10	$12 weekdays	$11

Course ratings:	Men	Par	Rating	Slope	Yardage	Women	Par	Rating	Slope	Yardage
Davis	Blue	66	63.1	107	4933	Blue	67	67.9	112	4962
	White	65	60.9	100	4349	Red	66	64.9	105	4422

Deep Cliff: Tired of whacking away on a windy course by the bay? Silicon Valley residents have only one place to play eighteen holes on a local, secluded, usually warm, public location. That's Deep Cliff, a short executive-type course wedged in a hollow below the northern hills of Cupertino. In the spring and summer, these hills are much warmer and inviting than any of the normal length courses along Bayshore Freeway.

It may be short, but that doesn't mean it lacks challenge. Narrow fairways, small greens, and trees standing very close to many of the fairways, provide its defining character. The park-like environment, similar to that of Berkeley's Tilden Park, is on a smaller scale. Walking is simple and flat. Fairways and roughs are maintained decently, greens are smooth and a pleasure, and traps stay well raked. Only thing missing, other than a lot of extra yardage, is a full sized driving range; they use nets (nice ones) instead. *Review based on play in July '07.*

Deep Cliff Golf Course

10700 Clubhouse Lane		Golf Shop:	408 253-5357
Cupertino, CA 95014		Fax:	408 253-4521
		www.playdeepcliff.com	
Managed by:	CourseCo	Architect:	Clark Glasson
Location:	Northwest of San Jose Airport about 10 miles. Take I-280 to Foothill Expressway exit in southern Los Altos. Turn south towards mountains and drive 1.5 miles to McClelland Dr. Turn left, then follow down around a steep hill to the course.		
Style:	Gently rolling terrain nestled against steep mountainsides. Short executive style course with tight fairways and lots of trees and doglegs. Fairways in decent condition, and greens are very nice. Best to play in summer when trees are full of leaves. A very easy walk.		

Greens Fees as of 10/08:	Weekends $38	Weekdays $28	Twilight $28/$21	Seniors $22 incl lunch	Carts/person $11

Course ratings:	Men	Par	Rating	Slope	Yardage	Women	Par	Rating	Slope	Yardage
Deep Cliff	Blue	60	59.7	99	3369	Blue	60	59.2	96	3369
						White	60	56.8	91	2938

Delta View: California's own version of Pennsylvania's city of Pittsburg sits

at the junction of the San Joaquin and Sacramento Rivers. Hills to the south form a perfect overlook for views of the Delta Region, spreading eastward with nearly 1500 square miles of croplands and wildlife habitat. Legendary course designer Alister MacKenzie was selected to work his magic here, back in the late 1940's. This icon, which worked as a camouflage specialist for the U.S. Army, lived temporarily at nearby (now defunct) Camp Stoneman. He is rumored to have made his first sketches for the original nine holes at Delta View on the back of a cocktail napkin.

Today, not much is left of his original vision. Only holes eleven, fourteen and sixteen continue to display his famous bunker designs around the greens. In 1991, prolific California architect Robert Muir Graves renovated the MacKenzie back nine, and added a new front of his own. The result is a composite, joining the gentler terrain covered by MacKenzie with hillier landscapes of Graves into a scenic venue.

Graves' work on the front side uses more manufactured contours and mounds than MacKenzie's natural appearing terrain, but the holes have good layouts. He takes golfers high up onto hills at the middle of this nine, for panoramic vistas of the Delta. Par-threes number six, going from hilltop to hilltop, and nine, needing a very long approach over a lake, show Graves is not afraid to bring his own brand of difficulty to a design.

Despite the pedigree given by two famous designers, Delta View comes up short of a ranking in the **Best 100**. Course condition is erratic, with slower greens than I expected. Little manicuring is done between holes, and dry spots showed on fairways and in roughs. Did the drought of '07-'08 have an affect on late summer play? Perhaps, but the same drought didn't have a similar impact on nearby Diablo Creek or Lone Tree. Also, rather than being a congruent series of well-designed holes, the layout is choppy and disjointed. Holes are nicely different from each other, but do not flow together as a unit. *Review based on play in October '08.*

Delta View Golf Course

2232 Golf Club Road
Pittsburg, CA 94565

Golf Shop: 925 252-4080
Fax: 925 439-8287
www.deltaviewgolfcourse.com

Managed by:	City of Pittsburg
Location:	Between Concord and Antioch. Take State Rt. 4 to the Bailey Rd. exit and turn south for 1/2 mile. Turn left (east) on W. Leland Ave. Drive 1.7 miles to Golf Club Drive. Turn right and clubhouse is just ahead. W. Leland can also be reached from Railroad Ave, if coming from the east via Rt. 4.
Style:	Hilly terrain, with some nice views of the Sacramento River. Doglegs and elevated greens or tees are typical of most holes. Side hill lies are common. Greens are sloped, but not severely. Trees border some fairways, mostly on the back nine. Fairways have spotty dry spots.

Architect: R. M. Graves/A. MacKenzie

Greens Fees	Weekends	Weekdays	Twilight	Seniors	Carts/person
as of 10/08:	$40	$25	$15	$15 weekdays	$14

Course ratings:	Men	Par	Rating	Slope	Yardage	Women	Par	Rating	Slope	Yardage
Delta View	Blue	70	71.3	133	6317	White	72	73.6	129	5775
	White	70	68.3	125	5775	Red	72	70.9	123	5261

Diablo Creek:

Back in the '60's Diablo Creek was just a flat, bare piece of windswept grazing land near Concord Naval Weapons Station. One could still see the old concrete weapons bunkers nearby, and the new golf course was a series of push-up greens, dry fairways and newly planted Monterey pines. Today, the topography is still flat, the old pines have been replaced by newer more durable varieties, and the course has grown into a very comfortable facility. If the original plantings had been stronger, they would now be fully-grown and the course would be that much more mature.

Despite the medium aged trees, Diablo Creek is a good course. Its fairways are well kept, reasonably soft, and a pleasure for both hitting and walking. Roughs are well maintained too, being evenly cut and green throughout the course. A few bare spots can be found, but they usually show markings as ground-under-repair. Large greens are very deep, so players need to add or subtract almost two clubs for front or rear pin positions. Well maintained greens usually run about a 9 Stimp speed, which is on the upper/medium side of the scale. Those golfers who hit from the white tee boxes will probably be surprised at the long, 6500-yards length. Yardage from the tips is close to 7000-yards.

The master layout puts most fairways up-wind or down-wind. When holes head into the breeze, 400-yards plays more like 450. This requires some real pokes for average golfers. Happily, landing zones are wide, especially on the longer front nine. It may take a few extra strokes to arrive at the green, but most can be reached without penalty. Rarely do mid-fairway bunkers impede progress, though a few holes have large ponds that tighten up landing areas.

This is a busy course. Though the pro-shop will usually find a way to wangle you a last minute starting time, plan on a five-hour plus round. And remember, Diablo Creek sits adjacent to the Delta, there are no hills or tall trees to keep the wind at bay. *Review based on play two times, last with interviews in September '08.*

Diablo Creek Golf Course

4050 Port Chicago Highway		Golf Shop:	925 686-6262
Concord, CA 94520		Fax:	925 681-1536
		www.diablocreekgc.com	
Managed by:	City of Concord	Architect:	Robt. M. Graves
Location:	Ten miles north of Walnut Creek near old Port Chicago Naval Weapons Station. Take State Rt. 4 to Port Chicago Hwy exit and head north 1/2 mile. Course is on the right.		
Style:	Flat terrain, with tree lined fairways. Plenty of distance on long, straight holes into the wind. Good bunker placement in fairways and around greens. Greens can be very deep. Good course condition but not much character to hole designs.		

Greens Fees	Weekends	Weekdays	Twilight	Seniors	Carts/person
as of 10/08:	$37	$28	$22/$19	$24 Fridays	$13

Course ratings:	Men	Par	Rating	Slope	Yardage	Women	Par	Rating	Slope	Yardage
	Blue	71	72.7	121	6885	Red	71	72.6	122	5683
Diablo Creek	White	71	70.5	117	6455					
	Gold	71	68.7	113	6072					

Diamond Mountain:
Susanville, about three hours north of Lake Tahoe, used to be known for its lumber mills. With the timber industry's decline, state and federal prisons took over as the major employer. Managers at Diamond Mountain, a local nine-hole muni, decided they needed to add an additional nine to support incoming golfing/prison-guard residents. Initially, the new concept did not work well, play slumped, and the course fell into disrepair. Then in 2008, a new management team came on board. Now, fertilizers, herbicides, new maintenance procedures, added manpower and better pricing slowly edge the course back to good condition.

The original front layout plays like many older muni's. Holes have straight fairways and low push-up greens, surrounded by bare desert landscape. The fairways and greens are in average condition, roughs are cut but otherwise un-groomed, and deep primary rough is filled with tall native wildflowers.

The newer back nine has the potential for much more character. It's shapes use modern design and up-to date construction techniques. Fairways have mounds and slopes; greens are smoother and faster. The first three holes remain in the desert meadow but flow nicely; the next six push into the surrounding forest. Interesting doglegs and small but sophisticated green complexes dominate the latter group. Greens may even be overly sloped to the point that pin location options are limited.

Unfortunately, as of July '08, immaturity still reigns in the new fairways, forcing lift-clean-and-place rules throughout. According to local residents, conditions are better than in '07, when they were mostly mud; and work continues to finish their development. New managers are working hard to re-earn the enthusiasm of players alienated the past few years, and seem to be making headway. *Review based on play in July '08.*

Diamond Mountain Golf Course

470-895 Circle Drive		Golf Shop:	530 257-2520
Susanville, CA 96130		Fax:	530 257-2523
		www.diamondmountaingolf.com	
Managed by:	Private, local	Architect:	Dave Tanner

Location: Northeastern California, 90 miles northwest of Reno. Once in Susanville on State Rt. 36, turn south on S.Weatherlow St, which shortly becomes Richmond Rd. Continue for four miles to Circle Drive. Turn right, course is on the right in 3/4 mile.

Style: Front nine is flat with a few creeks and a lake. It has open, firm fairways and mature greens. Back side is newly constructed with contoured fairways that need time to grow. Design here is much more sophisticated, with bunkers guarding highly sloped greens and several holes winding thru forests.

Greens Fees as of 5/09:	Weekends	Weekdays	Twilight	Seniors	Carts/person
	$30	$30	$20	$25	$13

Course ratings:	Men	Par	Rating	Slope	Yardage	Women	Par	Rating	Slope	Yardage
Diamond Mountian	Blue	71	70.4	124	6417	White	71	73.2	127	5914
	White	71	68.1	121	5914	Red	71	69.4	119	5118
	Red	70	64.5	112	5118					

Diamond Oaks:
This is the second, but shorter, of two municipal courses in Roseville. The other is Woodcreek, ranked No. 97 in the **Best 100**. In some ways Diamond Oaks is the better design, because of the variety of holes on the front nine. They show more grades, smaller landing areas, and more interesting natural terrain. Holes one through six are all very different, and if the rest of the course kept up this quality, it would have been much higher ranked. However, the course then flattens out and becomes ordinary, unlike Woodcreek—which maintains good character throughout. Maintenance conditions are generally good. The fairways are Bermuda grass, and crews pour on water in the summer, reducing roll significantly. Nice greens putt a bit on the slow side, but most are gracefully bunkered. Good approach shots become the key to success on this relatively short layout. *Review based on play in October '07.*

Diamond Oaks Golf Course			
349 Diamond Oaks Road		Golf Shop:	916 783-4947
Roseville, CA 95678		Fax:	916 783-3442
		www.golfroseville.com	
Managed by:	City of Roseville	Architect:	Ted Robinson
Location:	Central residential Roseville, fifteen miles northeast of Scaramento. Take I-80 to State Rt. 65 North and go to Exit #307. Turn south on Galleria Blvd, then go 1.1 miles and turn right on Roseville Blvd. Go 1/3 mile and turn left on Reserve Dr. Go another 1/4 mile and turn right on Diamond Oaks. Course is ahead on right in 3/4 mile.		
Style:	Front nine has rolling hills, back nine is much flatter. Trees line fairways but usually sit wide of landing areas. Small greens have good character. Front nine is lots of fun, back nine ordinary. Bermuda fairways are very soft in summer.		

Greens Fees	Weekends	Weekdays	Twilight	Seniors	Carts/person
as of 10/08:	$34	$28	$23/$18	$22 weekdays	$16

Course ratings:	Men	Par	Rating	Slope	Yardage	Women	Par	Rating	Slope	Yardage
Diamond Oaks	Blue	72	69.4	122	6179	White	73	73.7	124	5885
	White	69	68.1	117	5885	Red	73	71.5	119	5590

Dryden Park:
Dryden is the older of Modesto's two eighteen-hole municipal golf courses. It opened in the late 50's along the banks of the Tuolumne River, just west of State Rt. 99. Because of its age, the trees planted back then are fully grown, and offer welcome shade in hot summer months. Mushroom shaped Stone Pines add unusual silhouettes to tree-lines bordering fairways, and give unique visual character to the course.

The layout rests in a flood plain just above the river, with the clubhouse sitting atop the natural exterior bank. Good thing it's high up because back in 1997, a major flood completely engulfed the entire golf course, but only reached the basement of the buildings. Flat holes predominate with old-fashioned designs and no any hidden hazards or unusual obstacles. What you see is what you get. Rarely do fairway bunkers force drivers to be careful on tee shots, though the river does adjoin and parallel a few holes on the front side. Even trees lining fairways stand far enough back from play to cause few problems.

Most of Dryden's character comes from its old-style *push-up* greens. A "push-up" green is one where bulldozers gouge dirt from the fairways or surrounding area and push it up to greens which become slightly raised. (Modern greens add layers of gravel and sand to promote drainage and root growth.) Fortunately, Dryden's original 50-year old greens remain in good shape. Bunkers border most front corners, with shapes allowing pins to be placed behind the traps. As with many older courses, the greens surfaces adjacent to the traps have been heightened by sand accumulated over the years from thousands of bunker shots and years of top-dressing. The resulting mounds behind traps make approach shots into these greens the most interesting part of the game. *Review based on play and interview in March '08.*

Dryden Park Golf Course								
920 Sunset Avenue			Golf Shop:		209 577-5359			
Modesto, CA 95351			Fax:		209 578-1914			
			http://www.modestogov.com/prnd/facilities/golf.asp					
Managed by:	City of Modesto		Architect:		William P. Bell			
Location:	Take State Rt. 99 towards Modesto. Exit at Tuolomne Blvd (towards the south of town)and turn west. Take immediate left on Neece St. Go to the end, past Modesto Muni on the right to Dryden, on the left.							
Style:	Mostly flat terrain, with oaks lining many fairways. Medium sized greens are usually fronted by bunkers on both corners. Fairways in decent condition. With a couple of exceptions, hole designs show their 50 year age.							

Greens Fees	Weekends	Weekdays	Twilight		Seniors		Carts/person
as of 10/08:	$27	$21	$20/$17		$17 weekdays		$15

Course ratings:	Men	Par	Rating	Slope	Yardage	Women	Par	Rating	Slope	Yardage
Dryden Park	Blue	72	70.8	122	6531	White	74	75.2	121	6238
	White	72	69.2	121	6238	Red	74	72.9	116	5999

Dublin Ranch:
Hidden in the hills north of Interstate-580, above the Livermore Airport, is a new style golf course that is quite unusual. It sits between housing developments where huge homes jam so close together that they look like mansion versions of Daly City row houses. The course rises high enough on the hill you can look past the homes and see fabulous vistas of the Livermore Valley, Pleasanton, and mountains to the south and west.

Its uniqueness comes from several factors. First, instead of having four par-threes, like most courses, it has eleven of them. Second, fairways and roughs are maintained immaculately. Third, greens look huge and easy to approach, but beware: The aprons and fringe surrounding them can be so steep with thick grass that even short chips require a very firm swing. Fourth, windy afternoon weather adds or subtracts 30-yards per shot, especially on the front nine. And finally, hilly terrain makes walking a pleasure only for the purest of the old coots and strongest of young toughs. The resulting course rating of 64.6 on a par-63 course, proves it is a daring layout.

Don't let the low par-63 fool you into passing up Dublin Ranch. Long and extremely well bunkered par-fours provide a real challenge. The two par-fives are among the toughest, prettiest and best designs of any in the **Best 100.** The par-threes have full yardage plus some—three of them require a long wood or driver.

The course uses very few trees and the fairways are wide. This openness makes it easier for beginners, especially children, to play with adults, and not become frustrated by losing balls. At the same time, the best of golfers will have quite a time, particularly from the back tees. And since the course is nearly unknown—even after five years play remains light—it has flexibility for starting times and fast play. *Review based on play in August '07.*

Dublin Ranch Golf Course

5900 Signal Hill Drive	Golf Shop:	925 556-7040
Dublin, CA 94568	Fax:	925 556-7045
	www.dublinranchgolf.com	

Managed by:	Private, local	Architect:	Robt. T. Jones Jr.
Location:	East of I-680/I-580 junction about 5 miles. Take I-580 to Fallon Rd exit and turn north. Drive 2 miles up to Signal Hill Dr. Turn right and clubhouse is on the right.		
Style:	Short course with 11 par-threes, but longer than many executive style courses. Very hilly terrain, where huge homes line wide fairways. Very few trees on the course, but it has many bunkers and side hill lies. Entire course is in excellent condition and greens are huge. Beware of potential for strong afternoon winds.		

Greens Fees as of 10/08:	Weekends	Weekdays	Twilight	Seniors	Carts/person
	$65	$43	$45/$35	$38	Included

Course ratings:	Men	Par	Rating	Slope	Yardage	Women	Par	Rating	Slope	Yardage
	Blue	63	64.6	108	5073	White	63	64.6	106	4365
Dublin Ranch	White	63	61.5	105	4365	Red	63	61.9	100	3881
	Red	63	59.2	100	3881	Gold	63	59.3	95	3290

Eureka:
An arriving player's initial look at Eureka Golf Course may be disappointing. The layout appears to be in a mountain meadow, with wide-open, short holes, few trees and not much character. But this initial impression is inaccurate for two reasons. First, the front side has subtle turns of the fairways, and strategically placed bunkers or hidden creeks that make the course a lot less forgiving than it appears. Second, the meadow holds only the front nine, whereas the back side has several holes deep in a redwood forest.

The entire facility is maintained well, so hitting fairway shots is a pleasure. Greens are a little slow and predictable with their back-to-front slopes. With a few exceptions, approach shots can usually be played without tree interference, even when drives are well off line. You should score better than normal here, due to the diminutive 5600-yard length, but shooting to your handicap will be no easier than normal because the low 67.1 course rating rightly reflects the simple nature of the course.

Three holes starting the back nine are the best. Number ten requires an extremely straight, 230-yard drive, coming out of a long, highly elevated, narrow chute, to reach the corner of a 90-degree dogleg and a clear shot at the green. Number eleven, again has a highly elevated tee in the midst of 150-foot tall redwoods, but this time a lay-up drive of about 200-yards is needed to the 100-yard post. After that, a wedge around a corner to a green high on a hill must end up below the pin. If not, putts back down will likely fall off the green. Number twelve is a par-five requiring another lay-up drive to the corner of a sharp dogleg, and then about 250-yards up a slope, between the trees to a small green. Pass these holes successfully, and the rest of the round should be routine.

Eureka is California's western most golf course. *Review based on play in June '08.*

Eureka Golf Course

4750 Fairway Drive		Golf Shop:	707 443-4808
Eureka, CA 95503		Fax:	707 443-1003
		www.playeureka.com	
Managed by:	CourseCo	Architect:	Bob Baldock
Location:	Far Northern California coast. Take U.S. 101 towards Eureka to Exit #702/Herrick Ave., south of town. Follow Herrick east for .8 miles, it becomes Fairway Drive. Clubhouse is on left.		
Style:	Mildly hilly terrain. Front side sits in a meadow, back side has three holes surrounded by tall redwoods. Has wide fairways, with small greens, usually well-protected by bunkers. Fairways can be very wet in winter due to local flooding.		

Greens Fees as of 10/08:	Weekends	Weekdays	Twilight	Seniors	Carts/person
	$25	$20	$18$15	$18/$15	$12

Course ratings:	Men	Par	Rating	Slope	Yardage	Women	Par	Rating	Slope	Yardage
Eureka	White	70	67.1	116	5609	White	72	71.6	127	5609
	Red	67	65.4	110	5225	Red	71	69.5	121	5225

Fig Garden: Sitting on the on the northern edge of Fresno, Fig Garden is a throwback to country club styles of the thirty's. Instead of being overwhelmed by the modern mansions lining the entrance on Van Ness Ave., imagine you are entering an old oak filled valley, not changed in 70 years—one that was once the talk of the town.

Still fun to play, trees protrude into linear fairways and make players concentrate, just like on courses of yesteryear. The terrain is flat, but pinch points at the turn of doglegs make distance and direction control very important. Trees line fairways tightly enough that you are nearly guaranteed to need a few recovery shots.

All players, expert and novice alike, should enjoy its playability, and excellent maintenance. Fairways are green, pretty-much weed free, and as good as any that use common Bermuda grass for their turf. They are firm and allow long rolls. Hedges border many tee boxes . . . one reason the course has an old-time feel. Other reminders of days–gone–by include a few well-placed flowerbeds, nicely trimmed grass on aprons, and edge-trims along cart paths. These touches are not the norm for most public venues today.

My positive comments come despite the bad rap received in 2006 by the accidental burnout of many greens. They are now fixed and under the care of a consultant to make sure the repairs continue well. Though imperfect, because a little of the replacement bent grass sod died in a few out-of-the-way positions, greens are back to being very playable. By now, it's probably only a few disappointed members who are still grousing about the imperfections; most visiting players would never know there had been ever been a problem. *Review based on play in April '08.*

Fig Garden Golf Club

7700 North Van Ness Boulevard	Golf Shop:	559 439-2928
Fresno, CA 93711	Fax:	559 439-2129

www.figgardengolf.com					
Managed by:	Private, local		Architect:		Nick Lombardo
Location:	North central Fresno. Exit onto Herndon Ave from either State Rt. 99 or 41. Head 6 miles west from Rt. 41 or 5 miles east from Rt. 99. At Van Ness Blvd, turn north and go 1 mile to the end. Course is at end of the street at the bottom of the hill.				
Style:	Cassicly styled design, tailored to nearly match valley-style country club conditions. Has flat terrain without graded contours where mature pines protect most fairways. Greens are small with reasonably tight landing areas. Bunkers are well placed and shallow.				

Greens Fees	Weekends	Weekdays	Twilight	Seniors	Carts/person
as of 10/08:	$40	$40	$30	No savings	$19

Course ratings:	Men	Par	Rating	Slope	Yardage	Women	Par	Rating	Slope	Yardage
Fig Garden	Blue	72	71.6	124	6560	White	74	74.4	127	6091
	White	70	69.6	119	6091	Red	72	70.8	120	5441

Forest Lake:
Just north of Lodi, near State Rt. 99, is the town of Acampo, and the family owned Forest Lake Golf Club. This short, executive style golf course, was recently transferred to the Ring family's next generation. They are updating the layout, but it is a big job being done by a very small crew. Recently, new holes have been added to the front nine, but the old ones, plus their tees and signage, had not been removed when I played, making me wonder where to hit next. Even on the back nine, which is laid out in a more organized fashion, the foundations of old tee boxes still remain, covered in sand and dry grass.

With a men's par of 66, and a course rating of 61.1, it's is a good course for increasing one's handicap. It's much tougher than its rating, with sharp turns, tiny greens, and some very narrow fairway openings. The turf has settled in many spots, so uphill/downhill lies are common, despite the generally level terrain. Ultra slow greens result from infrequent mowing. Once the construction project on the front side is complete, grooming elsewhere will hopefully improve; if so, the short, tricky layout could become a fun experience. Until then its biggest assets are low greens fee specials. *Review based on play in September '08.*

Forest Lake Golf Club
2450 East Woodson Road
Acampo, CA 95220

Golf Shop: 209 369-5451
Fax: 209 369-8132

Managed by:	Private, local	
Location:	About 15 miles north of Stockton. From the south, take State Rt. 99 to Jahant Rd. Go back under freeway and veer right onto Woodson Rd. Course is on the left in 1.4 miles. From the north, take Rt. 99 to Liberty Rd. exit. Turn right and head .5 miles to Lower Sacramento Rd. Turn left and go 1.3 miles. Turn left on Woodson and course is on the right.	
Style:	Short executive course with rolling terrain and lots of trees. Fairways are tight, greens are small and extremely slow. Layout is confusing because alternate holes are played on rotating days. Fairways are in irregular condition and hardpan or dirt is common in roughs.	

Greens Fees	Weekends	Weekdays	Twilight	Seniors	Carts/person
as of 10/08:	$20	$16	$14/$11	No savings	$10

Course ratings:	Men	Par	Rating	Slope	Yardage	Women	Par	Rating	Slope	Yardage
Forest Lake	Blue	66	62.4	103	4586	Red-lg	67	65.9	106	5544
	Red	60	58.9	88	3709	Red-sh	62	60.4	94	3697

Forest Meadow:

Here is another short executive course, this time a well-designed layout. It's situated behind a housing development in the mountains, just east of the quaint mining town of Murphy's. Elevation is about 3100 feet, in gold country en route to Ebbett's Pass. Want a chance to shoot a low score, perhaps even shoot your age? This could be the ticket, but it won't be easy. Robert Trent Jones Jr. designed Forest Meadows in 1972, so one would not expect a pushover. One par-five, five par-fours and twelve par-threes are not easy: Par-five, number one requires a very straight drive, squeezed between a creek on one side, out-of-bounds on the other, and a culvert crossing in front of the green. The par-fours each have quirks that make them tougher than their distances, and about half of the par-threes are long, or long plus narrow. Every green has bunkers or other hazardous elements to make crooked shots perilous. Forests border most fairways, so, if you do shoot a good score, you have played very well.

Unfortunately, poor course condition means overcoming some pretty bad lies. Greens are marginal, and the rest of the course has become run-down over the years. Warm ups are hit into a well-used dusty net, with balls that look like they were pulled from an old mud-hole. *Review based on play several times, last in September '08.*

Forest Meadows Golf Course and Resort		
633 Forest Meadows Drive	Golf Shop:	209 728-3439
Murphys, CA 95247	Fax:	209 728-3430
	www.forestmeadowsgolf.com	
Managed by: Private, local	Architect:	Robt. T. Jones Jr.
Location:	In Sierra Foothills out of Stockton, above Angels Camp. Take State Rt. 4 past Murphys 3.5 miles. Turn right on Forest Meadows Drive, go through entrance gate and follow signs to course.	
Style:	Executive short course, well designed by R. T. Jones Jr. Has several elevated greens, sharp doglegs, and trees closely protecting fairways. Accurate shots needed to small greens. Fairways are not in particularly good condition, but greens are OK. No driving range.	

Greens Fees as of 10/08:	Weekends	Weekdays	Twilight	Seniors	Carts/person
	$32	$22	$22/$15	No savings	$13

Course ratings:	Men	Par	Rating	Slope	Yardage	Women	Par	Rating	Slope	Yardage
Forest Meadow	White	60	60.6	108	3870	White	60	62.3	109	3870
						Red	60	58.5	98	3221

Foxtail, North and South Courses:

These two courses, once known as Mountain Shadows Resort, sit behind the Doubletree Hotel in Rohnert Park, about ten miles south of Santa Rosa.

Since the name change in 2001, a lot of work has been done on the longer, tougher, North Course, their premier facility, to make it a good course. Changes include new drainage, fairway contouring, repaired tees, redesigned bunkers, and other minor adjustments. The first few holes on the front nine are routine, hit-it-down-the-middle affairs, but then creeks and lakes start adding interest and challenge. Fairway bunkers, staggered along the edges, usually allow players to aim at the opposite side and avoid landing in the sand. Due to lack of water and excessive summer heat, fairways lose enough grass to give lots of roll and occasional poor/thin lies. Aprons in front of the greens are very firm, so approach shots must allow for extra roll. Bunkers usually flank the front corners of greens; with their shape and height significantly different from hole to hole. This variation, combined with distinctive mounding, gives many green complexes a distinctive visual appeal. With more lush fairway grooming, Foxtail North could easily have been a top 100 course.

The South Course is shorter, with fewer improvements, and is used by golfers looking for an easier game. It has the same tree-lined fairways, and holes are routed in an appealing manner, making for an interesting adventure. However, it's a level course, with less challenge from water hazards, bunkers, or sloped greens.

Empire Golf Inc., the management company here, wants players to know that they should expect to have a lot of fun. During tournaments, they offer special games, on every hole if that's what organizers want, plus novice instruction and service out on the course. Managers actively try to increase women's golf skills and confidence to the point ladies can handle golf/business entertainment just as well as men. They also have special evening programs for singles and women called Sips and Tips, combining wine tasting with golf instruction. Call the course for further program details. *Review based on play and interviews in August '08*

Foxtail Golf Courses: North

100 Golf Course Drive		Golf Shop:	707 584-7766
Rohnert Park, CA 94928		Fax:	707 584-8469
		www.playfoxtail.com	
Managed by:	CourseCo	Architect:	Roger Baird

Location: Five miles south of Santa Rosa. From the north, follow U.S. 101 south to Wilfred Dr. Take the exit and turn right on Redwood, then right on Commerce and go under the freeway. Turn left on Golf Course Dr. and course is on the right in 1/4 mile. From the south, take Golf Course Dr. exit and turn left on Commerce, then right on Golf Course Dr.

Style: Flat terrain with some contouring and mounding. Trees, lakes and creeks create areas of trouble. Firm fairways and aprons make the ball hard to stop. Nicely shaped, well bunkered greens.

Greens Fees	Weekends	Weekdays	Twilight	Seniors	Carts/person
as of 10/08:	$52	$35	$38/$27	$26 weekdays	$15

Course ratings:	Men	Par	Rating	Slope	Yardage	Women	Par	Rating	Slope	Yardage
	Black	72	73.4	128	6851	White	72	73.4	126	5846
Foxtail: North	Blue	72	71.1	123	6394	Gold	72	69.9	116	5261
	White	72	68.5	120	5846					

Foxtail Golf Course: South

Style: Flat terrain with shorter holes and smaller greens, but similar trees and lakes as the North.

Course ratings:	Men	Par	Rating	Slope	Yardage	Women	Par	Rating	Slope	Yardage
	Gold	71	71.7	124	6492	White	70	73.8	129	5830
Foxtail: South	Blue	71	70.6	122	6224	Red	70	70.7	120	5343
	White	70	68.3	120	5830					

Franklin Canyon: Located in Hercules, on State Rt. 4 south of Vallejo—

about half way between Interstate-80 and Interstate-680—Franklin Canyon course is very centrally located. Thirty minute drives from Walnut Creek, Fairfield or Oakland, give quick and easy access to a very large golf population.

The course design provides reasonably wide fairways, plenty of native full-grown oaks, gently rolling topography and a meandering creek. They combined for a pleasant appearance, but not too much difficulty. Except for busy Rt. 4, which runs adjacent to a couple of holes, the setting is quite pastoral and relaxed. Native trees, brush and grass cover the surrounding hillsides. It's easy to feel you are out in the country, away from the hubbub of the city.

With a little added grading, narrowing of fairways, more sophistication in the green complexes, and better conditioning, Franklin Canyon could be a highly ranked venue. But it management seems to aim for a different customer niche. It merely tries to provide a convenient and relaxing setting, on a relatively short layout for those who want an easy walk, decent conditioning, playability, moderate temperatures, and less wind than other Delta golfing facilities.

These objectives are accomplished well but for two shortcomings. First, in drought years, irrigation water becomes unusually dear. Late summer finds dry fairways and roughs, causing balls to roll far off line into creeks or out-of bounds. True, the long bounces cause holes to become shorter, but straight shots and better knowledge of where not-to-stray are more important than extra distance. If not so firm the course would be much more relaxing. Second, September finds over-watered greens. Normal fast smooth surfaces turn into bumpy, slow quagmires. To see it at its best, avoid the end of the dry season. *Review based on play twice, last with interview in September '08.*

Franklin Canyon Golf Course

Highway 4	Golf Shop:	510 799-6191
Hercules, CA 94547	Fax:	510 799-3807
	www.franklincanyon.americangolf.com	
Managed by: American Golf	Architect:	Robt. M. Graves

Location: Between Oakland and Concord. Take State Rt. 4 exit off I-80 or I-680. From I-80 go east 3.2 miles to course exit on the right. From I-680, go west 9 miles to the Franklin Canyon exit. After exiting, turn left, go under freeway and turn left again, back heading east. Course is on right in about one mile.

Style: Rolling terrain with one hilly section. Trees are usually off to the side of playing areas. Bunkers sometimes protect driving zones; greens are usually protected too. Course can suffer for lack of water in drought years, affecting fairways, roughs and greens.

Greens Fees as of 10/08:	Weekends	Weekdays	Twilight	Seniors	Carts/person
	$49	$30	$32/$22	$25 weekdays	$14

Course ratings:	Men	Par	Rating	Slope	Yardage	Women	Par	Rating	Slope	Yardage
Franklin	Blue	72	71.5	129	6594	White	72	75.1	132	6152
Canyon	White	71	69.6	125	6152	Yellow	72	71.4	124	5482

French Camp: You will find this very short executive course just off State

Rt. 99, south of Stockton. It's one of the two in Northern California associated with an adjacent RV Park. Built in 1995, it contains all kinds of modern golf design features, such as elevated tees, mounding, ponds, deep bunkers, tiered greens and a decent driving range. Unfortunately, while the design elements remain, everything except the greens and the range have gone to seed. Tees are poorly maintained, fairways show mostly bare ground except on the few par-fours, and many bunkers are filled with grass or weeds. What remains is a nicely sculpted facility, with good greens and decent aprons, but minimal maintenance elsewhere.

Some holes are still a fun challenge. Number seventeen is a very tough par-three from the rear 191-yard tee-box. The approach must carry over a lake, about 180-yards to a narrow peninsula green surrounded by an ugly hazard. The par-four eighteenth hole is not long, at 250-yards, but offers a challenging forced-carry to a small landing area, and possibility of reaching the green if hit just right. Some other par-threes, which total twelve of the holes, also offer challenging approaches to small undulating multi-tiered greens.   Too bad the course condition is so poor or it could make a good executive play. *Review based on play in June '08.*

French Camp RV Camp and Golf			
3919 East French Camp Road		Resort:	800 350-5232
P. O. Box 1500		Golf Shop:	209 234-1938
Manteca, CA 95231		www.frenchcamp.com	
Managed by:	Private, local	Architect:	L. Zastre/S. Whitson
Location:	Just south of Stockton Airport. Take State Rt. 99 to French Camp Rd. Turn west on French Camp Rd and course is immediately on the right.		
Style:	Short executive course, mostly par-threes. Flat terrain that has been extensively graded to add slopes and mounds throughout. Greens are mini versions of terraced greens on bigger courses. Fairways and bunkers in very poor shape. Greens are OK. Easy to walk, popular driving range. Adjacent to RV Park.		

Greens Fees	Weekends	Weekdays	Twilight	Seniors	Carts/person
as of 10/08:	$17	$15	$8	$10	$10

Course ratings:	Men	Par	Rating	Slope	Yardage	Women	Par	Rating	Slope	Yardage
French Camp	Blue	57	59.4	93	3601	White	57	59	89	3313
	White	57	58.3	91	3313					

Furnace Creek: Furnace Creek is one of the most intriguing places to play

golf anywhere. Its site in Death Valley, at 208 feet below sea level, makes it the lowest elevation golf venue in the world. Here the average daytime high in the months between May and October is well above 120 degrees F, yet people still travel from all over the world to be there. During this hot season, the premier Furnace Creek Inn is not open, but the Furnace Creek Ranch, a nice motel/ranch/restaurant complex, caters to naturalists and visitors on National Park tours. Even with the heat it has a 75-plus percent occupancy rate. High season for the fancier resort is between mid-October and mid-May, but what fun is that?

Many wonder how the course stays green. In fact, Death Valley has an abundance of spring water, though the National Park Service is careful not to over-pump. These waters flow first into resort swimming pools and then directly from the pools out to the golf course ponds. This gives double usage for all golf water, and nearly eliminates chemicals needed in the pool. Extremely well manicured Bermuda grass fairways and roughs, and hybrid Bermuda greens, use grasses known to stay green in high heat/low water environments. The result is a fertile, but not overly watered course. Its appearance is no different than any well-kept San Joaquin Valley venue.

Did we mention the views? Everything obviously looks upward. Death Valley is over 50 miles long, five miles wide, a flat-bottomed canyon full of heat. Both rims stand 5000-6000 foot above, with striated colors changing depending on the time of day. They make a spectacular backdrop for views from the course. The ridges to the east are especially mystical at 6:00 am sunrise tee times for those playing off-season summer golf. Temperatures start at 85 degrees F for this early call, and remain easily playable till 10:00 am.

Perry Dye significantly modified the original 1931 design in 1997. He added subtle mounding to the fairway perimeters and re-constructed green complexes throughout. The front nine succeeded especially well, with several nicely designed holes, notably numbers two and six. The second hole is a par-three, over a reed edged lake to a small undulating green surrounded by medium sized hillocks. It's very easy to land in the lake, especially when driving into the prevailing 6:00 am breeze. Number six, a long par-four, starts over a series of ponds usually populated by waterfowl. Furnace Creek received an Audubon preserve rating, so a viewing stand has been installed near the pond to watch the wildlife. At dusk coyotes crouch behind the reeds, hunting coots. They are known to catch them mid-air, since the coot has a slow lumbering take-off . . . kind of like Tiger Woods catching Rocco Mediate in the 2008 U. S. Open.

Unfortunately the new Dye design features seem thwarted on holes twelve through seventeen, as their layouts are much less imaginative. Many are short featureless par-fours between 300 to 330-yards long. Some have moderate obstacles to deter long drives, but a 200-yard tee-shot and wedge can easily produce pars and birdies. Number eighteen makes up a little with several rare Raynor style bunkers guarding landing areas and the green. Their sand is very flat with a shallow lip, but a tall hump protrudes steeply on the far side to force highly elevated shots towards the green. This capstone hole teases the faithful to come back next year to this Mecca-in-the-desert. *Review based on play and interview in June '08.*

Furnace Creek Golf Course

Highway 190	Golf Shop: 760 786-3373
P. O. Box 1	Fax: 760 786-2762
Death Valley, CA 92328	www.furnacecreekresort.com
	Architect: William P. Bell

Managed by:	Xanterra Resorts — Perry Dye redesign
Location:	Death Valley at 208 feet below sea level. World's lowest golf course. From Northern California, take U.S. 395 south to State Rt. 190. Turn east and head 90 miles, first down 3500 feet, then up 3500 feet, and finally down 5000 feet to the resort.
Style:	Flat terrain with mature trees near many fairways. Short, nicely shaped holes and a couple of lakes. Bermuda fairways and greens kept in good condition despite the heat. In summer recommend starting time of 6:00 am. Easy walking, beautiful views of desert mountains.

Greens Fees as of 10/08:	Weekends	Weekdays	Twilight	Seniors	Carts/person
	$55	$55	$30	No savings	$13

Course ratings:	Men	Par	Rating	Slope	Yardage	Women	Par	Rating	Slope	Yardage
	Blue	70	69.7	117	6236	White	70	72.0	122	5873
Furnace Creek	White	70	68.0	113	5873	Yellow	70	69.1	116	5357
	Yellow	70	65.5	108	5357	Red	70	66.0	109	4724

Green Tree: Green Tree sits just south of Interstate-80 near Vacaville, and

is a strong candidate for the *Most Improved Golf Course* award. Back in the late 80's the fairways and roughs here were so terrible that the nickname *Green Weed* stuck for years. Perhaps it should have been *Green Weed & Crack City*, not for cocaine, but for the dried up clay soil.

What a turnaround! Fairways are now in very good condition as are the roughs and the greens. No cracks can be found. Unlike some courses that have become run-down, and then changed, here the original trees and layout remain pretty much intact. Put simply, this course is now in better condition than many average country clubs, a truly major accomplishment.

Is it a **Best 100** course? Not yet. The layout of the holes themselves is dated. Little grading was used in the original construction, and the green complexes are not near nearly as sophisticated as on modern courses. However, the course does have some good, challenging features. Par-five number one uses a very sophisticated drive landing-area. A lake sits at about 280-yards off the tee and reaching the green in two demands the drive be as close to it as possible. However, the landing zone is narrow peninsula into the lake, so anything crooked, over 210-yards off the tee (back tees), goes into the water. Par-five number nine is also a killer. It's almost 600-yards, often into the wind, and has a slough crossing directly in front of the green. It's very difficult to reach in three.

When asked how this resurrection was accomplished, pro shop staff offered that it was a matter of slow and steady changes over an eight-year period. Next scheduled improvement is to re-construct and enlarge the driving range. Following that, what's next, an upgraded restaurant? *Review based on play several times over the years, last with interview in September '08.*

Green Tree Golf Club: Championship Course

999 Leisure Town Road		Golf Shop:	707 448-1420
Vacaville, CA 95687		Fax:	707 446-0810
		www.greentreegolfclub.com	
Managed by:	Private, local	Architect:	William F. Bell
Location:	East of Vacaville, 25 miles from Sacramento. From I-80, take Liesure Town Rd south 1/2 mile. Course is on the right.		
Style:	Flat terrain with a few strategic lakes and creeks. Wide fairways, some bordered by homes, others by roads, and most by wide-set tree lines. Greens often well protected by bunkers. Recent maintenance has brought course into good condition. Also have short 9-hole executive course.		

Greens Fees as of 10/08:	Weekends	Weekdays	Twilight	Seniors	Carts/person
	$39	$29	$29/$23	$22 weekdays	$14

Course ratings:	Men	Par	Rating	Slope	Yardage	Women	Par	Rating	Slope	Yardage
Green Tree	Blue	71	69.9	119	6266	White	74	73.6	125	5881
	White	71	68.2	115	5885	Red	71	69.9	118	5261

Haggin Oaks, Arcade Creek:
According to managers of Morton Golf, who operate the McKenzie and Arcade Creek courses at Haggin Oaks, the Arcade Creek facility has a unique attribute: Players can sign up for a starting time on either nine, and if they want to play both, they need separate times for each. The course caters to players who want the experience of playing a normal course with the same kind of conditioning and design criteria as a high quality eighteen-hole venue, but only time or desire to play nine holes. Arcade Creek gives them all the options; they can get on quickly, play in half the time, and at about half the cost.

Quality of the course is not quite that of the bigger McKenzie course, but is better than many nine-hole competitors. It's also a great place for practicing lessons learned at the Haggin Oaks Academy. (See review No: 57, p.133 for more information about the Academy). Fairways and greens offer the same conditions as at the bigger eighteen, but greens are flatter and easier to putt. Mac McDonough, the same contractor who built the original McKenzie track, designed Arcade Creek in 1958, thereby cementing the similarities between the two separate venues.

Most holes are straight, with wide driving areas between the tree lines. Greens are in good condition and large, offering a chance for a wide variety of putting experiences. Bunkers often protect front corners of greens, giving new players a chance to practice stopping balls quickly after clearing the lips. Aprons are only OK , with several bare spots showing.

Number eighteen is by far the most distinctive hole on Arcade Creek. This 515-yard finisher has two creek crossings and the need for an excellently placed second shot, just short of the wide gully in front of the green. Without perfect placement, the second will end up wet, or leave a long shot home. The unique green has more slope and bunker protection than any on either Haggin Oaks course. It's similar to the old Alister MacKenzie greens, which had to be modernized because they were too difficult. Beginners get an idea here of what challenges lay ahead, when they move on to championship courses sure to be played soon. *Review based on play and interviews in October '08.*

Haggin Oaks, Arcade Creek Golf Course			
3645 Fulton Ave.		Golf Shop:	916 808-2525
Sacramento, CA 95821		Fax	916 808-2523
		www.hagginoaks.com	
Managed by:	Morton Golf	Architect:	Mac McDonough
Location:	Eastern Central Sacramento. Take I-80, U.S. 50, I-5 or SR. 99 to Capital City Freeway. Exit onto Fulton Ave. Course entrance is adjacent to northwest side of the freeway.		
Style:	Flat terrain, easy to walk. Wide fairways are shaped with distinctive rough contours. Trees line fairways, but well off playing areas. Greens less sloped than on the McKenzie Course. Though 18 holes, players must make separate tee times for each nine. This is a practice course.		

Greens Fees	Weekends	Weekdays	Twilight	Seniors	Carts/person
as of 10/08:	$35	$27	$24	No savings	$15

Course ratings:	Men	Par	Rating	Slope	Yardage	Women	Par	Rating	Slope	Yardage
Haggin Oaks: Arcade Creek	Blue	72	72	116	6889	Red	72	71.7	111	5786
	White	72	70.3	114	6552					
	Red	69	66.7	105	5786					

Hidden Valley Lake:
Back in the 1950's, Clear Lake provided a popular vacation destination for Sacramento and the Bay Area. Its beautiful warm, clean waters attracted swimmers, water skiers and bass fishermen. A few nine hole golf courses opened and well-known Konocti Harbor Resort followed soon thereafter. But in 1959, when Interstate-80 opened over Donner Pass, new investment money moved up to Lake Tahoe, where year round attractions and cooler summer weather stole the crowds.

Eventually, though, development matures, people tire of crowded freeways and rising costs; and they look for new venues. So, now, 50 years later, money and building are creeping back to Lake County. New restaurants have arrived, along with a myriad of wineries. Hidden Valley Lakes, a semiprivate country club started in 1968, is poised to take advantage. It's located about fifteen minutes from the south shore of Clear Lake, and 45 minutes north of Lake Berryessa. Ten years ago it was in ragged shape and just another place to play golf. But in 2000, a reclaimed water irrigation system was added, and the course shows vast improvement.

This is a nice course in an obscure location. Conditioning is good throughout most holes, at least when I played. It has reasonable length from the back tees, over 3500-yards on the front side and 3200 on the back, with the shorter nine being the heart of the course. Its middle four holes climb steeply over a hill, with doglegs, gullies, and elevation changes everywhere. Number twelve, a short par-five, begs golfers to take risk. Aiming your drive over oaks near the tee looks reasonable, but low shots easily hit the branches and usually squirt out-of-bounds. Next, if you try to hit across a creek on your second shot, you'll end up with an easy chip or a lost ball. Narrow fairways line the entire hole, and the next two are no wider or less risky. Number fifteen ends the hillside tour with a tee box elevated 150-feet above the fairway. It's so steeply perched your drive can be dizzying.

The rest of the course is more normal, with lava-colored bunker sand, strategically located oaks, and wide fairways bordered by vacation homes. Recently, more trees have been added to locations in need of added definition. Number six, is an example . . . a par-five that is 567-yards long, but plays longer because a creek, 180-yards from the green forces most players to lay-up their second shot. New trees will eventually close off openings that allow big hitters to cut through its dog-leg.

All and all, Hidden Valley is a surprising good course, with reasonable vacation-area pricing. It has enough length and character that, with a little maturity, and a bit more manicuring, could push it into the **Best 100**. For the money, I think it beats Yocha-de-he, its nearest competitor. *Review based on play twice, last in September '07.*

Hidden Valley Lake Country Club

19210 Hartman Road		Golf Shop:	707 987-3035
Hidden Valley Lake, CA 95467		Fax	707 987-4903
		www.hvla.com	
Managed by:	Private, local	Architect:	Willaim Bell
Location:	South of Clear Lake about 15 miles. On State Rt. 29, go 52 miles north from Napa or 10 miles south from Lower Lake to Hartman Road. Turn east and clubhouse is 1/2 mile on the left.		

Style:	Most of course is flat, but five holes near start of back nine head up and down a steep hill. Large oaks and creeks make accuracy important. Many side hill lies on holes 11 thru 15. Greens medium sized, in good condition; fairways OK too. Bunkers filled with red lava-colored sand.

Greens Fees	Weekends	Weekdays	Twilight	Seniors	Carts/person
as of 10/08:	$45	$35	No savings	No savings	Included

Course ratings:	Men	Par	Rating	Slope	Yardage	Women	Par	Rating	Slope	Yardage
Hidden Valley Lake	Blue	72	73	128	6695	White	76	76.6	135	6280
	White	70	70.9	125	6280	Gold	73	72.8	124	5658
	Gold	69	68.1	118	5658	Red	72	71.2	120	5349

Jack Tone:
Built in 1962 by owners George and Sharon Buzzini, this short par-62 golf course has seen good times and bad. Its location, off State Rt. 99 in Ripon is well suited for the population growth of the last decade; and its short, open layout provides a friendly layout to golfers at all levels. The facility is in better-than average condition, has low greens fees, and normally allows a fast round. Roughs are cut short, with most trees out of play. Small greens have interesting breaks, and are a pleasure to putt. The layout's eleven short par-threes, six short par-fours, one challenging par-five, and a good driving range, offers a convenient central location to meet Central Valley friends for a quick round.

Problem is that the 90-acre site is also flood plain of the Stanislaus River. Twice in 2006 floodwaters covered so many holes that only seven were playable for an extended period of time. The full course was re-opened in mid-2007 and somehow remains in pretty good shape. Evidence of flooding comes because Bermuda and other grasses contaminate the bent grass greens, rye grass fairways and bunkers on six or seven holes. To the owner's credit, his family worked hard to make greens throughout putt the same speed, even though the grasses are different. It's a good story about recovery against the odds, and, if you want a nice relaxing, quick game, is a good place to try for yourself. *Review based on play and interview in July '08.*

Jack Tone Golf			
1500 Ruess Road		Golf Shop:	209 599-2973
Ripon, CA 95366		Fax	209 599-1103
		www.jacktonegolf.net	
Managed by:	Private, local	Architect:	G. Buzzini & B. Ash
Location:	6 miles south of Manteca. Take State Rt. 99 south to Jack Tone Rd. Turn right and head 1 mile further south to W. Main St. Turn right and then quick left on Ruess Ave. Course is one mile south at end of street.		
Style:	Short executive course with flat terrain, easy to walk. Wide fairways and small greens place premium on good short irons. Very few trees in play. Course can flood in winter and holes affected have rougher fairways than the rest.		

Greens Fees	Weekends	Weekdays	Twilight	Seniors	Carts/person
as of 10/08:	$22	$18	$26/$13	$20/$18	$11/$9

Course ratings:	Men	Par	Rating	Slope	Yardage	Women	Par	Rating	Slope	Yardage
	Blue	62	58.8	85	3716	Blue	62	59.7	90	3715
Jack Tone	White	62	58.3	84	3513	White	62	58.6	87	3510
	Red	60	57.5	82	3290	Red	62	57.4	85	3292

Javier's Fresno West:

Back in the 1970's, Fresno West was a popular course. The Lady's PGA (LPGA) had a mini-stop here, and the course reputedly boasted "the best greens in the valley." But hard times hit, and the course deteriorated. Greens became the worst around, the driving range went to seed, lakes dried up, and the rest of the course and infrastructure didn't fare much better. Then Louie Duran, owner of the popular Javier's Restaurant on the east side of Fresno, bought the course in 2001. Slowly, he works to bring it back.

The basic layout is a true championship design, and can stretch to 7000-yards. Fairways have tree lines, with some pines protruding into the fairways at strategic spots. They are well bunkered, though the traps are flat and currently in poor condition. Roughs have many weeds, and course markers and signage need repair.

The first step towards renovation was to fix the greens, which vary tremendously in size and are reasonably well guarded by bunkers. They were re-seeded with Bermuda grass, a variety often used in valley fairways, but unusual in local area greens. The project succeeded well, and putts now roll true, if on the slow side, not unlike those in Hawaii. The greens hold and have consistent firmness. Golfers must take care to hit putts squarely and firmly, or the heavy grain will cause drift as balls slow down. Other course conditions have not improved much.

First Annual U. S. Mexican Open was scheduled for 2008 but did not take place, so the course will continue to operate as it does today until economic conditions improve. Fees are so low, it's a Top Value facility. *Review based on play and interview in April '08.*

Javier's Fresno West Golf Course

23986 West Whitesbridge Road   Golf Shop: 559 846-8655
Kerman, CA 93630   Fax   559 846-8694

Managed by:	Private, local Architect: B. Baldock/R. Baldock
Location:	Due west of Fresno by 23 miles. From State Rt. 99 take State Rt. 180 west. Golf course is on the right, one mile past left turnoff for S. James Rd.
Style:	Flat terrain, nicely designed course in need of major maintenance. Fairway condition erratic, bunkers full of weeds. Greens recently re-seeded with Bermuda grass. Fairways are tree lined but in need of trimming. New owners are trying to fix it up, slowly, on a low budget.

Greens Fees as of 10/08:	Weekends	Weekdays	Twilight	Seniors	Carts/person
	$25	$19	$12	$12	Included

Course ratings:	Men	Par	Rating	Slope	Yardage	Women	Par	Rating	Slope	Yardage
	Blue	72	72.1	119	6959	Red	73	74.1	122	6000
Javier's Fresno West	White	72	70.4	117	6607	Gold	72	71.3	116	5486
	Gold	70	65.3	105	5486					

Lake Chabot: This muni in the hills behind Oakland recently went

through a re-birth. Originally built in 1971, it had a run of good years, but players became frustrated with its poor condition in the mid '00's. The extremely hilly terrain is difficult to maintain, and the clay soil creates costly problems: poor drainage in winter and rock-hard patchy fairways in the summer. The course had to close for 6 months in late '06, and reopened in April '07 under new management. Project work included refurbishing the clubhouse, repairing irrigation lines, adding drains to soggy areas, and purchasing modern mowing equipment.

Work continues to this day on drains and irrigation, but the course is back to decent shape and worth a new look by players who became disenchanted. It remains a short, steep design but not the disheveled quagmire it had become.

Lake Chabot's hills make it a course for only the heartiest of walkers; some cynics have even surmised that Army Rangers must do their night training here, to shape up for mountain fighting. Fortunately cart rentals are cheaper here than at most courses and it's a good thing, since there is not a flat hole anywhere. In fact two are so hilly, they are unique among all in Northern California: Hole number nine, has the longest par-three elevation drop to a blind green (players cannot see the green from the tee). The drop is 115 feet and cuts about 25-yards off the distance on the card. Then, hole number eighteen is a par-six, the only men's par-six on a course reviewed in this book, at 673-yards. It has a dramatic drop of over 200 feet from tee to green.

Players who hit the ball short and straight, who can handle side-hill lies, and who want to play a mountain style course right in the city, will enjoy a morning at Lake Cabot. Otherwise, head over to Metropolitan near the airport and deal with the wind. *Review based on play several times, last in January '08.*

Lake Chabot Golf Course				
11450 Golf Links Road		Golf Shop:	510 351-5812	
Oakland, CA 94605		Fax	510 351-3418	
		www.lakechabotgolf.com		
Managed by:	Touchstone Golf, LLC	Architect:	William Lock	
Location:	East Bay Hills, above Oakland. Take I-580 to Golf Links Road exit. Head east, past Oakland Zoo, to the end of Golf Links Rd. Stay right at fork. Stone Pillars form the entrance gate.			
Style:	Very hilly terrain with uphill stretches on nearly every hole. Two holes, 9 and 18 have the most severe downhill slopes in Northern CA. Tree lined fariways can be soggy in winter, though drainage has inproved. Decent greens, mostly elevated. Short yardage, but need straight shots.			

Greens Fees	Weekends	Weekdays	Twilight	Seniors	Carts/person
as of 10/08:	$39	$29	$30/$18	$17 weekdays	$14

Course ratings:	Men	Par	Rating	Slope	Yardage	Women	Par	Rating	Slope	Yardage
Lake Chabot	Blue	70	68.9	119	5976	White	72	74.1	125	5681
	White	70	67.4	116	5681	Red	71	69.7	115	5234

Las Positas: Sandwiched between the local airport and Interstate-580 sits

Livermore's municipal golf course, Las Positas. The course opened in 1966, and for years looked like a hardpan ridden, wind-swept torture track to many zooming by on that well-ridden transportation corridor. But, 2003 brought the advent of a new maintenance philosophy; and investment in irrigation caused immense improvements. Fairways and greens now boast good, soft conditions and allow the basic design of the Robert Muir Graves course to show its true self.

Golfers homesick for Florida, or wondering what designs there are like, will enjoy holes number one, four and five. They have plenty of water, and fairways slope towards the ponds. A goose-chasing dog named Perk, marginally succeeds at keeping waterfowl poop off the fairways. He also works hole numbers eight and nine, where approaches and drives require good shot length and accuracy.

Forty-year-old trees are now full grown and line most fairways. They usually sit back far enough into the rough to interrupt only the most wayward shots. Grasses in roughs are very friendly and make balls sit-up, allowing for easier swings than usual. Even around greens the ball sits high on the turf, so chipping strokes go through the ball without grabbing. Greens are good in the summer and are said to be extraordinary in the winter, when groomed very fast to nearly U.S. Open speed.

The freeway noise on holes thirteen and fourteen is a bit much, and the afternoon wind often increases difficulty. But for these detractors, and the occasional private jet landing next door, a round at Las Positas is a walk in the park. And if you want a shorter walk, try their adjacent nine-hole Executive course. *Review based on play in July '07.*

Las Positas Golf Course

917 Clubhouse Drive		Golf Shop:	925 443-3122
Livermore, CA 94551		Fax	925 455-7838
		www.laspositasgolfcourse.com	
Managed by:	Private/local	Architect:	Robert Muir Graves
Location:	Near I-580 and the Livermore Airport. From I-580 take Airway Blvd/State Rt. 84 exit. Go south on Airway. Turn right after 1/4 mile onto Clubhouse Dr. Course lot is on the left.		
Style:	Mostly flat terrain, with lakes on several holes. Fairways lined by mature eucalyptus. Good fairways and nice greens, surrounded by modern-style bunkers. The well groomed 9-hole Executive course is also available. Can be windy, especially when fog shrouds San Francisco.		

Greens Fees	Weekends	Weekdays	Twilight	Seniors	Carts/person
as of 10/08:	$43	$35	$29/$25	$25 weekdays	$13

Course ratings:	Men	Par	Rating	Slope	Yardage	Women	Par	Rating	Slope	Yardage
	Blue	72	71.8	129	6677	White	72	76.2	130	6347
Las Positas	White	72	70.2	126	6331	Gold	72	72.8	125	5719
	Gold	72	68.1	114	5709	Red	72	70.7	117	5275

Lemoore:
Half way between Interstate-5 and State Rt. 99, about 35 miles south of Fresno, sits the town of Lemoore. Driving east from the I-5 turnoff, the 25-miles to Lemoore are bordered by bare fields in the spring, just awaiting new crops. Upon arrival, the Lemoore Golf Course seems like an oasis of green in a sea of flat brown freshly tilled dirt. Turns out that this region is smack dab in the middle of California's corporate farm heartland.

Primary employer in town is Naval Air Station, Lemoore. Like at all good military bases, personnel need an esoteric outlet for frustration, and what fits that bill better than hitting little white balls around the greenest turf they can find? Thus, 40 years ago a nine-hole course was built and ten years ago a second nine was added to the ride.

Lemoore's front nine is typical of its era . . . flat, eucalyptus and pine lined fairways, bunkers in predictable locations, on mostly straight holes. The exception comes at the greens, because all nine boast two tiers. Often, the second tiers appear to have been added at a different date than the original construction; but on others, the green flows nicely as one unit. Two have the odd feature of a back tier being lower than the front, and number four, a 160-yard par-three, is particularly unique. A tiny sunken peninsula, only 20' x 20', protrudes out front from the main surface. I had no clue the nicely shaped appendage was positioned in front of, and needed a shorter approach club than the rest of the green.

The new nine appears much more modern. Slopes and mounds were added at the edge of fairways, and large sculpted bunkers create focal images on each hole. However, the fairways themselves remain quite flat, and greens seem rather ordinary. In the end, the back nine gets character from bunkers, whereas greens define the front.

If this course gave its rough more care, and made the fairways as lush as the greens, those navy golfers and corporate farmers wouldn't ever think about driving elsewhere to find better golf adventures. *Review based on play and interview in March '08.*

Lemoore Golf Course

350 Iona Ave	Golf Shop:	559 924-9658
Lemoore, CA 93245	Fax	559 924-4131
	www.lemooregolf.com	

Managed by:	Sierra Golf Mgmt.	Architect:	Bob E. Baldock

Location: Central San Joaquin Valley, 35 miles due south of Fresno. Can be reached on State Rt. 41 from Fresno, or on State Rt. 190 from I-5 or State Rt. 99. Once in Lemoore, take Rt. 190 to S. Lemoore Ave. which becomes 18th Ave. Head south 1/2 mile to Ione Ave. Turn right, course is on the right.

Style: Flat terrain, easy to walk. Fairways are tree lined, but reasonably wide. Front side greens have multiple tiers. Back side is newer construction with younger trees and more fairway grading than the front. Roughs are often weedy, with hardpan.

Greens Fees	Weekends	Weekdays	Twilight	Seniors	Carts/person
as of 10/08:	$26	$20	$17/$14	$14 weekdays	$12

Course ratings:	Men	Par	Rating	Slope	Yardage	Women	Par	Rating	Slope	Yardage
Lemoore	Blue	72	70.9	125	6591	White	72	74.2	125	6131
	White	72	68.9	119	6131	Red	72	68.7	116	5194

Likely Links:

The first question is, "Why name a town Likely?" Answer: For the U. S. Post Office to give a zip code, a new town's name must be unique in that State. Residents of this tiny community in the high desert, 20 miles south of Alturas, tried for years to come up with an original name, but all were rejected. They finally concluded it would be "unlikely" to get one. Then someone at a town meeting said,

"Wait a minute . . . if its 'un'-likely we will get one, lets try and be more positive, how about 'Likely?'" . . . and 90 residents finally had their zip code.

Next question is, why build a golf course in a spot 165 miles north of Reno and 125 miles east of Redding? Answer: You have to see it to believe it. The property sits at the edge of a broad, high desert valley, surrounded by steeply sloped forests, and has great golf topography. Slight inclines, natural moderate-sized swales and a small plateau give views panoramic perspective. The local habitat is called "sage brush steppe," a natural landscape covered with sage, pine and juniper. And a major bonus comes from abundant water supply by the South Fork of the Pitt River. How could one not place a golf course out here in the boondocks?

Originally, Likely Place was just a nine-hole course with an adjacent RV Park. The owners felt there was a market not being served: retirees wanting very low cost second homes. Their location in Likely might fit this market well, with its plentiful fishing, relaxed outdoor life, and a surrounding eighteen-hole wildlife friendly golf course. They added nine more holes to what was there, and a remote summer community was formed.

The course design strives to be golfer friendly. Traits include relatively flat fairways, natural terrain, nearly non-existent bunkers, and small, level greens elevated only a foot or two above the normal plain. Good fairways sown with rye grass allow balls to sit up well. Rather narrow landing zones follow contours in the hills beautifully, with wide roughs manicured well enough to keep stray shots from bounding into the sagebrush. No, its not Pebble Beach quality, but golf in this pristine location, with a well-designed layout, is as unique as the town's name would imply. *Review based on play and interview in April '08.*

Likely Links Golf Course

County Road 64	Mail to: P. O. Box 1772	Golf Shop:	530 233-6676
Likely, CA 96116	Alturas, CA 96101	Fax	530 233-4466
		www.likelyplace.com	
Managed by:	Private, local	Architect:	S. MacIlraith/R. Hamel

Location:	Far Northeastern California, twenty miles south of Alturas. From U.S. 395 in Likely, turn east on Don's Rd/Jess' Rd. Go 1/2 mile and turn right at signs for Likely Place Resort. Course is 1/4 mile ahead.
Style:	True Heathlands style. Rolling terrain surrounded by high desert and vistas of distant mountains. Course has few trees,wide open fairways; its great for long hitters looking to swing away. Fairways and greens are in good shape, with few bunkers. Wildlife abounds. Elevation is 2400 feet.

Greens Fees	Weekends	Weekdays	Twilight	Seniors	Carts/person
as of 10/08:	$23	$20	No savings	No Savings	$9

Course ratings:	Men	Par	Rating	Slope	Yardage	Women	Par	Rating	Slope	Yardage
	Blue	72	69.8	119	6702	White	74	74.2	127	6356
Likely Links	White	72	68.4	116	6380	Red	72	72.6	123	6050
	Red	72	67.0	111	6046	Yellow	72	67.4	112	5130

Lincoln Hills: Hills and Orchard Courses: Lincoln

Hill Golf Club, thirty minutes northeast of Sacramento, runs a two-course complex originally built by Dell Webb. The courses, named Hills and Orchard were completed in phases over a five to six year period, finally opening as two separate eighteens in 2005. Recently, Billy Casper Golf took ownership and management control of the operation. The facility primarily serves members living in the surrounding active-adult community, but courses are also open to the public.

Dell Webb Co. put plenty of space between golf holes and homes, so only *really* crooked shots fly out-of bounds. Fairways run through shallow ravines, overlooked by homes on low ridges. Plenty of creeks and tall grasses add even more barriers for the golf.

Green complexes are the notable strength of both courses, good enough for top tournament competition. They are large, with mounded aprons, multiple terraces, significant long slopes and picturesque bunkers. Putting conditions are consistent and smooth, except that newer greens are understandably firmer than older ones. The LPGA used the facility in 2003 as a last minute replacement venue for the Long's Drug Challenge.

I like the Hills course more than the Orchard. Its holes seem more mature, almost like they were designed for tournament play rather than retirement golf. Number two, a short par-five, gives a good idea of the style . . . Drives must first clear a lake, which is not too difficult even from the back tees, and stay short of the first bunker, 230-yards out. The second shot is tricky because another bunker protects one side of the fairway, and a sloping grade and creek protect the other. Finally, a creek, a hill, and a large face-bunker guard the small, steeply double-tiered green. This is not your average retiree golf hole.

Others must agree with me because the Orchard Course is not as popular as the Hills, even though it contains wider fairways more typical of active-adult golf. Fairways show less maturity, *i.e.* they are firmer and have less grass; but the course measures longer, with a higher course rating. More water hazards and longer par fours create several long carries for approach shots. Waterfowl and reed-covered lakes bring a pastoral feel to one short set of wildlife sanctuary bounded holes. Despite its name, no orchard can be found.

One major flaw at both courses: because of the housing and distance from several greens to the next tee, carts are mandatory. That's a shame, because walking these venues would be good exercise and not too difficult. *Reviews based on play in September of '07 and '08.*

Lincoln Hills Golf Club: The Hills			
1005 Sun City Lane		Golf Shop:	916 543-9200
Lincoln, CA 95648		Fax:	916 434-7905
		www.lincolnhillsgolfclub.com	
Managed by:	Billy Casper Golf	Architect:	Billy Casper & Steve Nash
Location:	Twenty miles northeast of Sacramento. Take I-80 to State Rt. 65 North exit. Go 8.5 miles up Rt. 65 to Sterling Pkwy. Turn east and then turn right on Parkway Pt. Go a few hundred yards and turn right again on E. Lincoln Pkwy. After 1/4 mile turn left on Del Webb Blvd. Follow it 3/4 mile and turn right on Sun City Lane. Clubhouse is dead ahead.		

Style:	Rolling hills with golf holes in canyons between homes. Wide fairways lead to sophisticated greens surrounded by large bunkers and sweeping aprons. Course is usually in good condition.

Greens Fees as of 10/08:	Weekends $69	Weekdays $57	Twilight $45/$35	Seniors No savings	Carts Included, mandatory

Course ratings:	Men	Par	Rating	Slope	Yardage	Women	Par	Rating	Slope	Yardage
Lincoln Hills: Hills Course	Black	72	73.1	128	6876	White	73	73.7	125	5895
	Blue	72	70.6	124	6369	Red	72	70.5	117	5411
	White	72	68.2	119	5895					

Lincoln Hills Golf Club: The Orchard

Style:	Rolling hills with golf holes in canyons between homes. Course is slightly longer than The Hills, but greens are not as elegant and fairways are not as well defined.

Course ratings:	Men	Par	Rating	Slope	Yardage	Women	Par	Rating	Slope	Yardage
Lincoln Hills: Orchard Course	Black	72	73.4	131	7046	White	72	73.4	125	6071
	Blue	72	70.9	121	6516	Red	72	70.9	120	5401
	White	72	69.3	115	6071					

Lincoln Park:
Unfortunately, this different, short, hugely scenic, fun golf course is shamefully maintained in very poor condition. The location between the Golden Gate Bridge and San Francisco's Palace of the Legion of Honor Museum, gives many spectacular views of the City. Its layout winds through huge cypresses, pines and so many hills that walking is more work than one would expect on a short course. At par 68, and total distance of only 5100-yards from the back tees, many short par-fours tempt big hitters to try and hit greens with their drives. Fairways narrow sharply though, so shorter accurate tee shots usually yield better scores. Greens look nice and would be in good shape . . . but their grass is purposely cut long; so they are very slow, firm, and difficult to putt. Many fairways are in such poor condition that their *poa anna* turf plays more like deep un-groomed rough.

Despite the course maintenance problems, one hole, number seventeen is one of the best and most picturesque in Northern California. The par-three looks out at the Marin Headlands, with a spectacular panoramic view of the Golden Gate Bridge. Being 240-yards along the cliffs, to an elevated, well-bunkered green, it almost makes playing the often ragged course worth the effort. *Review based on play several times, last in September '07.*

Lincoln Park Golf Course

34th Avenue & Clement Street		Golf Shop:	415 221-9911
San Francisco, CA 94121		Fax	415 221-1519
		www.lincolnparkgc.com	
Managed by:	City of San Francisco	Architect:	Tom Bendelow
Location:	In SF, west of Golden Gate Bridge. From south: take 19th into GG Park. Veer left at Crossover Drive and then turn left on Fulton. Take it west to 34th Ave. Turn right and go up to course lot across 34th. From north: take Park Presidio to 34th. Turn right and drive east to Clement.		

Style:	Very hilly, short course. Tight fairways bordered closely by pines and cypress. Greens are small with long grass and slow putting. Some fairways in very poor condition. Contrast the condition with many gorgeous views of the City and Golden Gate Bridge.

Greens Fees	Weekends	Weekdays	Twilight	Seniors	Carts/person
as of 10/08:	$38	$34	$25/$20	No savings	$13

Course ratings:	Men	Par	Rating	Slope	Yardage	Women	Par	Rating	Slope	Yardage
	Blue	68	65.5	107	5146	Blue	70	68.3	110	5146
Lincoln Park	White	68	64.6	105	4948	White	70	67.2	108	4948
						Red	70	66.0	105	4732

(The) Links at Vista del Hombre: Formerly know as

The Links at Paso Robles, this layout has the potential to be in the **Best 100**. It was originally designed as a true links course—no trees, flat terrain, plenty of big bunkers, and very wild native-grass roughs. Then ownership changed, most traps were filled with grass and w, and the roughs were cut to normal length. In late 2007 a program began to re-design bunkers and construct a clubhouse, but both projects were stalled as of April '09.

In spite of this turmoil and use of trailers for the pro-shop, the course remains a good golf experience because the basic layout is well conceived. The course truly imitates the feel of golf at some of Scotland's seaside courses. Four to eight foot high coyote bushes, very similar in appearance to Scottish gorse, rim the fairways. Huge greens, often over a quarter acre in size, make good putting skills much more important than on most of our California courses. Fairways and greens remain in good condition. Several holes demand blind drives, another common trait of the Scottish links style. It's also a great place to practice blasting the ball as far as you can, because, except for a few remaining bunkers, obstacles and hazards are currently out of play.

What kind of result will follow, when the renovation is complete, remains to be seen. *Review based on play in October '07.*

The Links at Vista del Hombre			
5151 Jardine Rd		Golf Shop:	805 227-4567
Paso Robles, CA 93446		Fax	805 227-1596
		www.linkscourseatpasorobles.com	
Managed by:	Private, local	Architect:	Rudy Duran
Location:	Just east of Paso Robles, thirty miles north of San Luis Obispo. From U.S. 101, take State Rt. 46 five miles east towards Fresno. Turn left on Dry Creek Rd. and then make quick right on Jardine Rd. Go 1.4 miles north to the course entrance on left.		
Style:	Flat/rolling terrain, bordered by desert-type bushes similar in color and size to Scottish gorse. Huge greens, kept in good condition. Sand has been removed from many bunkers, now filled with weeds. Good course for long hitters to bang-away.		

Greens Fees	Weekends	Weekdays	Twilight	Seniors	Carts/person
as of 10/08:	$40	$30	$27/$22	$30/$20	$13

Course ratings:	Men	Par	Rating	Slope	Yardage	Women	Par	Rating	Slope	Yardage
Links at Vista del Hombre	Gold	72	72.2	115	6937	Red	72	72.1	121	5610
	Blue	72	70.8	112	6642					
	White	72	68.9	109	6254					

Lockeford Springs:

Surrounded by vineyards and nut orchards, Lockeford Springs' location, just north of Stockton, provides easy access to a large population of Valley residents. It seeks to attract outsiders touring Lodi's fifteen new wine-tasting rooms, hoping such enological adventurers are also potential golfers.

Building a good golf course in the flat topography of the Central Valley is no mean feat. Construction finished in 1994, so modern standards were in place for both foundations and style. The early '90's must have been a peak period for adding undulating features to courses, since nearly every fairway shows distinct contours, mounds or trenches. Some of these affect drive placement, some just add visual framing to fairway appearance. Today's fashion would consider their extensive use dated, since the mounds and hillocks display sharply angled slopes rather than flowing natural shape. However, the features are fun to negotiate, and are certainly more interesting than old-style flat fairways. Unfortunately, the condition of turf-grass could be better. Dry spots prevail almost to the point that winter rules should be used in the middle of summer.

The dominating feature at Lockeford Springs is the enormous depth and character of its greens. Putting surfaces extend at least one-half longer than normal, often 45 to 50-yards rather than a normal 32-yards. The extra span can mean forty yards difference between front and back flag positions. Even experienced golfers need to think carefully about approach club selection. Steep slopes and multiple terraces complicate the longer putting distances. The greens and mounding make Lockeford Springs a course where experience and/or awareness of the right distance to the day's pin placement, is a key to success. *Review based on play and interview in August '08.*

Lockeford Springs Golf Course			
16360 North Highway 88		Golf Shop:	209 333-6275
Lodi, CA 95240		Fax	209 333-6277
		www.lockefordsprings.com	
Managed by:	Private, local	Architect:	Sandy Tatum and Jim Summers
Location:	Just north of Stockton, east of Lodi. From State Rt. 99, take: 1) State Rt 88 north 11 miles to the course, or 2) take State Rt. 12 east 5 miles and then turn south on Rt. 88 for .7 miles.		
Style:	Flat terrain, extensively graded, with mounds and hollows throughout. Greens are highly distinctive, well bunkered and extra deep with multiple slopes. Fairways are tree lined but wide; their condition can be ragged.		

Greens Fees as of 10/08:	Weekends	Weekdays	Twilight	Seniors	Carts/person
	$45	$35	$35/$25	No savings	$20/$15

Course ratings:	Men	Par	Rating	Slope	Yardage	Women	Par	Rating	Slope	Yardage
Lockeford Springs	Gold	72	73.1	127	6858	White	72	74.3	123	5975
	Blue	72	71.4	123	6482	Red	72	72.1	118	5583
	White	71	68.9	120	5975					

Lone Tree:

Antioch's Lone Tree Golf Course is the Delta's oldest public golf venue. The original nine, built by the WPA in 1934, sat near a huge old oak used by local farmers as a shady meeting place to discuss the day's affairs. Hence, the name Lone

Tree emerged. Another nine was added in 1962 and then, earlier this decade, John Harbottle (designer of Stevinson Ranch) revamped several greens and bunkers.

The Harbottle changes augmented a 1991 irrigation system and brought the entire facility to current standards for design and maintenance. The irrigation system now keeps nearly the whole property green, rather than just the playing areas. By 2010 re-claimed water will replace East Bay MUD supply, to help preserve course condition and water supply into the future.

Today's product presents a surprisingly modern and very playable course. Yardage at 6427 from the blue tees may not be long, but well-bunkered greens, mature trees, good fairways and gently rolling topography make for a park-like experience. Straight fairways allow young bucks to pound the ball toward the green. Terrain of the front side resides along low hillsides so elevation changes rule its style. The flatter back nine uses bunkers, doglegs and well-placed trees to keep the game interesting.

Some conditions could be improved. Traps were poorly maintained, needing trimming and raking. Roughs showed bare spots and were covered with leaves, both of which could have been caused by late-year water restrictions and heavy winds. High popularity brings in a busy 70,000 rounds per year, so play is slow when large groups are on the course.

The heavy play comes for a reason though—good layout, playability for all levels of golfer, good greens and fairways, all at a competitive price—so its still a good golfing choice and excellent value. *Review based on play and interviews in October '09.*

Lone Tree Golf Club

4800 Golf Course Road		Golf Shop:	925 706-4220
Antioch, CA 94509		Fax	925 706-7709
		www.lonetreegolfcourse.com	
Managed by:	City of Antioch	Architect:	Bob Baldock and John Harbottle
Location:	From State Rt. 4 take the A St./Lone Tree Way exit south. Drive 1.7 miles to Golf Course Road. Turn right (west) and proceed 1/2 mile to club entrance.		
Style:	Rolling terrain with trees lining several holes. Well maintained fairways, greens and roughs. Compact course has flatter front nine than back. Fewer bunkers than on other nearby courses.		

Greens Fees	Weekends	Weekdays	Twilight	Seniors	Carts/person
as of 10/08:	$35	$25	$20/$17	$20 weekdays	$15

Course ratings:	Men	Par	Rating	Slope	Yardage	Women	Par	Rating	Slope	Yardage
	Blue	72	71.1	124	6446	White	75	74.9	131	6098
Lone Tree	White	72	69.5	121	6098	Gold	72	73.3	128	5935
	Gold	72	68.0	118	5935	Red	72	72.1	126	5608

Los Lagos: San Jose's newest course opened in 2002. Los Lagos (*The Lakes*)

sits in south-central San Jose between Capitol Expressway and Tully. Its construction responded to the demand created by the closure of Oakridge golf course in western San Jose. Some say its creation and immediate popularity hastened the demise of nearby Pleasant Hills in the eastern part of town.

The course design provides a significant upgrade for golf quality in central San Jose. One well-maintained, very interesting test of skill replaced two crowded, older unimaginative tracks. Par on Los Lagos may only be 68, two short of the standard needed to attract open tournaments, but golf here is neither dull nor easy. Just the contrary, as soon you drive through the entrance gates, the course appearance invites a challenge.

Hole number one starts with a bang, a double dogleg par-five, well protected by bunkers and mounds along the way, ending at an unusual double-green (shared with number eight). Don't worry; enough room separates the two sections of green to play both safely at the same time. The long sculpted putting surface adds an artistic element portending more unusual features to come. Several par-threes and par-fours continue the travel through well-tended fairways, mounded green complexes and strategically placed hazards. Short par-four number four confronts the first of four lakes. Like a little risk? Fly the ball 200-yards over water from the back tees, and you may end with a chip and one-putt or even hit the green.

Other features also distinguish Los Lagos. The well-manicured property maintains and a verdant green color throughout, similar to high quality Eastern courses in summertime. The rough presents a real challenge because the evenly cut heavy rye grass both stops roll and also kills club-head speed on recovery shots. These traits add 50 yards to distances on holes where drives wander off the fairway. Huge greens are deceptively deep, making approach distances hard to judge. Finally, all four par-fives show exceptional designs. Each plays long and tight, and distinct doglegs require good distance control. They also tantalize players to risk approach shots that easily end up in hazardous locations.

For the money, this relatively unknown course provides one of the best deals for good golf in the Santa Clara Valley. Its also very crowded, even on weekdays, so don't expect a quick round. *Review based on play and interview in August '07.*

Los Lagos Golf Course

2995 Tuers Road	Golf Shop:	408 361-0250
San Jose, CA 95121	Fax	408 361-0255
	www.playloslagos.com	
Managed by: CourseCo	Architect:	JMP Golf Design
Location:	Central San Jose. From U.S. 101, take Capitol Expy exit and head west. Go 1/2 mile to Tuers Rd. Turn right (north) and course entrance is one block up on the left.	
Style:	Flat terrain, easy to walk. Fairways are graded to have significant contours and mounds at the edges. Short yardages balanced by deep rough and nicely terraced green complexes. Course is in good condition and green throughout.	

Greens Fees	Weekends	Weekdays	Twilight	Seniors	Carts/person
as of 10/08:	$46	$32	$28/$23	$20 weekdays	$14

Course ratings:	Men	Par	Rating	Slope	Yardage	Women	Par	Rating	Slope	Yardage
Los Lagos	Blue	68	65.6	118	5393	White	68	68.1	113	4922
	White	68	63.6	111	4922	Red	68	65.3	109	4490

Mace Meadow: Jackson Rancheria operates a highly advertised casino five miles up State Route 88 from the gold country town of Jackson. Ten miles further east, towards Carson Pass, and above the small town of Pioneer, you find Mace Meadows. It competes with Castle Oaks in Ione for golfers visiting the casino.

While not quite in the same league with mountain courses such as Sierra Meadows, Mount Shasta Resort and Pine Mountain Lake, Mace Meadows presents a good layout, worth the trip from up from gold country. At 3300 feet, summer temperatures read somewhat cooler than the Valley, and the design boasts relatively flat fairways, plus plenty of trees and shade. Overall yardage is fairly short, but the 6300-yard tips bring some special challenges. They are positioned off line, and significantly increase the need for accuracy. For instance the rear tee position at par five number six forces your drive to be hit low, under limbs, through a narrow chute, with a slight hook. No hook and it goes into trees right of the fairway; if pulled left even a little, it hits trees next to the tee and falls immediately into heavy brush about 20-yards from the blocks. The rest of the hole also needs shots almost as accurate as the drive!

Course condition is only average, with roughs and fairways showing occasional dry spots and thin grass. Greens are good and tricky. A few have double plateaus and many show subtle spines down their centers. It's tough to know whether they will hold approaches, because some are softer than others. Bunkers were in poor shape when I played, needing additional sand and better care to prevent balls rolling onto washed-out, un-sanded bottoms.

Several people recommended the restaurant next to the golf shop as a good one. But, a great alternative is back down Rt. 88 at the St. George hotel/restaurant/bar in the little town of Volcano. It's a gold country experience you won't forget, and a good top-off to your day at Mace Meadow. *Review based on play in June '08.*

Mace Meadows Golf & Country Club

26570 Fairway Drive		Golf Shop:	209 295-7020
Pioneer, CA 95666		Fax	209 295-1557
		www.macemeadow.com	
Managed by:	Private, local	Architect:	Jack Fleming
Location:	Central Valley Sierra foothills. Take State Rt. 88 out of Jackson,head east 18 miles. Five miles past the small town of Pioneer, turn left on Fairway Dr. and follow signs to course.		
Style:	Rolling terrain. Several holes are in meadows, others are in forest. Straight drives needed on tree-lined holes. Greens can be elevated and are usually well bunkered. Course condtions are marginal, with decent fairways, OK greens but unkept bunkers.		

Greens Fees	Weekends	Weekdays	Twilight	Seniors	Carts/person
as of 10/08:	$37	$27	$25/$20	$24 weekdays	$12

Course ratings:	Men	Par	Rating	Slope	Yardage	Women	Par	Rating	Slope	Yardage
Mace Meadows	Blue	72	69.9	128	6294	White	72	73.8	132	5947
	White	72	68.5	124	5947	Red	72	70.4	125	5355

Madera:
Weekends are packed on this course, located just off State Rt. 99, twenty miles north of Fresno. It is one of the best deals in the Fresno area, especially for seniors who get the same low rate on both weekdays and weekends.

Madera Golf Course opened in 1991, with many features updated over typical San Joaquin Valley public courses located to the south. A system of ponds was chosen to assure better water storage. They not only create nice looking hazards and better irrigation options, but also provided excess dirt for raised bunkers and greens. The fairways don't have much slope or contour; so these elevated traps add contrast to the flat landscape. Their distinctive shapes, ranging from pot bunkers to large clover-leafs are a big improvement to the otherwise featureless landscape.

Green complexes also have modern qualities. They use mounds and firm slopes to make golfers think before hitting approaches. Standard lofted shots at the pin don't work well because balls likely roll off to wayward positions. Rather, pitch-and-run shots do the trick from the fairway, and should be targeted at the flat parts of greens.

The course's weakness comes in care of the fairways and roughs. Weeds abound and, though they make a decent hitting surface in the spring, are unsightly. Local rumors suggest that the city of Madera may authorize construction of a new casino nearby, with negotiations including money for a new course irrigation system and other city services. If the water could be distributed more evenly by a modern system, herbicide control would improve and golfers could enjoy softer, more standard fairways underfoot.

In the mean time, the layout is OK, the greens are interesting, the fairways are greenish and trees planted 25 years ago have finally taken hold. Good luck on finding weekend tee-time. *Review based on play and interviews in April '08.*

Madera Golf Course

23200 Avenue 17		Golf Shop:	559 675-3504
Madera, CA 93637		Fax	559 661-1936
		www.maderagolf.com	
Managed by:	City of Madera	Architect:	Robert Putnam
Location:	Twenty minutes north of Fresno, two miles north of Madera. Take State Rt. 99 to Avenue 17 exit and head one mile west to the course.		
Style:	Flat terrain, easy to walk. Wide fairways are bordered by half grown trees. Holes towards the end have bordering lakes and more mature vegetation. Greens are modern, with multiple bunkers and interesting terraces. Course condition suffers from wind and uneven grass growth.		

Greens Fees	Weekends	Weekdays	Twilight	Seniors	Carts/person
as of 10/08:	$36	$31	$31/$27	$22	Included

Course ratings:	Men	Par	Rating	Slope	Yardage	Women	Par	Rating	Slope	Yardage
	Blue	72	72.8	124	6831	White	74	75.3	122	6369
Madera	White	72	70.5	121	6369	Red	73	70.6	112	5513
	Gold	69	66.3	111	5545					

Manteca Park:
Owned by the city of Manteca, ten miles south of Stockton, this course adjoins the civic center, very near the heart of town. Dense housing and roadways encircle its perimeter, but the course itself sits internally to the suburban hubbub. Beautiful trees line nearly every hole, and when fully-grown in a few years, the fairways will narrow into an interesting and difficult layout. For now, trees don't intrude much, and crooked shots can easily be found if they make it to the adjacent fairway.

Despite flat terrain and minimal fairway contouring, Manteca Park provides a surprisingly good test. Lush fairways receive attentive maintenance; and their soft textures minimize roll on a fairly short course (6500-yards from the tips). Roughs are kept longer than on most muni's to toughen up the challenge a bit. This practice also results in a more natural, rustic appearance. Lakes border several holes, adding difficulty to certain shots. The whole property appears manicured and green; so, with the shade offered by plentiful trees, even the hottest valley afternoons stay reasonably comfortable.

Busy is a good word for activity on Manteca Park. At 68,000 rounds per year, it is one of the most heavily played courses in the Central Valley. High school golf teams use it for practice and competition. The flat, wide layout attracts new and younger golfers learning the game. The serenity of the locale, and the good quality of fairways and green complexes bring in many amateur tournaments. Locals get a great deal on monthly greens fees. However, all this play means frequent long, slow rounds. *Review based on play and interview in September '08.*

Manteca Park Golf Course

305 North Union Road	Golf Shop:	209 825-2500
Manteca, CA 95337	Fax	209 825-2506
	www.mantecagolf.org	
Managed by: City of Manteca	Architect:	Jack Fleming

Location: Twenty minutes south of Stockton in central Manteca. Take State Rt. 120 to S.Union Rd. exit. Go north one mile. Course is on the left, two short blocks north of W. Yosemite Ave.

Style: Flat terrain, easy to walk. Tree lined fairways and lots of shade. Roughs heavier than normal, but evenly cut. Smallish greens in good shape. External perimeter surrounded by homes but internal grounds very park-like.

Greens Fees	Weekends	Weekdays	Twilight	Seniors	Carts/person
as of 10/08:	$28	$21	$25/$21 incl. cart	$10 sometimes	$15/$14

Course ratings:	Men	Par	Rating	Slope	Yardage	Women	Par	Rating	Slope	Yardage
	Blue	72	71.2	123	6478	White	74	75.0	132	6131
Manteca Park	White	72	69.7	118	6131	Red	72	71.9	125	5564
						Gold	70	68.6	118	4982

Mather:
Originally a private military course on Mather Air Force Base, this property transferred to the City of Sacramento in 1994. It is now public, managed by CourseCo. Original construction took place in the late '50's and the simplicity of those days still shows. Most fairways are straight, with only a few gently bending doglegs. Mature trees, including ash, hackberry, mulberry and sweet gums, line their edges. On this old-fashioned classically styled course, greens are moderate size, putt at average speed and usually have one or two large bunkers protecting the front corners. Occasionally a creek crosses a fairway, but that's rare; so water hazards rarely come into play. Exterior holes have some out-of-bounds markers, but even they are well off to the side.

The real pleasure here is the expansive, evenly green coloration and park environment. No houses rim property lines, since the facility is bordered by 1400-acre Mather Regional Park. The trees graciously provide plenty of cooling shade in summer. Unlike at oak-laden golf courses in nearby California foothills, green roughs run right up to the trunks of Mather's trees. The result is serenity throughout the property, except perhaps, for those who are swinging poorly. Oaks are now being planted in various natural dry-grass spaces that are interior-to-the-course. These off-line areas receive no irrigation, and exhibit a more rustic appearance. (Oaks can't stand the constant watering required for grass, or they would die of fungus problems.) They contrast nicely with the green of the course itself and mirror the feel of the surrounding park.

With the good maintenance provided for tees, greens, cart paths and bunkers, Mather provides an enjoyable though somewhat routine design, and a relaxed round of golf. *Review based on play and interviews in October '08.*

Mather Golf Course				
4103 Eagles Nest Road		Golf Shop:	916 364-4354	
Mather, CA 95655		Fax	916 364-4360	
		www.playmather.com		
Managed by:	CourseCo	Architect:	Jack Fleming	
Location:	Ten miles southeast of Sacramento. Take U.S. 50 to Sunrise Highway exit. Head south on Sunrise fiour miles. Turn right on Douglas and drive one mile to Eagles Nest Rd. Course is on left.			
Style:	Flat terrain, easy to walk. Wide fairways have few contours but are bordered by mature trees. Water on a few holes. Nice fairways and greens.			

Greens Fees	Weekends	Weekdays	Twilight	Seniors	Carts/person
as of 10/08:	$35	$28	$22/$20	$23 weekends	$15

Course ratings:	Men	Par	Rating	Slope	Yardage	Women	Par	Rating	Slope	Yardage
Mather	Blue	72	71.5	123	6730	White	75	75.8	132	6431
	White	72	70.1	120	6431	Red	74	72	124	5873

Monterey Pines: Situated just east of Del Monte golf course, across State Rt. 68, Monterey Pines closed for extensive re-construction in late 2007. This military course is operated by the Dept of Defense, but is open to the public. Re-opening is scheduled for late July '09 with par at 69 and yardage of 5600-yards. *Comments based on phone interview in April '09.*

Morro Bay: Central Coast promotional brochures give high complements to this coastal park-surrounded golf venue. It really does have the panoramic views advertised of the coastline and ocean—from almost every hole. One in particular, 410-yard par-four number fourteen, displays an elegant design, descending down a cypress-lined fairway to a green framed with a backdrop of forest and beach.

But beyond these highlights, Moro Bay, known years ago as The Golden Tee, disappointed me greatly. Mature eucalyptus, pine and cypress trees border the rest of fairways too, but many have died or blown down in storms and not been replaced. Though the view mentioned above provides a great panorama, the appearance looks identical from each fairway, and eventually the vista looses impact. Similarly, designs of holes other than fourteen have little inspiration; many fairways just traverse back and forth across the 500-foot high hillside slope where the course is located. Nearly every lie seems to have the same degree of incline, whether going up, down, left or right across the hill. Tough Kikuyu grass permeates the fairways, and makes iron-play and chip shots more difficult than most Northern Californians expect. Roughs are full of hardpan and droppings from eucalyptus trees. Greens run slow but show good grooming. The entire layout uses only five bunkers.

And, as the *coup de grace*, strong summer afternoon winds usually make a cold and un-relaxed experience. For my money, this course does not live up to its billing. *Review based on play over the years, last in October '07.*

Morro Bay Golf Course

201 State Park Road
Morro Bay, CA 93442

Golf Shop: 805 782-8060
Fax 805 772-8752
www.centralcoastgolf.com

Managed by:	Fairway Management
Architect:	Russell Neyes & Al Lape
Location:	On the coast, eleven miles west of San Luis Obispo. Take State Rt. 1 exit from U.S. 101 and head west, following signs for Morro Bay. Drive 11 miles and then turn at exit for South Bay Blvd. Go left (south) on South Bay for .7 miles. Turn right onto State Park Rd. At "Y" veer right onto Park View Dr. Clubhouse is 3/4 mile ahead.
Style:	Side hill terrain throughout most of course. Trees line fairways, though many have died or blown down in storms. Wiry Kikuyu grass on all fairways. Small greens with moderate breaks. Very few bunkers. Often windy and cool, so wear a hat that fits tightly. Nice views of Morro Bay and the Pacific Ocean.

Greens Fees	Weekends	Weekdays	Twilight	Seniors	Carts/person
as of 10/08:	$48	$39	$24/$20	$26 weekdays	$16

Course ratings:	Men	Par	Rating	Slope	Yardage	Women	Par	Rating	Slope	Yardage
	Blue	71	70.7	118	6358	Gold	72	72.9	118	5633
Morro Bay	White	71	69.5	116	6100	Red	72	69.7	111	5055
	Gold	69	67.3	111	5633					

Napa at Kennedy Park: The city of Napa renamed Kennedy Park

in 1969, as a memorial to Robert F. Kennedy, after his assassination. Several recreation facilities locate within its borders, including the municipal Napa Golf Course. In a town surrounded by expensive and semi-exclusive golf venue's, such as Chardonnay, Eagle Vines, and Silverado, it's refreshing to have a lower cost, decent quality, muni course available for normal everyday play.

For decades, floods on the Napa River have made news on Northern California TV stations. Unfortunately, Napa Golf Course sits right on the edge of the flood plain and regularly gets a dose of the same water. Maintenance crews work hard to recover quickly from these unfortunate events, and put the four or five flooded holes in decent playing conditions by May 1. However, because floodwaters bring aberrant grass and weed seeds, fairways on these holes consistently show a different texture than those on the rest of the course.

Layout at Napa varies from exceptional to average. Holes number one, eight, nine, ten, and eighteen have good interest, picturesque settings and require skillful shots. They make excellent use of changing fairway elevations; and trees protrude into fairways to create beauty, challenge, variation and distinction. Other holes show less character, with straight fairways and wide-set water hazards. Course brochures say water impinges on fifteen holes. This may be fact, but the hazards rarely come into play except on long or very crooked shots.

Despite its somewhat irregular condition, and inconsistent layout, the course provides a good challenge for city and county tournaments. The soft fairways, occasional hazards, severely sloped greens and ever-present breeze mean a good score must be well earned. *Review based on play and interviews in August '08.*

Napa Golf Course at Kennedy Park

2295 Streblow Drive		Golf Shop:	707 255-4333
Napa, CA 94558		Fax	707 255-4009
		www.playnapa.com	
Managed by:	CourseCo	Architect:	Bob Baldock and Jack Fleming
Location:	Southern Napa, just east of the Napa River. From State Rts. 12 & 29 take the exit for State Rt. 221 and head north toward downtown. After one mile, turn left on Streblow and follow signs for the course.		
Style:	Gently rolling terrain, fairly easy to walk. Lots of trees and water, but these obstacles only directly affect play on half the holes. Small greens can be severely sloped. Fairways and greens in average condition. Course oftens floods in winter and needs time to dry out in spring.		

Greens Fees	Weekends	Weekdays	Twilight	Seniors	Carts/person
as of 10/08:	$43	$33	$28/$22	$22 weekdays	$14

Course ratings:	Men	Par	Rating	Slope	Yardage	Women	Par	Rating	Slope	Yardage
Napa At Kennedy Park	Black	71	73.3	130	6698	White	74	75.0	132	6299
	Blue	71	72.6	128	6519	Gold	73	73.0	128	5690
	White	71	70.1	126	6299					

Oakmont: West and East Courses:

The Oakmont active-adult community originated in the early '60's, and sits in the hills southeast of Santa Rosa, on the road to Sonoma. It consists of 3500 homes, plus shops, restaurants, commercial offices, and various recreational facilities, including two well-manicured golf courses. Golf construction began in 1963 and finished in 1980, built one nine at a time. Near the beginning, residents formed a private golf club, but the public has always been welcome to play. Today, the membership continues and owns the course, though in a different format than the original contract. These days over half of the private members come from outside the Oakmont community. Many starting times remain available to the public, and management always searches for new members.

The two separate courses, named West and East, are managed and maintained by Empire Golf. Summer weather finds both courses in excellent condition, with mildly undulating greens, soft, lush fairways, and wide, friendly roughs. Bunkers are also maintained well and were recently renovated. Fairways receive an annual dose of heavy sand top-dressing, a process that has improved drainage significantly over the years. Earlier this decade a member donated a new driving range. Large, mature oaks sit prominently at strategic spots to create narrow gaps on three or four holes of each course. They add good challenge to other shots here and there, but open landing zones and approaches represent the norm. The design strives to be friendly for those who want a casual game, and beautiful for those who appreciate mature oaks and views of nearby Mayacama Mountains.

These sister courses maintain similar conditions, appearance and style, but for one significant difference. The West Course measures a full 6400-yards, the East Course an executive 4300-yards. The East deserves some special comments . . . While not long, nor particularly difficult for players less than a twenty handicap, it is a rare example of a public short-course, designed and maintained to compete with the condition and style of a full sized course. Except for Dublin Ranch in the Livermore Valley, Northern California's executive courses (so named because they take less time for busy executives to play) are either in disrepair or home grown. They are not as sophisticated in their appearance as their championship counterparts. Oakmont East is an exception, and if you want the ego-boosting pleasure of breaking your personal record score, on a gracefully designed short course, it's a great choice.

The bigger West Course is a pleasure too, with gentle doglegs winding through oaks and other full-grown trees. Occasionally a water hazard or fairway bunker adds a good distraction, and the medium sized greens can be sped up if a tournament is scheduled. The course can be set-up to be more difficult, but that's not usual. Most members want a tranquil walk or ride through a park-like setting, hoping their golf swing is as nice as the scenery. *Review based on play and interviews in August '08.*

Oakmont Golf Club: West Course

7025 Oakmont Drive		Golf Shop West:	707 539-0415
Santa Rosa, CA 95409		Golf Shop East:	707 538-2454
		Fax:	707 539-0453
		www.oakmontgc.com	
Managed by:	Empire Golf	Architect:	Ted Robinson
Location:	Southeastern Santa Rosa, on the way to Sonoma. From U.S. 101, take State Rt. 12 exit east. Drive 8 miles to Oakmont Drive. Turn right and follow Oakmont 1.5 miles. Then look for signs.		
Style:	Gently rolling terrain. Fairways bordered by mature oaks, with a few lakes and water hazards thrown in. Country Club type conditions on fairways and greens. Mild bunkering, mostly at greens.		

Greens Fees as of 6/08:	Weekends	Weekdays	Twilight	Seniors	Carts/person
	$50	$32	$35/$22	No savings	$16

Course ratings:	Men	Par	Rating	Slope	Yardage	Women	Par	Rating	Slope	Yardage
Oakmont: West	Blue	72	70.8	128	6313	White	72	74.3	129	6059
	White	72	69.5	124	6059	Yellow	72	71.7	123	5573

Oakmont Golf Club: East Course

Style:	Short, executive course but with all the style, good conditions and manicuring of the full-sized West Course. Nine par threes, many long and tight. Nine par-fours, short but need accuracy.

Course ratings:	Men	Par	Rating	Slope	Yardage	Women	Par	Rating	Slope	Yardage
Oakmont: East	White	63	61.5	101	4293	White	63	63.5	100	4293
						Yellow	63	62.2	97	4067

Old River.
This short flat course in Tracy is owned by a local couple, and seems to be a work in progress. The front nine just finished construction in 2006 and fairway grasses still need more thatch. It's designed for beginning, struggling, or ego

seeking golfers to increase their confidence. The front nine fairways are flat, as are the greens; trees are small; and few, if any, bunkers can be found. Golf on this new nine would only be easier if it were more mature or shorter.

The back nine, developed in 1999, presents an entirely different style. Narrow fairways and mounds permeate all the holes. Some are so twisted I had to guess what direction to hit tee shots. Making matters more difficult, hazards are close to fairways, and some drives demand very precise accuracy. Mounds, bunkers and occasional water hazards surround sophisticated green complexes, where some putting surfaces show extreme undulations and tucked-away pin positions. Their slow speed, same as on the front nine, is a blessing, because speedier Stimp readings would really cause havoc.

The extreme style difference between nines may make the course seem schizophrenic, but the second nine is lots of fun if you hit the ball straight. I recommend trying it. Some of the back tees (which are at only 6100-yards in total length) use narrow strips of grass on the top of narrow levees, and augment the course's Delta charm. One hole, the sixteenth, is a particularly outstanding design. Comparing it to Augusta's famous par-three twelfth hole may be heresy, but the similarity is there, in mirror image, if the pin is on the back left plateau of the green. Shot length, at 155-yards is similar, as is the mounding and fear of hitting into hazards both front and back. Purists may disagree, but the hackers amongst us, who don't have access to that great Georgia venue, get a good feel for the difficulty of the real hole. *Review based on play and interview in March '08.*

Old River Golf Course and Range

18007 MacArthur Drive		Golf Shop:	209 830-8585
Tracy, CA 95304		Fax	209 832-8585
		www.oldrivergolf.com	
Managed by:	Private, local	Architect:	L. Zastere, T. Donahue, C. Matsuno
Location:	Twenty miles southwest of Stockton. From I-205, Tracy's connecting freeway between I-5 and I-580, exit onto McCarthur Ave. Drive north 2.3 miles to the course on the left, past the driving range.		
Style:	The two nines are wildly different in style. Front side is new, open and flat, including the greens. The back side is contoured, tight, has lots of water, trees, and greens with steep slopes and terraces. The area can be windy and fairway conditions are marginal.		

Greens Fees	Weekends	Weekdays	Twilight	Seniors	Carts/person
as of 10/08:	$25	$18	$12/$10	$10 weekdays	$10

Course ratings:	Men	Par	Rating	Slope	Yardage	Women	Par	Rating	Slope	Yardage
	Blue	72	69.7	118	6198	White	72	74	135	5885
Old River	White	72	68.8	110	5885	Gold	72	72.4	131	5530
	Gold	72	67.7	105	5530	Red	70	67.4	108	4530

Pacific Grove: Many publications give high praise to this local muni

course. Perhaps most notable, Chris Santella includes it in his 2005 book, *Fifty Places to PLAY GOLF Before You Die*. Golf Digest lists it in their *Top 50 US courses under $50*.

Pacific Grove has lots of interesting attributes. The first and second holes are par-threes bordered on the right by an unfenced graveyard. Skip to holes five and six; these adjacent, down-and-back par-fives, have cypress trees lining the rough between fairways, and trees and screens guarding homes on the other side. Balls hit into the adjacent fairway are subject to a local rule: "Bring shots back to the centerline of your current fairway and drop without penalty." Wouldn't that be a nice rule on your home course?

The course's famous notoriety comes because of the back nine. Jack Neville, designer of Pebble Beach, put it together in 1960, after 28 years of just nine holes. Here, wind from the Pacific Ocean meets the dunes of the Monterey Peninsula. A nice stretch of six holes, from eleven through sixteen, traverse across that prevailing westerly wind, and create a brief but authentic links experience. Hole number twelve is the jewel, a par-five dogleg right, and then right again. The cross-wind often requires drives to be aimed out-of-bounds left, in order to keep them from bounding into the sand and ice-plant lining the entire right side of the fairway. The next several holes are all cut from the same natural mounding, with occasional views of the ocean. A lighthouse internal to the course dominates a nearby hill and regularly surveys Neville's nine. Wide, firm fairways undulate gently, styled with very closely cut grass. This pitch-and-run country requires some specialized links-style golf skills.

The lighthouse and holes 11 through 16 give golfers a true links experience at Pacific Grove. Jack Neville, designer of Pebble Beach designed the back nine in 1960.

So, why didn't Pacific Grove make the **Best 100**?
While the six links-y back nine holes are picturesque, interesting and fun, they only represent one third of the course. The other two-thirds are short and ordinary by today's expectations. Totals length is a maximum of 5700-yards, par 70. The greens are in good shape and have enough character to make putting difficult, but are erratic in firmness. Roughs throughout are littered with tree debris and a lot of hardpan; and unsightly screens or cyclone fences often border the holes. A magnificent view of Monterey Bay on number six is partially blocked by a tall cyclone fence. What a shame.

Nevertheless, it is still a famous course, and a great chance to experience the true links game for a few holes. Greens fees are up recently, but remain far less than nearby

Monterey Peninsula courses. And, when you play Pacific Grove, bring a hat that stays tight or it may blow into the bay! *Review based on play several times, last in March '08.*

Pacific Grove Golf Links

77 Asilomar Boulevard	Golf Shop:	831 648-5775
Pacific Grove, Ca 93950	Fax	831 648-5779
	www.ci.pg.ca.us	
Managed by: City of Pacific Grove	Architect:	J. Neville and H. Chandler Egan
Location:	Just east of Monterey, on the northern tip of the Montery Peninsula. From State Rt. 1, use exit 399A for Pacific Grove/State Rt. 68.Turn right (north) and follow to the ocean. Rt. 68 becomes Forest Dr. in town and requires a left turn on Lighthouse Ave and a right on Asilomar Blvd. Clubhouse is on the right a few blocks from the water.	
Style:	Rolling terrain, easy to walk. Front nine is short, inland, with tight, tree lined holes. Back nine has several true links-style fairways and greens amongst the sand dunes and ice-plant. It's exposed directly to the ocean. Course condition dissapointing on the front nine.	

Greens Fees	Weekends	Weekdays	Twilight	Seniors	Carts/person
as of 10/08:	$45	$40	$20	No savings	$17

Course ratings:	Men	Par	Rating	Slope	Yardage	Women	Par	Rating	Slope	Yardage
Pacific Grove	Blue	70	67.5	118	5732	White	72	71.9	120	5571
	White	70	66.8	116	5571	Red	72	70.2	116	5299

Pajaro Valley: Located about a half mile east of State Rt.1, just south of

Watsonville, Pajaro Valley opened in 1928. The irregular topography appears to be part of an ancient riverbed or coastal reef, with many steep inclines and sharp drops. The topsy-turvy terrain creates an uneven balance of hole designs, varying from flat, open fairways, some with 90-degree doglegs, to forested linear chutes. The par-fives are short and relatively easy. But approaches to other small sloping greens mean approaches must be very accurate, because putts are hard to judge. Three pars are most difficult because their medium lengths require shots over bunkers to the same style small greens.

Two consecutive holes stand out from the rest. Number eleven is 185-yards long, with a narrow triple-decker green tightly guarded by bunkers on both sides. Hitting the green at the correct level is a real cause for celebration. Next, number twelve, a 420-yard par-four, has an open drive but the approach must skim by tall eucalyptus to a long, very narrow green, sitting on a hillside, bunkered tightly all around.

Some times of the year—surrounding tournaments in the spring and summer—Pajaro is decently maintained and fun to play. However, other times maintenance seems to lapse: The greens get heavy and soggy, fairways turn spotty, and rough becomes hard and weedy. A safety warning: beware when walking from the third green to the fourth tee; balls from the driving range can land nearby, past the nets. *Review based on play several times throughout the years.*

Pajaro Valley Golf Club

967 Salinas Road	Golf Shop:	831 724-3851, ext. 2
Royal Oaks, CA 95076	Fax	831 724-9394
	www.pajarovalleygolf.com	
Managed by: Private, local	Architect:	Floyd McFarland

Location:	Between Santa Cruz and Monterey. From State Rt. 1 turn east on Salinas Rd, just south of Watsonville. Drive one mile and course is on the right.
Style:	Mildly hilly terrain, with most holes easy to walk. Wide fairways, many lined by mature pines. Fairways usually in good shape, but roughs get dry and weedy. Greens use poa anna grass, which can be heavy and bumpy certain times of the year.

Greens Fees	Weekends	Weekdays	Twilight	Seniors	Carts/person
as of 10/08:	$80	$60	$50/$40	No savings	$18

Course ratings:	Men	Par	Rating	Slope	Yardage	Women	Par	Rating	Slope	Yardage
Pajaro Valley	Blue	72	70.2	121	6261	White	72	74.4	125	6008
	White	72	69.2	117	6008	Red	72	72.7	121	5757

Palo Alto Muni:

The City of Palo Alto was one of the first San Francisco Peninsula suburbs to build a golf course after completion of the Bayshore Freeway (U.S. 101) in the mid '50's. Even back then, the only affordable land sat near the bay in the salt marshes, adjacent to their municipal airport. Salt and turf grass don't mix, so the builders added acres and acres of wood chips to the lowest areas in an attempt to soak up the salt. It was quite an adventure in those days hitting through the chips. Thankfully, they are gone now due to a re-design in the 80's, but the holes nearest the bay continue to show the impact of underground salt seepage. The evidence includes spotty grass growth and lack of trees lining the edge of fairways. Pines and other varieties have died or blown down over the years, and replacements have been delayed.

This flat course has few doglegs and little textured rough or dramatic bunkering; but it still gives players a good test. Yardage from rear tees is challenging, augmented by soft fairways that yield minimal roll. The greens are big and usually stay in good, consistent condition. The fairways and roughs on the back nine are much better than those on the front, perhaps because of their further distance from salt seeping underground from the bay. Bunkers throughout are raked regularly and kept well trimmed. The annual Palo Alto City Open tournament is very popular with Bay Area residents, and attracts a good field.

With its exposed location next to the bay, the wind can be very strong in the afternoon. Want to score well? Try teeing off before 7:00 am, especially in the summer. *Review based on play several times, last in August '07.*

Palo Alto Golf Course		
1875 Embarcadero Road	Golf Shop:	650 856-0881
Palo Alto, CA 94303	Fax	650 746-7484
	www.paloaltogolfcourse.com	
Managed by: City of Palo Alto/ Brad Lozarez	Architect:	William F. Bell
Location:	Mid-San Francisco Peninsula. From U.S. 101, take Embarcardero Rd. East exit. Head east towards Palo Alto Airport. Golf course is at end of street, on the left.	
Style:	Flat terrain, easy to walk. Wide fairways, often windy, trees usually far from landing areas. Very nice greens but grass growth suffers from salt seepage, especially on front nine.	

Greens Fees	Weekends	Weekdays	Twilight	Seniors	Carts/person
as of 10/08:	$48	$37	$32/$28	$32 weekday	$13

Course ratings:	Men	Par	Rating	Slope	Yardage	Women	Par	Rating	Slope	Yardage
	Black	71	72.4	121	6833	White	74	74.7	126	6227
Palo Alto Muni	Blue	71	71.2	120	6580	Red	72	71.8	119	5679
	White	71	69.8	117	6249					

Paso Robles:
Originally built in 1960 as a private course, Paso Robles Country Club once acted as cornerstone to new housing development. But thirty-five years later, demographics changed and exclusive membership could no longer sustain the facilities. To generate more income, play opened to the public.

This section of southeastern Paso Robles presents relatively flat terrain, but creeks, trees and gentle slopes provide a measure of character. Fairways meander through home sites, especially on the front nine, and routes take advantage of the natural topography whenever possible. This first nine shows imaginative use of doglegs and diagonal creek banks to create several well defined, tight landing zones. Number nine (and later number eighteen) find the same wide creek/pond hidden at the bottom of a rise, ready to catch 200-yard tee shots from unsuspecting first-timers.

The back side abruptly changes, containing fewer distinctive features. The setting opens to wider spaces so most drives can be blasted with impunity. Many holes sit in a featureless field where it looks like designer Bert Stamps ran out of ideas or money, or maybe trees have since blown down or died.

The course is not as difficult as the 71.0 course rating (at 6200 yards) implies, provided one hits shots reasonably straight and cuts a couple of corners. Smooth, relatively flat greens hold shots well, and bunkers surrounding them are not too punitive. Bermuda and Kikuyu grass fairways run firm, so expect good roll on drives. Wide roughs stop most balls from rolling into homes or hazards. Too bad the back nine driving areas lack more definition, or those holes would be fun too. *Review based on play in October '07.*

Pas Robles Golf Club

1600 Country Club Drive		Golf Shop:	805 238-4722
Paso Robles, CA 93446		Fax:	805 238-2547
		www.centralcoast.com/pasoroblesgolfclub	
Managed by:	Private, local	Architect:	Bert Stamps

Location: From the north, exit U.S. 101 onto Riverside. Turn left and then left again on 13th St. From the south, exit onto Paso Robles St. and turn right on 13th St. Once on 13th, cross the river, it becomes State Rt. 229/Creston Rd. Continue for 1.9 miles, turn right on Niblick, then left on Country Club.

Style: Gently rolling terrain, easy to walk. Bermuda fairways usually very wide, but trees obstruct a few drives. Beware of hidden creeks. Front nine has more doglegs and more interest than the back.

Greens Fees	Weekends	Weekdays	Twilight	Seniors	Carts/person
as of 10/08:	$27	$20	$18/$15	$23/$16	$12

Course ratings:	Men	Par	Rating	Slope	Yardage	Women	Par	Rating	Slope	Yardage
Paso Robles	Blue	71	71	122	6260	White	73	74.9	129	6032
	White	71	69.9	120	6032	Red	73	73.5	126	5748

Poplar Creek:
Years ago known as San Mateo Muni, Poplar Creek underwent total renovation in the mid 1990's. The layout was dressed-up extensively. Hallmarks of the change include new lakes, concrete lined creeks, a few altered fairway routes, new green complexes, and improved conditioning everywhere. Prices went up too; and now, instead of the old local municipal trade, the crowd seems more business-oriented. A non-golfing lunch set fills the clubhouse restaurant frequently; so don't expect a seat to be available for a quick, casual sandwich after a morning round.

Poplar Creek remains a short course, in good shape, with green fairways and roughs on all but the extreme perimeters of the property. A series of steel power-transmission towers march through the middle of the course, but do not seriously impact play. Mature eucalyptus remains the dominant tree variety, and closely lines some of the fairways. However, a couple of holes now feature young live oaks as obstacles in front of greens on shorter par-fours. They provide a pleasant change from the constantly shedding eucalyptus stands.

It's location at Coyote Point, adjacent to U.S. 101, sits five miles south of the San Francisco Airport and gives easy access to the SF Peninsula's large and affluent population. The site and its compact size create one big plus and one big minus. On the plus side, if you are playing well and hit the ball 250-yards, the short par-fours present a real scoring opportunity. In late 2008, high school senior Adam Ichikawa shot a tournament record 58, with ten birdies and one eagle, to break the course record by several shots. Talk about a hot game! The minus is the afternoon wind. It comes straight down from Daly City and can be cold and harsh, even in the summer. *Review based on play several times over the years, last in July '07.*

Poplar Creek Golf Course

1700 Coyote Point Drive		Golf Shop:	650 522-4653, ext.2
San Mateo, CA 94401		Fax	650 522-7511
		www.poplarcreekgolf.com	
Managed by:	City of San Mateo	Architect:	Steve Halsey
Location:	Mid-San Francisco Peninsula at Coyote Point. From U.S. 101 take Peninsula Avenue exit and follow signs for Coyote Creek Blvd or the golf course. This exit is under re-construction in late 2008, so alternate routing may be needed.		
Style:	Flat terrain, easy to walk. Short, course, often very windy in afternoons. Fairways and greens in good condition. Trees come into play on some holes, and greens are well bunkered, but it's a good place to shoot a low score.		

Greens Fees	Weekends	Weekdays	Twilight	Seniors	Carts/person
as of 10/08:	$45	$35	$29/$24	$23 weekends	$13

Course ratings:	Men	Par	Rating	Slope	Yardage	Women	Par	Rating	Slope	Yardage
	Black	70	70.1	117	6042	Gold	72	73.1	120	5645
Poplar Creek	Gold	70	67.8	115	5645	Silver	70	70.8	116	5220
	Silver	70	65.7	111	5220	Yellow	70	67.8	112	4768

Rancho Cañada East:
Adjacent to the better known West course sits the shorter, and somewhat easier Rancho Cañada East. Despite wider fairways and flatter greens, the course is no pushover, since slope ratings read above 120 from both

the women's and men's (back) tees. Views of Carmel River bluffs and the river itself remain serene and bucolic. Weather may even be a bit warmer and winds somewhat softer than on the West because the East's location sits a quarter mile farther into the Carmel Valley. Don't forget, it's often *much* warmer at Rancho Cañada courses than on the nearby Monterey Peninsula venues.

The East measures 200 yards less than the West, with fewer trees. Pines and oaks are present, but in less strategic spots, and sometimes stand so far out of play that bunkers make holes seem almost links-like. Par-fives give the greatest challenges because yardage on these few holes are longer than on the West, trees come much closer to line of play, and fairways have sharper doglegs. Another plus . . . fewer rounds are played here, so it's not quite as crowded.

Fortunately, spring and summer bring the same excellent playing conditions maintained throughout the entire facility. *Review based on play in September '08.* See "Rancho Cañada West," ranked No. 74 on p.163, for more information.

Rancho Cañada Golf Club, East Course

4860 Carmel Valley Road		Resort:	800 536-9459
P.O. Box 22590		Golf Shop:	831 624-0111
Carmel, CA 93922		Fax	831 624-6635
		www.ranchocanada.com	
Managed by:	Private, local	Architect:	Robert Dean Putnam
Location:	South of Monterey. Drive south on State Rt. 1 to Carmel Valley Road. Turn left (east) and go one mile to course entrance on the right.		
Style:	Gently rolling terrain, easy to walk. Wide fairways are bordered by mature trees, but not as closely as on the West Course. Nicely maintained fairways and greens. Shorter and easier than the West.		

Greens Fees	Weekends	Weekdays	Twilight	Seniors	Carts/person
as of 10/08:	$70	$70	$40	No savings	$18

Course ratings:	Men	Par	Rating	Slope	Yardage	Women	Par	Rating	Slope	Yardage
Rancho	Blue	71	69.5	122	6085	White	72	73	121	5714
Canada: East	White	71	67.6	116	5714	Red	72	67.7	114	5278

Rancho Del Rey: Atwater, a Central Valley town located half way between Merced and Modesto, used to be home of Castle Air Force Base and a wing of the Strategic Air Command. The end of the Cold War shut this major employer down, hitting the local economy hard. Then, the Merced Campus of the University of California opened nearby, propelling a boom in housing . . . which has now also gone bust, sending a second major shock to the local area. Through it all, Rancho Del Rey followed a steady path, keeping itself in good condition, and providing an affordable outlet for good golf recreation.

In fact, many people travel here just to play an old fashioned, traditional layout. The flat course is easy to walk, has tree-lined fairways and keeps nicely green throughout the entire property. On warm summer days plenty of shade cools temperatures, and both roughs and fairways stay in good condition. Raised moderate-speed greens, protected by bunkers on the front flanks, show moderate breaks, usually heading back-to-front. A couple of them use double tiers, and pins sometimes hide in corners behind the front bunkers.

Golf at Rancho Del Rey is relaxing. Wide landing areas and minimal fairway bunkers create little angst for drives. However, several water hazards cross some fairways or protect both their flanks and the greens, so you have to be careful with strategy on these holes. In recent years, the club added shorter lady's tees, to make a friendlier challenge from the front. However, back tees sometimes hide in remote, off-line locations, adding distance, angle, and more interest for longer hitters. These rear tees become particularly challenging on par-threes, where shots range in distance from 180 to almost 220-yards. Even the big dogs think that's enough on three-shot holes. *Review based on play and interview in July '08.*

Rancho Del Rey Golf Course

5250 Greensands Avenue		Golf Shop:	209 358-7131
Atwater, CA 95301		Fax	209 358-3803
		www.ranchordr.com	
Managed by:	Private, local	Architect:	Bob Baldock
Location:	Southern Atwater, 32 miles south of Modesto. Take Ashby turnoff north towards Bulach Rd. Turn right on Bulach, and immediate left on Green Sands Ave. Course is 1/4 mile on the right.		
Style:	Flat terrain, easy to walk. Moderate width fairways with green, evenly cut rough. Small moderately sloped greens with traps at the front corners. Nice trees throughout make a relaxing layout.		

Greens Fees	Weekends	Weekdays	Twilight	Seniors	Carts/person
as of 10/08:	$37	$27	$27/$21	No savings	$11

Course ratings:	Men	Par	Rating	Slope	Yardage	Women	Par	Rating	Slope	Yardage
Rancho Del Rey	Blue	72	72.1	123	6708	Gold	72	74.4	128	5930
	White	72	70.3	120	6317	Red	72	72.4	124	5601
	Gold	72	68.6	116	5930					

Rancho Maria: This southern-most venue in the **Best 100** lies just south

of the Santa Maria River, not far from the Pacific Ocean. It completes our coverage of the wonderful courses in Central California . . . before heading too far into Southern California Golf Association territory and deeper into LA living styles.

From the entrance road, Rancho Maria appears rather flat and mundane; except that large trees—many mature eucalyptuses—portend something grander may be hidden. In fact, there is. After a few unexciting, level warm-up holes, Rancho Maria heads up the side of a hill not readily seen from the parking lot, towards all sorts of adventure. Fairways traverse slopes moderately up, down, or across; and some show crowned declines at the side where balls hit in the rough head down side-slopes towards gulches, pastures and other unfriendly golfing terrain. Long par-fives wind around corners; good medium length par-fours cross barrancas; and par-threes all see tall bunkers guarding the front edges. Greens-keepers boldly place pins directly behind the yawning pits. Too bad they haven't learned how to cut cups cleanly, as regular players confirm their ragged edges are a common problem. Back on the flats again, a beautifully trimmed eucalyptus with the largest trunk I've ever seen, guards the approach to the sixteenth green. Its grandeur turns routine par four into a thought provoking challenge.

Other than the poorly cut cups, course maintenance is good. Greens may be a little slow, but putts generally roll true. Fairways are green and evenly cut, though edges are sometime indistinct, showing no transition into the rough. It's is an enjoyable course, a real surprise, and definitely a good value, worth a try on your trip to Santa Barbara. *Review based on play in September '08.*

Rancho Maria Golf Club

1950 Casmalia Rd	Golf Shop:	805 937-2019
Santa Maria, CA 93455	http://ranchomariagolf.com	

Managed by:	Private, local	Architect:	Bob Baldock
Location:	Northern Santa Barbara County. From U.S. 101 take E. Clark Ave exit just south of Santa Maria. Head west 3.3 miles to State Rt. 1/Cabrillo Hwy. At junction turn right and go 1.7 miles to course.		
Style:	Combo of hilly and flat terrains. Large trees line fairways and bunkers block some landing areas. Fairways are in good condition. Greens are a bit slow, and cups can be cut with ragged edges.		

Greens Fees	Weekends	Weekdays	Twilight	Seniors	Carts/person
as of 10/08:	$35	$28	$26/$22	$23 weekdays	$12

Course ratings:	Men	Par	Rating	Slope	Yardage	Women	Par	Rating	Slope	Yardage
Rancho Maria	Champ	72	70.7	124	6390	Forward	73	70.9	119	5504
	Regular	72	69.7	119	6148					

(The) Reserve at Spanos Park: Just north of Stockton, about

a half mile west of Interstate-5's Eight Mile Road exit, lies a young course that gets good marks from players in the Central Valley. The topography is flat, flat, flat; so constructing a golf course with pizzazz was a challenge. Andy Raugust, a designer-gone-solo from the Jack Nicklaus organization, gave it a shot and came up with a nice links style look.

Played in late spring, the Reserve is in excellent condition. Consistent fairways match smooth roughs. Despite being constructed in wheat and alfalfa fields, contractors moved enough dirt to simulate a real links environment. Winds coming from the West off Mt. Diablo add to that feeling, especially in the afternoon.

The course can be stretched out to a hearty 7132-yards and 74.0 rating, so it has plenty of challenge. However, Raugust let the reigns loose for tee-shots. Most fairways have wide landing zones, and if bunkers or hazards sit ominously on one side, those on the other can be cleared or not be reached (except for 270+ yard hitters). Water hazards usually sit far enough from greens and landing areas that minor shot miss-directions usually stay safe.

The strong point of The Reserve is styling around the greens. Here the *links* moniker really shows because greens are consistently firm, fast and undulating. Their hills, valleys and breaks are not severe enough to be visually dramatic, but golfers need to understand where to miss or not miss. Surrounding dips, grass bunkers, mounds and bunkers, often hidden from fairway view, make balls careen to spots from which recoveries can be very difficult. Good chipping, and management of shots around the green, is critical. Newcomers cry "fowl" at the surprising bounces on a few holes. But the locals counter, "come back again, and bring some friends. Then you can take *their* money." *Review based on play and interview in June '07.*

The Reserve at Spanos Park

6301 West Eight Mile Road		Golf Shop:	209 477-4653, ext. 21
Stockton, CA 95219-8702		Fax	209 477-0169
		www.thereserve.americangolf.com	
Managed by:	American Golf	Architect:	Andy Raugust
Location:	Northwestern Sacramento. Tale I-5 to Eight Mile Road Exit and turn west. Go one mile to course on the right.		
Style:	Flat terrain, planned for housing, but no homes yet. Fairways well bunkered at corners of doglegs. Trees very young and not much of a factor. Lakes come into play on several holes. Nice, large, modern green complexes. Can be breezy in afternoons.		

Greens Fees	Weekends	Weekdays	Twilight	Seniors	Carts/person
as of 10/08:	$67	$55	$35	$41 weekdays	Included

Course ratings:	Men	Par	Rating	Slope	Yardage	Women	Par	Rating	Slope	Yardage
Reserve at Spanos Park	Gold	72	74.3	131	7000	White	72	74.3	126	6060
	Blue	72	71.8	126	6550	Red	72	69.9	118	5294
	White	72	69.1	125	6060					

Ridgemark: Diablo and Gabilan Courses: These

two Hollister courses, along with Santa Teresa and the old Riverside in southern San Jose, were the quality standards for decades of play in the Santa Clara/San Benito Valleys. Only since the late 90's have San Juan Oaks, Cinnabar, Eagle Ridge, CordeValle, Coyote Creek and The Ranch taken over as the premier choices. Ridgemark, the southernmost course in this area, and the lowest in greens fee prices, continues to attract many players; but it also languishes in course condition and style.

Owners are currently considering big changes: elimination of one nine, addition of an executive short course, and building a series of new residences. Whether or not these or any concept is accepted and implemented, remains unknown. With maintenance costs rising and an oversupply of courses throughout Northern California, some kind of change certainly makes sense.

In the meantime, golf operations go on, and the current courses remain. Public golfers need to understand that their access to the two courses alternates. One day Gabilan opens to the public, the next Diablo becomes available, and this sequence continues throughout the year. Private member play rotates daily too, on the *other* course.

The original Ridgemark design opened in 1972, and the second eighteen came in 1990. When the newer holes were finished, the original course was split apart, half of the holes going to Diablo and the other half going to Gabilan.

Diablo is now the shorter course, at a max of 6600-yards, and offers a more pastoral setting. Mature trees line all fairways; and the new holes from the 1990 construction give more challenge and undulation than the older ones. Hilly elevations dominate the middle of this eighteen, providing good views of the California's grassy rolling landscape in the valley south of Hollister.

Gabilan, longer at 6720-yards, took the more sophisticated designs from the original course. In particular, current number fourteen offers a distinct challenge. Its 430-yard length, often into the wind, has OB stakes and a pasture closely guarding one side at both the drive landing zone and the green. The approach shot sets-up dangerously because a creek, trees and the OB all protect its well-bunkered green. The following four holes also see similar challenges with OB stakes protecting nice looking wide-set homes.

Unfortunately, the entire facility needs a facelift. Fairways find Kikuyu grass encroaching; this evil wiry grass makes hitting balls much more difficult than normal. Grooming looks inconsistent, with roughs sometimes lush, other times dry and irregular. Greens no longer have the fast dangerous surfaces once boasted by the Santa Clara Valley's one-time best golfing facility. Now they putt slowly and can be bumpy. We all wait to see if any future changes can bring Ridgemark back into a **Best 100** ranking. *Review based on play several times over the years, last in September '08.*

Ridgemark Golf and Country Club: Gabilan and Diablo Courses

3800 Airline Highway		Golf Shop:	831 637-1010
Hollister, CA 95023		Fax:	831 637-5392
		www.ridgemark.com	
Managed by:	Private, local	Architect:	Richard Bigler
Location:	Southern reaches of the Santa Clara Valley. From Hollister, take State Rt. 25 three miles south of town to the golf course, on the right.		
Style:	Rolling terrain. Gabilan Course is flatter, Diablo is hillier. Both tree lined with medium width fairways and greens protected by bunkers on the front corners. Gabilan course has more character, due to doglegs and more creative bunkering. It is also often in better condition. Diablo has several very tight holes, some with blind landing areas.		

Greens Fees as of 1/09:	Weekends $65	Weekdays $55	Twilight $40/$30	Seniors No savings	Carts/person Included

Course ratings:	Men	Par	Rating	Slope	Yardage	Women	Par	Rating	Slope	Yardage
Ridgemark: Gabilan	Blue	72	72.8	131	6721	White	72	75.8	129	6336
	White	72	71.0	128	6336	Gold	72	73.7	124	5949
	Gold	70	69.2	123	5949	Red	72	71.3	118	5624
Course ratings:	Men	Par	Rating	Slope	Yardage	Women	Par	Rating	Slope	Yardage
Ridgemark: Diablo	Blue	72	72.6	126	6582	White	72	75.4	129	6099
	White	71	70.3	124	6099	Gold	72	73.6	126	5807
	Gold	71	68.9	122	5807	Red	72	71.8	122	5441

River Oaks (in Ceres): This executive-style golf course, just south

of Modesto, measures a short 2855-yards. The front nine uses short par-threes exclusively, on flat terrain, with only one over 135-yards long. Greens are in good shape, but putting is on the slow side, about 7 on the StimpMeter. Most have simple shapes, just slightly elevated above the fairways

The back side shows much more variety, interest and character, but fairways conditions are irregular in condition and appearance. Number ten tee, elevated about 40 feet above the flood plain below, aims players past a narrow tree line to a green 286-yards distant. The twelfth and fifteenth holes, also par-fours, are fun because they closely follow the curving contour of the Tuolumne River. Drives must be hit over the river, or around trees lining the overgrown bank. This means reward for good tee shots, or very long approaches if aimed safely. By and large, the holes on this lower nine are also flat, and again the par-threes are routine. Being down at river level, looking up at surrounding cliffs, makes a much more scenic setting. After the final hole, a rope tow (the only one in the **Best 100**) assists the climb back up to the clubhouse. It's a good touch, to end a scenic adventure along the river. *Review based on play in March '08.*

River Oaks Golf Course

3441 Golf Links Road	Golf Shop:	209 537-4653
Ceres, CA 95307	Fax	209 537-4705

Managed by:	Private, local	Architect:		Jim Phipps
Location:	Just south of Modesto. From State Rt. 99 take E. Hatch Rd. exit and head east 2 miles, past Mitchell Rd. Turn left on Golf Links Rd. into course.			
Style:	Short executive course on two separte playing levels. Upper front nine is short par threes. Back nine drops to river plain along the Tuolumne River and requires many target style drives and approaches.			

Greens Fees	Weekends	Weekdays	Twilight	Seniors	Carts/person
as of 10/08:	$20	$18	No savings	No savings	No power carts

Course ratings:	Men	Par	Rating	Slope	Yardage	Women	Par	Rating	Slope	Yardage
River Oaks, Ceres	White	58	58.6	96	3472	Red	58	54.3	75	2855

River Oaks (formerly Rio La Paz): Northwest of

Sacramento's airport by about 15 miles, this River Oaks course huddles against the Feather River's eastern levee. Like Teal Bend, ten miles to the south, it course takes advantage of excellent soils and plentiful water to create good conditions for year-round golf. Course length is moderate, with men's tees ranging from 5400 to 6500 yards, and ladies at 4700. While many wide-open holes reduce the challenge, scores will add up if a player's game is not sharp. Small greens, soft, and in excellent condition, have very few slopes or mounds, so putts don't break much. Despite generously wide fairways, drives must be placed to navigate around mature oaks situated near or in front of many greens. Bunkers, though rare in the fairway, do catch bad shots, rather than just make holes look pretty. Reed-filled lakes border several holes, gobbling up anything hit toward them. Water hazards present the biggest danger on the first three holes, so make sure your game is warmed-up before heading out.

If your game is on, and your putter is working, you should score well. If not, relax and enjoy the ambience of a river setting. The fees are priced right but the course is not well known in either Sacramento or Yuba City. *Review based in play in July '08.*

River Oaks Golf Club, in Nicolaus (Formerly Rio La Paz Golf Club)

201 Lee Road	Golf Shop:	916 488-4653
Nicolaus, CA 95659	Fax	530 656-2185
	http://riveroaksgolfclub.net	
Managed by:	Private, local	Architect:	Ted Robinson
Location:	Thirty miles north of Sacramento. Take State Rt. 99 exit from I-5 and drive 16 miles to Garden Highway. Exit and head southwest 2 miles to the course.

Style:	Flat terrain in the Feather River flood plain, graded to add contours and lakes. Medium width fairways with occasional trees blocking shot placement. Modern greens, well bunkered. Fairway condition is erratic due in part to patchy appearance of different grass varieties.

Greens Fees	Weekends	Weekdays	Twilight	Seniors	Carts/person
as of 10/08:	$35	$23	$20/$17	$29/$20	$12

Course ratings:	Men	Par	Rating	Slope	Yardage	Women	Par	Rating	Slope	Yardage
River Oaks:	Black	71	71.1	128	6487	Blue	71	74.1	132	6006
	Blue	71	68.8	123	6006	White	71	70.6	124	5383
Nicolaus	White	69	66.0	114	5383	Red	71	66.9	115	4722

Riverside:

Home to Northern California's second largest City Amateur tournament, Fresno's Riverside Golf Course has been a mainstay for years. A major overhaul took place in 1982, but additional improvements are constantly underway. Mid-2008 saw completion of a $2.5 million irrigation system and improved fairway and rough conditions. New greens come on stream at the rate of about one per year, and some bunker modification are planned for 2009.

The course sits adjacent to the San Joaquin River, just east of State Rt. 99. A couple of fairways dip down into the river basin, but the bulk lie well above the banks. Undulations and hillocks, added over the years to upper level holes, appear artificially constructed. However, they still add character to the naturally flat farmland. Trees throughout the course are mature, and those that die are diligently replaced. They not only add visual and shot making interest, but also provide shade and wind protection.

The layout uses narrow fairways, lined with bunkers to keep golfers honest. Drives must be hit down one side or the other of each fairway, to avoid the sand. At the green sand traps become quite distinctive. They are set deep with taller lips than normal, protruding high enough to partially hide the putting surfaces. Yardages, long for both white and red tees at 6400 and 5500-yards respectively, measure only 6650-yards for low handicappers. So in tournaments, the course's primary defense comes from narrow greens, narrow fairways, and heavy rough—much like on old-time PGA tournament courses.

Compared to more modern facilities on the northeastern side of town, Riverside is a simpler, classic style of the game. Green fees stay low, keeping it popular, and the scheduled improvements will certainly keep the players coming. *Review based on play and interview in April '08.*

Riverside Golf Course

7672 North Josephine Avenue		Golf Shop:	559 275-5900
Fresno, CA 93722		Fax	559 275-0492
		www.playriverside.com	
Managed by:	CourseCo	Architect:	Willaim P. Bell
Location:	Just off Herndon Ave. in northwest Fresno. From State Rt. 99, take Herndon exit and head east. Go 1/3 mile and turn left on Weber Ave, then right on N. Elgin Ave. Veer right at bend onto N. Josephine and follow signs to course.		
Style:	Flat terrain except for a couple of holes next to the San Joaquin River. Tree lined fairways. Small greens protected closely by deep bunkers. Recently, mounding, contours and new irrigation have been added to add character and modernize the layout.		

Greens Fees	Weekends	Weekdays	Twilight	Seniors	Carts/person
as of 10/08:	$35	$27	$24	No savings	$15

Course ratings:	Men	Par	Rating	Slope	Yardage	Women	Par	Rating	Slope	Yardage
Riverside	Blue	72	71.0	123	6629	Red	72	73.0	124	5924
	White	72	70.0	121	6411	Gold	72	71.2	121	5504

Salinas Fairways:

Golfers unfamiliar with this course don't realize what they are missing. For the price, Salinas Fairways is probably the best value in Monterey County. It's located off Airport Blvd, near the freeway, in the southern part of town. The property is a well-watered haven apart from the arid airport and industrial scenes surrounding it. The front nine has good landscaping and fairway contours, cut from the generally flat local terrain. Holes layouts offer scenic doglegs and tailored par-threes. The more open back side exhibits straighter holes, which can be windy, but it's also kept in good condition. Greens use bent grass, in very good shape, and have mild but varying breaks.

The major negative here is that densely cut Kikuyu grass covers most fairways and roughs, especially on the second nine. When cut short, fairways of Kikuyu significantly reduce club-head speed and shorten shot distances. Players new to this kind of fairway need to beware of frustration, especially when hitting touchy chip shots. Other than the Kikuyu, Salinas is a very good play, one of Northern California's real value gems. *Review based on play in September '07.*

Salinas Fairways Golf Course

45 Skyway Boulevard		Golf Shop:	831 758-4653
Salinas, CA 93905		Fax	831 758-4656
		www.salinasgc.com	
Managed by:	Sierra Golf Management	Architect:	Jack Fleming
Location:	Southern Salinas, adjacent to airport. From U.S. 101 take exit 326B/Monterey Peninsula. After exiting, turn the opposite direction from Monterey, northeast on S. Sanborn Rd. Make a quick right on St. John and go 1/2 mile. Turn right on Alisal and quick right again on Skyway. Clubhouse lot is immediately on the left.		
Style:	Flat terrain, easy to walk. Front nine has treelined fairways which are slightly contoured to add shape and depth. Back side is more open, next to the airport with wiry Kikuyu grass fairways. Greens are excellent, with nice slopes and good bunkering. Foggy days can be windy.		

Greens Fees	Weekends	Weekdays	Twilight	Seniors	Carts/person
as of 10/08:	$32	$21	$20/$16	$20 weekdays	$11

Course ratings:	Men	Par	Rating	Slope	Yardage	Women	Par	Rating	Slope	Yardage
Salinas	Blue	71	70.5	120	6479	Gold	72	69.7	109	5460
Fairways	White	71	69.3	118	6230	Red	71	67.9	105	5121

San Jose Muni:

This high volume course, known for good deals and heavy play, offers a nice place to learn, practice and get some decent exercise. Holes offer a mixture of straight/linear fairways and mild doglegs. Only a few on the back nine have slopes, mounds, large trees or obstacles to add difficulty or character. Despite the several varieties of grass found in them, fairways stay in decent condition, and usually get good roll. Greens are OK, but nearly every one has the same identical slope, going steeply from back to front. The back nine uses more trees and a few elevation changes, but most landing zones are wide-open compared to other courses in the area. Best known features here are the low greens fees, the club fitting and swing clinics, and the discount pro-shop. *Review based on play several times, last in September '07.*

San Jose Municipal Golf Course

1560 Oakland Road		Golf Shop:	408 441-4653
San Jose, CA 95131		Fax	408 453-8541
		www.sjmuni.com	
Managed by:	Mike Rawitzer Golf	Architect:	Robert Muir Graves
Location:	Northeastern San Jose. From I-880 take the Brokaw Rd. exit. Turn east on Brokaw, towards the East Bay hills. Go 1/2 mile to Oakland Rd. and turn right. Course entrance is on the left in 1/4 mile. For other directions see the website above.		
Style:	Flat terrain, easy to walk. Wide fairways, some with wide tree lines. Small greens are sloped back-to-front, with bunkers on the front corners. Hole designs are standard without much character or difficulty.		

Greens Fees	Weekends	Weekdays	Twilight	Seniors	Carts/person
as of 10/08:	$50	$36	$32/$25	$22 weekdays	$14

Course ratings:	Men	Par	Rating	Slope	Yardage	Women	Par	Rating	Slope	Yardage
	Gold	72	71.8	119	6700	Black	74	75.2	126	6304
San Jose Muni	Black	72	70.0	117	6304	Silver	72	71.2	116	5568
	Silver	72	66.7	109	5568	Orange	69	63.6	100	4200

San Ramon: San Ramon Golf Course opened in 1962 as one of the first golf/real estate developments in Contra Costa County. It began as a public venue and remains that today, with the original course design pretty much in tact. While the terrain is flat, the front and back nines run through varying types of developments. The front side has fewer homes on fairway perimeters, bigger trees, and more space between holes. It straddles the Iron Horse Trail, widely used by bicyclists, hikers and walkers throughout the area. The back nine complexion changes because it's definitely in the middle of the housing. Walks from green to tee cross streets several times.

During the fall of '07, construction equipment came in to add mounds at the edges of two par-five fairways on the second nine. The project was supposed to bring variety to shot-making, and improve the visual appearance for both homes and golfers. It succeeded on number fifteen, but the grass hasn't yet taken hold on much of the fourteenth. Little has really changed to the nature of play on either. The back side continues to keep a more tailored appearance, compared to the more rustic look of the longer front side. Greens throughout are groomed very well, almost to country club standards.

As for unusual holes, number nine stands out, with an island green at the end of a medium length par-four. Number eighteen plays the most difficult, due to a long approach over a lake. It's one hole where hitting a good drive, long down the middle, makes a big difference in score. It makes a nice finish to a relaxing, mildly interesting round of golf. *Review based on play and interview in June '09.*

San Ramon Golf Club

9430 Fircrest Lane	Golf Shop:	925 828-6100
San Ramon, CA 94583	Fax	925 828-3743
	www.sanramongolfclub.com	

Managed by:	Private, local
Location:	South of Walnut Creek in residential area on east side of I-680 corridor. Take Alcosta Blvd. exit from I-680 and head east. Drive 1.2 miles to Fircreat Ln. Turn left, course is 1/3 mile ahead.
Style:	Flat terrain, but walking longer than normal due to streets between some holes. Tree lined fairways with many doglegs. Holes 9 and 18 both have lakes in front of greens. Most of course is in good condition, especially the greens.

Greens Fees	Weekends	Weekdays	Twilight	Seniors	Carts/person
as of 10/08:	$44	$34	$26/$18	$28 weekdays	$14

Course ratings:	Men	Par	Rating	Slope	Yardage	Women	Par	Rating	Slope	Yardage
San Ramon	Blue	72	71.3	125	6451	White	74	75.0	130	6103
	White	72	70.0	119	6103	Red	73	72.7	126	5781

Santa Clara Golf and Tennis: Santa Clara's muni golf facility

sits adjacent to the Convention Center, across from Great America amusement park. The conservatively designed course mostly uses sharply angled doglegs to distinguish the layout. However, architect Robert Muir Graves made good use of a prominent hill, left over from an old garbage landfill, to create two nice elevated holes that give good views of South Bay. Back down on the flats, pine and eucalyptus trees create windscreens on most fairway edges, and clustered traps nicely defend greens and dogleg corners. Long hitters who fly the ball 230-250 yards, can cut the corners from the gold (men's) tees and rarely need more than wedge to par-four greens. The rest of us have much longer approaches.

Putts need to negotiate multiple terraces to widely varying pin positions. Condition of the greens varies from date to date, ranging from slow and rough one year to smooth and wonderful the next. I cannot predict what you will find when you play, except to say that odds favor good conditions.

Maintenance crews keep the fairways green and smooth enough that players do not need to invoke *winter rules* in the summer. Unfortunately, the dreaded Kikuyu grass, a tough species of turf-grass that decelerates club speed, encroaches on many. Unless impeded, it will degrade the experience here. *Review base on play several times, last in September '07.*

Santa Clara Golf and Tennis Club

5155 Stars & Stripes Drive	Golf Shop:	408 980-9515
Santa Clara, CA 95054	Fax	408 980-0479
	www.santaclara.americangolf.com	

Managed by:	American Golf	Architect:	Robert Muir Graves
Location:	At south end of the Bay, adjacent to Great America Amusement Park: From U.S. 101, take the Great America Pkwy exit and head east. From State Rt. 237 take Great America Pkwy and head south. At the Santa Clara Convention Center, turn east on Tasman, and course is on the left.		

Style:	Rolling terrain, with several nice holes built on top of an old waste disposal site. Many dogleg holes with bunkers and trees at the corners. Well bunkered greens which fluctuate from fast to slow. Can get heavy bay breezes.

Greens Fees	Weekends	Weekdays	Twilight	Seniors	Carts/person
as of 10/08:	$46	$24	$28/$26	No savings	$13

Course ratings:	Men	Par	Rating	Slope	Yardage	Women	Par	Rating	Slope	Yardage
	Green	72	72.1	118	6704	Black	72	73.3	118	6026
Santa Clara	Gold	72	70.2	116	6420	Gray	72	71.1	114	5525
	Black	71	68.2	114	5918					

Santa Teresa:
Surrounded on two sides by south San Jose housing developments, and on the others by turkey and deer populated rolling hills, Santa Teresa was originally built in 1962. The flat front nine has wide fairways lined with trees grown mature over the past 45 years. The back side sees more elevation change, with six holes wandering the lowest slopes of Mt. Umunhum. A large set of PG&E power line towers crosses both nines. The course does its best to minimize the impact of these wires and towers but they do come into play on a couple of holes on the front side, detracting from the otherwise graceful setting.

The last five years have been good to Santa Teresa. A new irrigation system made fairways and roughs a consistent and solid green color, unlike years past. In addition, greens, tees and some greenside bunkers were rebuilt starting in the early '00's. Now all the construction is complete and the result makes for significant challenge, interest and atmosphere.

While most fairways are free of obstacles and the roughs are cut short to speed play, the greens really make this course. They are very large, with multiple pin locations near their perimeter. The extra size allows greens-keepers to move flagsticks frequently, giving each spot a rest. During the week, when play is not as heavy as on weekends, more difficult placements are used. Reading greens can be quite challenging too. The *poa anna* grass surfaces are mowed daily with a target speed of about 10 on the StimpMeter, which is quick. Players cannot be too aggressive with the long putts often faced because well-hidden drainage slopes and subtle terracing turn many a par opportunity into a three-putt double-bogey.

Management operates Santa Teresa as a high volume, good quality, affordable golf venue that encourages new and young golfers. For the quality, it is truly a good deal. It also maintains a beautiful short nine-hole golf course. The extra nine gives beginners the feel and quality of the real track, but not the length or difficulty. *Review based on play and interview in July '07.*

Santa Teresa Golf Course

260 Bernal Road		Golf Shop:	408 225-2650
San Jose, CA 95119		Fax	408 226-9598
		www.santateresagolf.com	
Managed by:	Mike Rawitzer Golf	Architect:	George Santana
Location:	Southern San Jose. From State Rt. 85 South or U.S. 101, take Bernal Rd. exit. Head south on Bernal for 2 miles. Course entrance is on the left just past Santa Teresa Blvd.		

Style:	Mostly flat terrain with six rolling holes on the back nine. Fairways have medium width, are mostly tree lined, and in good condition. Greens are big, in excellent condition, with multiple moderate slopes.

Greens Fees	Weekends	Weekdays	Twilight	Seniors	Carts/person
as of 10/08:	$60	$40	$34/$25	$24 weekdays	$14

Course ratings:	Men	Par	Rating	Slope	Yardage	Women	Par	Rating	Slope	Yardage
	Black	71	72.5	126	6738	Blue	75	76.8	132	6419
Santa Teresa	Blue	71	70.9	125	6419	White	73	74.4	126	6026
	White	71	69.1	122	6026	Forward	68	62.8	99	4046

Seascape:
Located south of Santa Cruz in the town of Aptos, this course has been around since the 1930's. Beautiful Monterey pines and cypress trees line its fairways and the use of natural terrain rather than manufactured grades is a refreshing throw-back to the good old days.

The setting could be idyllic, except that the course condition is not kept up to the standards I would expect from such serenity. The fairways and roughs are often over-watered or dry, varying from wet near the sprinkler heads to thin under the eucalyptus groves. The design itself shows its vintage. Holes are much shorter than on modern courses.

Greens are small, as are bunkers protecting them. This means accurate iron play is needed to score well, though the shorter holes ease difficulty. The *poa anna* greens are kept soft, and in good shape. They are moderately sloped, with few having multiple tiers, so a hot putter can really bring scores down. *Review based on play several times over the years.*

Seascape Golf Club

610 Clubhouse Drive
Aptos, CA 95003

Golf Shop: 831 688-3214
Fax: 831 688-3587
www.seascapegc.com

Managed by:	American Golf	Architect:	Willie Locke
Location:	Ten miles south of Santa Cruz: From State Rt. 1, take exit for Rio Del Mar, just south of Aptos. Go south, towards the ocean then make quick left onto Clubhouse Drive. Continue .6 miles to the course.		
Style:	Hilly terrain, but a short course with greens close to next tee. Many narrow fairways, lined by eucalyptus and pine. Small greens, well protected. Fairways usually in good condition, but rough can be hardpan, dirty from tree droppings.		

Greens Fees	Weekends	Weekdays	Twilight	Seniors	Carts/person
as of 10/08:	$72	$50	$41/$31	No savings	$17

Course ratings:	Men	Par	Rating	Slope	Yardage	Women	Par	Rating	Slope	Yardage
	Black	68	70.1	128	6029	Black	72	75.6	133	6029
Seascape	Gold	68	69.2	125	5813	Gold	72	73.3	125	5813
	Silver	68	67.9	122	5514	Silver	72	71.5	122	5501

Selma Valley:
Driving down the narrow, worn driveway past old sheds and dilapidated equipment I wonder . . . is this place as run-down as everybody says?

A clubhouse and a food counter do exist, but just barely. The driving range uses ancient balls, well-worn mats, and old cloth advertising banners so faded and frayed that company names are mostly unintelligible and probably out-of business. The course itself also needs major maintenance. The roughs and trees show little evidence of care or trimming. The fairways and bunkers look better, but need huge amounts of work. Greens play okay because they are smooth, but intermittent bare spots and multiple varies of grass create an uneven appearance.

Yet, the course design is decent, and has plenty of character for a 5300-yard layout. Most importantly, the trees planted back in 1963 have grown to full size and give good shape to most of the holes, though they need major pruning. Some protrude into the fairways and easily block slightly errant drives. The layout's natural undulations and side-hill lies are quite unusual for a Central Valley course. Slopes and contours, shaped like the area was once a quarry or sink-hole, force drives to bounce away from the direction of the doglegs. But such positions don't necessarily hurt your score, because many of the greens hide behind tree branches at the end of fairways, and approaches need to be on the far side to find an opening.

With a lot of work, and a few simple structural changes, Selma Valley could be improved tremendously. Although the course is short, it could easily be stretched another 400 yards. Customers must have complained about excess difficulty, because management moved distance markers up towards the front of tee boxes, rather than use their full potential.

So, would an investment pay off soon? Probably not, in this time of oversupply . . . and new Ridge Creek just down the road. *Review based on play several times over the years, last in April '08.*

Selma Valley Golf Course

12389 East Rose Avenue		Golf Shop:	559 896-2424
Selma, CA 93662		Fax	Same as above

Managed by:	Private, local
Location:	Fifteen miles southeast of Fresno: From State Rt. 99, take Exit 115 onto Mountain View Ave. Turn east towards Dinuba and go 1.3 miles to Bethel Ave. Turn left and head north 1.5 miles. Turn right on E. Rose and course is .4 miles ahead on the right.
Style:	Surprisingly rolling terrain surrounded by flat valley vineyards. Course is short but tightly lined by trees on most holes. Greens and fairways are Bermuda grass. Trees need lots of trimming and the course needs considerable overall maintenance.

	Architect:	Bob Baldock

Greens Fees	Weekends	Weekdays	Twilight	Seniors	Carts/person
as of 10/08:	$20	$16	$12	No savings	$12

Course ratings:	Men	Par	Rating	Slope	Yardage	Women	Par	Rating	Slope	Yardage
Selma Valley	White	69	65.0	112	5332	White	70	70.6	118	5332
						Red	70	69.0	114	5038

Sharp Park: Alister MacKenzie, one of the world's most famous golf

architects, designed the original layout of this Pacifica ocean-side track back in 1924. Unfortunately, population growth and political pressure caused a major roadway to be built through some of its fairways on the front side, and then a major 1982 storm took a hole from the back nine. New holes replaced those affected, but the course was then said to be too difficult for average public play. This meant several of the remaining MacKenzie bunkers were filled with grass. All this bastardization created a course the shell of its original self.

Sharp Park could still be a good course if investment or private management were allowed. Cypress trees line many of the fairways and well-bunkered, artistically shaped greens make good targets. As it is, the City of San Francisco manages the facility. While its partial ocean-side setting remains scenic and challenging, the greens and roughs have deteriorated. Greens here and at Sunnyvale Muni on the SF Peninsula are probably the slowest of all courses described in the **Best 100**. Kikuyu grass infiltrates many of the fairways. Recently, environmentalists lobbied to close the facility and stop the inadvertent poisoning of endangered California red-legged frogs and San Francisco garter snakes.*

It will be interesting to see what happens to this once-revered MacKenzie design. With much of its classic character gone, only the most stalwart souls, and local advocates, brave the fog and wind associated with its seaside location. *Review based on play in September '07.*

*From the *San Francisco Chronicle*, dated 9/24/08. Article "Rare Frog, Snake at center of golf dispute," by Marisa Lagos.

Sharp Park Golf Course

Highway 1, Foot of Sharp Park Road	Golf Shop: 650 359-3380
Pacifica, CA 94044	Fax 650 355-8546
	www.sharpparkgc.com

Managed by:	City of San Francisco Architect: Alister MacKenzie
Location:	On the coast, 5 miles south of San Francisco: Take I-280 to State Rt. 1 exit and head 4 miles south, first up and then down the hill to the ocean. At the bottom, course is at junction of Rt. 1 and Sharp Park Rd.
Style:	Rolling terrain. Tree lined fairways, with one hole along the ocean. Once dotted with beautiful bunkers, many have now been filled with grass. Very small greens, usually protected by scenic bunkers, are cut long to make them slow. Kikuyu grass prevalent in many fairways. Often foggy.

Greens Fees	Weekends	Weekdays	Twilight	Seniors	Carts/person
as of 10/08:	$36	$31	$23/$19	$19/$12	$13

Course ratings:	Men	Par	Rating	Slope	Yardage	Women	Par	Rating	Slope	Yardage
	Blue	72	71.5	121	6476	White	74	75.4	125	6239
Sharp Park	White	72	70.4	118	6239	Red	72	72.9	120	5793
	Red	72	68.4	114	5793					

Sherwood Forest: Looking for a respite from the hot, dusty Central

Valley? Sherwood Forest sits about twenty miles due east of Fresno, just off State Rt. 180. OK, it's still hot, but not nearly so dusty. The locale, near the base of the Sierra foothills, straddles Minkler Creek, and trees of all varieties line the fairways. Now 40 years old, they have grown large enough to provide pleasant relief from the summer sun, and narrow conduits for many golf-shots. The wooded setting creates a very picturesque backdrop for a casual round of golf.

The course has several routine flat holes, like those found on many golf courses in the Valley, interspersed with a few that have real personality. For example, short, straightaway 320-yard number one looks at a wide-set tree line and a couple of broadly spaced bunkers at the green. But the next hole adds two deep and intimidating bunkers in line with the front of the green, plus trees in much closer, making it much more interesting.

Minkler Creek meanders along the back nine but just provides ambience until reaching the fourteenth hole. On this par-five it crosses the fairway about 130-yards from the green, creating a high risk second shot for medium-length hitters. Do I try to blast it over, or lay-up and leave a 165-yard third shot to another tightly tree protected green? Later, number seventeen gives a signature photo-op on a good par-three. The 175-yard drive (back tees) heads over a railroad-tie and river-stone framed lake, to an elevated green, also protected by trees and bunkers . . . a pretty, but risky shot, at any distance.

Despite the short overall yardage, varying from 5500 to 6250-yards, Sherwood Forest gives Fresno golfers a good change of pace. *Review based on play in April '07.*

Sherwood Forest Golf Club

79 North Frankwood		Golf Shop:	559 787-2611
Sanger, CA 93657		Fax	559 787-2662
		www.sherwoodforestgolfclub.com	
Managed by:	Private, local	Architect:	Bob L. Baldock

Location: East of Fresno Airport, near Sierra foothills: Follow State Rt. 180 east fifteen miles, from either State Rts. 99 or 41. The highway turns right at Clovis Ave. and left at Kings Canyon Road, but stays Rt. 180. Past tiny town of Minkler, turn left on N. Frankwood Ave. Course is 1/2 mile ahead.

Style: Flat terrain, easy to walk. Wide fairways bordered by mature oaks and sycamores. A few holes on the back nine nestle up to the Minkler Creek, others are crossed by narrow streams. Small greens well protected on front corners by bunkers. Greens are on the slow side.

Greens Fees	Weekends	Weekdays	Twilight	Seniors	Carts/person
as of 10/08:	$28	$21	No Savings	$21 Wed. only	$13

Course ratings:	Men	Par	Rating	Slope	Yardage	Women	Par	Rating	Slope	Yardage
Sherwood	Blue	71	69.2	125	6247	White	72	74.6	126	6050
Forest	White	71	68.3	124	6050	Red	72	71.0	122	5487

Shoreline:
The City of Mountain View operates this 1982 Robert T. Jones designed SF Peninsula course. It adjoins Shoreline Amphitheater, behind Google's headquarters, on part of an old county dump. Soon after it was opened, the city hosted a mini-tour precursor event to what is today called the Nike Tour. Tom Lehman, now a well-known PGA pro and Ryder Cup Captain, nicknamed it "home of the Methane Open" because of decomposing garbage.

Those days of tournament hype, journalistic hyperbole, and flammable gases are now gone, and Shoreline gives one of the better options for public golf along the SF

Bay's western shore. Its hybrid design sits somewhere between the straight fairway style of the '50's and '60's, and the extreme contouring and long yardage of the '90's. Modestly graded roughs have only a few minor slopes and shallow mounds. Bunkers on the corners of doglegs are moderate sized. Simpler green complexes use fewer bunkers, flatter aprons and fewer undulations than are now seen in more recent designs. Ponds sit in off-track locations that make them more cosmetic than threatening, at least for short hitters.

One lingering concern remains and it's not the methane. Despite good roughs, all irrigated and mown to maintain a consistent green appearance, and good maintenance on fairways and greens, water drainage remains an issue. The low-lying bayside location still creates soggy winter fairways. The city installed new drain-lines in 2002 and improved conditions, but certain fairways remain wet sometimes even in summer. Unless fixed properly, Silicon Valley residents may be tempted to scoot down south to Morgan Hill and Gilroy for a crack at some of the top rated **Best 100** courses. On the other hand, its decent design, relatively low greens fees (especially if you are a Mt. View resident), improving conditions and nice restaurant setting, make it awfully convenient. *Review based on play several times, last in June '09.*

Shoreline Golf Links

2940 North Shoreline Boulevard		Golf Shop:	650 903-4653
Mountain View, CA 94043		Fax	650 969-8383
		www.ci.mtnview.ca.us	
Managed by:	Private, local	Architect:	Robert Trent Jones, Jr.
Location:	Southern SF Peninsula, near the bay: From U.S. 101, take Shoreline Blvd North exit. Turn north, towards the bay, and drive 2 miles, till you see signs for the course.		
Style:	Flat terrain. Relatively wide fairways and even wider closely cut green roughs. Most holes have doglegs and bunkers near landing areas. Greens are designed with slopes and terraces. Course can be soggy in winter, and afternoons are often windy.		

Greens Fees	Weekends	Weekdays	Twilight	Seniors	Carts/person
as of 10/08:	$54	$38	$28/$25	$28 weekdays	$12

Course ratings:	Men	Par	Rating	Slope	Yardage	Women	Par	Rating	Slope	Yardage
	Black	72	73.5	129	6988	White	72	75	131	6053
Shoreline	Blue	72	71.9	127	6600	Red	72	71.1	123	5429
	White	72	69.3	123	6053					

Skywest: This course, near the Hayward Airport is currently undergoing an extensive renovation project. As of May '09, the project was partially completed and the course re-opened at full greens fees. *When I visited in March '08, it was still under construction so a review could not be completed.*

Southridge: Ever wonder about that outcropping of volcanic hills in the middle of the Sacramento Valley, west of Yuba City? They are called Sutter Buttes, and Southridge Golf Club takes golfers up-close-and-personal. It sits on the southeastern edge of this small mountain range and the back nine climbs up into its lower hills.

There, golfers will get beautiful views of its many crags as well as the outstretched valley below.

Unfortunately, Southridge's golf attributes are a study in contradiction. The scenery is great, and its Heathland style goes from gently rolling fairways on the front to very hilly grasslands on the back. Once upon a time it was a really good track, with plans for housing, a big hotel, tournaments, *etc.* Those days are gone though, and all that remain are the basics of the good design. The hot, windy summer days have taken their toll on course conditions. Blotchy fairways show patches of dry grass and even dirt. Roughs look worse, due in part to the ubiquitous gopher holes and gopher mounds. Who knows what other critters use these same burrows. The tee at the range is green, but a dried grass field collects the shots. Greens are the highlight and a pleasure to putt.

The course presents a tough walk, especially on the back nine. Plan on a 600-yard climb between the eleventh green and the twelfth tee-box. Add another steep climb up to the fifteenth tee, after the beautiful downhill par-three fourteenth.

Reputedly, course owners look to improve maintenance. An additional employee was hired the day I played to cut the fairways and roughs at decent regular intervals. A new greens-keeper will presumably bring updated techniques for feeding and managing the various turf surfaces. But these new employees have a big job on a very spread-out facility. Good luck on bringing maintenance back to conditions when they hosted the Sacramento Valley Championships in 1993. *Review based on play in June '08.*

Southridge Golf Club

9413 South Butte Road		Golf Shop:	530 755-4653
Sutter, CA 95982		Fax	530 755-1404
		www.southridge.com	
Managed by:	Private, local	Architect:	Cal Olson
Location:	West of Yuba City, at base of Sutter Buttes: 1) From I-5 take exit 578, near Williams and head east on State Rt. 20, through Colusa to southern edge of the Buttes. At Southridge Rd turn left, then turn right on S. Butte Ave; course is ahead on the left. 2)From State Rt. 99 drive to Yuba City, then turn west on Rt. 20. Drive 8 miles to Wyncoop Rd. Turn right, then left on S. Butte. Course is ahead on the right.		
Style:	Front nine has mild, rolling terrain, back side is very hilly. Well designed doglegs, mounding and contours on most holes. Greens also very modern with slopes and terraces. Course condition does not match the quality of the design.		

Greens Fees	Weekends	Weekdays	Twilight	Seniors	Carts/person
as of 10/08:	$55	$45	$34/$26	$28	Included

Course ratings:	Men	Par	Rating	Slope	Yardage	Women	Par	Rating	Slope	Yardage
	Gold	72	73.7	129	7047	White	72	74.4	131	6105
Southridge	Blue	72	71.6	126	6611	Red	72	71.3	122	5541
	White	72	68.9	121	6105					

Spring Hill: The road from Watsonville to Gilroy is off the beaten track; but golfers looking for a fun, speedy, inexpensive round may find the trip worth the effort. And if one can hit the ball straight, this short 6000-yard track makes for some good scores. Back in the early 80's Spring Hill lapsed into terrible condition with rock-hard

fairways, roughs and greens. But then original owners re-entered the scene, added modern irrigation, and the course came back to life.

Layout here is a mix of flat terrain on the first few holes and hillsides the rest of the way. All sorts of obstacles make certain sections rather tricky. These start with a 170 to 200-yard approach shot on number one, where ball flight must clear the corner of a hill, several trees, a steep apron and several bunkers, to find a tiny green. That's pretty tough for a starting hole. Numbers two and three have burns (a Scottish term for a stream or creek, similar to a large drainage ditch) crisscrossing the fairway near the green and require good placement skill just to stay dry. Although the remaining holes on the front side are short, many have creeks or hazards alongside roughs, forcing players to be careful on at least one shot per hole.

The back nine starts with a 175-yard par-three where a large oak protects an elevated green. Then players climb higher to an adjacent ridge and a series of gentle doglegs and undulating fairways. Again, the holes are relatively short, so a couple of bunkers have been added to toughen up approach shots. If drives are too crooked, they hit hardpan and bound off hills into real trouble or out-of-bounds.

Additional improvements take place regularly, a sign that the management once again cares to attract more play. If they would just extend their irrigation lines further into the rough, and slow those hardpan rolls, Spring Hill could become even more enjoyable. *Review based on play several times over the years, last in October '07.*

Spring Hills Golf Course

501 Spring Hills Drive
Watsonville, CA 95076

Golf Shop: 831 724-1404
Fax: 831 724-1474
www.springhillsgolf.com

Managed by:	Private, local	Architect:	Hank Schimpler
Location:	South of Santa Cruz, east of State Rt. 1, near route over Hecker Pass: From Rt. 1 southbound, take Airport Blvd exit and turn left on Green Valley Rd. From northbound Rt. 1 take Green Valley Rd exit and drive through Airport Blvd intersection. Continue on Green Valley Rd. east four miles. Turn right on Casserly, go 1 mile, then turn left on Smith. Entrance is on left. See website for directions over Hecker Pass or from U.S. 101.		
Style:	Rolling and hilly terrain. Short course but lots of narrow landing areas and creeks to gobble up stray shots. Small greens with bunkers usually on front corners. Many sharp doglegs. Fairways in OK condition, but roughs can be soggy or hardpan, take your pick.		

Greens Fees	Weekends	Weekdays	Twilight	Seniors	Carts/person
as of 10/08:	$45	$35	$30/$23	$25 weekdays	$15

Course ratings:	Men	Par	Rating	Slope	Yardage	Women	Par	Rating	Slope	Yardage
	Blue	71	70.0	127	6015	White	71	74.7	128	5883
Spring Hills	White	71	69.6	125	5883	Gold	71	73.1	126	5585
						Red	71	72.0	123	5397

Spring Valley: High above the hills of Milpitas, where State Rt. 237 becomes a rural route, sits a small valley with a golf course. The moderately level terrain makes Spring Valley a respite from other severely hilly courses in these same East Bay Hills.

Several factors combine to make it a pretty easy track: Yardage is short and fairways are firm. Trees provide borders but leave wide-open landing areas. Even when shots go off-line, hardpan adds roll, and branches are trimmed high enough that players can easily recover. Bunkers are widely spaced, including around the greens, and lakes come in to play on only three drives. The toughest challenges come on par-threes, at distances varying between 150 and 200-yards. Breaks on their large surfaces can be steep enough to test the patience of any golfer.

Course condition is not quite average, with some fairways soft and others firm, though the ball sits-up pretty well on most. Narrow roughs, bordered by hard ground find lotsof weeds mixed with the grass. On many holes, dropped leaves remain under the trees, meaning most lack a manicured appearance. Greens, by comparison, are in adequate shape and hold well. Several have been rebuilt; but the new ones, those with the more extensive terracing and bunkers, putt at different speeds than the older ones. *Review based on play several times over the years.*

Spring Valley Golf Course			
3441 East Calaveras Boulevard		Golf Shop:	408 262-1722
Milpitas, CA 95035		Fax	408 262-3260
		www.springvalleygolfcourse.com	
Managed by:	Private, local	Architect:	Anderson/Taylor; G. Jetter re-design
Location:	North of San Jose in southern East Bay Hills: From I-680 or I-880, take State Rt. 237/Calaveras Blvd east into foothills. Course entrance is on the left just past turnoff for Ed Levin County Park.		
Style:	Gently rolling hills. Wide fairways, occasionally bordered by mature trees. Greens small, though newer ones are larger. Short course, with easy par-fours and fives, but tough par-threes. Fairways in OK condition, but roughs have hardpan under trees and beyond.		

Greens Fees	Weekends	Weekdays	Twilight	Seniors	Carts/person
as of 10/08:	$54	$36	$29/$26	$28 weekdays	$14/$13

Course ratings:	Men	Par	Rating	Slope	Yardage	Women	Par	Rating	Slope	Yardage
Spring Valley	Blue	70	68.4	113	6009	White	72	72.5	120	5783
	White	70	67.4	110	5783	Red	72	70.4	116	5503

Squaw Creek: A broad meadow, full of wetlands, waterfowl and all variety

of native animals covers the small valley at the base of the 1960 Winter Olympic ski slopes. In the late 1980's, local communities approved construction of a golf course and resort, and Robert Trent Jones Jr. was selected to design the golfing section of the project. But, with the development agreement came a serious restriction: Environmental conditions were so delicate, that only a bare minimum of fill material and drainage lines would be allowed. To this day, maintenance crew can use little fertilizer or herbicides.

The result is one of the most *organic* courses in the state, if not the nation. This means players must adjust their expectations about conditions of play. Extremely firm fairways make balls bounce hard and far, easily careening into surrounding marshes. Weeds show in fairways and on greens. Players who understand the reasons for these differences, and who change their golfing tactics and expectations, have a lot more fun and appreciation of this special locale.

The course has two sections. Holes one through four traverse the hills near the lower ski slopes. They are mountainous in nature and picturesque, with fairways winding through the firs and pines. Beware, shots hit crooked to the low side of the fairways often continue bounding down into heavy forest.

Then the course reaches the flatlands. Background scenery of snowy peaks and ridges provide spectacular beauty, but play is different. Instead of trees framing the shots, low lying marshes—filled with long grasses, water, and reeds—border almost every hole.

It is here that golfers discover how the original landfill restrictions impact their game. Often fairways and tees are set so low that it's difficult to see where to hit your drive. The roughs slope down into the marsh grasses; so, without extra dirt fill, it is difficult to know where land stops and unplayable rough or environmentally protected areas begin. The tee-shot on number eleven is totally blind because marsh-grasses, almost as high as your head, extend out 150-yards in nearly all directions. Only the tip-top of a white aiming stake provides a sense of which direction to aim, and no idea where fairway boundaries stop or what length of hit is needed to cross the hazard. Be prepared for forced drive carries of well over 100-yards on these holes, and some may require lay-ups too.

Target golf in an environmentally pristine setting would be an apt description of the game at Squaw Creek. *Review based on play and interview in September '07.*

(Resort at) Squaw Creek

400 Squaw Creek Road		Resort:	800 327-3353
P. O. Box 3333		Golf Shop:	530 581-6637
Olympic Valley, CA 96146		Fax	530 584-4058
		www.squawcreek.com	
Managed by:	Destination Hotels and Resorts	Architect:	Robert Trent Jones, Jr.
Location:	North Lake Tahoe, adjacent to Squaw Valley Ski slopes. From I-80, exit at State Rt. 89 South. Follow signs at traffic circles for Rt. 89 South. Go south 8.5 miles to traffic light a Squaw Creek Rd. Turn right (west) and follow signs to golf course. Pro shop on back lower level of hotel.		
Style:	First four holes mountain style with fairways sloped in forest along base of mountain. Balance are in open marshy alpine meadow. Very firm fairways mean lay-up shots needed often, or balls easily roll into hazards.		

Greens Fees	Weekends	Weekdays	Twilight	Seniors	Carts/person
as of 10/08:	$115	$100	$60	No savings	Included

Course ratings:	Men	Par	Rating	Slope	Yardage	Women	Par	Rating	Slope	Yardage
	Gold	71	72.4	135	6931	White	71	74.2	139	6010
Squaw Creek	Blue	71	70.0	131	6453	Red	71	69.1	127	5097
	White	71	68.2	122	6010					

Stockton Muni's: Swenson Park and Van Buskirk Park

Swenson Park is the older of two municipal courses in Stockton. Built in 1952, the property actually houses two courses: an eighteen-hole Championship course, where the San Joaquin County Championships are held annually, and a nine-hole executive par-three course, which can be played in about an hour. The course is located three miles north of downtown, on the east side of Interstate-5. Stockton's other muni, Van Buskirk Park, sits three miles south of downtown, on the west side of I-5.

Swenson is far more popular, with over double the amount of play. Located in a purely residential area, it's near Stockton's primary population center. The lush green Bermuda fairways, heavily irrigated all summer long, keep players coming. Fairways are wide, with mature trees set far back from the line of play, and rarely do players need to hit over water. On the other hand, guys and gals used to hitting from short front tee boxes won't find any here. Regular men's tees measure a very long 6500-yards. The women's short tees, at 6000-yards, are the longest in Northern California. The extra length gives long-hitting youngsters a big advantage in tournaments on the soft, slow-rolling fairways.

I like Van Buskirk's more sophisticated layout better. It is somewhat more difficult because of longer yardage, narrower fairways, closer tree lines and faster greens. Hole layouts may show the same flat surfaces as Swenson, but fairways offer more twists, turns and variations in shape. Well-protected greens, with bunkers closer to pin locations, are kept in better condition. Fairways too, are much firmer, often even to the point of being about one-quarter burned out in the late summer. But even with this defect, Van Buskirk has better design and interest, and requires more strategy, finesse, and subtlety on approach shots.

Those who hit it long should stay at Swenson, if you have good accuracy, choose Van Buskirk. *Review based on play and interviews in September '08.*

Swenson Park Golf Course

6803 Alexandria Place	Golf Shop:	209 937-7360
Stockton, CA 95207	Fax	209 937-7328
	www.stocktongov.com/golf/	
Managed by: City of Stockton	Architect:	William Bell
Location:	North Central Stockton: From I-5 take exit for N. Benjamin Holt Dr. Head east .7 miles to N. Alexandria Place. Turn left (north), course is on the left.	
Style:	Flat terrain. Wide Bermuda grass fairways, kept soft and slow in the summer. Mature trees line roughs. Greens have some modern shape and bunkering. Very long women's tees.	

Greens Fees	Weekends	Weekdays	Twilight	Seniors	Carts/person
as of 10/08:	$29	$24	$18/$16	$19/$15	$13

Course ratings:	Men	Par	Rating	Slope	Yardage	Women	Par	Rating	Slope	Yardage
Swenson Park	Blue	71	70.6	115	6704	White	75	76	125	6431
	White	71	69.4	111	6431	Red	74	73.6	120	6036

Van Buskirk Golf Course

1740 Houston Avenue	Golf Shop:	209 937-7357
Stockton, CA 95206	Fax	same
	www.stocktongov.com/golf/	
Managed by: City of Stockton	Architect:	John Dominick and Larry Nordstrom
Location:	Southwestern Stockton: From I-5 take the exit for W. 8th St. Go west on 8th one mile to S. Fresno St. Turn left there and go to the end. Course is dead ahead, across the street.	

Style:	Flat terrain, easy to walk. Some fairways are links-like, others bordered with trees. Fairway bunkers are usually small, but doglegs and trees create some interesting landing zones. Greens vary in size and design but have subtle breaks. In summer fairways get hard, with many dry spots.

Greens Fees as of 10/08:	Weekends	Weekdays	Twilight	Seniors	Carts/person
	$29	$24	$18/$16	$19/$15	$13

Course ratings:	Men	Par	Rating	Slope	Yardage	Women	Par	Rating	Slope	Yardage
	Blue	72	72.9	123	6949	White	75	76.8	128	6511
Van Buskirk	White	72	70.8	118	6511	Red	73	73.3	120	5882
	Red	70	67.7	113	5882					

Summitpointe:

Years ago known as Tularcitos, Summitpointe sits just above Interstate 680, east of Milpitas. Expensive homes can be seen high above the fairway's rolling terrain, but few actually adjoin the playing areas. Grazing land and grassy canyons frame scenes on most of the course. Many expansive views of the south bay add enjoyment to your day in the hills.

Layouts vary, so each hole has a different look. Some head steeply up-hill, some steeply down. Many require shots across lakes or gullies, or have small creeks running at their edge. The toughest holes run across side-hill slopes, where bounces go hard left or hard right, rather than straight. Greens often mirror the heavy breaks of these fairways. Add multiple tiers plus decent conditioning and they bring a good challenge for your short game.

Inconsistent quality on fairways and roughs are the course's weakness, probably from its age and the challenge of watering hilly, windy terrain. Also, clay based soils make for more difficult irrigation that leaves both soft and wet spots on the same fairway. Summers yield big rolls and winters can be mushy. One unusual feature: the driving range, which uses mats on concrete, aims you into a lake where the range balls float! *Review based on play several times, last in September '07.*

Summitpointe Golf Club

1500 Country Club Drive	Golf Shop: 408 262-8813
Milpitas, CA 95035	Fax 408 262-5867
	www.summitpointe.americangolf.com
Managed by: American Golf	Architect: No record

Location:	East Bay foothills above northern Milpitas: Take I-680 to Jacklin Rd. Exit and turn east, towards the foothills. Make a quick left on N. Park Victoria Rd. and then right again on Country Club Dr. Go up the hill 1 mile to course parking lot on the right.
Style:	Hilly terrain, a walking challenge. Mostly wide fairways, with few trees but sloped so ball will easily roll into rough. Short rough is in good shape but past that it's hardpan and weeds. Fairways vary from moist to firm. Small greens often severely sloped but in good shape; bunkered on front corners.

Greens Fees as of 10/08:	Weekends	Weekdays	Twilight	Seniors	Carts/person
	$66	$46	$39	No savings	Included

Course ratings:	Men	Par	Rating	Slope	Yardage	Women	Par	Rating	Slope	Yardage
	Blue	72	71.3	133	6329	White	72	75.6	138	6061
Summitpointe	White	72	70.1	131	6061	Red	72	72.7	132	5530

Sunnyvale:

The heart of Silicon Valley, adjacent to U.S. 101, provides the setting for 40-year old Sunnyvale Muni. As recently as the late '90's player's backswings were interrupted by P-3 Orion anti-submarine aircraft, landing at nearby Moffet Field. Nowadays most of the air traffic is gone. Landing lights in the ninth fairway and the strong prevailing crosswinds are a reminder that we used to live in a country that feared and hunted for Russian subs nearby.

Sunnyvale's course conditions have seen the impact of its windy environment for years. Though not designed as a links layout, holes on the north side of State Rt. 237 play almost like an oceanside course. Originally designed for traditional tree-lined play, enough trees have died or been blown down that keeping up with the carnage appears nearly fruitless.

On the plus side, fairways are now wide, their *poa anna* grass is green and in good shape, and hitting off their textured turf is a pleasure. Too bad management doesn't care for *poa* on the greens with the same success. It grows long, creating slow and bumpy putts. Only San Francisco's Lincoln and Sharp Parks have slower greens.

The back side at Sunnyvale, although shorter, is more fun to play because holes wander through parts of an old walnut orchard. Well-rooted trees protect shots from breezes, add better depth perception to shot making, and provide more visual interest to the surroundings. Number eighteen has the most modern design on the course, and its 360-yard distance can be quite challenging when hitting over a lake, into the wind, and the pin is far back on a tiny terrace surrounded by tall bunkers and water. Its a tough shot at the end of a windy afternoon. *Review based on play several times, last in July. '07.*

Sunnyvale Golf Course

605 Macara Lane		Golf Shop:	408 738-3666
Sunnyvale, CA 94085		Fax	408 738-3670
		www.sunnyvale.ca.gov	
Managed by:	City of Sunnyvale	Architect:	Clark Glasson
Location:	Across U.S. 101 from Moffet Field airbase: 1)From U.S. 101 take Matilda Ave South exit, and go .8 miles to Maude. Turn right and then right again on Macara. 2)From east or west, take State Rt. 237 to Maude Ave exit. Turn south and then turn left on Macara. Course is ahead on left.		
Style:	Flat terrain, easy to walk. Wide fairways, not contoured, some lined closely with mature trees. Small greens cut to putt very slowly are often well bunkered, especially on shorter holes. Location exposed to strong afternoon breezes.		

Greens Fees	Weekends	Weekdays	Twilight	Seniors	Carts/person
as of 10/08:	$47	$35	$30/$26	Discount card	$13

Course ratings:	Men	Par	Rating	Slope	Yardage	Women	Par	Rating	Slope	Yardage
Sunnyvale	Black	70	70.2	118	6255	White	71	72.5	121	5740
	White	70	67.6	113	5740	Gold	71	69	114	5170

Sunol Valley: Palm and Cypress Courses:

This 36-hole facility is owned by the City of San Francisco but operated privately. It is located in a valley about 40 miles southeast of the Bay Bridge, on Interstate-680, between Pleasanton and Fremont. The two courses are similar in style and difficulty, with The Palm running around the perimeter of the property and Cypress covering the inside. Due to the central South Bay location and easy freeway access, both usually keep busy all day. Fairway maintenance is reasonably good; and greens putt on the slow side, but also stay in decent condition. Downside is that the holes line up close together, and many have dated, relatively unimaginative designs. Most of the course's character comes on par-fives that can be reached in two shots by 250-yard hitters, and have interesting mounded bunker/green complexes.

Those who hit the ball wildly will find Sunol a friendly venue, as crooked shots often end up playable in adjacent fairways. Even though the layouts are rather short, hills and occasional trees add enough interest to challenge good players and give lesser players success too. It's a great place for teambuilding in an office *scramble* tournament, because all levels of golfers have a chance: The long hitters can be heroic, and novices can keep the ball in play. *Review based on play many times, last in February '07.*

Sunol Valley Golf Club: Palm and Cypress Courses

6900 Mission Road		Golf Shop:	925 862-0414
Sunol, CA 94586		Fax	925 862-2250
		www.sunolvalley.com	
Managed by:	Private, local	Architect:	Clark Glasson
Location:	In the SF South Bay, adjacent to I-680, between Pleasanton and Fremont: Take I-680 to Andrade Rd. exit and turn north, course entrance is immediately on the right.		
Style:	Both courses similar in style. Rolling/mildly hilly terrain. Wide fairways, some loosely bordered by trees. A few greens are terraced, but most have uniform break from back to front. Courses are kept in moderately good condition.		

Greens Fees	Weekends	Weekdays	Twilight	Seniors	Carts/person
as of 10/08:	$67	$57	$57/$45	No savings	Included

Course ratings:	Men	Par	Rating	Slope	Yardage	Women	Par	Rating	Slope	Yardage
Sunol Valley:	Blue	72	72.3	121	6895	Red	74	74.8	126	6083
Palm	White	72	71.0	120	6458					

Course ratings:	Men	Par	Rating	Slope	Yardage	Women	Par	Rating	Slope	Yardage
Sunol Valley:	Blue	72	69.2	120	6086	White	72	73.5	124	5763
Cypress	White	72	68.0	117	5764	Red	72	71.5	120	5479

Table Mountain: This is an easy course, in good condition, which is popular with locals as a place to enjoy a little exercise or learn the game. Table Mountain, located just south of Oroville, has a good junior program, fair greens fees, and a decent but small practice area. Plenty of trees surround the old clubhouse, and keep its central meeting area shady on hot summer days. The course layout, made back in 1957, is what one might expect on a muni course of this vintage. Holes first head out around the perimeter of the property, then often parallel each other on very flat topography. Fairways are green, with decent lies, as are the first 10 yards of rough. After that, the rough becomes dry, sometime turning to hardpan. Balls hit off-line should expect rolls far in the wrong direction, sometimes far enough to give an open

recovery shot. Lovely small greens have Bent grass that's kept soft, making chips and putts are a real joy.

Bottom line: Table Mountain offers easy putting plus fairways green—where they need to be green—and an easy walk. It has few, if any, truly challenging holes, but is a good place to boost the ego and have a relaxing afternoon. *Review based on play in July '08.*

Table Mountain Golf Course

2700 Oro Dam Boulevard		Golf Shop:	530 533-3922
Oroville, CA 95965		Fax	530 533-0550
		www.tablemountaingolf.com	
Managed by:	Private, local	Architect:	Bob Baldock
Location:	Seventy miles due north of Sacramento: Take State Rt. 99 sixty miles north from I-5 exit to Oro Dam Blvd West. Turn east and drive 3.4 miles. Course is on the right.		
Style:	Flat terrain, easy to walk. Wide fairways, loosely tree lined. Plenty of room for stray shots. Greens slope back to front, with bunkers usually at front corners. Relaxing, easy course.		

Greens Fees	Weekends	Weekdays	Twilight	Seniors	Carts/person
as of 10/08:	$30	$25	$20/$15	$16 weekdays	$13

Course ratings:	Men	Par	Rating	Slope	Yardage	Women	Par	Rating	Slope	Yardage
	Black	72	71.4	120	6690	White	72	71.6	116	5739
Table Mountain	Blue	72	69.1	114	6254	Gold	72	67.7	108	5068
	White	69	66.6	110	5713					

Tahoe Paradise:
This short executive course is quite unusual. Straight hitters will love scoring here, and new golfers will enjoy its short length. It's located in South Lake Tahoe, a few miles north of the junction of U.S. 50 and State Rt. 89. The layout runs up and down the lower stretches of the same mountain ridge as Heavenly Valley ski area, a few miles north. Fairways are in good condition, lined with tall pines. Par-fours often measure only 225 to 290-yards, but that doesn't make them pushovers. Some use doglegs to force lay-ups or big slices/hooks from the tee. Wise players go with mid-length irons from the tee and set up 100-yard approach shots, rather than trying for the green. Those using a 240-yard club to hit tiny, elevated, extremely well protected greens, usually end up lost in the trees. Even well hit drives, just a bit off-line, can yield impossible chips. Small greens mean short putts, so birdies (or eagles) can be had, because the surfaces are smooth and true. Total course length measures only 4000-yards, so walking is not too challenging. But remember, elevation of 6500 feet means high altitude pre-conditioning would be wise. *Review based on play in July '08.*

Tahoe Paradise Golf Course

3021 U.S. Highway 50		Golf Shop:	530 577-2121
South Lake Tahoe, CA 96150		Fax	530 577-1813
		www.tahoeparadisegc.com	
Managed by:	Private, local	Architect:	Harold S. Prescott
Location:	South Lake Tahoe, south of the airport: On U.S. 50, .7 miles north of junction with State Rt. 89.		
Style:	Executive course, in the forest, with several hilly holes. Small greens, sharp doglegs requiring many lay-up drives and accurate approaches. In reasonable condition.		

Greens Fees	Weekends	Weekdays	Twilight	Seniors	Carts/person
as of 10/08:	$42	$42	$30	$34	$18

Course ratings:	Men	Par	Rating	Slope	Yardage	Women	Par	Rating	Slope	Yardage
Tahoe Paradise	White	64	61.7	103	4034	Red	66	59.3	99	3572

Tilden Park:
High atop the East Bay hills, directly above the UC Berkeley campus, sits an old fashioned, long esteemed golf course, built with funds from Roosevelt's old WPA. Despite it's age, and lack of major modernization projects, Tilden remains highly popular, is a natural beauty, and has a place for golfers of all abilities.

Recently some improvements have been made. American Golf Company started managing in 2003 and added drainage to the shady fourteenth, fifteenth, seventeenth and eighteenth holes. They also changed a couple of hole-designs and continue to re-work bunkers, while keeping the basic layout the same.

A day at this course is a special experience. No homes line the fairways. Heavy natural vegetation and full sized trees augment the reclusive feel of the area. Steep hillside canyons surround the course, creating a golfing get-away only a few miles from the heart of the Bay Area's urban sprawl.

At a maximum length of only 6300-yards, the course measures short by modern standards. However, steep uphill holes and a few sharp doglegs on others, create more challenge than might be expected. Right at the start, number one stamps its image as the toughest starting par-four in the **Best 100**. The fairway goes up, up and then more up, about 410-yards, playing 460. The green sits on a ledge near the top of the hill; players need to be careful not to putt back off the front edge, or it seems the ball might trickle back to the clubhouse. The following two holes give added indelible memories: Number two's dogleg comes so abruptly that players need a 160-yard drive followed by a 200-yard approach. Isn't that backward? Three is a long skinny tree-lined chute down a 460-yard par-four before holes ease up at the bottom of the hill. Straight driving remains important throughout and small greens put a premium on good short iron play and chipping.

Unusual is Tilden's lack of bunkers, totaling only eleven. Their absence does not diminish interest, character or difficulty, because hills, trees, creeks or steep aprons take their place to the point that more traps might be punitive. However, bunkers create shadows that can augment the appearance of length, height, or drama of a shot. Tilden's old-fashioned design misses some of this extra texturing seen in its modern competitors.

Course condition varies with the season. Winters remain wet, though the new drainage has improved playability. Even though summer brings the best conditions, both damp and dry spots remain. Greens are in good, not great condition, and run at medium speed. Play is so heavy, they see lots of wear; but that's the consequence at such a well-revered locale. *Review based on play in January '08.*

Tilden Park Golf Course		
Grizzly Peak Blvd and Shasta Road	Golf Shop:	510 848-7373
Berkeley, CA 94708	Fax	510 848-2726
	www.tildenparkgc.americangolf.com	
Managed by: American Golf	Architect:	William P. Bell

| Location: | In the East Bay Hills above Berkeley: 1)Take State Rt. 24 to the east end of the Caldecott tunnel. Exit onto Fish Ranch Rd. and head up to Grizzly Peak Blvd. Turn right on Grizzly Peak and go north 3 miles to Golf Course Rd. Turn right and clubhouse is 1 mile ahead. 2)See website for alternate routes from I-80. |
| Style: | Hilly terrain, especially on first three holes. Trees and forest border most holes. Doglegs and creeks also affect many shots. Course in good shape during summer, but can be wet in winter. Greens are small, so require good accuracy. |

Greens Fees	Weekends	Weekdays	Twilight	Seniors	Carts/person
as of 10/08:	$57	$34	$30/$24	$29 weekdays	$15

Course ratings:	Men	Par	Rating	Slope	Yardage	Women	Par	Rating	Slope	Yardage
	Blue	70	70.8	124	6282	Blue	73	75.7	132	6282
Tilden Park	White	69	68.8	119	5813	White	71	73.1	126	5813
	Red	69	67.2	115	5452	Red	71	71	121	5452

Trilogy at Rio Vista:
Trilogy Co. competes with Del Webb Corp. for sale of retirement homes throughout the country. It purchased the Rio Vista Golf Course and development project from Blackhawk Development in 2004. The course was built in 1996, but fell on hard times. Trilogy has been shouldering renovations ever since.

Now the course is back in good condition. Its style appears similar to those of quality desert resort hotels. Sunken fairways lie below the level of surrounding homes, and sculptured banks line the sides. Homes sit well back from the playing area. Ponds and water hazards definitely come into play, often placed close to greens and drive landing-zones. Deep bunkers, tight to the greens, force shots away from their sand towards more open parts of the greens. Sometimes, when these shots land short, steep aprons bounce balls well off line. This course is not designed for beginners, though wide fairways give players a good chance at the start of each hole, and hazard drop zones sit *across* the hazards, usually near the greens.

Course length of 6700 to 5300-yards plays shorter than it sounds because fairways allow long rolls. Fairways and roughs stay in good shape, with their rye grass cut so the ball sits up nicely. Subtle breaks and large putting surfaces mean players need good putting skills, but slow 7 to 8 Stimp speed insure balls do not zoom past the hole.

If the wind is blowing, as it is most of the time, difficulty increases exponentially. In the spring, and any time a fog bank hovers above San Francisco, the wind whips through the Delta at 20-30 miles per hour. Under these conditions—which are common at all times of the day—every shot, except the down-wind drives, presents a challenge. Crosswinds blow shots 20-50 yards off line. Headwinds add two to three club lengths to every shot. Tail winds make control of green approaches extremely difficult. Even down-wind wedges and chip shots can careen out of control and routinely add many extra strokes for the best of golfers. To play this course well on a windy day takes a lot of practice; even putting is tough when the wind is howling around your head.

The course offers many pretty and challenging approach shots, such as lakes at nine and eighteen, but they usually come after wide-open drives down the same old recessed fairway. More creativity in landing zone design, and less impact of wind would easily have moved it into the **Best 100**. *Review based on play in June '08.*

Trilogy Golf Club at Rio Vista

1000 Summerset Drive	Golf Shop:	707 374-2900
Rio Vista, CA 94571	Fax	707 374-4405
	www.trilogygolfclub.com	
Managed by: Trilogy	Architect:	Ted Robinson

Location: In the Sacramento River Delta region, on State Rt. 12, three miles east of the junction of State Rts. 12 and 160. It's about one hour southwest of Sacramento, and 30 minutes east of Fairfield.

Style: Layout runs between housing, on fairways often excavated below the level of homes. Lakes come into play on several holes. Fairways are reasonably wide but narrow at greens, which are well protected by modern bunkering. Course is in good condition and well landscaped but very windy.

Greens Fees	Weekends	Weekdays	Twilight	Seniors	Carts/person
as of 10/08:	$50	$40	$40/$30	No savings	Included

Course ratings:	Men	Par	Rating	Slope	Yardage	Women	Par	Rating	Slope	Yardage
Trilogy at Rio Vista	Blue	72	73.6	131	6800	Green	72	72.4	124	5330
	Gold	72	71.9	124	6393					
	White	72	70.0	119	5971					

Tulare Golf Course:
This is the best of the Northern California Golf Association's older courses along State Rt. 99 in the southern San Joaquin Valley. Its distinction comes from care given by its owners, Bob and Don Clark. These ex-farmers bought the course in the mid seventies, ten years after it was built as Tulare Country Club. They still manage it with the attention they would give their own fields. Roughs are in much better shape than their competition, and fairways have more grass under the ball, even in early spring.

A few other features also set it apart: (1) Fairways on the front nine show small undulations. Such a style is unusual on older farmland courses. These ridges and shallow trenches may exhibit only a couple of feet in elevation change, but any texturing of the flat farmland adds visual interest. (2) Greens are unusually small, some with narrow double tiers. Those on most par-threes measure no more than 40 feet across. (3) The course has decent length, a welcome feature for those wanting a few more shots for the dollar. (4) Finally, its lakes use curious styling. Normally, cattails, reeds or heavy grasses mark the edge of golf ponds. Also, water levels normally lie several feet below the fairway, and banks make lake boundaries clearly visible. Not true here. At Tulare, the rough ends and most pond water sits at the same level as the fairway . . . no banks no borders, only yellow and red markers indicate their presence. Any golfer who regularly strays off the fairway or who wants to take a short cut, best watch closely for the stakes. *Review based on play and interviews in April '08.*

Tulare Golf Course

5320 South Laspina Street	Golf Shop:	559 686-5300
Tulare, CA 93274	Fax	559 686-0590
Managed by: Private, local	Architect:	Bob Baldock and Wayne Hanson

Location:	Southern San Joaquin Valley: 1) From State Rt. 99 southbound, take Exit 85. Turn left on E. Paige, then right on Laspina St. Head 1.8 miles to the course. 2)From northbound Rt. 99, take Exit 83. Turn left on Tax Dr., the frontage road, and go north to Laspina. Turn right (south) and course is on the left in .4 miles.
Style:	Flat terrain, easy to walk. Wide treelined fairways have minor contouring here and there. Greens are very small and can be well bunkered. Lakes border many fairways, adding interest and need for accuracy. Course is in good condtion during summer months.

Greens Fees	Weekends	Weekdays	Twilight	Seniors	Carts/person
as of 10/08:	$30	$24	No savings	Monthly card	$12

Course ratings:	Men	Par	Rating	Slope	Yardage	Women	Par	Rating	Slope	Yardage
Tulare	Blue	72	71.9	123	6788	Gold	72	74.4	129	6008
	White	72	71	120	5969	Red	72	72.3	125	5672

Tuscan Ridge:
This is one of two Chico-area public eighteen-hole golf courses, and in the summer of 2008, it played a heroic role in local history. A huge forest fire threatened to burn east through local blue-oak and grass-covered hills, and create serious damage in nearby Paradise, CA. But Tuscan Ridge provided a wide, green firebreak and enough water from its irrigation pond, to help stop the advancing flames. Golf courses apparently do have a public function other than providing serenity, exercise and maybe a little tax revenue.

But the fire, which did almost no physical damage to the course itself, highlighted the area's lack of irrigation water. Instead the 800,000 gallons per day needed to maintain the course, only half that was available for the rest of the summer. This meant water rationing for fairways, to keep greens and tees healthy. Owners cut off all water to the first 100-yards of each hole, and reduced usage on the rest. Brown spots showed up everywhere except on greens and some fairway areas turned bone dry.

The upside for players was that hard ground made five-pars reachable in two, even by medium length hitters. The greens and their surrounds stayed in excellent shape and highlighted their good design. One in particular, number seventeen, stands out as unique in the **Best 100**. The short 485-yard (back tees) par-five requires an approach across a long diagonal hazard-like gully. My good drive, downwind on a hard fairway, left an attempt at the green in two. But the long approach leaves a dilemma: The green splits into two sections, at different heights, connected by a narrow putting isthmus. The top level gives an easier target because it's closer, and has no bunkers protecting the front. The lower level, about 30-yards farther carry, gets protection from multiple bunkers plus the deep creek, so it's often out-of-reach. But when the pin sits on the back/lower level, a shot ending on top leaves a nearly impossible putt. It must be stroked at just the right speed to catch the down-slope to the other section, and even then the hill doesn't generate enough speed to carry the ball to the hole. Oh well, its still a fun hole with a possible fifteen-foot birdie putt. A par still beats an opponent who tries to hit directly to the lower pin position and loses it in the creek! *Review based on play in July '08.*

Tuscan Ridge Golf Club		
3100 Skyway	Golf Shop:	530 624-7006
Paradise, CA 95967	Fax	866 653-6217
	www.tuscanridgeclub.com	

Managed by:	Private, local			Architect:		Algie Pullet		
Location:	Ten miles south of Chico: From State Rt. 99, take Skyway exit towards town of Paradise. Drive 5 miles east, course entrance is on the right.							
Style:	Rolling terrain with deep creeks and lakes. Fairways medium width, with some well placed bunkers, depressions and mature oaks. Greens are good modern designs with terraces and bunkers all around. Drought had severe impact on course conditon in 2008.							

Greens Fees	Weekends	Weekdays	Twilight	Seniors	Carts/person
as of 10/08:	$36	$29	$24/$21	$26/$19	$12

Course ratings:	Men	Par	Rating	Slope	Yardage	Women	Par	Rating	Slope	Yardage
Tuscan Ridge	Blue	72	71.2	126	6434	White	72	73.4	125	5887
	White	72	68.7	122	5887	Red	71	67	112	4738

Ukiah:

Your first look at Ukiah Muni generates a mixture of expectations. The old clubhouse shares a building and rooms with other organizations at the municipal park complex. Yet, grounds of both park and course are green and clean. The first hole is very short, rather open and straight up a steep hill, but it's difficult to tell much about the rest of the course.

In fact, Ukiah Muni is a surprisingly good experience. No, it doesn't have a restaurant, and no, it doesn't have a driving range, but the layout uses varying terrains, good conditioning, and can be very challenging. The first hole may measure only 250-yards, but it plays 320, and is an unusual start. It's not as dramatic as number one at Tilden Park, but walkers still get a good stretch on their Achilles tendons in the early part of a trek through the oaks. And your walk will be a hike, not a stroll. Hill climbs and descents abound, but the reward is beautiful scenery and the thrill of pounding the ball down many steep precipices.

Only one par-four, number fourteen, measures over 400-yards, but architect Paul Underwood found ways to overcome the lack of distance. A myriad of elevated greens, water hazards, sharp doglegs and side-hill lies add the equivalent of 300 to 400-yards, making a round here much longer than the 5800-yards listed on the card.

Ukiah's most unique feature is its tiny greens. They stay quite soft, and those on shorter holes find extensive protection from large bunkers. Accurate irons are needed on nearly every approach, and players who find the small surfaces often have short, easy putts. Shots that miss the green--and the bunkers--will find soft aprons, very cleanly cut, so chip-and-one-putt is a realistic expectation.

Despite the need for accuracy, it's a good place for inexperienced players. The abbreviated layout boosts their egos and confidence. If the city would add a driving range, get a new restaurant approved, and improve water distribution on fairways, Ukiah has the design and character to move into **Best 100** rankings. *Review based on interview and play in July '08.*

Ukiah Municipal Golf Course		
599 Park Boulevard	Golf Shop:	707 467-2832
Ukiah, CA 95482		
	www.ukiahgolf.com	
Managed by: Private, local	Architect:	Paul Underwood

Location:	In residential Ukiah, 60 miles north of Santa Rosa: From U.S. 101 take the Central Ukiah exit. Go west on E. Perkins then right on N. State. Turn left on C.W. Smith St. and right on N. Barnes. Finally, veer left onto Park and proshop is ahead on the right.
Style:	Rolling and hilly terrain amongst native mature oaks. Several short holes, but enough distance and narrow fairways to make an interesting round. Small greens usually well bunkered.

Greens Fees	Weekends	Weekdays	Twilight	Seniors	Carts/person
as of 10/08:	$35	$27	$24	No savings	$15

Course ratings:	Men	Par	Rating	Slope	Yardage	Women	Par	Rating	Slope	Yardage
Ukiah	Blue	69	69.2	124	5793	White	70	72.1	125	5657
	White	69	68.6	123	5702	Red	70	70.5	119	5312

Valley Oaks: Valley Oak's original eighteen-hole course, known today as nines named The Valley and The Oaks, was completed in 1977. Hole-count went from 18 to 27 in 1990, when a new nine called The Lakes came on line. Located just a mile east of State Rt. 99, near the freeway to Visalia, this complex has easy access for golfers from throughout in the mid-San Joaquin Valley.

The old course and new nine offer significantly different styles of play. The original holes are flat with well-developed trees lining fairways. As with nearly all San Joaquin Valley courses, fairways and roughs utilize Bermuda grass. Nowadays, this grass variety comes in all kinds of hybrids. Newer varieties exhibit narrower, thinner blades of grass that stay green at lower temperatures and need less irrigation. But all of them eventually turn brown in cold Central Valley winters and die back to thinner turf. At Valley Oaks, if rain is light in winter, balls roll a long way in and lies become very tight (*i.e.* the ball sits close to the ground). Around May 1, as temperatures increase, grass greens up, fills-in, and lies become thicker and heavier.

The Valley nine displays old-fashioned, uninteresting, straight/linear fairways with few fairway bunkers. However, greens show good character. Nearly all have double terraces and some contain unusual small plateaus or basins where pins are hard to reach. The Oaks nine has more doglegs and a couple of holes with small greens tucked into picturesque spots. It is the more difficult of these original nines, with tighter landing areas.

On the newer Lakes, instead of farm-flat fairways, graders excavated large depressions below the valley floor, and built up mounds along the sides. Their style mimics Palm Desert courses, without the floral landscaping. Number-three, a par-five double-dogleg shows particularly good shaping. Drives head between two large modern bunkers, where a slope easily bounces pulled shots into the sand. A small grove of trees then blocks the fairway on one side, and OB and deep rough guard the other. Finally an elevated green, well protected by deep bunkers beyond the trees, forces a high approach. Other designs on this nine are neither as tight nor as elegant, but have a similar feel. Young trees on The Lakes mean much less shade in the summer. Nevertheless, interest and character makes this new nine the popular choice at Valley Oaks. *Review based on play in April '08.*

Valley Oaks Golf Course

1800 South Plaza Drive	Golf Shop: 559 651-1441
Visalia, CA 93277	Fax 559 651-1349
	www.playvalleyoaks.com
Managed by: CourseCo	Architect: Robert Dean Putnam

Location: Next to Visalia airport and State Rt. 99, about 60 miles south of Fresno: From Rt. 99, take State Rt. 180 exit and head east. At first exit, go south on Plaza Drive. At "T" into airport, turn left and follow Plaza around the airport to the course.

Style: Course has three nines: The first two, Valley and Oaks, are older in style, with level fairways and trees lining all holes. Course condition is mediocre and holes lack imagination. The newer nine, named the Lakes, has contours in fairways and roughs, with modern greens and bunkers. It's much better maintained. *Each nine can be played as a distinct unit; so eighteen hole stats are not listed in the chart below.*

Greens Fees	Weekends	Weekdays	Twilight	Seniors	Carts/person
as of 10/08:	$31	$25	$19/$17	$17 weekdays	$12

Wildhawk:

South of Sacramento, just off State Rt. 16, Wildhawk was originally set up as a real estate venture. But the housing crisis of the late '00's hasn't helped bring in planned local building. The course holds on because it has a decent design and greens fees priced to attract.

Lots of soil movement went into making this course. Excavated fairways and mounded perimeters show on almost every hole. The depth, height and placement vary from one to the next, but designer J. Michael Poellot used significant contouring and height to eliminate the pancake-flat natural terrain. In fact, without the planned housing, the design, location and environment seem almost rural.

Green complexes are a strength of the overall design, surrounded with well-placed sand bunkers, hollowed-out collection areas and the occasional lake. If water and fertilizer were plentiful, the result would be a pleasant, green, rolling course that's typical of designs built in the late 90's. However, the late '00' drought faded fairways and brought rock-hard rolls. The day I played, long rough—within just feet of greens—caused balls to disappear in deep Bermuda grass. September leaves from young deciduous trees were not regularly swept.

If the course gets a chance . . . with wet winters, more maintenance, and additional home sales, it could be a good one. For now it's a decent play at a reasonably low price. *Review based on play in October '08.*

Wildhawk Golf Club

7713 Vineyard Road	Golf Shop: 916 688-4653
Sacramento, CA 95829	Fax 916 688-9489
	www.wildhawkgolf.com
Managed by: Southgate Recreation and Parks	Architect: J. Michael Poellot

Location: Southeastern Sacramento: 1)From the south, take State Rt. 99 north to Grant Line Rd. Exit and turn right. Then turn left at Bradshaw and drive 6 miles to Gerber Rd. Turn right and then right again on Vinyard. 2)From the north, take U.S. 50 east to State Rt. 16. Exit and follow Rt. 16 southeast 4 miles to Bradshaw. Turn right and go to Gerber Rd. Turn left and then right on Vineyard.

Style:	Flat terrain graded extensively to create rolling fairways, contours and mounds. Layout flows well, with medium width fairways and nicely bunkerd greens. Trees are still immature and fairways have blotchy green appearance. Roughs are very heavy, especially around greens.

Greens Fees	Weekends	Weekdays	Twilight	Seniors	Carts/person
as of 10/08:	$41	$31	$28/$21	$24 weekdays	$12

Course ratings:	Men	Par	Rating	Slope	Yardage	Women	Par	Rating	Slope	Yardage
	Gold	72	70.9	125	6573	White	72	73.1	123	5770
Wildhawk	Blue	72	69.4	120	6202	Green	71	67.1	111	4793
	White	72	67.5	114	5770					

Willow Park:

About three miles north of downtown Castro Valley, right on its main Redwood Drive, this fun little golf course gives players a simulated mountain experience. Mature trees line the fairways; creeks meander the roughs, and suburbia seems far removed. No, it's not truly in the mountains, just a level ravine in the Oakland Hills. Fairways sit at the base of steep oak and bay tree covered hills, suggesting similar canyons in steep parts of the Sierra foothills. The layout even simulates old-style alpine courses, with trees and brooks closely bordering narrow landing areas. Small slightly elevated greens sit at the base of sloping hills, where missed approaches bound off into creeks. Other than these obstacles, the course is flat and short. Low handicappers can shoot great scores if they chose direction, not distance, as their shot-making priority. Even middle and high handicappers can have a good time and make good scores, if they can keep the ball in play. Greens appear in decent condition, hold fairly well, and bunkers loosely protect them.

Unfortunately, fairways and roughs are spotty. Both wet and dry areas make rolls unpredictable. Perhaps these flaws are the result of occasional winter floods. But such detractors happen on Sierra courses too; so why not just play Willow Park and save the three-hour drive to gold country? *Review based on play and interviews in August '08.*

Willow Park Golf Course

17007 Redwood Road		Golf Shop:	510 537-8989
Castro Valley, CA 94546		Fax:	510 537-6775

Managed by:	Private, local		Architect:	Bob Baldock
Location:	In the East Bay hills, north of Castro Valley: Take I-580 towards Castro Valley. Exit at Redwood Road and turn north, through town about 2.5 miles. Course is just off the road in a rural canyon.			
Style:	Rolling terrain along two creeks, at the base of forested hillsides. Bays, sycamores and oaks line narrow fairways. Greens offer small targets, kept in good shape. Roughs and aprons can be very firm, so missed shots will roll into trouble. Yardage is short so good scoring possible.			

Greens Fees	Weekends	Weekdays	Twilight	Seniors	Carts/person
as of 10/08:	$35	$24	$15	No savings	$12

Course ratings:	Men	Par	Rating	Slope	Yardage	Women	Par	Rating	Slope	Yardage
Willow Park	Blue	71	68	120	5846	White	71	71.8	124	5516
	White	71	66.6	118	5516	Red	71	70.3	120	5241

Woodlake Ranch: Known locally as *Hank's Swank Woodlake Ranch*, or

its prior name, *Sawtooth on the St. Johns*, this course is fifteen miles northeast of Visalia. It has a couple of distinctions among the **Best 100**, the most bizarre being the 200-foot long eighteenth green. The large surface has several full sized trees growing right in its middle. In addition, it's the only design laid out in an actively harvested walnut orchard, where a functioning concrete standpipe hovers ten feet above the fringe of the eighth green. (The owner, Hank, is thinking of cutting down many of the current trees and replacing them with redwoods. I hope he doesn't do so because that could hurt much of its current unique charm.)

All three of the course pumps failed in 2007 and a shortage of repair contractors prevented a quick fix. As of '08, the Bermuda grass fairways were still recovering from the long dry spell, and construction is now active on several new greens. Tees remain in good condition, but directional signage, explaining how to get from certain greens to the next tee, is sometimes missing. Hole routing can also be confusing, so find a knowledgeable partner or an experienced local to point the right direction. Roughs are just natural orchard ground, often hardpan under the walnut trees, so errant shots must be tracked long distances if they haven't already disappeared into a squirrel hole. Be careful to avoid bunkers; the course was designed with many, but most have gone to seed and play more like waste-bunkers overgrown with wiry weeds.

Despite its shortcomings, Woodlake Ranch can be fun and is certainly interesting. Many greens have good designs and modern bunker shapes. Maybe it's the ego-boosting roll, the quirky-ness of the orchard, the design of that eighteenth green or the constant improvements being made, but I'll continue to be interested in this work-in-progress. *Review based on play and interviews in June '08.*

(Hank's Swank) Woodlake Ranch Golf Course

21730 Avenue 322
Woodlake, CA 93286

Golf Shop: 559 564-1503
www.woodlakeranchgolfcourse.com

Managed by:	Private, local
Location:	Northeast of Visalia by 22 miles: From State Rt. 99, take State Rt. 198 east. Drive 16 miles, well past Visalia, to State Rt. 245/Road 204. Turn left (north) and follow Rt. 245 for six miles, thru two turns. At Avenue 332 turn right (east) and go 1/2 mile to the course.
Style:	Flat terrain, easy to walk. Built in a walnut orchard where direction to hit is sometimes unclear. Course is recovering from lack of water in '07-08, so fairways, roughs, bunkers and greens are in irregular condition. Some interesting hole designs, especially on the back nine.

Architect: Ed Dobson

Greens Fees	Weekends	Weekdays	Twilight	Seniors	Carts/person
as of 10/08:	$20	$10 Mon-Wed	No savings	$16 Friday	$15

Course ratings:	Men	Par	Rating	Slope	Yardage	Women	Par	Rating	Slope	Yardage
Woodlake Ranch	Blue	71	70.1	123	6393	No				
	White	71	68	119	5984	data				
	Gold	71	65.2	112	5363					

Chapter 4:
Not-So-Public Courses

Two hundred nineteen publicly accessible eighteen-hole courses operate in Northern California. These courses, all of which are reviewed in Chapters 2 and 3, offer tee times to the public-at-large, provided space is available and greens fees are paid. Another 100 courses are classified as private clubs. About 90 of these restrict play to members and member-sponsored guests. The other 10-or-so open their doors non-members, but only on occasion. A few in this small group require golfers to stay at expensive lodges or hotels to gain entry, making play both time-consuming and expensive. (Even Pebble Beach courses will let non-Lodge guests play when last-minute space becomes available, usually as singles joining twosomes or threesomes.) Others seek outside revenues for various reasons—to augment membership dues and entrance fees, or generate extra income for their management companies. Their openings for non-member play are so restrictive that I label them *Not-So-Public.*

Including and ranking this group is important, because they give excellent golf experiences, worthy of recognition and comparison. However, adding them to the **Best 100** rankings in Chapter 2 wouldn't have been fair to the *truly* public venues. Instead, I created this separate chapter to highlight five courses and assign ranking positions as though they had been included in Chapter 2. For example, Granite Bay and CordeValle, if included in Chapter Two, would have been ranked No. 4 and No. 5, respectively, pushing Poppy Hills to No. 6. All the other courses behind it would also have been pushed back two notches. Similarly, adding the three other courses, Grizzly Ranch and the two at Silverado—numbers 27, 30 and 49 respectively—would have moved courses behind them a total of five spots; so, Micke Grove, our 100th course, would have become No. 105.

At the end of this chapter, I acknowledge that there were a few *Not-So-Public* courses that I did not play, either because they were not interested in publicity, or because their status was in some degree of transition when I visited the area. Indeed, given today's recessionary economic conditions, even more courses may open their doors to the public. Readers will have to call the courses I skipped to find the current status of their non-member play restrictions.

No. 4: Granite Bay

Granite Bay represents one of Sacramento's finest golf courses, public or private. It opened in 1994 as a private club, with layout by architect Robert Trent Jones Jr., and Kyle Phillips as the lead designer. Since then Phillips has gone on to become an independent architect who designed the highly acclaimed Kingsbarns Golf Links near the Old Course in St Andrews, Scotland. Certainly the success of Granite Bay's design augmented the reputation of both architects.

The town of Granite Bay is an exclusive community about twenty-five miles northwest of Sacramento, just south of Auburn. The club remains a successful private facility, an enclave within an area of multimillion-dollar homes. However, non-members are able to play on-occasion at Charity tournaments held on Mondays, when the club is closed to members. Club Corp manages operations here, so individuals associated with other Club Corp facilities outside the Sacramento area, also have limited access.

The course and its environs are genuinely up-scale. Well planned park-like landscaping adorns roads outside the club complex. Cobblestone walls protect privacy on many outside fence-lines; and the clubhouse and pro-shop are faced by granite exteriors and Tudor-style interiors. The driving range adjacent to the pro shop looks so pristine it reminded me of a formal grass tennis-court.

But that's where the formality stops, since the course itself displays a much more natural appearance. The front nine winds amongst landscaping that appears much like an informal English garden. Plantings appear casual on the surface, but are located in exactly the correct place. Only within the last couple of years have golf cart paths been installed to commercialize the look. The club insures outstanding maintenance for all aspects of the course. Fast greens stay reasonably firm, and have a tradition of subtly tough pin placements.

As with many modern courses, the first hole runs a short-to-medium length and appears un-intimidating. Water sits on the left, but not close enough to cause heartburn. However, unbeknownst to the newcomer, the green has turns and slopes that easily send a potential birdie wedge directly to double bogey three-putt. The balance of the front nine runs through gently rolling terrain, among specimen trees purchased originally at a massive nursery fire sale. Drives need to be hit accurately enough to avoid trees, but bunkers often sit just out of range for 220 to 230-yards hitters. Unlike many Sacramento area courses, where turf under oaks stays dry for fear of oak-root-fungus, roughs here are populated by other kind of trees and remain green. Well-tended aprons make chipping a delight. Par-three number seven sits atop the pinnacle of the front side with glorious views of foothills northeast toward Lake Tahoe.

The back nine changes significantly. Golfers now hit to fairways winding through heavy oak forest and hilly topography. Doglegs have sharper corners and shot-length must be controlled to keep the balls rolling through fairways. Fourteen, an especially demanding 200-yard par-three (portrayed above) heads across a wooded barranca, to an elevated green surrounded by deep bunkers and down hill slopes. Miss anywhere but short and the ball bounces into the woods.

Granite Bay's 200-yard par-3 number fourteen demands your approach hits the green or front apron. Otherwise, shots will bounce off the hill into the surrounding bunkers, oaks, or out-of-bounds.

The crowning glory comes on the final hole. Listed as a par-four, 455-yards, it plays more like 410. The blue tees require a climb up a steep landscaped path, the equivalent of 5 flights of stairs. Players are then rewarded with a broad view, southeast towards Placerville and beyond. The tee shot drops about 70 feet to a fairway bordered by trees and bunkers. Then the approach needs another 200-yards, across a deep fairway gully to the side-hill perched green. Par is a wonderful end to a great day, followed by a beer in the English-style pub. *Review based in play in October '07.*

Granite Bay Golf Course

9600 Golf Club Drive		**Golf Shop:**	916 791-5379
Granite Bay, CA 95746		**Fax:**	916 791-3214
		www.granitebayclub.com	
Managed by:	ClubCorp	**Architect:**	Robt.T. Jones Jr.

Location: 25 miles northwest of Sacramento, between I-80 and U.S. 50. From I-80 take Douglas Blvd east 1.5 miles to Eureka Blvd. Turn right and go .8 miles to E. Roseville Pky. Turn right after 2.3 miles into the club on Golf Club Dr. From U.S. 50, take Folsom Road north. It becomes Folsom-Auburn Rd. Go 7 miles to Eureka Blvd. Turn left and go 1/2 mile to Barton. Turn left on Barton and go another 1/2 mile to E. Roseville Pky. Turn right, then turn left on Golf Club Dr.

Style: Flat and rolling terrain on front nine, hillier on the back. Surrounded by mansions. Fairways throughout are tree lined, so acccuracy is needed. Course is in excellent shape.

Other info: Private course except for company and charity tournaments on Mondays.

Course ratings	Men	Par	Rating	Slope	Yardage	Women	Par	Rating	Slope	Yardage
	Tournament	71	73.6	142	6909	Cobble	71	74.1	135	5750
Granite Bay	Granite	71	72.0	135	6520	Combo	71	72.2	131	5393
	Club	71	70.1	131	6100	Pebble	70	70.3	127	5046

No. 5: CordeValle

First class golf courses fill the central Santa Clara Valley, just south of San Jose. At the top of this list perches Robert Trent Jones Jr.' local masterpiece, CordeValle in the small town of San Martin. Another, Eagle Ridge, sits in Gilroy, just four miles south on Santa Teresa Boulevard, and illustrates Johnny Miller's top **Best 100** design. Cinnabar, The Ranch and Coyote Creek also receive rankings in the top 50.

The two at the top, CordeValle and Eagle Ridge, may be close in proximity but exist worlds apart in style. Eagle Ridge offers a moderately priced shot makers dream, with 90 deep bunkers tightly protecting the greens and landing areas. Sloping fairways wind amongst housing developments and over nearby hills. CordeValle, on the other hand, exudes understated elegance. Rosewood Resorts runs operations and requires that non-members be registered room guests. Those who can afford the cost will appreciate the beautiful clubhouse architecture, the flowing style of the course, and pervasive yet unostentatious service provided by their staff.

For example, if one chooses not to use valet parking, a crew of carts descend to take guests to the pro-shop or clubhouse. Uniformed caddies then provide courteous service and excellent advise on the course. Caddy quality is as good or better than that on the Monterey Peninsula. At the end of the first nine a cart greets walkers and transports them 400 yards to a rest stop and then to the 10th tee. And after play, guests have access to fabulous dining facilities.

Of course, it's not just the look of the place and the service that make CordeValle special. It was originally created as a haven for a breed of affluent golfers spawned in Silicon Valley. New entrepreneurs wanted a beautiful private course and all the trappings. But the heady times of its opening in 1999 did not last. When the 2001 DotCom bust hit the area, techies and realtors alike had to go back to work, and the hour drive from the Peninsula became a bit much. The elegant set-up retained enough members to stay a viable operation, but soon opened for guests who use the resort.

Similar to the service, Jones' course design is elegant and understated. Topography of the lower Santa Cruz Mountains allow fairways to meander gently around and between ridges rather than climbing too far up the slopes. Pastoral views of vineyards and green/golden foothills, find few homes cluttering their vistas. Steep lies rarely exist in the main field of play. Even the shape and placement of bunkers have a subtle crafting; sand shines with a gorgeous bright white color, encased in classic Jones' multi-fingered shapes. Walking is much easier than other courses nearby, as the distance from green to tee is manageable, almost old-fashioned by modern cart-driving standards. Even breezes are minimized, since hills to the north form an effective barrier.

The par-four seventeenth at CordeValle overlooks a small niche in hills that protect the course from prevailing winds in the adjacent Santa Clara Valley. Illustration modeled from photo provided by CordeValle.

Most memorable hole on the course comes at seventeen. It has the only truly elevated view of the small valley, which contains much of the course. The drive aims players down a funnel shaped fairway and the second shot—a long one from a downhill lie—goes further down to a beautifully crafted, subtly elevated green. Bunkers and sloping aprons protect it well, and once on, a long side-hill slope with subtle breaks makes even the shortest putts more difficult than they appear.

Naturally, course condition is excellent. Fairways are as good as any in the Valley, though not as lush as at courses along the coast. Greens are big and well guarded by elevation and bunkers, but not to the extreme. They still contain nearly 100% bent grass, a real rarity on Bay Area golf courses.

The course is not easy, but most of our best courses aren't. It's the ambience that puts this young course right next to the top of my rankings. *Review based on play twice, last in August '07.*

CordeValle, A Rosewood Resort

One CordeValle Club Drive	Resort:	888 767-9663
San Martin, CA 95046	**Golf Shop:**	408 695-4590
	Fax:	408 695-4592
	www.cordevalle.com	
Managed by: Rosewood Resorts	**Architect:**	Robt. T. Jones Jr.

Location:	Fifteen miles south of San Jose. Take U.S. 101 to San Martin Exit. Take San Martin Road west, through town 1.6 miles to Santa Teresa Blvd. Turn left (south) and head .8 miles. At CordeValle Club Drive, turn right and drive one mile to the clubhouse. Valley Parking.
Style:	Gently rolling grass and oak covered hills. Wide, expertly contoured fairways with bright white, deep bunkers. Greens are sloped and terraced, requiring good accuracy. Walking very comfortable.
Other info:	Resort and member guests only. Must use caddy or forecaddie.

Greens Fees	All days							
as of 10/08:	$390-$420, depending on whether caddies or forcaddies are used. Extra tip expected.							

Course ratings	Men	Par	Rating	Slope	Yardage	Women	Par	Rating	Slope	Yardage
	Back	72	75.1	138	7114	Silver	72	74.6	128	6032
CordeValle	Middle	72	73.1	134	6642	Gold	72	71.0	120	5385
	Forward	71	70.0	127	6032					

No. 27: Grizzly Ranch

Built as a private club—not normally open to public play—the late '00's slowing economy and real estate slump affected the membership and luxury development surrounding this 2005 course . Non-member starting times began being offered in 2008. They can be difficult to get and are usually limited to weekday afternoons, but anyone who has the chance, should try it while they can. It is a beautiful facility.

Grizzly Ranch operates in a gated community, near Portola, about 50 minutes north of Truckee, at an elevation of 5100 feet. This small region sits adjacent to Graeagle, a five hour drive from San Francisco, and is one of the least traveled areas for low-cost, high quality golf in Northern California. Five excellent 18-hole courses, most with comparable quality but lower greens fees than in the Tahoe area, attract players north. (See Chapter 5, Region 7 for a listing of the other courses.) Fishing, hiking, camping and a lack of crowds provide additional appeal. Major area shortcomings are two: lack of lodging and few winter activities. Plumas Pines Resort condominiums remain the primary spot for groups and families. A few motels and bed-and-breakfast locations can be found in Portola, and the course itself offers some very-upscale rentals.

Golf at Grizzly Ranch is a first class experience, even better than at nearby highly touted Whitehawk Ranch. My rating system puts Whitehawk ahead in the **Best 100** rankings because Grizzly's young age lacks the pedigree of tournament play. But the layout is a joy, the scenery special, course condition fabulous, and unusual greens are superbly designed. It is one of my personal favorite courses.

Except for a couple of holes, where trees, long fescue grasses and bunkers protect the drive landing area, wide fairways encourage players to hit away. However, slopes and grades makes certain landing spots much more friendly than others. Architect Bob Cupp, who also designed Pumpkin Ridge in Oregon, created gracious greens with multiple putting levels joined by long, relatively gentle slopes. Speed judgment becomes difficult, especially when on the wrong part of a green, and re-enforces the need for accurate approach shots from those subtle landing zones.

Grizzly Ranch's finishing hole heads uphill 525-yards, with a large lake on the left, hidden from the tee. As players come closer they find a stream cascading down the left rough just below the green.

While all holes are good, and often unique, three in particular stand out from the rest. Number twelve makes the **Best 100** list of toughest par-fives, with its 621-yard length being just one of the problems. Drives start down a narrow fairway with a 225-yard lay-up, due to a crossing barranca. The next shot must carry 175-yards to clear a second hazard, and also fade slightly to catch the curve of the right sloping fairway. Finally, the approach shot of 125 to 175-yards goes over a deep creek to an elevated smallish green. And the green is hard to hit because a false front easily allows balls to roll off, far down its steep aprons. At least three good shots, a good chip and a good putt are all needed for par.

Number seventeen is another excellent design, where a lay-up drive short of a diagonal crossing stream, leaves about 175-yards. The trick here is to reach the correct part of a highly unusual green. A three-foot deep putting trench cuts diagonally across the front third of the putting surface, somewhat like the "valley of sin" in front of St Andrews' Old Course number eighteen green. The middle of the main surface is elevated, triangular shaped, and firm; so hitting that small hard space with a long approach shot requires a lot of skill or a lot of luck.

Finally, the eighteenth is a wonderful, up-hill, 525-yard par-five, picturesquely set below a mountain backdrop. An elevated lake, blind from the tee, sits about 300-yards out on the left side, and comes into play for big drives and many second and third shots. A stream accents the setting's beauty with waterfalls cascading below greenside bunkers, down to the lake. Its rocks and ponds trap many errant shots trying to approach a small, elevated putting area, but who cares at this point? The mesmerizing scenery has finally overtaken all but the most serious competitors. *Review based on play and interview in July '08.*

Grizzly Ranch Golf Club

4375 Grizzly Road		**Toll free:**	866 901-1010
P. O. Box 2107		**Golf Shop:**	530 832-4200
Portola, CA 96122		**Fax:**	831 655-8792
		www.grizzlyranch.com	
Managed by:	Private, local	**Architect:**	Bob Cupp
Location:	About 1 hour north of Truckee. Take State Rt. 89 exit from I-80 and head north through Sierraville. Eight miles past Sierraville, turn right (east) on Calpine Rd. Go 1.7 miles and turn left on Westside Rd. This terminates at State Rt. 70 after 12 miles. Turn left 1.6 miles to Grizzly Rd, then turn right. Go 1.7 miles to turnoff and gates for the club, on the right.		
Style:	Rolling terrain, with some hilly holes, but many fairways are reasonably level. Straight shots are a big advantage, as is good distance. Trees rarely come into play near fairways; but hills, slopes and forced carries present the biggest obstacles. Greens have big slopes.		
Other info:	Private course, available to non-members if approved by the proshop in advance.		

Greens Fees	Check proshop for times available to public and updated pricing.
as of 10/08:	$125 for the 2008 season, including cart. Public play usually limited to weekday afternoons

Course ratings	Men	Par	Rating	Slope	Yardage	Women	Par	Rating	Slope	Yardage
	Black	72	74.9	140	7411	White	72	73.9	139	6024
Grizzly Ranch	Green	72	72.2	133	6782	Red	72	71.1	129	5411
	White	72	69.0	120	6024					

No. 30: Silverado, North Course
No. 49: Silverado, South Course

Silverado has for years been one of Northern California's premier resorts. Its location in the heart of Napa Valley wine country is a magnet for active families, get-away weekends, business retreats, and the wealthiest, most discerning culinary connoisseurs in the world.

In addition to fine restaurants, a spa, a tennis facility, and accommodations of all varieties, the resort is home of two renowned golf courses. Both have serious pedigrees and were Robert T. Jones Jr.' first commission after leaving his father's firm. He redesigned the North Course and added the new South Course. The North Course soon became home to a PGA tour stop, first called the *Kaiser Open,* and then changed to the *Anheuser Busch Golf Classic.* That string of tournaments ended in 1980. Then the South Course became home to a Senior PGA event, *The Transamerica,* from 1989 through 2002. Famous golfers such as Jack Nicklaus, Johnny Miller, Tom Watson, Tom Kite and Lee Trevino won one or both these tournaments. Tiger Woods was too young to play in pro tournaments those days but did have dinner in one of the resort's restaurants with Arnold Palmer, while still an amateur. As the story goes, in order to keep his amateur status he had to reimburse Arnie with a $25 check to pay for his share of dinner.

1966 was the year Silverado eliminated its status as a semi-private golf course. Since then, the only ways to gain access are by:
- Being a Silverado member or guest of a member.
- Being a guest of the resort.
- Being a private golf club member or guest of that member.
- Playing in occasional charity tournaments or NCGA Members-Only-Outings.

Number eleven on the North Course is one of Silverado's most picturesque holes. The par-three displays how R. T. Jones, Jr. combined magnificent oaks, gentle elevation changes and picturesque hazards, to embody the aura of the area.

Today, Xanterra Parks and Resorts, the same company that oversees Furnace Creek in Death Valley and other high quality National Park lodges, manages the entire facility. Golf courses cover most of the property's 360 acres and have benefited from recent re-investment, including a new clubhouse, pro shop and $3.5 million dollar upgrade to the irrigation system. The new watering system allows even distribution across golf fairways and roughs, and cuts down on waste.

Otherwise, the courses remain very similar to the ones played by the pros back in the tournament era. The shorter South Course measures 6685-yards from the blues and 5600 up front. It sports more lakes, water hazards,, and tighter fairways than the North, but still offers rather generous landing areas, at least by modern standards. The North Course, 200-yards longer, has even wider landing zones which are very friendly to everyone. But dogleg corners on its longer par-fives cannot be cut as readily as on the South course, thereby increasing its course rating. In addition, tree location on the North Course block green approach shots more often.

But, let's face it; Silverado's are resort courses. They are mildly challenging, very pretty, and nicely maintained, so guests can relax and have a good time. Northern California's everyday tough golf challenges are located elsewhere. Greens and aprons are especially beautiful and built to a high quality standard. Their structure allows speeds to be increased or decreased depending on current needs. If a tournament dictates, greens can be made extremely fast, roughs lengthened, and fairways narrowed. Under these conditions, not normal for everyday guests, Silverado's courses can become a true test of the game. But on a day-to-day basis, Silverado concentrates on good course maintenance and keeping guests happy. Golf operations boast superb customer service: shop personnel, the pro, his assistants, the starters, and course restaurant personnel all go out of their way to make guests happy.

The critique of the courses is that fairways may be good, often great, but are also variable. Depending on the time of year, a few have areas that appear burned or diseased and diminish the overall good appearance of the course. At the time of this writing, number eighteen, South Course, had this affliction. Hopefully, a month later all will be back to perfect. However, Kikuyu grass is also beginning to encroach on many holes. It has not really impacted play much yet, but it could. *Last played in August '08.*

Silverado Resort, North Course

1600 Atlas Peak Rd.		**Resort:**	800 532-0500
Napa, CA 94558		**Golf Shop:**	707 257-5460
		Fax	707 257-5400
		www.silveradoresort.com	
Managed by:	Xanterra	**Architect:**	Robt T. Jones, Jr.

Location:	Just north of Napa. Take State Rt. 12 or State Rt. 29 to their junction west of Napa. Go north on Rt. 29 seven miles to Trancas Rd. Turn right (east) and go 1.7 miles to State Rt. 121. Veer left on Rt. 121 (becomes Montecito Rd) and go 1.2 miles to Atlas Peak. Turn left and Resort is one mile up the road, on the right
Style:	Mostly flat terrain, easy to walk. Classic oak tree lined design, but with broad fairways. Greens have some terracing.
Other info:	Usually, players must be a member or resort guest.

Greens Fees	Weekends	Weekdays	Twilight	Seniors	Carts/person
as of 10/08:	$160	$160	$85	No savings	Included

Course ratings	Men	Par	Rating	Slope	Yardage	Women	Par	Rating	Slope	Yardage
Silverado North	Blue	72	73.2	135	6883	White	72	76.6	136	6299
	White	72	70.3	130	6299	Red	72	73.9	130	5847
	Red	72	68.0	124	5847					

Silverado Resort, South Course

See North Course (above) for contact information **Architect:** Robt T. Jones, Jr.
and greens fees.
Style: Mildly rolling terrain, hillier than the North course. Greens can be more severe in their slopes

Course ratings	Men	Par	Rating	Slope	Yardage	Women	Par	Rating	Slope	Yardage
Silverado South	Blue	72	72.0	129	6649	White	72	76.6	136	6205
	White	72	70.0	126	6205	Red	72	72.7	131	5702
	Red	72	67.5	118	5702	Bronze	72	71.9	129	5497

Other Courses

The real estate slump of '08 hit metropolitan Sacramento hard. Several private courses decided to allow some public play or switch to a semi-private status. Starting times on those listed below may be restricted, so call the pro shops. I have not played the following group and cannot personally vouch for their quality, but others say good things about them:

Winchester Country Club		
3030 Legends Drive	**Golf Shop:**	530 878-3001
Meadow Vista, CA 95722	**Fax:**	530 878-9515
	www.winchestercountryclub.com	
Location: Northeast of Auburn.	**Architect:**	Charles Maud

Morgan Creek Golf and Country Club		
8791 Morgan Creek Lane	**Golf Shop:**	916 786-4653
Roseville, CA 95747	**Fax:**	916 771-8566
	www.morgancreekclub.com	
Location: 15 miles northeast of Sacramento	**Architect:**	Kyle Phillips

Auburn Country Club		
8800 Auburn Valley road	**Golf Shop:**	530 269-1837
Auburn, CA 95602	**Fax:**	530 268-1727
	www.auburncountryclub.com	
Location: North of Auburn, off State Rt. 49.	**Architect:**	R. Bisset/ L. Curtola

Lake of the Pines		
11665 Lakeshore North	**Golf Shop:**	530 268-8337
Auburn, CA 95602	**Fax:**	530 268-8014
Location: North of Auburn, off State Rt. 49.		

A few additional noteworthy Northern California courses can be played only by staying at resorts not necessarily owned or operated by the course itself. I have not reviewed the following two, both located in Sonoma County:

Fountaingrove Golf and Athletic Club		
1525 Fountaingrove Parkway	**Golf Shop:**	707 521-3214
Santa Rosa, CA 95403	**Fax:**	707 544-3109
Reservations: Call Fountaingrove Inn at 800 221-6101 for lodging and golf reservations.		
Location: Northern Santa Rosa	**Architect:**	Ted Robinson

Sonoma Inn		
17700 Arnold Drive	**Golf Shop:**	707 996-0300
Sonoma, CA 95476	**Fax:**	707 996-8464
	www.fairmont.com	
Reservations: Call Fairmont Sonoma Mission Inn at 866 540-4499 for lodging and golf reservations.		
Location: One hour north of San Francisco	**Architect:**	S. Whiting/W. Watson

One other eighteen-hole public course opened in 2008, but county permit issues reputedly restrict the amount of golfers allowed to play per day. I wait to play and review Trinitas after it opens officially, without restrictions:

Trinitas		
9209 Ospital Road	**Golf Shop:**	209 887-9150
Valley Springs, CA 95252	**Fax:**	209 887-9140
	www.trinitasgolf.com	
Reservations: Call the pro shop for starting times and pricing		
Location: Thirty miles north east of Stockton, off State Rt. 26	**Architect:**	Mike Nemee

Chapter 5:
Trip Planning and Value Courses

This chapter gives readers suggestions on where to play golf in Northern California if . . .

- You want to know my recommendations for the cheapest places for quality golf.
- You are traveling to Oregon, Reno, Santa Barbara, or Palm Springs and want to play on the way.
- Your business needs a unique meeting venue.
- Your club/charity needs a place for an outing.
- Buddies are bored with the same old course.
- You've just discovered a new friend is a golfer.
- A destination wedding is in the offing.
- You are planning a golf getaway.
- Visitors are coming to town.

Most of us have not traveled extensively in this territory, and are unfamiliar with weather, terrain or driving distances. Consequently, we could certainly use some maps and a list of courses in each individual region to help us plan golfing trips or outings. The following few pages provide such information, in addition to a ranking of the quality and value you can expect to find on 18-hole courses you encounter. I also provide a few other helpful travel tips.

Course descriptions for all the courses listed can be found in the prior chapters. Refer to the Index following Chapter 6 to find the corresponding page number. Also, I use some shorthand notations in parentheses following the name of courses that indicate special course features. "(2x18)' means the course complex contains two 18-hole courses. "(18+9)" means a course has 27-holes. "(Executive)" means the course has shorter than normal yardage, usually with a par of 65 or below.

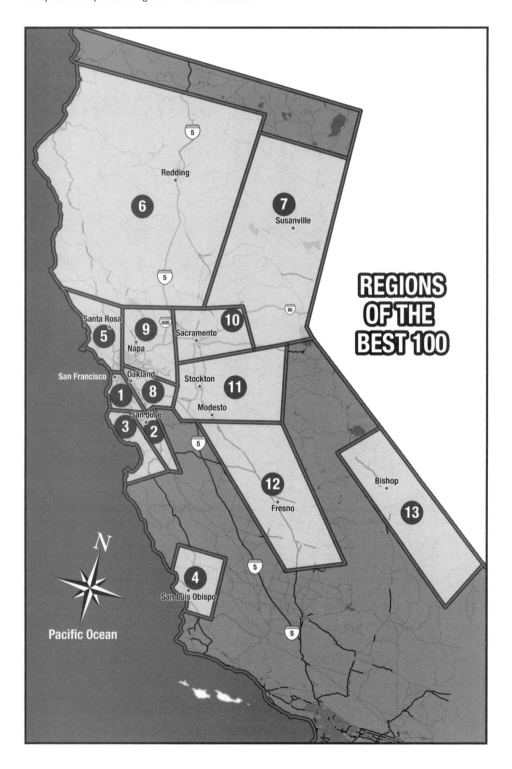

Regions of the **Best 100:**

This chapter divides Northern California into thirteen Regions, generally based on Northern California's primary highway transportation routes. Locations for 221 public-access eighteen-hole golf courses are included, enough to satisfy the most itinerant of souls:

Region 1: **San Francisco and SF Peninsula**, where U.S. 101 is the main route.
Region 2: **San Jose and Milpitas to Hollister**, also near U.S. 101.
Region 3: **Santa Cruz to Carmel Valley and Salinas**, where State Rt. 1 is the main road.
Region 4: **San Luis Obispo and the Central Coast**, continuing down U.S. 101 towards Santa Barbara.
Region 5: **Golden Gate Bridge and north to Marin and Sonoma Counties**, also on U.S. 101.
Region 6: **North Central Valley and North Coast**, where Interstate-5 and State Rt. 99 provides most access to public golf courses.
Region 7: **Tahoe and Northern Sierras**, with most golf available from Interstate-80 and State Rt. 89.
Region 8: **East Bay and Livermore Valley**, mostly near Interstates-880, 580 and 680.
Region 9: **Napa and the north and south Delta**, near Interstate-80 and State Rt. 4.
Region 10: **Sacramento, east to the Sierra foothills** off Interstate-80 and U.S. 50.
Region 11: **Stockton and Patterson, east to Sierra foothills**, via Interstates 5 and 205, plus State Rts. 99, 49 and 4.
Region 12: **San Joaquin Valley, east to Sierra Foothills**, near State Rt. 99.
Region 13: **Southeastern Sierras**, down U.S. 395.

The Regional sections begin with brief discussions on topography and/or climate as they impact play. Listings include all 224 courses reviewed in the book. Those ranked in the **Best 100** are noted and ranked regionally, so readers know those I believe to be the best. Top value courses are listed too.

Selected Getaway Suggestions:

Next comes a listing of resorts or hotel/lodges, which offer stay-and-play golf packages at select courses as of April '09. "Stay-and-play" usually means that a lodging facility subsidizes golf, cart fees or food in return for players staying in their rooms. Savings range from under $20 per person, to free golf, or big room discounts. Sometimes, the advertiser adds a box lunch or promotional item such as a hat. In truth, good on-line shoppers can often find better deals if they spend time and effort using the discount web sites mentioned in Chapter 6. However, the recommended facilities are a safe bet for good quality rooms located nearby. Many of these inns or resorts are adjacent to or affiliated with the referenced courses.

This Getaway listing is incomplete because I write about and try to understand golf, not hotels. As with greens fee pricing, stay-and-play packages come and go with the wind. Web sites cannot even keep up-to-date listings, since deals are often seasonal. Check Google: "Golf Stay-and-Play Offers" in the locations you plan to visit for more options. Very few pro-shops are aware of the local motel offers. Check my website, www.best100golf for more complete/current listings.

Highest Value Courses.

Finally, I identify the Top Value courses in each Region. Golf *value* is a subjective, personal matter. Some people want to play courses with the least expensive greens fees, period. Others want the quickest round, the toughest course, the best weather, the nicest walk, or the most beautiful location. Some look for fast greens, soft fairways, and lots of shade or clean air. You name it; the list goes forever.

Rather than deal with all these disparate needs, I define *value* by a calculation, using two numbers already developed in the prior Chapters. The first of these numbers is the **Quality Rating** described in Chapter 1. It assigns points for each course, based on my own personal experience, objective analysis, and discussions with the pro and local players. See Chapter 1 for more details.

The next number is the **Cost to Play***. It is derived from the Greens Fees shown in charts at the end of the course reviews in Chapters 2 thru 4. (Remember, the greens fees shown are subject to change at any time. They are not a listing of all the possible variations or specials available, but represent the main categories of play. To give an element of consistency, most were based on peak season rates in 2008.)

Value is then a simple calculation, dividing the Quality Rating by the Cost to Play. In other words, **Value equals Quality per dollar spent**. Such a formula may be oversimplified or theoretical, but that's what happens when my simple engineering mind goes to work. It gives readers a guide to courses that:

- Are a good quality at a low price, or
- Know they are lesser quality but price themselves accordingly , or
- Price the greens fees low to meet the needs/demands of their regular customers.

Each Region offers a different price players are willing to pay for greens fees. San Francisco, the SF Peninsula, and Monterey average the highest greens fees. This makes their average Value Rating lower than other areas, despite being home to many top courses. I believe these often exorbitant prices result from some of the highest costs for land, construction, insurance, environmental, and labor costs in the country. Also, high demand for play a Pebble Beach Company courses may add an extra local bump to greens fees in the immediate Monterey vicinity.

In the end, Regional markets vary so much I make no direct value comparisons *between* them, but stick to comparisons *within* each Region. In order to focus on just the *best* values, only the top 20% of each region receive recognition.

Have fun looking through the options and suggestions that follow. If you head off the main freeways you will find some beautiful scenery, unique small towns, great little inns and play wonderful golf courses too. Have a great trip!

* Cost to Play is a weighted average calculation as follows: 35% of weekend greens fee + 35% of weekday rate + 20% of twilight rate + 10% of senior rate + 60 to 90% of the cart fee. The cart cost is adjusted based on my estimate of the percentage of people who pay for carts on each separate course.

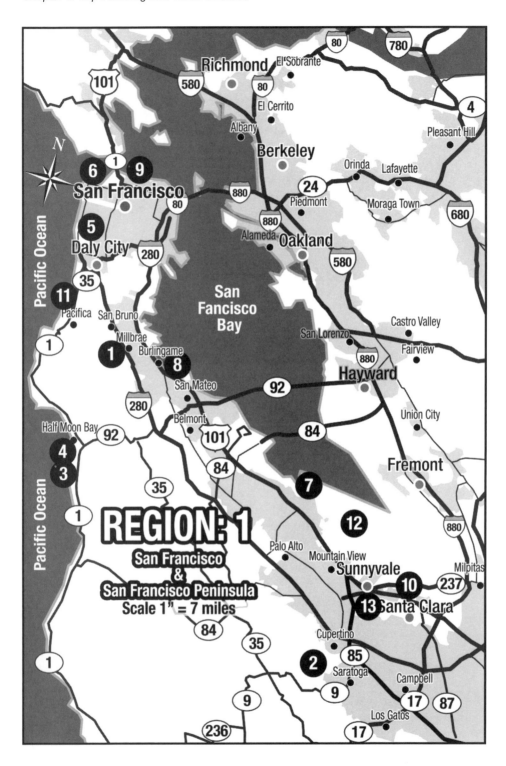

REGION: 1
San Francisco
&
San Fancisco Peninsula
Scale 1" = 7 miles

Region 1: San Francisco and SF Peninsula:

Our first region sees a mixture of climates. Six courses sit near the Pacific Ocean and are directly affected by seaside storms, fog and wind. Another five, all along San Francisco Bay or near its reaches, see similar impacts from fog on summer mornings and wind on many afternoons. Even Crystal Springs, inland on a Peninsula ridge-crest, nudges the edge of these summertime fog banks. Only Deep Cliff, an executive-style short course in Cupertino, gets less influence from the Coastal climates. Country clubs along the Peninsula foothills seem to have a monopoly on the area's famous mild Mediterranean climate.

Courses included in this region:

		Best 100	Region 1
		Rankings	
1.	Crystal Springs		
2.	Deep Cliff (executive)		
3.	Half Moon Bay: Ocean Course	19	1
4.	Half Moon Bay: Old Course	56	4
5.	Harding Park	32	3
6.	Lincoln Park		
7.	Palo Alto		
8.	Poplar Creek		
9.	Presidio	25	2
10.	Santa Clara		
11.	Sharp Park		
12.	Shoreline		
13.	Sunnyvale		

Selected Getaway Recommendations:

- **Half Moon Bay Ocean and Old Course,** savings @ Ritz Carlton Hotel, 650 712-7000; or Half Moon Bay Lodge, 800 710-0778.

Top 20% of Value Courses in Region 1:

1. Crystal Springs
2. Santa Clara Golf and Tennis

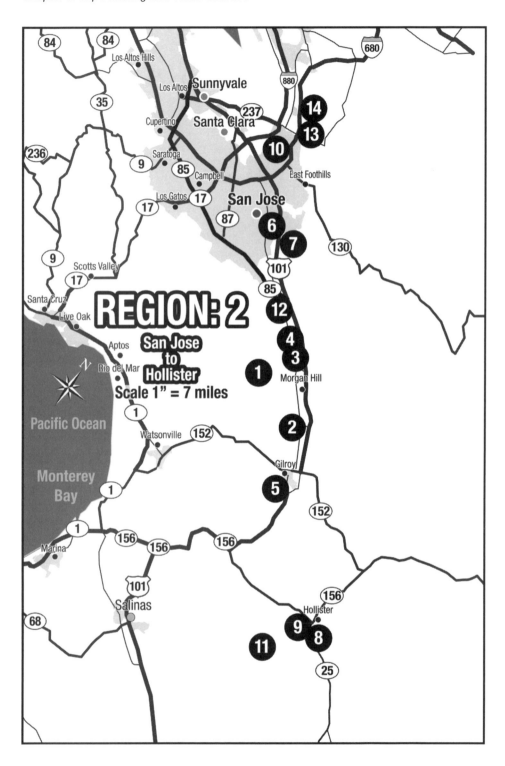

Region 2: San Jose and Milpitas to Hollister

The southern end of Santa Clara Valley extends almost 60 miles south from San Jose. A few courses, such as Coyote Creek and San Jose Muni, sit within flatlands of the valley basin; others climb around the surrounding foothills. Unless protected by protruding ridges, many catch fog or wind blowing down through the Valley from the Bay or across from Monterey.

Courses included in this region:		Ranking	
		Best 100	Region 2
1.	Cinnabar..28		4
2.	CordeValle..5		1
3.	Coyote Creek Tournament Course........................50		6
4.	Coyote Creek Valley Course....................................76		7
5.	Eagle Ridge..11		2
6.	Los Lagos		
7.	Ranch, The...43		5
8.	Ridgemark, Diablo Course		
9.	Ridgemark, Gabilan Course		
10.	San Jose Muni		
11.	San Juan Oaks..27		3
12.	Santa Teresa		
13.	Spring Valley		
14.	Summitpointe		

Selected Getaway Recommendations:

- **CordeValle**, a Rosewood Resort in San Martin, 408 695-4500.
- **Eagle Ridge** savings @ Hilton Garden Inn in Gilroy, 408 840-7000.

Top 20% of Value Courses in Region 2:

1. **Los Lagos**
2. **Santa Teresa**
3. **San Juan Oaks**

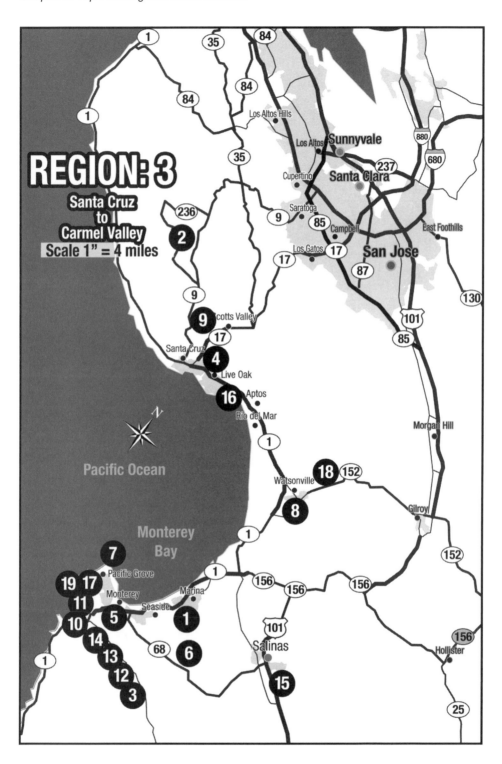

Region 3: Santa Cruz to Carmel and Salinas

Monterey Bay dominates the views, weather and topography of this Region. Since most courses sit near the coast, morning fog is a common issue. Those in the Carmel Valley or near the road to Salinas generally escape these patterns. Due to popularity of Pebble Beach Co.'s highly rated and high cost courses, greens fees in the region are the highest in Northern California.

Courses included in this region:

	Ranking Best 100	Ranking Region 3		Ranking Best 100	Ranking Region 3
1. Bayonet	15	6	11. Poppy Hills	4	4
2. Boulder Creek			12. Quail Lodge	39	8
3. Carmel Valley Ranch	34	7	13. R. Cañada East		
4. De Laveaga	96	12	14. R. Cañada West	72	9
5. Del Monte	88	11	15. Salinas Fairways		
6. Laguna Seca	82	10	16. Seascape		
7. Pacific Grove			17. Spanish Bay	9	5
8. Pajaro Valley			18. Spring Hill		
9. Pasatiempo	3	3	19. Spyglass Hill	2	2
10. Pebble Beach	1	1			

Selected Getaway Recommendations:

- **Pebble Beach, Spyglass Hill, Spanish Bay and Del Monte** savings @Lodge at Pebble Beach or Inn at Spanish Bay, 800 654-9500.
- **Quail Lodge** Resort, Carmel Valley. 888 828-8787.
- **Carmel Valley Ranch** Resort, 866 282-4745.
- **Boulder Creek** Golf and Country Club, Lodging: 831 338-2111.
- **Pasatiempo** savings @ Chaminade Resort in Santa Cruz. 800 283-6569.
- **Del Monte** savings @ Hyatt Regency Monterey. 831 372-1234
- **Bayonet** savings @ Sanctuary Beach Resort in Marina, 866 359-3863

Top 20% of Value Courses in Region 3:

1. Salinas Fairways
2. Poppy Hills for NCGA Members
3. Pacific Grove
4. De Laveaga

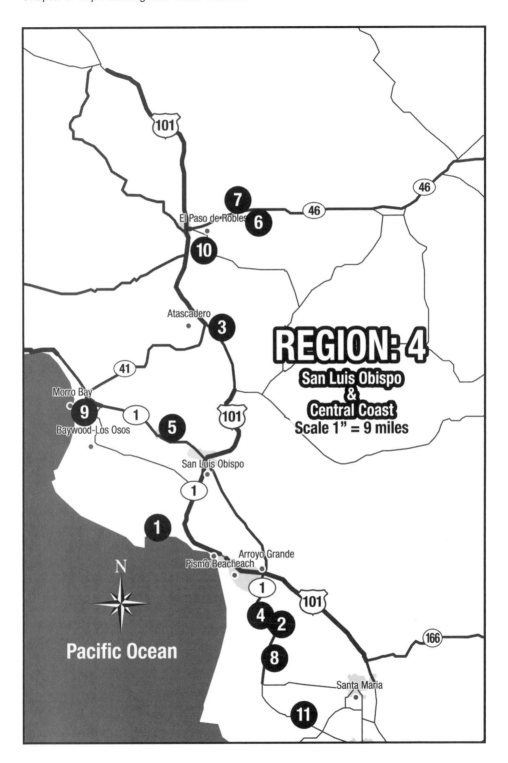

Region 4: San Luis Obispo and the Central Coast

San Luis Obispo County extends from the inland areas of Paso Robles and Atascadero, west across the Santa Lucia Mountains to the coast, and south to the Santa Maria River. Course terrains vary from gently rolling to reasonably hilly, providing all with good visual interest. Hunter Ranch and courses in the north, feel temperatures in the high 90's F in summer, but Moro Bay on the coast can be foggy, windy and cool. Other courses south of San Luis Obispo sit in between these extremes, and can be quite comfortable nearly year round.

Courses included in this region:

		Ranking	
		Best 100	Region 4
1.	Avila Beach	85	5
2.	Blacklake (18+9)		
3.	Chalk Mountain		
4.	Cypress Ridge	17	3
5.	Dairy Creek	77	4
6.	Hunter Ranch	12	1
7.	Links @ Vista del Hombre		
8.	Monarch Dunes (18+12)	14	2
9.	Moro Bay		
10.	Paso Robles		
11.	Ranch Maria		

Selected Getaway Recommendations:

- **Avila Beach, Blacklake and Monarch Dunes** savings @ The Cliffs Resort in Pismo Beach, 866 292-4670.
- **Morro Bay and Dairy Creek** savings @ Embarcadero Inn in Morro Bay, 888 223-5777.

Top 20% of Value Courses in <u>Region 4</u>:

1. **Rancho Maria**
2. **Dairy Creek**
3. **Links @ Vista del Hombre**

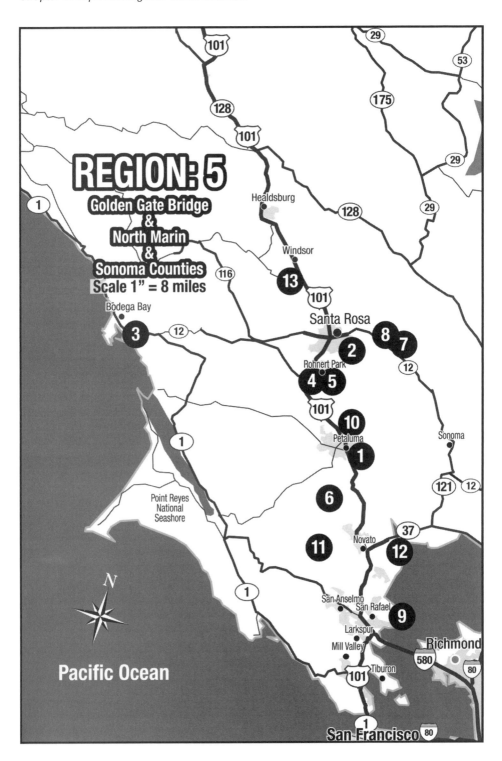

REGION: 5
Golden Gate Bridge
&
North Marin
&
Sonoma Counties
Scale 1" = 8 miles

Region 5: Golden Gate Bridge north to Marin and Sonoma Counties

Climate and terrain vary tremendously in the counties north of San Francisco. From the foggy hills of Bodega Harbour to the warm summer afternoons on the flats of Petaluma, just about any golf-friendly temperature can be found. Half the courses are located on hillside slopes, with the balance on flatlands around U.S. 101. Multitudes of wineries and excellent restaurants can be found too, especially in the valleys and small towns west of U.S. 101.

Courses included in this region:

	Ranking Best 100	Region 5			Ranking Best 100	Region 5
1. Adobe Creek			8.	Oakmont West		
2. Bennett Valley			9.	Peacock Gap 6	5
3. Bodega Harbour.....36	1		10.	Rooster Run 74	. 6
4. Foxtail North			11.	San Geronimo.........91	7
5. Foxtail South			12.	StoneTree.................45	2
6. Indian Valley...........47	3		13.	Windsor...................52	4
7. Oakmont East (executive)					

Selected Getaway Recommendations:

- **Bodega Harbour** savings @ Bodega Bay Lodge and Spa, 707 875-3525.
- **StoneTree** savings @ Inn at Marin in Novato, 415 883-5952.

Top 20% of Value Courses in <u>Region 5</u>:

1. **Indian Valley**
2. **Windsor**
3. **Rooster Run**

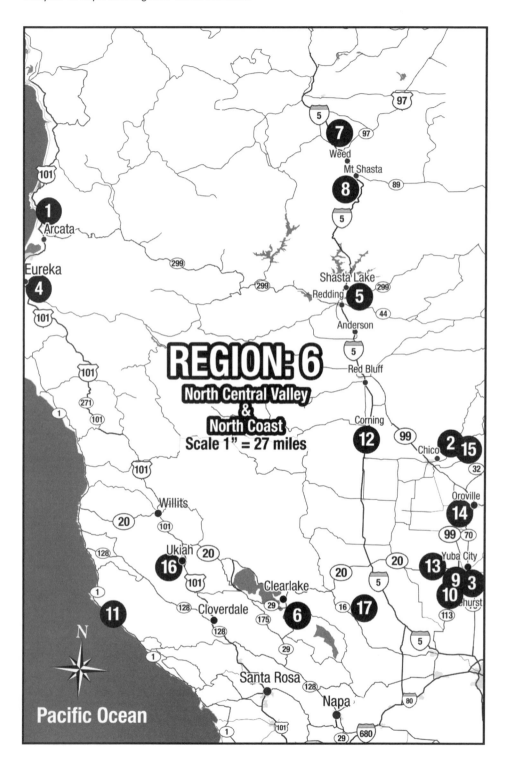

REGION: 6
North Central Valley
&
North Coast
Scale 1" = 27 miles

Pacific Ocean

Region 6: North Central Valley and North Coast

By far the largest Region in the state, it extends over 200 miles south-to-north: from the Sacramento Airport to Mt. Shasta, along Interstate-5 and State Rt. 99; and from Ukiah to Eureka along U.S. 101. Many courses find homes near levee-protected flood plains of the Feather River; others spread far and wide through golden foothills on either side of the Valley. Except on courses along the coast, summers are hot and winters are cool, but golfers play all year long.

Courses included in this region:

	Ranking Best 100	Region 6		Ranking Best 100	Region 6
1. Beau Pre			10. River Oaks		
2. Bidwell Park			11. Sea Ranch	92	6
3. Coyote Run			12. Sevillano Links	10	1
4. Eureka			13. Southridge		
5. Gold Hills	55	3	14. Table Mountain		
6. Hidden Valley			15. Tuscan Ridge		
7. Lake Shastina	93	7	16. Ukiah		
8. Mt. Shasta Resort	83	5	17. Yocha-de-he	35	2
9. Plumas Lakes	79	4			

Selected Getaway Recommendations:

- **Lake Shastina** savings @ Lake Shastina Resort in Weed, 800 358-4653.
- **Mount Shasta** savings @ Mount Shasta Resort, 800 958-3363.
- **Sea Ranch** savings @ Sea Ranch Lodge, 800 732-7262
- **Sevillano Links** savings: call the pro shop, 530 528-4600 for lodging deals @ The Lodge, Vagabond Inn in Corning.
- **Tuscan Ridge** savings @ Hotel Diamond in Chico, 866 993-3100.
- **Yocha-de-he** savings @ Cache Creek Casino in Brooks, 888 772-2243

Top 20% of Value Courses in <u>Region 6:</u>

1. **Plumas Lakes**
2. **Tuscan Ridge**
3. **Beau Pre**
4. **Sevillano Links**

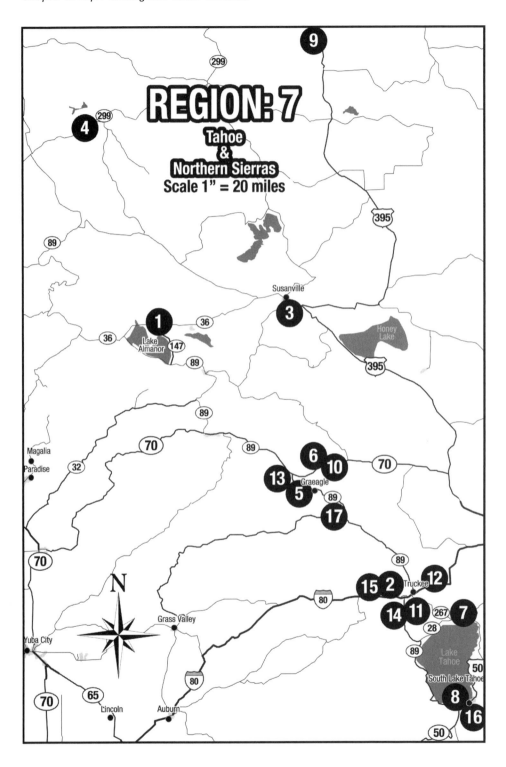

Region 7: Lake Tahoe and Northern Sierras

Golf in Region 7 centers around the towns of Truckee, just north of Lake Tahoe, and Graeagle, about an hour north of Truckee. Altitudes range from 4200 to 6400 feet, with either forested or meadow-like landscapes. Most courses close for the winter, from mid-October to mid-April, but feature mild temperatures and low humidity the rest of the year. Sunny skies turn a clear deep blue so be sure to wear plenty of sunscreen at these altitudes. This Region has Northern California's greatest concentration of **Best 100** courses.

Courses included in this region:

		Ranking Best 100	Ranking Region 7			Ranking Best 100	Ranking Region 7
1.	Bailey Creek	41	7	9.	Likely Links		
2.	Coyote Moon	7	2	10.	Nakoma (Dragon)	65	12
3.	Diamond Mountain			11.	Northstar	58	9
4.	Fall River Valley	67	13	12.	Old Greenwood	5	1
5.	Graeagle Meadows	53	8	13.	Plumas Pines	59	10
6.	Grizzly Ranch	27	4	14.	Squaw Creek		
7.	Incline Champion	30	5	15.	Tahoe Donner	33	6
8.	Lake Tahoe	63	11	16.	Tahoe Paradise (executive)		
				17.	Whitehawk Ranch	23	3

Selected Getaway Recommendations:

- **Bailey Creek,** savings at Bailey Creek Cottages in Chester, 866 959-7829.
- **Fall River Valley,** savings @ Fall River Hotel, 530 336-5500.
- **Plumas Pines,** savings @ Plumas Pines Golf Resort, 530 836-1420.
- **Whitehawk Ranch,** savings @ Whitehawk Ranch Resort, 877 945-6343.
- **Squaw Creek,** savings @ Resort at Squaw Creek, 800 327-3353.
- **Northstar,** savings @ Northstar Resort, 800 466-6784.

Top 20% of Value Courses in <u>Region 7:</u>

1. **Fall River Valley**
2. **Likely Place**
3. **Nakoma**
4. **Graeagle**

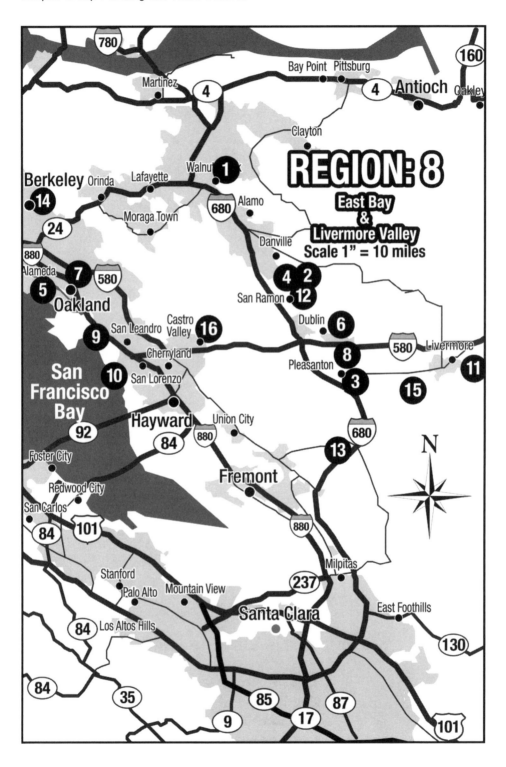

Region 8: East Bay and Livermore Valley

The East Bay offers multiple microclimates and several types of terrain. All courses see some impact from fog and wind coming through the San Francisco Bay, off the Pacific Ocean, unless protected in a small valley. In summer, afternoon breezes may be warmer than those along the ocean, but are still just as strong. Play early in the day if you prefer calm weather.

Courses included in this region:

		Ranking				Ranking	
		Best 100	Region 8			Best 100	Region 8
1.	Boundary Oak			9.	Metropolitan	71	5
2.	Bridges	44	3	10.	Monarch Bay (18+9)	75	6
3.	Callippe	37	2	11.	Poppy Ridge	62	4
4.	Canyon Lakes			12.	San Ramon		
5.	Chuck Corica (2x18)			13.	Sunol (2x18)		
6.	Dublin Ranch (executive)			14.	Tilden Park		
7.	Lake Chabot			15.	Wente Vineyards	18	1
8.	Las Positas (18+9)			16.	Willow Park		

Selected Getaway Recommendations:

- **Poppy Ridge, Wente,** savings @ Hawthorne suites in Livermore, 925 606-6060; or La Quinta Inn, 925 373-9600

Top 20% of Value Courses in Region 8:

1. **Boundary Oak**
2. **Callippe**
3. **Monarch Bay**
4. **Dublin Ranch**

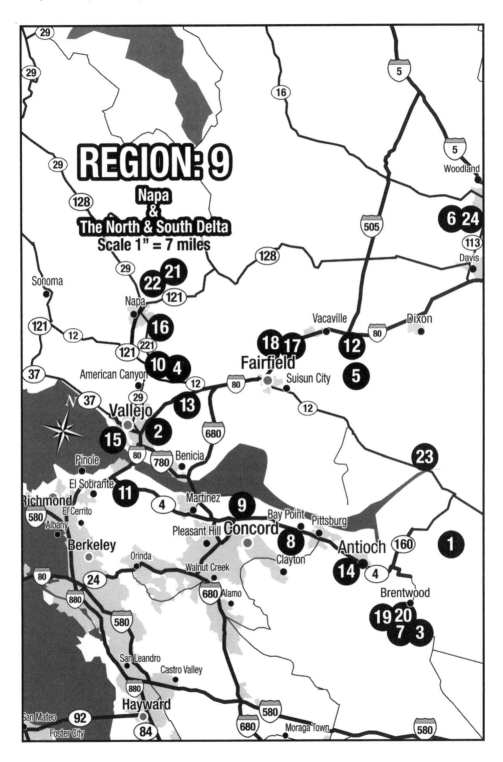

Region 9: Napa County and the north and south Delta

The San Joaquin and Sacramento Rivers join together near the town of Pittsburg. The surrounding the area, what we in California call the Delta, occupies over 1500 square miles. The land golf courses here often experience significant winds, euphemistically called the Delta breeze, due to significant temperature differences between the Pacific Ocean and vast Central Valley farther east. Courses near the rivers run flat, but many sit nestled in nearby hills. Napa's courses, further to the north, offer similar topography, sometimes encircled by local vineyards.

Courses included in this region:

		Rankings				Ranking	
		Best 100	**Region 9**			**Best 100**	**Region 9**
1.	Bethel Island			13.	Hiddenbrooke	31	3
2.	Blue Rock Springs (18x9)			14.	Lone Tree		
3.	Brentwood			15.	Mare Island	81	11
4.	Chardonnay (27)	20	1	16.	Napa at Kennedy Park		
5.	Cypress Lakes			17.	Paradise Valley	49	6
6.	Davis			18.	Rancho Solano	48	4
7.	Deer Ridge	68	8	19.	Roddy Ranch	90	12
8.	Delta View			20.	Shadow Lakes	70	9
9.	Diablo Creek			21.	Silverado North	30	2
10.	Eagle Vines	78	10	22.	Silverado South	49	5
11.	Franklin Canyon			23.	Trilogy at Rio Vista		
12.	Green Tree			24.	Wildhorse	60	7

Selected Getaway Recommendations:

- **Silverado, North and South Courses** @ Silverado Resort, 800 532-0500
- **Brentwood, Shadow Lakes,** savings @ Comfort Inn, 925 516-2837
- **Chardonnay,** savings @ Napa River Inn in Napa 707 251-8500
- **Rancho Solano,** savings @ Hampton Inn in Fairfield, 707 469-6200

Top 20% of Value Courses in <u>Region 9</u>:

1. **Wildhorse**
2. **Lone Tree**
3. **Paradise Valley**
4. **Delta View**

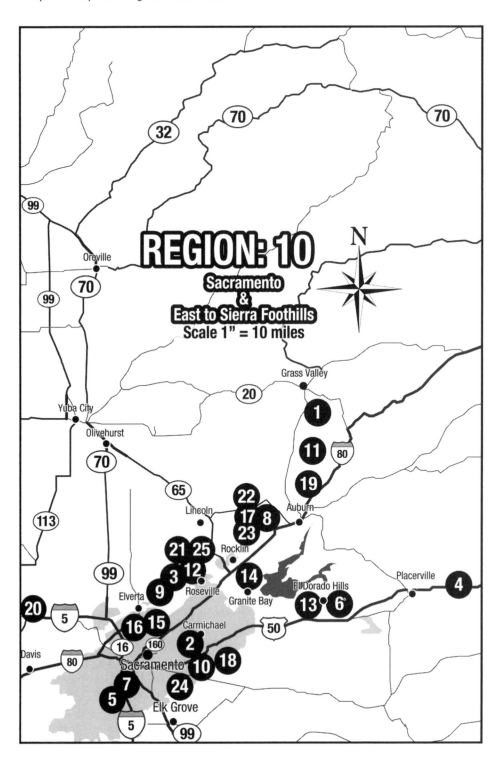

Region 10: Sacramento and east to Sierra Foothills

This Region covers metropolitan Sacramento east to Auburn and Placerville. Due to fierce competition over the last few years, many offer great golfing value, with their high quality and reasonable greens fees. Winter weather is cool to mild, and summers usually run in the high 90's to 100 F. Topography varies from flat valley and river basins near Sacramento to rolling slopes and steep climbs in the foothills.

Courses included in this region:

	Ranking				Ranking	
	Best 100	**Region 10**			**Best 100**	**Reg. 10**
1. Alta Sierra				14. Granite Bay	4	1
2. Ancil Hoffman	61	10		15. Hag. Oaks Arcade		
3. Antelope (executive)				16. Hag. Oaks M.Kenzie	57	9
4. Apple Mountain	22	4		17. Lincoln Hills (18x2)		
5. Bartley Cavanaugh				18. Mather		
6. Bass Lake				19. The Ridge	8	2
7. Bing Maloney				20. Teal Bend	89	11
8. Catta Verdera	26	5		21. Timber Creek	94	12
9. Cherry Island				22. Turkey Creek	42	7
10. Cordova (executive)				23. Whitney Oaks	40	6
11. Darkhorse	13	3		24. Wildhawk		
12. Diamond Oaks				25. Woodcreek	97	13
13. Empire Ranch	54	8				

Selected Getaway Recommendations:

- **Darkhorse, Lincoln Hills, The Ridge, Turkey Creek, Whitney Oaks,** small savings on case-by-case basis @ Rocklin Park Hotel & Spa, (888) 630-9400
- Few Stay-and-Play packages are available due to already-low golf prices.

Top 20% of Value Courses in <u>Region 10</u>:
1. **Ancil Hoffman**
2. **The Ridge**
3. **Apple Mountain**
4. **Cherry Island**
5. **Darkhorse**

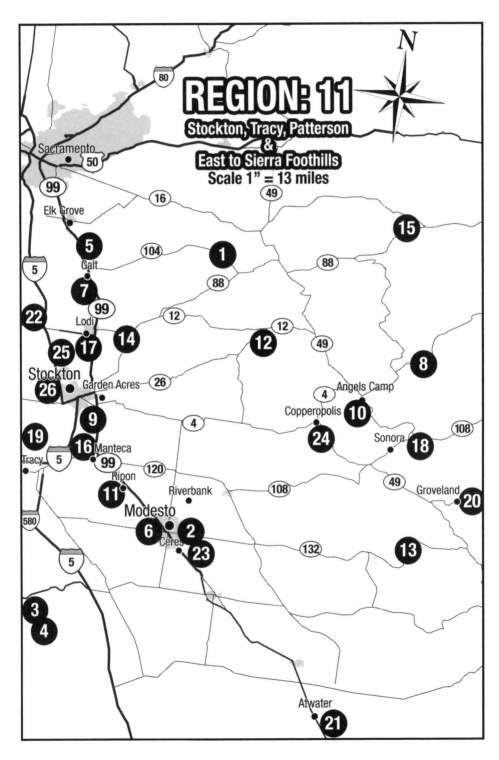

Region 11: Stockton and Patterson east to Sierra foothills

Like Region 10, topography ranges from flatter courses near Stockton and Modesto to hillier locales on both sides of the Valley. Courses on the west side feel Delta winds, but as you travel east others become much calmer—and warmer. East side foothills in this part of the valley start a very slow climb to the mountains, so courses there often have wonderful gently rolling terrains, perfectly suited for good golf architecture.

Courses included in this region:

		Ranking				Ranking	
		Best 100	**Reg. 11**			**Best 100**	**Reg. 11**
1.	Castle Oaks	38	4	14.	Lockeford Springs		
2.	Creekside			15.	Mace Meadows		
3.	Diablo Gr. Legends	24	3	16.	Manteca Park		
4.	Diablo Gr. Ranch	16	1	17.	Micke Grove	100	11
5.	Dry Creek	87	8	18.	Mountain Springs	84	7
6.	Dryden			19.	Old River		
7.	Forest Lake (exec)			20.	Pine Mountain Lake	80	6
8.	Forest Meadow (exec)			21.	Rancho Del Rey		
9.	French Camp (exec)			22.	Reserve at Spanos Park		
10.	Greenhorn Creek	66	5	23.	River Oaks (exec)		
11.	Jack Tone (exec)			24.	Saddle Creek	21	2
12.	La Contenta	99	10	25.	Swenson Park		
13.	Lake Don Pedro	98	9	26.	Van Buskirk Park		

Selected Getaway Recommendations:

- **Diablo Grande,** savings @ Villa del Lago in Patterson, 866 744-2358.
- **Greenhorn Creek Resort** in Angels Camp, call 209 736-8175
- **Saddle Creek** in Copperopolis, call 800 611-7722

Top 20% of Value Courses in <u>Region 11</u>:

1. **Castle Oaks**
2. **Dry Creek**
3. **Micke Grove**
4. **Creekside**
5. **Van Buskirk**

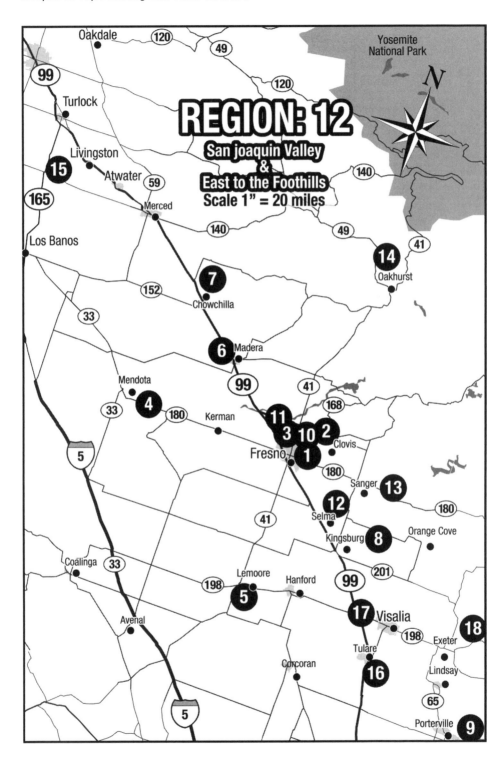

REGION: 12
San joaquin Valley
&
East to the Foothills
Scale 1" = 20 miles

Region 12: San Joaquin Valley east to Sierra Foothills

This southernmost region extends from Merced to Porterville, 130 miles along State Rt. 99. With a couple of exceptions, courses in Fresno and south are older, often very flat and routine in layout. Courses to the north show more modern design elements, since many were built within the last 20 years; several of these are found in foothill terrain. Weather can be foggy and cool in winter and is usually hot and dry (around 100 F) in summer. Fairways commonly utilize Bermuda grass varieties that turn partially brown from November thru April.

Courses included in this region:

	Ranking Best 100	Ranking Region 12		Ranking Best 100	Ranking Region 12
1. Airways			10. Riverbend	51	3
2. Brighton Crest	64	4	11. Riverside		
3. Fig Garden			12. Selma Valley		
4. Javier's Fresno West			13. Sherwood Forest		
5. Lemoore			14. Sierra Meadows	90	7
6. Madera			15. Stevinson Ranch	6	1
7. Pheasant Run	73	5	16. Tulare		
8. Ridge Creek	46	2	17. Valley Oaks		
9. River Island	86	6	18. Woodlake Ranch		

Selected Getaway Recommendations:

- **Riverside,** savings @ Spring Hill Suites in Fresno, 559 431-0004
- **Valley Oaks,** call the course at 559 431-0004 for savings @ Holiday Inn, Comfort Suites or Hampton Inn, all in Visalia.

Top 20% of Value Courses in Region 12:

1. **Javier's Fresno West**
2. **Tulare**
3. **Pheasant Run**
4. **Stevinson Ranch**

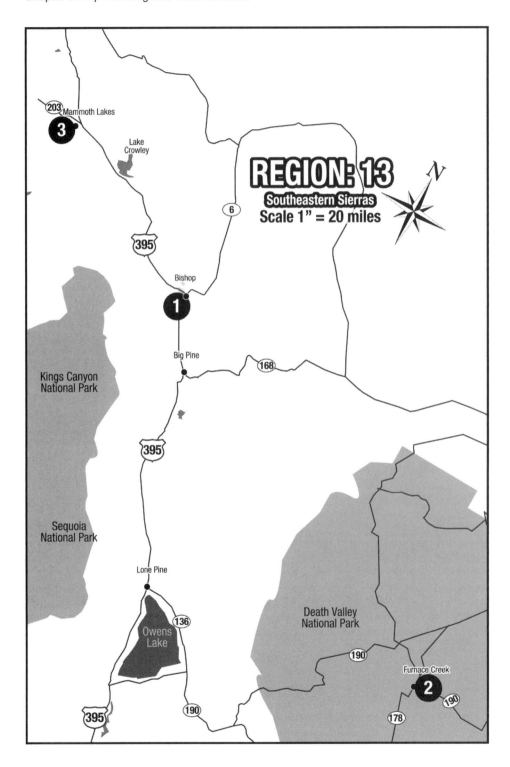

REGION: 13
Southeastern Sierras
Scale 1" = 20 miles

Region 13: Southeastern Sierras

Only three eighteen-hole public courses straddle the 350-mile stretch of highways heading south from Carson Pass (30 miles south of Lake Tahoe) to Furnace Creek in Death Valley. The scenery on this trek is some of the most spectacular in the entire United States. To the west of U.S. 395, the high altitude spine of the Sierra Nevada Mountains overlooks the route. Peaks and ridges rise five to ten thousand feet above the roadbed. They form an imposing edifice, far enough away for perspective, yet close enough to see rocky details.

To the east, more mountain ranges appear, mostly in Nevada. These reach high altitudes too, but sit farther away and display less rocky spires. Close by the road's edge run several rivers, brim full in June, next to desert and alpine wildflowers. The flora here, which usually lies low, close to the rocky soil, is much different from that we see elsewhere in the state. It's colorful, fragile, and though sometimes small, a precious joy to behold.

At the southern outpost of Lone Pine the scene changes after turning east, off U.S. 395, for the final 110-miles down to the minus 200 foot elevation of Furnace Creek. Trees diminish, replaced by striations of colored rock decorating 5000-foot ridges. Dry asphalt and salty flats on the valley floor reflect back searing heat to the underside of passing cars.

From the highest golf course in the state at Mammoth Lakes' Sierra Star, to the lowest course in the world is about a four hour drive. Two diverse extremes, one cool and crisp, the other hot and dry, form a fitting conclusion to the golf experiences of Northern California.

Courses included in this region are:

		Rankings	
		Best 100	Region 13
1.	Bishop		
2.	Furnace Creek		
3.	Sierra Star	29	1

Selected Getaway Recommendations:

- **Sierra Star,** savings @ Mammoth Mountain Resorts, 800 626-6684
- **Furnace Creek.** Furnace Creek Inn, the premier 4-Diamond facility, is open mid-October thru early May. Furnace Creek Ranch, the more casual facility stays open all year round. Call 800 236-7916.

Chapter 6:
Glossary and Local Golf Trivia

Golfers are like any other sport junkies, they like to know as much as possible about the facts and figures, and the more trivial or obscure, the better. Some of us like to bet, some to argue, some to show off, and some of us are just plain number freaks: Where is the longest hole; which is the hardest course; where is the toughest par-three; which course has the highest elevation? Many of these questions were answered in the prior chapters, but below is a refresher list, in addition to several other world-saving facts and even some useful golf definitions. As throughout the **Best 100**, the course data only relates to eighteen-hole public access courses in Northern California.

Approach shots: When a player shoots directly at the green with the expectation of reaching it, he is said to be hitting an *approach* shot. The club used can be a driver from the tee or a 3/4 sand-wedge from the rough. If using less of a swing, because the shot is shorter—generally from about ten to fifty yards—the shot would be called a *pitch*

Par-five holes reached in 3 shots, par-fours reached in two shots and par-threes reached in one shot, are said to have been reached *in regulation. Hitting the green* means an *approach shot* stays on the putting surface in the *regulation* number of shots for the hole. If an *approach* hits the green on the fly, and then rolls off, a player did not *hit the green.*

Architects, top in Northern California: Due to the extensive volume of success he has had in building high quality courses, Robert Trent Jones, Jr. has to be considered the best of our architects. He has lived on the SF Peninsula for over thirty years and five of his designs rank in our top ten. Robert Muir Graves is the next most prolific designer. Johnny Miller, Brad Bell, John Harbottle, Jack Nicklaus, and Robert T. Jones, Sr. each find a high percent of their designs with **Best 100** rankings. The data below chronicles these and others' work on public 18-hole courses in Northern California:

	Number of Courses	Number in Best 100*	Top Ten* Courses
Architects with 4 designs or more:			
Robert Trent Jones, Jr.	18	13	Granite Bay, CordeValle, Poppy Hills
(some shared w/Jones Sr. or others)			The Ridge, Spanish Bay**
Robert Muir Graves	16	7	
R. L. and/or R. E. Baldock	15	1	
William F. Bell	7	5	
William P. Bell	7	0	
Ted Robinson, Sr.	7	0	
Johnny Miller	6	6	
Brad Bell	6	6	Coyote Moon
Jack Fleming	6	1	
John Harbottle	5	4	Stevinson Ranch**
Robert Putnam	5	1	
Jack Nicklaus	4	4	Old Greenwood
Alister MacKenzie	4	2	Pasatiempo
Robert Trent Jones, Sr.	4	4	Spyglass Hill
Richard Bigler	4	2	
Clark Glasson	4	1	
Others with multiple Best 100 or Top 10 ratings:			
Gary Baird	3	3	
Fred Bliss	2	2	
Homer Flint	2	2	
Robin Nelson	2	2	
Jack Neville	2	1	Pebble Beach
Arnold Palmer	2	2	
Algie Pullet	3	2	
Stark/Daly	1	1	Sevillano Links
Tatum/Summers	3	2	
Others			
29 architects		28	
		105*	

*Includes courses listed in both Chapters 2 and 4. By including both Chapters, the totals in this Table create a **Best 105** and a **Top 12.**

**Additional primary architects collaborated on the designs; see reviews for more detail.

Blind shot: Often a golfer must aim to a location where the landing area cannot be seen. Such *blind shots* usually occur on drives, though greens can be hidden too. Our best courses have a few good examples . . . **At Pebble Beach,** the second shot up the hill on number six and drives on number eight, eleven, fourteen and fifteen are *blind*. **At Spyglass Hill** the drive on number one (if hit it very long or around the corner), the approach to number two. and the back pin location on number four are *blind* shots. Most golfers consider a few such shot circumstances to be exciting, but dislike their overuse.

Bogey Rating: See **Course Slope.**

Bunker: *Bunkers* are depressions in areas of the fairway, roughs or around greens that are filled with sand. (Often the word *trap* is used as a colloquial term for the word *bunker.*) The *lip* forms the exterior border of a bunker and is usually well trimmed, creating a grassy-mounded edge and distinctive outline for the appearance of the bunker. Texture of the sand varies, depending on the closest and least expensive supply. Bunkers normally fall under the rules of golf as a kind of *hazard* where players are not allowed to touch their club to the ground (i.e. the sand in a bunker) before swinging down at the ball in an attempt to hit it. Golf etiquette dictates that players should rake the sand smooth after they have entered or hit out of bunkers so that following players find a consistent surface.

Many bunker styles receive special names, but such designations are seldom used in this book. Exceptions would be: 1)*Waste bunker*, a large flat area covered with shallow sand, often populated with tufts of grass or low shrubs. *Waste bunkers* are usually un-raked, so grounding the club and taking practice swings are allowed. 2) *Grass bunker*, a depression similar in shape to a sand bunker, but filled with long grass or *rough*. Grass bunkers are not treated as *hazards*, so grounding of clubs is allowed, and rarely are they styled with *lips*. Typically, the careful raking and grooming of sand bunkers makes hitting from them easier than grass bunkers or waste bunkers.

Chip shot: See **Pitch shots.**

Cost to play: See **Value Rating.**

Course Rating: The current Course Rating system, developed early in the 20th century, was golf's first attempt to create a worldwide system of standardized *difficulty* measurements for varying styles of courses, and handicaps. Without such a system, fair handicapped competition between players from opposing clubs would be difficult. Neither *par* nor *distance* provided good standards because hazard placement, course condition, fairway shape and obstacle position vary tremendously on different courses.

The Course Rating measures "the score a scratch golfer should make on an eighteen-hole course." A male scratch golfer, *i.e.* one with a "0" handicap, is described as one who hits drives 250 yards and is capable of reaching greens with two shots on holes measuring 470-yards. A female scratch golfer hits drives 210 yards and regularly reaches 400-yard holes with two shots. A scratch player may be expected to shoot 70 on an easy par-72 course, but shoot 74 on a tougher one. These expected scores, the 70 and 74 respectively, became the *course rating.*

Teams of trained course-raters, usually volunteers, descend on a course at least every six years to re-evaluate its ratings. Not only do they play the course and check overall yardage, but they also measure distances to hazards, distances to recovery points from hazard relief spots, depth of bunkers, locations of obstacles such as trees, size and speed of greens, average wind strength and direction, amount of fairway roll, depth of roughs, etc.

Once a course rating was established, and until the addition of the Slope Rating in the late 1980's, the *handicap* was calculated using a three-step process:

1) The *differential* (i.e. difference) between posted scores and the *course rating* on each course played was calculated.
2) The differential was multiplied by .96; and results were posted.
3) The average of the lowest ten *differentials* became the monthly *handicap*.

Nowadays, most courses in the U.S—and some others throughout the world—recognize that using *course rating* alone as the method of *handicap* calculation is unfair for most golfers, and, as explained in the following *Course Slope* definition, a further modification transpired. The number resulting from the calculation described above is now called a player's *Index* rather than his *handicap*.

Course Slope: The Slope Rating was added to further refine the handicapping system because The *Course Rating* uses hole length as the primary gauge of difficulty. Even today, most pros and statisticians would argue that these distances make by far the best forecaster of scores for scratch players.

However, we lesser golfers know from experience that scores well above our norm come much more frequently when playing difficult courses than easy ones. Under the old course rating handicap system, players who earned a 20 handicap on an easy course were not nearly as competent as those who achieved the same 20 handicap on more difficult one. Competition between players from opposing courses was still unfair.

The *Slope Rating* takes this disparity into account by adding another number to the handicap soup. To get the modern *handicap*, course raters start by creating a new calculation, the *Bogey Rating*. A *bogey rating* is defined as what a twenty handicapper would expect to shoot on the course. A bogey player is further defined as a male who drives 200 yards and reaches 370-yard holes in two strokes, or a female who drives 150 yards and reaches 280-yard holes in two shots.

Once both the *Bogey Rating* and the *Course Rating* are finally determined, the course *Slope* can be calculated. Mathematically, *Course Slope* equals *Bogey Rating* minus *Course Rating* times 5.381 for men, and times 4.24 for women. (Ask a USGA statistician if you need to know how these particular multipliers were developed.). With the Course Slope calculated, your *handicap* can be finally be determined:

1) First each player must determine what set of tees to be played that day, and know his/her current monthly home-course *index*. NCGA members can also find their *index* on the NCGA posting computer in the course pro shop or at www.ncga.com.

2) Next they need to ask the pro shop for the *handicap table* related to that set of tees. It's usually placed somewhere in the vicinity of the posting computer.

3) Find your index on the chart, and your handicap will be next to it.

Any other questions?

Course Styles: Golf course styles mentioned in **Best 100** reviews include:

Desert courses abound in the Southwest and other arid sections of the West. Palm Desert, CA, and both Scottsdale and Tucson, AZ, are famous for this style. They use natural rock outcroppings, sandy unimproved roughs and natural desert vegetation as contrast to their bright green irrigated grassy roughs and fairways.

Executive courses use shorter yardage and many more par-three holes than normal full-length courses. Often par is between 58 and 63, rather than the normal 70-72 (for men). The name comes from the idea that business executives needed courses where they could play a quick 2-3 hour game instead of a normal 4-5 hour round. I have noted several such short courses in the **Best 100** Table of Contents and in the articles of Chapter 5.

Heathland courses originated in Scotland and other European countries, with terrain similar to links courses (see below), but at inland locations rather than sites on the coast. They usually appear flat or gently rolling, with arid vegetation in the rough. Sand dunes and waste areas covered in gorse (a spiny evergreen bush) and heather are typical in Europe because no commercial crops would grow there. In the U.S. we don't have indigenous British Isle brush species, so mesquite, sage, and similar low shrubs provide an adequate substitute. California courses such as Poppy Ridge or Roddy Ranch use tall wild grasses, vineyards and scrub oaks to simulate the original European flora.

Links designs are few and far between in the U.S., according to European purists. They describe links-land as "coastal strips of land between the beaches and inland agricultural areas . . . usually unsuited for crops . . . typically having sandy soil, dunes, undulating topography . . . often with an out-and-back routing for the golf holes." This quote comes from the Internet site, www.about.com and commentary from the British Museum. In the U.S we have modified the term Links Style to include gently rolling or flat courses, along the ocean or not, which have few trees, firm fairways, firm greens, and a good deal of wind.

Mountain courses usually have steeper hills, tall evergreen trees and broad vistas of surrounding ridgelines. Often these courses use shorter yardage and sharper doglegs, caused by the irregular topography. They also have cooler temperatures and thinner air, so the ball travels farther than at sea level. Rule of thumb for extra distance is 1% longer ball-flight for every 1000 feet of elevation increase. However, this only applies if balls are hit high in the air. Low-hit balls get little assistance from thin air.

Parkland is the normal name associated with courses found on lush inland properties. Such courses may have lakes, creeks, trees, or any of the vegetation we would expect to find in a park. In Scotland, "Parkland" usually refers to inland courses not designed in a Heathlands style.

Resort courses typically have wide fairways, excellent maintenance conditions, relatively flat greens, and excellent after-golf facilities. Years ago this meant easy, fairly unchallenging golf, but resort built in the last 15 years have become more difficult.

Stadium courses provide improved audience-viewing locations for large public tournaments. Often green positions sit near hills where crowds can easily view the competition. Northern California has no, public courses in this style.

Dawson's personal favorite courses: After playing 220-plus courses in Northern California, people usually want to know which were my favorites. To some extent the answer depends on cost. So I give you my top six, regardless of cost, and then the ones I would like most to go back and play regularly.

My favorites are all *playable.* That is, they are not too long and roughs are cut relatively short most of the time. They are maintained well; have very interesting bunkers around the greens, and greens-keepers put pins in interesting/unusual positions. Many have twists and turns in the fairways that take away the advantage of long hitters; so good chipping and putting skills give me an advantage. Unfortunately, few are easy to walk. The group below, titled "for regular play" cost $60 or less mid-week, and have even lower senior and afternoon rates.

Regardless of cost:	Coyote Moon	Incline Champion	Pebble Beach
	Grizzly Ranch	Pasatiempo	Sierra Star
For regular play:	Bailey Creek	Fall River Valley	(The) Ridge
	Callippe	Greenhorn Creek	Sierra Meadows
	Deer Ridge	Hunter Ranch	Wildhorse
	Dry Creek	Indian Valley	Windsor

Discounts: See the **Websites** section of the glossary for Internet access to discount sites. Golf management companies such as American Golf and CourseCo also offer discounts on the web. Independent courses sometimes do the same if you join their website mailing list. The best discounts are often available on the spur-of-the-moment because your local course is trying to fill an unexpected series of last minute openings. Other regularly published sources are:

Bay Area & Northern California Golf Guide, a free booklet available in many pro-shops.
West Coast Golf Value Book, a coupon book that can be purchased at www.2for1golf.com.

Dog friendly courses: Such facilities are rare. Quail Lodge allows walking golfers to have their pooch on a leash while playing. Ancil Hoffman allows non-golfers to walk the course's exterior pathways with a dog-on-leash. Others may be available but you will need to ask.

Draw: See **Shot trajectory.**

Extreme Statistics: Here is some golf trivia, accurate as of April 1, 2009. The elevation gain/loss estimates come from readings measured on Google Earth.

Longest holes:
 Sevillano Links, Corning: #18, 561 to 686 yards (par-5).
 Lake Chabot, Oakland: #18, 644 to 673 yards (par-6).
 Fall River Valley, Fall River Mills: #3, 554 to 672 yards (par-5).
 Ridge Creek, Dinuba: #15, 498 to 648 yards (par-5).
 Likely Place, Likely: #5, 506 to 630 yards, with room to expand to 780 yards. (par-5)
Longest course:
 Back tees ("Daly tees") @ Sevillano Links, Corning: 7823 yards. Under special tournament conditions can be expanded to 10,000 yard @ par 90.
 Front tees ("Ladies) @ Swenson Park, Stockton: 6036 yards.
Steepest uphill hole: Cinnebar: #7, on Canyon Nine. Par 4, up 100' over 341 yards.
Most drop from tee to green: Lake Chabot: #18, a 200' drop over 673-yards.
Most drop from tee to green on a par-three: Lake Chabot: #9, 115' drop over 182 yard hole length.
Hilliest walking course: Lake Chabot, Oakland, CA.
Steepest climb from green to tee: Wente's "Lombard Street." Goes up nearly 190'.
Only rope tow assist: Following #18 green at River Oaks in Ceres.
Only cable car for bag carriers and pull carts: Following #13 green @ Indian Valley.
Courses with extreme walking or riding distance from green to tee:
 Whitney Oaks, Roseville, designed by Johnny Miller and Fred Bliss.
 The Ranch, San Jose, designed by Casey O'Callaghan and Wade Cable.
 Bridges, San Ramon, designed by Johnny Miller.
 Nakoma (The Dragon), Clio, designed by Robin Nelson.
Oldest public access courses:
 Mare Island, Vallejo, 1892, became an 18-hole course again in 2000.
 Presidio, San Francisco, 1895, became public in 1995.
 Del Monte, Monterey, 1897; "Oldest continually operating 18 hole course west of the Mississippi."
Courses first opened in 2007, 2008 and 2009:
 Likely Place, Likely (near Alturas) added 9 holes to become 18.
 Ridge Creek, Dinuba.
 Sevillano Links, Corning (at Rolling Hills Casino).
 Yocha-de-he, Brooks (at Cache Creek Casino).
 Trinitas, Valley Springs (not yet open for review as of May '09).
Courses closed in 2007 and 2008:
 El Dorado Hills (east of Sacramento).
 Mountain House (near Tracy).

Fade: See **Shot Trajectory.**

Fairway: the smooth, closely cut area of the golf playing field. Golf balls at rest in the *fairway* sit on top of short turf, so that grass blades do not come between the face of the club and the ball when a shot is hit. *Fairways* lie between the *tee* and the *green*, and usually provide the target for drives and intermediate shots. *Roughs* and *hazards* border their sides.

False Front: The term usually refers to the surface of a green, where the front portion is constructed with such a steep break that balls landing on it roll back off the front edge.

Flop Shots: See **Pitch Shots.**

Forced Carry: The need for a drive to carry or fly across a long distance of rough or hazard before landing. Many modern courses, especially hilly designs by Johnny Miller require ball flights of over 150 yards, or the ball will be lost and need to be re-hit.

Golf, derivation of the word: Contrary to popular male mythology, the word "golf" is not originally an acronym created by the Scots to mean Gentlemen Only, Ladies Forbidden. Rather most scholars believe it is derived from the words "chole and kolf, which were names for a variety of medieval stick and ball games in Britain and Europe." *

* From *Scottish Golf History 2003-2007*. Internet Version: Scottish Golf History.net/Golf word, version 3.33.

Golf Digest **ranking criteria:** The **Best 100** uses a one-of-a-kind ranking system, designed to appeal to golfers with good, not superb golfing skills, and who enjoy the social side of the game as much as competition. Golfers in the handicap range between 5 and 20 are my target audience. I stress course design and course condition as the most important criteria in evaluating the **Best 100,** but add quality of facilities (such as the practice areas and clubhouse), walkability, beauty of surroundings and tournament history as lesser features. Other ranking systems, such as that used by *Golf Digest*, take a more pure approach to ranking, one that applies more to top-notch players and only to the golf course itself. Here are their criteria, from 2008:

Shot Values: How well does the course pose risks and rewards and equally test length, accuracy and finesse? (Author note: Points earned for this item are double the values of other ranking criteria listed below.)
Resistance to scoring: How difficult, while still being fair, is the course for a scratch player from the back tees?

Design variety: How varied are the golf course's holes in differing lengths, configurations, hazard placements, green shapes and green contours?

Memorability: How well do the design features (tees, fairways, greens, hazards, vegetation and terrain) provide individuality to each hole, yet a collective continuity to the entire 18?

Aesthetics: How well do the scenic values of the course (including landscaping, vegetation, water features and backdrops) add to the pleasure of a round?

Conditioning: How would you rate the playing quality of the tees, fairways and greens when you last played the course?

Ambience: How well does the overall feel and atmosphere of the course reflect or uphold the traditional values of the game?

Green Complex: the area of the green, including the various physical features immediately surrounding it. Differing styles of complex can impact scores and affect play significantly, because of varying chip and recovery shot requirements. Also called the *green surrounds*, the features include:

The green: an extremely short, smooth, evenly cut grass surface, which surrounds the cup. Green designs vary tremendously from small, flat and soft . . . to huge mounded surfaces so firm balls bounce waste high.

Collar: a narrow band of grass that touches the green; sometimes called the fringe. Usually only 1-2 feet across, it can be wider like at Stevinson Ranch. It is normally cut so closely that players use putters rather than chipping irons.

Apron: broader term for the area of semi-closely cut, usually well conditioned grass that allows balls to be cleanly hit within 10-20 yards of the green. Since apron grass is shorter cut than fairways, chipping and pitching from it can be more difficult for many players. If aprons are mowed very close around elevated greens, shots missing the green often roll far down slopes into deep rough.

Bunker: see the definition on p. 369.

Mounding: small rounded hills, covered with rough or apron. Mounds perform many functions, including keeping balls from squirting too far away from the green, creating interesting stances for chips, adding visual framing to the green area, and breaking the wind when constructed very tall.

Collection area: depressions next to the green, with grass cut short like on aprons, for balls to roll in lieu of falling into a bunker. They often sit between high mounding and add a different type of challenging shot or contrasting appearance.

Greens fees: The admission cost to play on a golf course. On any one course fees vary depending on time of day (prime time is usually in the morning), weekend or weekday, players age (seniors and juniors often get lower prices), whether you play nine or eighteen holes, and time of the year. Power carts are sometimes included in the price if a course is difficult to walk, but not always. Pull carts, caddies, range balls, equipment rentals, drinks and food are usually add-ons. Typically, use of practice putting greens is free.

Handicaps: These numbers are used to allow golfers of different skills to compete together fairly. Normally, lower handicap players give the higher handicap player the number of strokes equal to the difference between their

handicaps. For instance, if I am a 6 handicap, and John is a 21, I give John (21-6)=15 strokes. In *match play*, where we play hole by hole, we look at the scorecard and find the row or column marked "Handicap." On each hole where the number printed is 15 or less, John gets to reduce his score by one shot to determine who wins the hole. In *medal* (or stroke) play, where only the total 18-hole score counts, I subtract 6 from my score to determine my *net* score. John then subtracts 21. So, if he shoots 92, his *net* score is (92-21)=71. My *net* score, if I shoot 78 is (78-6)=72. Therefore John wins, after adjusting for handicaps because his *net* 71 is lower than my *net* 72. See *Course Ratings* and *Course Slope* on pp. 371 and 372 for information about calculation of handicaps.

Hazards: bunkers, plus very rough terrain marked by either red or yellow stakes. Includes lakes, creeks, gullies, and other areas where hitting balls would be difficult. Players are allowed to drop out of *hazards* or replay shots that land in hazards under specific rules and penalties. If a player chooses to hit from within the hazard, their clubhead may not touch the vegetation or ground surface until he/she swings downward in an attempt to hit the shot. Objects within *hazards* may not be moved in an attempt to make swinging easier.

Heathlands: See **Course Styles.**

Hook: See **Shot trajectory**.

Index: The *index* was called a player's handicap before development of the *Slope* handicapping system. See **Course Ratings** and **Course Slope**.

Lay-up shots: See **Target golf.**

Links: See **Course Styles.**

Lip: See **Bunkers.**

Longitude and latitude, course locations: These longitude/latitude estimates come from Google Earth readings.

Highest course: Sierra Star, Mammoth Lakes. 8050 ft.
Lowest course: Furnace Creek, Death Valley. -208 ft.
Northern most: Lake Shastina, Weed. Latitude 41 deg, 31'11."
Eastern most: Furnace Creek, Death Valley. Longitude 116 deg, 51'08."
Southern most*: Dairy Creek, San Luis Obispo. Latitude 35 deg 20'12."
Western most: Eureka, Eureka, CA. Longitude 124 deg 10'20."

*Dairy Creek is the southernmost course in the NCGA. The southernmost course reviewed in this book is Rancho Maria, Santa Maria, Latitude 34 deg 52'24."

Management companies: Local owners often subcontract course management to outside specialty companies. Even city owned muni's do this. In some cases, players can purchase discount programs from companies that that offer substantial savings at all their affiliate courses. The following list includes only those organizations managing three or more public eighteen-hole public courses in Northern CA. The list is subject to change at any time.

American Golf
Bidwell Park
Franklin Canyon
Lake Tahoe
Monarch Bay
Reserve at Spanos Park
San Geronimo
Santa Clara
Tilden Park

Castle & Cook Prop.
Coyote Creek Tournament
Coyote Creek Valley
Saddle Creek

Empire Golf
Ancil Hoffman
Cherry Island
Darkhorse
La Contenta
Oakmont East
Oakmont West

Touchstone Golf, LLC
Boulder Creek
Mare Island
Roddy Ranch

CourseCo
Boundary Oaks
Callippe
Deep Cliff
Eureka
Foxtail North & South
Los Lagos
Mather
Metropolitan
Napa at Kennedy
Riverside
Stonetree
Valley Oaks

Sierra Golf Mgmt.
Diablo Grande Legends
Diablo Grande Ranch
Lemoore
Pheasant
Salinas Fairways

Morton Golf
Bartley Cavanaugh
Bing Maloney
Haggin Oaks Arcade
 & MacKenzie

KemperSports
Bodega Harbour
Bridges
Chuck Corica (36 holes)
Harding Park
Hiddenbrooke
Monarch Dunes
Paradise Valley
Rancho Solano
Ridge Creek

Pebble Beach Co.
Del Monte
Pebble Beach
Spanish Bay
Spyglass Hill

ClubCorp
Airways
Empire Ranch
Granite Bay
Teal Bend
Turkey Creek

Xanterra
Furnace Creek
Silverado North & South

NCGA and other golf associations in Northern CA: The Northern California Golf Association (NCGA) governs men's amateur golf—both public and private—in Northern California. Several Reno/Tahoe courses also affiliate with the NCGA. The association has between 165,000 and 175,000 members.

The NCGA and other groups listed below all provide handicapping and other golf related services to their members.

The city of San Luis Obispo on the Central Coast (Latitude 35 degrees 20'), and southern borders of Tulare and Inyo Counties form the dividing line with the **Southern California Golf Association (SCGA).** The southernmost public eighteen-hole golf courses are Dairy Creek on the coast, River Island in

Porterville, and Furnace Creek in Death Valley. (Bakersfield is an SCGA affiliate region.) Northernmost courses are Beau Pre in McKinleyville, Lake Shastina in Weed and Likely Links, just south of Alturas.

The **Pacific Women's Golf Association (PWGA)** governs public women's golf on the West Coast and the **Women's Golf Association of Northern California (WGANC)** covers private Northern California clubs. However, many lady members of both public and private clubs join the NCGA. By doing so they get lower cost golf at Poppy Hills and Poppy Ridge and can play in different tournaments with varying groups of friends.

The **Northern California Professional Golf Association (NCPGA)** has jurisdiction over professionals in Northern California and parts of Nevada, Idaho and Oregon. Membership includes over 4000 professionals.

Out-of-bounds (OB): Course's exterior perimeters, access roads, parking lots, clubhouse structures, pools, courts and walkways are usually marked as *out-of-bounds*. Balls hit past the white stakes, which identify the boundaries, must be re-hit, with penalty strokes added. Some courses add OB stakes on the interior of course to protect against golfers taking short-cuts or unsafely encroaching where others may be playing.

Par: The score a "scratch" or zero handicapper should shoot on a hole is called "par." The length of a hole normally determines the number. Holes up to 250-yards are par-three; holes on up to 470-yards are par-four; and holes on up to 650 yards are par-five. Women's length for a par-five is adjusted down to 400-yards and above. Unfortunately, par, which is based on distance alone, is not a good measure for handicapping. Many other factors, such as hazards, terrain and course condition, affect scores achieved on a hole. See **Course Rating** and **Course Slope** for further information.

Parkland: See **Course styles.**

Pitch shots: *Pitch* shots include all short shots, (except for blasts out of a hazard) hit with irons from distances up to 50 yards from the edge of the green. Players usually employ a partial swing for *pitches*. Due to the range of results possible, from landing the ball next to the hole, to running it over into a lake, they often make or break a good score. *Pitches* fit into several sub-categories:

Chip Shot: is very short pitch, usually hit within 10 yards of the green. Often backspin *checks* (or stops) the ball from rolling too far. A *chip-and-run* is a longer chip shot, hit without backspin so the ball is free to roll further. Harvey Penick, the famous golf coach of the 60's and 70's teaches *chipping* the ball no higher than "the bottom of a bench."* He advises players to use a low-lofted club such as a 5 to 9 iron, and hit the ball no higher than a foot to keep it under control.
Pitch & run/Bump & run: a longer shot, often 20 to 50-yards, where the player expects the ball to roll a long distance after it lands on or short of the green. A *run-up* shot refers

more broadly to all shots hit low to force the ball to bounce up or around various surfaces.

Flop shot: Made famous by Phil Michelson, this term refers to a shot normally within the range of a pitch, but hit with a full swing and open clubface to make a high trajectory that stops quickly on the green.

*Harvey Penick's Little Red Book: Lessons and Teachings from a Lifetime in Golf: Harvey Penick, Bud Shrake, Edwin Shrake. Published by Simon & Schuster, 1999.

Push-up greens:
Today, contractors use exacting standards, including layers of different rocks, sands and specialized soils, to build greens. The resulting porous sub-foundations allow grass roots to delve deep into the ground and survive periods of drought and/or stress. Greens made to such standards can run hard and fast yet survive, and minimize the need for chemicals and water. Sophisticated drainage systems and sloping techniques insure good drainage in winter.

Less sophisticated processes were commonly used until about 1960. Instead of layering special foundation soils, bulldozers scraped topsoil from nearby ground or bunker wells and *pushed it up* to form greens raised slightly above the natural grade of the surroundings. Higher elevations at the back made approach shots hold well. Some such greens still exist today, especially on older tracks in Central Valley.

Such *push-up* greens tend to be smaller with one-dimensional front-to-back slopes, except for mounds created by years of blasting sand from bunkers. Because they lack unusual character and are more susceptible to drought or drainage problems, most have been replaced.

Quality Rating: see Value rating.

Reference Guides for golf travelers:
I have found the following guides very useful for travel, trip and golf planning in Northern California. Also refer to the maps and tips included in Chapter 5 of the **Best 100**.

Best Western Guidebook. Best Western is an affiliation of hotels and motels throughout the US. They attempt to make sure that all members maintain high and consistent standards for quality at their properties. The guide is free to all and can be picked up at any Best Western affiliate motel.

AAA Traveling With Your Pet. A very good guide to hotels, motels and B&B's that allow pets in some of their rooms. Includes the AAA rating system, contact info, directions and price ranges.

Northern California Golf Association (NCGA) Bluebook. This guide is published annually, in winter of each year. It lists all course names, contact information, and basic statistical information. Members get it free. Non-members should call (831) 622-0560 to purchase it.

Northern California Golf Getaways: Susan Fornoff & Cari Kenicer; distributed by Avalon Travel Publishing, 2001. Although a bit outdated, it guides readers to high quality restaurants, good lodging, various activities and some golf courses in almost all areas of Northern California. The book is a bit dated and excludes some areas covered by the **Best 100.**

Foghorn Outdoors CALIFORNIA GOLF, 2002 edition, edited by George Fuller. A good source for statistics and short course descriptions on all CA golf courses. Unfortunately, it has not been updated since January '02.

Fodor's Golf Digest's Places to play in the Southwest, 1998 edition. Another good abbreviated source on less than half the courses in Arizona, California, Colorado, Nevada, New Mexico, Texas and Utah. It uses a 4-Star rating system and includes some short subjective critiques. As with Foghorn's book, it excludes new courses and comments are outdated by eleven years.

California State Park System. Join the California State Parks Foundation at www.calparks.org, and get eight free passes to the parks, in addition to maps and information about the system. Not interested in joining? Go to www.parks.ca.gov for answers to many questions. Phone number for questions and recorded info is (800) 777-0369.

Rough: Areas of a golf course where grass is longer and thicker than fairways is called *rough.* Sometimes rough is cut and groomed, sometimes not. Trees and other varieties of vegetation commonly grow in the same area. The *first cut* is a strip of short cut rough, often 12" to 24" wide that borders the edge of fairways. The *second cut* comes next, usually mowed about 1 to 2 inches longer than fairways. (These days most courses keep roughs trimmed short in order to speed up play, and only let them grow long for special tournaments.) *Primary rough,* another common term, identifies a course's dominant rough style. In some cases the *second cut* and *primary rough* are one-and-the-same because maintenance crews mow all roughs to the same length. But on newer, grander courses *primary rough* applies to the long uncut grasses and vegetation outside the *second cut.*

Run-up shot: This term applies to a type of shot usually perfected on links courses in the British Isles. When aprons and greens dry out to become hard and fast, high shots, even with good spin, are difficult to stop. Instead, low shots, hit short of the green, *run-up* to the hole. During times of drought in the U.S., use of such shots becomes more common. See **Pitch Shots** for more information.

Signature hole: This is usually the most photogenic hole on a golf course, not necessarily the prettiest or best or most difficult. It usually appears in advertising or on the cover of the scorecard. Some courses have several signature holes and interchange them over time.

<u>Shot trajectory</u>: Golf lingo includes several terms to describe the shape and direction a ball travels. The related terms included in the **Best 100** include *hook*, *draw*, *slice* and *fade*. Their meaning depends on whether a player is left-handed or right-handed. For a right-handed player, a *hooked* shot curves sharply to the left and a *slice* sharply to the right. A *draw*, on the other hand curves only slightly, usually less than fifteen yards from the original line of the shot, and normally not until the shot reaches near the peak of its arc. A *fade* curves only slightly to the right, usually less than fifteen yards.

If a player is left-handed, all the directions are opposite from those of the right-handed player. For instance, *hooks* and *draws* turn right, and *slices* and *fades* curve left.

<u>Slice</u>: See **Shot trajectory.**

<u>Slope</u>: See **Course Slope.**

<u>StimpMeter</u>: Named after its creator, Eddie Stimpson, this simple tool is used to measure the distance golf ball roll on the green. In golf parlance, they measure the *speed of the green*. It is a box with a short ramp: a ball rolls down the ramp and the number of feet rolled on the grass is measured and recorded. The resulting number of feet is called the *Stimp* speed. A *fast* green, with roll distance of 10 to 12 feet, means players must hit putts softly because they will roll far. A *slow* green, where the ball rolls only 5 to 7 feet requires a much stronger stroke to reach the cup. For further details see:

www.usga.org/turf/articles/management/greens/stimpmeter.html

<u>Target golf</u>: Courses, usually the more modern ones, often limit the distance players can hit before reaching hazards or rough. The obstacles require shots to *lay-up* short, rather than be hit with full power and the longest clubs. Indeed, sometimes fairway landing zones are no larger than greens, and drives must be hit far enough to clear one type of trouble and short enough to stay out of another. If enough of these *target zones* populate a course, players would refer to it as a *target course* and say they are playing *target golf*.

<u>Tee</u>: This word is used in several ways on the golf course:

1) A *tee*, or *driving-tee*, is a 2-3 inch long wooden or plastic prong, which has a small cup on one end, and point on the other. Its used to elevate the ball above the ground for easier hitting of the first shot, or drive, on each hole.
2) The *tee*, or *tee-box*, is the location designed to hit from at the start of each hole. *Tees* are graded to be level and usually stand elevated above the plane of the surrounding ground. Their grass is cut short, at fairway length or less. Ideally, they are soft enough for easy insertion of *driving tees*, yet are firm enough that these same *tees* easily stand up straight and balls set on them don't fall off. *Tee-*

boxes contain *yardage medallions*, which mark the starting point for distance measurements on each hole.

3) *Tee-blocks*, or *tee-markers* are small moveable wooden, plastic, rock or metal monuments, which indicate the place greens-keepers want players to *tee-off* on a particular day. They are switched from time to time in order to give grass time to re-grow. Players of different skill levels play from different colored *tee-blocks*, at distances that can vary up to 150 yards.

4) To *tee-off* means to hit the initial shot, or drive, on any particular hole.

5) A *tee-time*, *tee-off time*, or *starting-time*, is the time of day reserved with the pro-shop for starting a round of golf.

Tips: are the most rear position that tee-blocks can be set on the tee-box, thereby extending course distance to its maximum. Often the *tips* are behind and longer than the longest distance indicated on the score-card.

Toughest Courses:

Most professionals believe that Course Ratings are the best gauge of course difficulty. Theur measurement relies on yardage as the prime component. Those of us who hit the ball shorter often feel that the Slope Rating is a better measure because it adds emphasis on location of hazards, impact of weather, and difficulties around greens.

I have even gone one step further and created a Toughness Rating, which combines Rating and Slope together with a simple formula, giving equal importance to both (2 x Course Rating plus Course Slope). Take a look at the following lists and decide for yourself the one that best measures the toughest courses.

Rankings on the next page all come from published numbers in the NCGA Golf 2009 Bluebook. I list different tee options to show the different degrees of difficulty available, since the numbers range widely, depending on which tee is used. Rather than duplicate rankings and lists, I chose to include lady's data from the front tee position only.

As a reminder to readers, my rankings for quality and value use the tee-blocks and ratings closest to 6500-yards, usually the men's blue set.

Toughest by Rating

Men's back tees		Men's blue tees		Men's white tees		Women's front tees	
Wente	75.8	Diablo Gr. Ranch	74.1	Stevinson Ranch	72.7	Ancil Hoffman	74.2
Spyglass Hill	75.5	Bayonet	73.4	Coyote Crk. Ch.	72.2	Pheasant Run	74.2
Diablo Gr. Ranch	75.4	Bridges	73.4	H. Moon Bay, Old	72.0	Pasatiempo	73.6
Bayonet	75.3	Eagle Vines	73.4	Diablo Gr. Ranch	71.6	Swenson Park	73.6
Eagle Vines	75.3	H. Moon Bay, Old	73.4	Spyglass Hill	71.4	Boundary Oaks	72.3
H. Moon Bay, Old	75.2	Coyote Crk., Tmt.	73.2	Bayonet	71.3	Van Buskirk	73.3
Old Greenwood	75.2	Spyglass Hill	73.2	Boundary Oaks	71.2	Alta Sierra	73.2
Stevinson Ranch	75.2	Cordevalle	73.1	Pebble Beach	71.2	Eagle Vines	73.2
CordeValle	75.1	Poppy Hills	73.1	Bridges	71.1	Napa @ Kennedy	73.0
Darkhorse	75.0	Poppy Ridge	73.1	Eagle Ridge	71.0	Spyglass Hill	72.9

Toughest by Slope

Men's back tees		Men's blue tees		Men's white tees		Women's front tees	
The Ranch	150	Spyglass Hill	144	Bridges	139	Pasatiempo	133
Bridges	147	Diablo Gr. Ranch	142	Spyglass Hill	137	Spyglass Hill	133
Diablo Gr. Lgnds.	147	The Ranch	142	Coyote Crk. Tmt.	134	Alta Sierra	132
Spyglass Hill	147	Bridges	141	Pebble Beach	134	Summitpointe	132
Spanish Bay	146	Poppy Hills	141	Poppy Hills	134	Brentwood: Crk/Hil	130
Wente Vineyards	145	Eagle Ridge	139	Bayonet	133	Pajaro Valley	130
Coyote Crk. Tmt.	144	Hiddenbrooke	139	Diablo Gr. Ranch	133	Paso Robles	129
Diablo Gr. Ranch	144	Apple Mountain	138	Eagle Ridge	133	River Island	129
Poppy Hills	144	Coyote Crk. Tmt.	137	Hiddenbrooke	132	Grizzly Ranch	129
Stevinson Ranch	143	Diablo Gr. Lgnds.	137	Diablo Gr. Lgnds.	131	Dry Creek Ranch	128

Toughest by Dawson formula

Men's back tees		Men's blue tees		Men's white tees		Women's front tees	
Spyglass Hill	298	Spyglass Hill	290	Bridges	281	Pasatiempo	280
Diablo Gr. Legd.	297	Diablo Gr. Ranch	290	Spyglass Hill	280	Spyglass Hill	279
Wente	297	Bridges	288	Coyote Crk. Tmt.	278	Alta Sierra	278
Bridges	296	Poppy Hills	287	Pebble Beach	276	Summitpointe	277
The Ranch	295	Eagle Ridge	284	Diablo Gr. Ranch	276	Rancho Del Rey	277
Diable Gr. Ranch	294	Coyote Crk. Tmt.	283	Poppy Hills	276	Paso Robles	276
Spanish Bay	294	The Ranch	283	Bayonet	276	Pajaro Valley	275
Coyote Crk. Tmt.	294	Diablo Gr. Lgnds.	282	Eagle Ridge	275	River Island	275
Stevinson Ranch	293	Bayonet	282	Stevinson Ranch	274	Ancil Hoffman	274
Poppy Hills	293	Eagle Vines	282	H. Moon Bay, Old	274	Pheasant Run	274

<u>**Twenty toughest golf holes,**</u> as played from the tees closest to 6500-yards. I exclude Pebble Beach and Spyglass Hill from the list below because their holes have been well reported by both my reviews and many other writers. The choices are purely my personal opinion, and do not take advantage of tournament statistics, handicap ranking or Course Rating and Course slope data.

Par-fives:
De Laveaga, Santa Cruz: Number ten, 590-yards @ back tees. Slightly downhill and can be down-wind. Drive is extremely tight, between oaks. Second shot must clear a deep ravine and avoid creek on left and out-of-bounds on right. Final shot is easier, but to an elevated green protected on sides and back by hazards and bunkers.
Diablo Grande Ranch, Patterson: Number twelve, 621-yards @ blue tees. Double dogleg, first right, then sharply left. Cannot hit drive more than 235 yards, then must cross a 180-yard wide ravine on second shot. Trees usually block the third shot to green

which is still over 200-yards away. Green is well sloped and well bunkered to the sides.

Mount Shasta Resort, Mt Shasta: Number four, 570-yards @ back tees. Uphill drive though an opening in the pines aims directly at towering Mt. Shasta. Second shot must carry over a wide creek, through a narrow side-hill opening, about 150 yards from the green. Final shot is uphill to green tightly protected by tall pines on the right, and traps both left and right.

Ridge Creek, Dinuba: Number fourteen, 597-yards @ middle tees. Hole has treeless, level terrain, with a normal crosswind. Drive is open, but second shot must be laid-up short of wetland or hit well to the right, adding 40 yards to the hole. From an approach location 210-yards more yards are needed to an unobstructed green. Shots hit further and to the right must clear multiple bunkers and land on down-slope at the green. Green is very large with multiple moderate undulations.

San Juan Oaks, Hollister: Number fifteen, 523-yards @ middle tees. Uphill double dogleg through heavy oaks to long highly elevated green. Drive must hit a shallow fairway short of a wide creek. Second shot is critical. It's uphill, must clear the creek, and find a landing area less than thirty yards wide. Shots hit long go over and down to another creek. Shots short or to the other side bound into the first creek. Approach is a short iron but the green is long, highly sloped and narrow, well protected by bunkers and steep aprons.

Par-fours:

Bayonet, Seaside: Number nine, 449-yards @ middle tees. Relatively open drive to corner of mild dogleg, with out-of-bounds and trees deterring shots towards the corner. Second is steeply up, over multiple cluster and cross-bunkers to a highly elevated green. Once on, a prominent spine divides two sections of green.

Castle Oaks, Ione: Number eighteen, 416-yards @ middle tees. Hole plays like a par five if one takes the safe approach around perimeter of three lakes. Otherwise, for medium length hitters, landing areas are tiny, and anything crooked or the wrong length gets wet. The approach on a direct route at the green needs at least 210-yards in the air to clear water and/or bunkers.

Catta Verdera, Lincoln: Number eighteen, 412-yards @ middle tees. Drive heads over deep gulch to narrow fairway opening between trees. Second must then head up over a hill and a wide pond just in front of the green. Lay-up approaches still leave nearly 100-yards often from downhill lies.

Cinnabar Hills, Morgan Hill: Number seven on the Canyon Nine, 340-yards @ middle tees. Drive landing area is small. Hole climbs nearly 100 feet in elevation, mostly on the second shot, which must clear a deep bunker to a blind green from a steep lie. Distance judgment for the approach is difficult.

Coyote Moon, Truckee: Number four, 426-yards @ middle tees. Two difficult shots: the drive must hook around a hill and trees on the left, or it will head down a steep embankment into the woods. The approach is to a highly elevated green, usually 200-yards away, where the surface is so steep that three-putts are normal.

Eagle Vines, Napa: Number five, 424-yards @ middle tees. Very pretty hole around a lake on the left to a green elevated on a hillside. The drive must be close to the lake to cut off approach distance. The green is two-tiered, with a big elevation between the two, and protected by the lake, and deep bunkers.

Pasatiempo, Santa Cruz: Number eleven, 390-yards @ back tees. Drive heads uphill to a narrowing fairway, tightly guarded on left by a deep barranca. Second shot is up even more, over the diagonally angled hazard, to an elevated green. Green is closely protected by bunkers, the creek, and has sharply inclined putting surface.

Peacock Gap, San Rafael: Number eleven, 435-yards @ back tees. A creek on one side and out-of-bounds on the other guards a narrow tree-lined fairway. Approach needs to clear several tall traps and then hit a very long, undulating, narrow green where the back half slopes away from incoming shots.

San Juan Oaks, Hollister: Number eighteen, 439-yards @ middle tees. The drive must be hit to the right side of the fairway to avoid a row of large oaks from blocking the green approach. But the right side is well trapped and guarded by nasty waste areas. The long second shot must also clear a wide hazard and large bunker fronting the green.

Tilden Park, Berkeley: Number one, 411-yards @ back tees. A steep hill faces drives on what many say is the **Best 100's** toughest starting hole. Elevation climbs over 80 feet to the green. The drive is wide-open but the second is long, with a steep final assent to a shallow green with a steep back-to-front break. Hit a downhill putt too hard and your headed 30 yards off the front edge.

Par-threes:

Avila Beach, near San Luis Obispo: Number two, 233-yards @ back tees. The shot heads uphill, over a bunker about 40-yards in front of the green, and then up an embankment covered by heavy Kikuyu grass. Full-length shots are difficult to hold and usually roll over the back, down 10-15 yards.

Monarch Bay, San Leandro: Number seven, 207-yards @ gold (second from back) tees. A monster, usually into the wind, the back two sets of tees play really long. The slightly elevated green is narrow and guarded by deep bunkers right and mounds left.

Pasatiempo, Santa Cruz: Number three, 217-yards @ back tees. The tee shot heads uphill to a green elevated even higher. Balls rarely bounce up to the putting surface, so any drive landing there is a good one. Bunkers above left and below right catch anything crooked. Fast running putts need to contend with big breaks and a two-tier green.

Pheasant Run, Chowchilla: Number four, 185-yard @ middle tees. An island green represents their signature hole. Drives go dead into the prevailing breeze. Even though the green is big, any draw or fade is likely to be pushed off line into the water or a front bunker.

Wente Vineyards, Livermore: Number fourteen, 166-yards @ Gold (second from back) tees. A short, deceptively simple looking shot, slightly downhill to a green surrounded by steep downhill slopes and heavy rough. Breezes usually head towards the tee. Drives missing the aprons, bunkers or green should be re-hit. The rough looks playable but even pros easily reach double-digit scores if they keep trying to whack out of the lousy lies below the green.

Value Ratings: *Value*, as a topic, is discussed at the end of the introduction to Chapter 5. Here I simply add the formulas used for calculation in more detail. These formulas and definitions are based on my belief that *value* is directly related to both *quality* (discussed at length in Chapter 1) and the *Cost to Play*.

Value = Quality Rating divided by Cost to Play

The *quality rating* was created from objective reviews written immediately following play and screening that same day. Points were assigned to 29 separate attributes grouped into the following categories:

Attributes:	Max Score
Design elements: overall layout and design, special holes, hazard position, green's character, walk-ability, ease of losing golf balls, impact of weather.	120
Beauty: location and surroundings.	50
Course condition: fairways, roughs, bunkers, greens, aprons, tees.	100
History: tournament play and contribution to the community.	24
Uniqueness: variation of hole designs on course being reviewed, and unusual character compared to other courses.	24
Facility features and condition: proshop, caddy availability, clubhouse facilities, cleanliness, toilet access, staff friendliness, speed of play, practice facilities, cart quality and access to fairways and lots.	<u>72</u>
Total	**390**

The *Cost to Play* is a weighted average calculation: 35% of weekend greens fee + 35% of weekday rate + 20% of twilight rate + 10% of senior rate + 60 to 90% of the cart fee. (The cart cost varies, depending on my estimate of the percentage of people who pay for carts on each individual course.)

<u>**Waste bunkers**</u>, see Bunkers, p. 369.

<u>**Websites:**</u> The following list could find you discount greens fees, more information about courses, or definitions of golf terms not listed in the glossary:

www.bestbuyteetimes.com	Discount tee times throughout the country
www.golfnow.com	Same discount info as www.bestbuyteetimes.com
www.golfnortherncal.com	Another golf site, hooked up with American Golf
www.ezlinks.com	Discounts on limited courses throughout US, hit "Tee Time Specials"
www.golflinks.com	Course reviews and info
www.americangolf.com	E-mail specials, including discount greens fees.

www.greenskeeper.org	Course reviews and info
www.ncga.org	Home site of the Northern CA Golf Assn
www.hookedongolf.com	Forum for discussion about Nor Cal golf and TV show
www.2for1golf.com	Site for purchase of discount golf coupon book
www.centralcoastgolftrail.com	Info on Central Coast Golf Courses
norcalgolfguide.com	Summary data on Northern CA courses
http://golf.about.com/od/ golfterms/a/golfglossary.htm	Great glossary of golf terms

<u>Winter rules:</u> Unlike Scotsmen, who would never dream of moving the ball to improve a lie under any conditions, most Americans are not such purists. We like soft greens that hold approaches, and fairways where the ball sits high on the turf rather than down in a divot. We want the best chance of low scores and good shots. By and large, we understand the rules of the game and respect the traditions of golf etiquette. This means we know that golfers cannot pick-up or clean their ball after teeing off on a hole, until it reaches the green. We cannot move it unless we are actually hitting it.

However . . . we don't think it's fair to be subjected to the poor fairway conditions that most courses find during periods of poor weather, usually in winter. Therefore, an exception is often made by local clubs to allow players to lift-clean-and-place their ball to an improved lie, no closer to the hole, at times of the year when conditions are poor. Some courses allow movement of 6 inches, some a club length. Some allow this movement only in the fairway of the hole being played; others allow it *through the green*, which includes roughs and other fairways, but not hazards. The rules of golf frown on *winter rules*, but the relaxation of purism sure makes the game a lot more enjoyable when fairways are damaged from lack of care or poor weather. Even today's pro tournaments occasionally allow players to lift, clean and place.

Index

Dye, Pete: 84, 86

E & J Gallo: 242
Eagle Ridge GC: 36-38, 169, 291, 326, 343,
        382, 383
Eagle Vines GC: 55, 174-176, 182, 279, 357,
        382, 383, 385
Earl Fry Course: 239-240
Edgewood CG: 145
Egan, H. Chandler: 284
El Dorado Hills: 373
Empire Golf summary: 377
Empire Ranch GC: 102, 127-128, 198, 222.
        359, 377
Eureka GC: 252, 351, 376, 377
Executive course style: 371
Extreme statistics: 373

Facilities and Service: 9
Fade, see Shot Trajectory: 381
Fairway definition: 373
Fairway Mgmt: 174, 279
Fall River Valley GC: 153-155, 353, 372, 373
False front definition: 374
Fig Garden GC: 253, 363
Fleming, Jack: 195, 234, 275, 277, 278, 280,
        295, 368
Flint, Homer: 100, 102, 138, 368
Flop Shot: See Pitch Shots: 379
Fodor's Golf Digest's Places to play in the
        Southwest, 1998 edition: 380
Foghorn Outdoors CALIFORNIA GOLF,
        2002 edition: 380
Foley, Stephen: 134
Forced carry definition: 106, 374
Forest Lake GC: 254, 361
Forest Meadow GC: 255, 361
Fought, John: 111, 112.
Fountaingrove: 334
Fowler, William Herbert: 243, 244
Foxtail North GC: 255, 349, 377
Foxtail South GC: 255, 349, 377
Franklin Canyon GC: 257, 355, 377
Fream, Ron: 38
Fresno West: See Javier's Fresno West: 264
French Camp RV Camp & Golf: 258, 361
Furnace Creek GC; 72, 73, 231, 258, 332,
        365, 376, 377

Geiberger, Al: 46
Getaway Suggestions: 337
Gibson Golf Management: 139, 140
Gill, Garrett: 218,219
Glasson, Clark: 155, 246, 310, 311, 368

Golden Tee: 278
Gold Hills CC: 35, 129-130, 351
Golf Digest ranking criteria: 374
Golf Websites, see Websites: 387
Golf Solutions: 157, 158, 222
Golf, derivation of the word: 374
Graeagle Meadows GC: 7, 125-126, 149, 353
Granite Bay CC: 98, 102, 198, 323, 324, 359,
        368, 377
Graves, Robert Muir: 95, 97, 118, 136, 137,
        203, 205, 213, 214, 233, 235, 238,
        239, 247, 248, 257, 266, 296, 297, ·
        367, 368
Green and Green complex definitions: 374
Green Tree GC: 260, 357
Greenhorn Creek GC: 57, 93, 151-153, 363,
        372
Greens Fees definition: 375
Greenway Golf: 177
Griffiths, Dennis: 48
Grizzly Ranch GC: 328-330, 353, 372, 383
Guidebooks, see Reference Guides: 380

Haggin Oaks Arcade GC: 133, 261, 359, 377
Haggin Oaks McKenzie GC: 133-135, 142,
        230, 261, 359, 377
Half Moon Bay GC, Ocean: 53-55, 341
Half Moon Bay GC, Old Course: 131-132,
        341, 383
Halsey Daray Golf: 243
Halsey, Steve: 287
Hamel, Rick: 268
Handicap: 375. See also Course Ratings,: 369
Handicapping by hole: 236
Hank's Swank Woodlake Ranch: 321, 363
Hanson, Wayne: 315
Harbottle, John: 26, 72, 163, 173, 273,
        367, 368
Harding Park GC: 11, 66, 79-81, 341, 377
Hardy, Jim: 49.
Harling, Don: 226, 227
Harmon, Ben: 227
Harvey Penick's Little Red Book: 379
Hazards definition: 376
Heathlands: 143, 371, 375
Hidden Hills: 215
Hidden Valley Lake CC: 87, 262, 351
Hiddenbrooke GC: 77-79, 182, 359, 377, 383
High Value courses: 338
Hills, Arthur: 55.
History and Tournaments:11
Hitchcock, Alfred: 89
Hogan, Ben: 19, 20
Hook, see course trajectory: 381

Ordering Information

for

Northern California's
Best 100
Public Golf Courses

by
Doug Dawson

E-mail: sureshot12@comcast.net

Internet: www.best100golf

Phone: 650 559-7873